The Future of National Development Banks

THE INITIATIVE FOR POLICY DIALOGUE SERIES

The Initiative for Policy Dialogue (IPD) brings together the top voices in development to address some of the most pressing and controversial debates in economic policy today. The IPD book series approaches topics such as capital market liberalization, macroeconomics, environmental economics, and trade policy from a balanced perspective, presenting alternatives, and analyzing their consequences on the basis of the best available research. Written in a language accessible to policymakers and civil society, this series will rekindle the debate on economic policy and facilitate a more democratic discussion of development around the world.

OTHER TITLES PUBLISHED BY OXFORD UNIVERSITY PRESS IN THIS SERIES

Fair Trade for All
Joseph E. Stiglitz and Andrew Charlton

Economic Development and Environmental Sustainability
Edited by Ramón López and Michael A. Toman

Stability with Growth
Joseph E. Stiglitz, José Antonio Ocampo, Shari Spiegel, Ricardo Ffrench-Davis, and Deepak Nayyar

The Washington Consensus Reconsidered
Edited by Narcís Serra and Joseph E. Stiglitz

Capital Market Liberalization and Development
Edited by José Antonio Ocampo and Joseph E. Stiglitz

Industrial Policy and Development
Edited by Mario Cimoli, Giovanni Dosi, and Joseph E. Stiglitz

Time for a Visible Hand
Edited by Stephany Griffith-Jones, José Antonio Ocampo, and Joseph E. Stiglitz

Debates on the Measurement of Global Poverty
Edited by Sudhir Anand, Paul Segal, and Joseph E. Stiglitz

Overcoming Developing Country Debt Crises
Edited by Barry Herman, José Antonio Ocampo, and Shari Spiegel

Good Growth and Governance in Africa
Edited by Akbar Noman, Kwesi Botchwey, Howard Stein, and Joseph E. Stiglitz

The Economic Development of Latin America since Independence
Luis Bértola and José Antonio Ocampo

Law and Economics with Chinese Characteristics
Edited by David Kennedy and Joseph E. Stiglitz

Intellectual Property Rights
Edited by Mario Cimoli, Giovanni Dosi, Keith E. Maskus, Ruth L. Okediji, Jerome H. Reichman, and Joseph E. Stiglitz

Global Governance and Development
Edited by José Antonio Ocampo

The World Economy through the Lens of the United Nations
Edited by José Antonio Ocampo, Anis Chowdhury, and Diana Alarcón

The Future of National Development Banks

Edited by
Stephany Griffith-Jones and
José Antonio Ocampo

OXFORD
UNIVERSITY PRESS

OXFORD
UNIVERSITY PRESS

Great Clarendon Street, Oxford, OX2 6DP,
United Kingdom

Oxford University Press is a department of the University of Oxford.
It furthers the University's objective of excellence in research, scholarship,
and education by publishing worldwide. Oxford is a registered trade mark of
Oxford University Press in the UK and in certain other countries

First Edition published in 2018

Published in the United States of America by Oxford University Press
198 Madison Avenue, New York, NY 10016, United States of America

British Library Cataloguing in Publication Data
Data available

Library of Congress Control Number: 2018938178

ISBN 978–0–19–882794–8

Preface

Stephany Griffith-Jones and José Antonio Ocampo

For a long time, the topic of development banks was largely neglected in the academic literature, or was limited to a debate between admirers and detractors of these institutions, often inserted in a more general debate between states and markets. Since the 2007/9 North Atlantic financial crisis, not only has interest in and support for these institutions broadly increased, but also it has become clearer that the key issues are understanding how such development banks work, what their main aims are, what instruments, incentives, and governance work better in general and in particular contexts, and importantly what are their links with the private financial and corporate sector, as well as with broader government policies.

As long-term supporters of 'good' (well-functioning) development banks, we thought an in-depth study of several cases of national development banks, as well as horizontal issues such as their role in innovation and structural change, infrastructure financing, financial inclusion, environmental sustainability, the countercyclical role of development financing, and the financial regulation that is appropriate for these institutions, would be valuable, both for academics and policymakers. We hope this book contributes to such knowledge, and encourages further research in this important topic.

We would like to warmly thank BNDES and the Development Bank of Latin America (CAF) for their valuable financial and intellectual support to the research project on national development banks, which resulted in this book. Joao Ferraz, then Vice President, gave us key initial support; when he left BNDES, Vinicius Carrasco continued supporting our work. Throughout the project, we had extremely valuable collaboration with Lavinia Barros de Castro from BNDES and Pablo Sanguinetti from CAF in all phases and aspects of the project. Lavinia, given her in-depth expertise on financial regulation and her academic activities, also contributed a valuable paper to the research project, resulting in a chapter of the book. We also want to thank Columbia University's Global Policy Initiative, which cooperated in the final stages of elaboration of this book, which contains the major results of the project.

We are very grateful to all the authors of the chapters, all well-known experts in their countries and in their fields, who have worked so hard and well to produce such valuable research. We appreciate the support given by BNDES, where the first workshop in Rio de Janeiro was so successfully hosted, and to Carnegie Endowment in Washington DC, where we held our second conference. The latter was followed by a public panel, held during the 2017 Spring Meetings of the IMF and World Bank, which was kindly and insightfully chaired by Otaviano Canuto, who is Executive Director at the World Bank for Brazil and several other Latin American countries. In both meetings we received valuable comments from a very informed audience.

A number of colleagues have made valuable contributions to this project, but besides the above-mentioned we would like to highlight the contribution and commitment of Paola Arias and Felipe Rezende. We are also grateful to Jiaming Ju and Laila Staudinger Pedroza for excellent administrative support. We are thankful to Tom Trebat and Bruno Pantaleao, who gave valuable support to the BNDES meeting, and who organized a preliminary meeting in Rio in September.

December 2016

Contents

Part II. Thematic Issues

List of Figures

List of Tables and Box

Tables

Box

Endorsements

'Once considered a key vehicle for national advancement, development banks have come to be regarded as relics of a bygone age. This volume, however, reveals that these banks have in fact played highly positive roles in many countries. Moreover, it shows their best days may be ahead of them, as the need for large-scale, long-term finance grows with the challenges of climate change and techno-paradigm shift. Weaving together focused thematic analyses and rich, well-contextualized case studies, this excellent book presents a rigorous, balanced, and pragmatic discussion of one of the most important tools of economic development. Highly recommended.'

Ha-Joon Chang, Reader in the Political Economy of Development, University of Cambridge, UK, and author of *Kicking Away the Ladder* and *23 Things They Don't Tell You About Capitalism*

'This book is an excellent historical analysis of the positive role of national development banks worldwide. A clear incentive for these institutions to expand their products and services in line with the challenges of this new era, it is essential reading for researchers as well as national and international policy-makers dealing with economic development, and especially with development finance.'

L. Enrique García, Former President of the Development Bank of Latin America (CAF)

'This book is an outstanding and pioneering contribution to knowledge on national development banks' valuable roles to help achieve countries' economic, social and environmental aims. The in-depth analysis of their activities, especially in major Latin American countries, shows their positive support for private and public investment, and for the development of the financial sector. This book clarifies, thanks to its comprehensive analysis, the positive impact of these development banks, which are increasingly important but not sufficiently known and valued. This book is a must read for all concerned with the role of the financial sector in development.'

Enrique Iglesias, Former President of the Inter-American Development Bank.

'The reputation of national development banks (NDBs) has waxed and waned as policy fashions have evolved over the years. The case studies included in this book demonstrate that NDBs continue to have an important function. They offer valuable lessons on how to enhance the contributions of NDBs to development and the conditions that are most conducive to their success.'

Dani Rodrik, Ford Foundation Professor of International Political Economy at the John F. Kennedy School of Government, Harvard University

List of Abbreviations

4G	fourth generation
AAAA	Addis Ababa Action Agenda
ABC	Agricultural Bank of China
ABDIB	Brazilian Association of Infrastructure and Basic Industry
ABS	asset-backed security
ADBC	Agricultural Development Bank of China
ABCP	Asset-Backed Commercial Paper
AIIB	Asia Infrastructure Investment Bank
AMA	Advanced Measurement Approach
ANI	Agencia Nacional de Infrastructura
ANVISA	Agência Nacional de Vigilância Sanitária
APESEG	Peruvian Association of Insurance Companies (Asociación Peruana de Empresas de Seguros)
ASA	Alternative Standardized Approach
BA	Banco Agropecuario
BANCOLDEX	Banco de Comercio Exterior
BANOBRAS	Banco Nacional de Obras
BCIE	Central American Bank for Economic Integration
BCRP	Banco Central de Reservo del Perú
BDC	Business Development Corporation
BDC	Business Development Bank of Canada
BIS	Bank for International Settlements
BMZ	Federal Ministry for Economic Cooperation and Development
BN	Banco de la Nación
BNDES	Banco Nacional do Desenvolvimento Economico e Social/National Development Bank of Brazil
BNDESPAR	BNDES Participações S.A.
BOT	build–operate–transfer
BRICS	Brazil, Russia, India, China, and South Africa

CAB	Cyclically Adjusted Balance
CAF	Construcciones y Auxiliar de Ferrocariles
CAF	Development Bank of Latin America
CAP	steel enterprise
CARG	Compound Annual Growth Rate
CCB	China Construction Bank
CDB	China Development Bank
CDB	Community Development Bank
CDF	CDB Development Fund
CEPLAN	Centro Nacional de Planeamiento Estratégico
CFD	Corporacion Financiera de Desarrollo
CIC	city investment company
CIFES	Centre for Innovation and Development of Sustainable Energy
CNBV	Comisión Nacional Bancaria y de Valores
CNCA	Comisión Nacional de Crédito Agropecuario
CNIC	National Council for Innovation and Competitiveness
CONICYT	Comisión Nacional de Investigación Científica y Technológica
CORFO	Corporación de Fomento de la Producción or Production Development Corporation
CPI	consumer price index
DARPA	Defense Advanced Research Projects Agency
DB	development bank
DBJ	Development Bank of Japan
DEG	Deutsche Investitions- und Entwicklungsgesellschaft
EBP	Estruturadora Brasileira de Projetos S.A.
EFSI	European Fund for Strategic Investment
EIB	European Investment Bank
EIBC	Export-Import Bank of China
EIF	European Investment Fund
EMDE	emerging markets and developing countries
ENAP	oil enterprise
ENDESA	enterprise for electricity distribution
ENSI	European National Securitization Initiative
ENTEL	telecommunications
ERP	European Recovery Program
FAG	Fondo Agropecuario de Garantias

FDN	Financiera de Desarrollo Nacional
FEN	Financiera Eléctrica Nacional (before 1990)
FEN	Financiera Energética Nacional (after 1990)
FGI	Guarantee Fund of Free Investment Credit
FINAGRO	Fondo para el Financiamiento del Sector Agropecuario
FINAME	financiamento de máquinas e equipamentos
FINDETER	Financiera de Desarrollo Territorial
FMR	Fondo para las Microfinanzas Rurales
FMV	Fondo MiVivienda
FOGAPA	Fondo de Garantía para la Pequeña Agricultura/Guarantee Fund for Small-Scale Agriculture
FOGAPE	Fondo de Garantía para el Pequeño Empresario
FOGASA	Fondo de Garantía para el Campo y del Seguro Agropecuario/ Countyside and Agricultural Insurance Guarantee Fund
FONADE	Fondo Financiero de Proyectos de Desarrollo
FSI	Fund for Strategic Investments
G-SIBS	Global Systematically Important Banks
GAAP	Generally Accepted Accounting Principles
GDP	gross domestic product
GDR	German Democratic Republic
GFC	Global Financial Crisis
GIZ	Deutsche Gesellschaft für Internationale Zusammenarbeit
GS	Goldman Sachs
I&L	infrastructure and logistics
IAA	International Actuarial Association
IABE	Inter-American Development Bank
IANSA	sugar beet processing
IB	infrastructure bank
IBRD	International Bank for Reconstruction and Development
ICF	Innovation and Competitiveness Fund
ICO	Official Credit Institute
ICR	Incentivo a la Capitalización Rural
ICT	information, technology, and communications
IDU	Investment Units
IFC	International Financial Corporation
IFI	Instituto de Fomento Industrial

IFRS	International Finance Reporting Standards
IGF	Investment Guarantor Fund
IGR	Reciprocal Guarantee Institution
IMF	International Monetary Fund
INEGI	National Institute of Statistics and Geography
INEI	Instituto Nacional de Estadística e Informática
IPD	Initiative for Policy Dialogue
IRB	Internal Rating Models
IRC	Incremental Risk Charge
ISI	import substitution industrialization
JBIC	Japanese development bank
JFC	Japan Finance Corporation
JPM	J.P. Morgan
KfW	German development bank
KSM	Keynesian, Schumpeterian, and Minskyan approach
LAN	national airline
LCR	short-term liquidity risk indicator
LGD	Loss Given Default
LGFV	local government financial vehicle
MAR	Ministry of Agriculture and Irrigation
MDB	multilateral development bank
MDG	Millennium Development Goal
MEF	Ministry of Economy and Finances
MFT	Market Failure Theory
MS	Citibank Morgan Stanley
MSME	micro-, small, and medium-sized enterprises
NAFINSA	Nacional Financiera
NASA	National Aeronautics and Space Administration
NBD	national development bank
NCRE	Non-Conventional Renewable Energy
NDB	national development bank
NDB	New Development Bank
NDRC	National Development and Reform Commission
NIH	National Institutes of Health
NPB	national promotional bank
NPL	non-performing loan

NRDC	Natural Resources Defense Council
NSF	National Science Foundation
NSFR	long-term liquidity risk indicator
ODA	official development assistance
OECD	Organization for Economic Cooperation and Development
PAC	Growth Acceleration Programme
PADEMER	Programa de Apoyo al Desarrollo de la Microempresa Rural
PBoC	People's Bank of China
PD	Probability of Default
PDP	Programa de Desarrollo de Proveedores
PIL	Logistics Investments Programme
PIP	Pensions Infrastructure Platform
PPI	Public Procurement for Innovation
PPP	public–private partnership
PROFO	Programa de Proyectos Asociativos de Fomento
PSI	Programa de Sustentação do Investimento
PSL	pledged supplementary lending
PV	photovoltaic
PWC	PricewaterhouseCoopers
R&D	research and development
RES	renewable energy sources
RET	renewable energy technologies
RMBS	residential mortgage-backed securities
ROA	return on assets
ROE	return on equity
SBCI	Strategic Banking Corporation of Ireland
SBIC	Small Business Investment Company
SBIR	Small Business Innovation Research
SBS	Superintendence of Banking and Insurance
SIC	Southern Interconnected Power System
SELIC	Sistema Especial de Liquidação e Custodia
SING	Northern Interconnected Power System
SMA	Standardized Measurement Approach
SMBC	Sumitomo Mitsui
SME	small and medium-sized enterprises
SOE	state-owned enterprise

SPC	State Planning Commission
SPSS	Strategic Programme of Smart Specialization
SUS	Brazilian National Health System
SVAR	Stressed Value at Risk
SWF	Sovereign Wealth Fund
TBN	public TV
TDA	Títulos de Desarrollo Agropecuario
TFP	Total Factor Productivity
TJLP	Taxa de Juros de Longo Prazo (long-term interest rate)
TLP	long-term interest rate
VaR	Value at Risk
VAT	value-added tax
WTO	World Trade Organization
WUCI	Wuhu Urban Construction Investment Co. Ltd
WWB	Women's World Bank

List of Contributors

Stephany Griffith-Jones is Financial Markets Director at the Initiative for Policy Dialogue at Columbia University, Emeritus Professorial Fellow at the Institute of Development Studies, Sussex University, and Senior Research Associate at the Overseas Development Institute. She is an economist researching and reforming international and national financial architecture, from a development perspective, and development finance, especially national, regional, and multilateral development banks. Griffith-Jones has written or edited over twenty-five books and many articles, including *Time for a Visible Hand* (2010), coedited with José Antonio Ocampo and Joseph Stiglitz. She advises many international organizations, including the European Parliament, World Bank, IADB, various UN agencies, and several governments.

José Antonio Ocampo is a member of the board of Banco de la República (the central bank of Colombia), Professor in the School of International and Public Affairs at Columbia University, and Chair of the Committee for Development Policy of the United Nations. He has been UN Under-Secretary-General for Economic and Social Affairs, Executive Secretary of the UN Economic Commission for Latin America and the Caribbean (ECLAC), and Minister of Finance, Minister of Agriculture, and Director of the National Planning Office of Colombia. He has published extensively on macroeconomic theory and policy, international financial issues, economic and social development, international trade, and Colombian and Latin American economic history.

Paola Arias is head of the Research Unit at Banca de las Oportunidades, the Colombian national programme for financial inclusion. She has a broad knowledge of financial system stability issues, in particular financial crises, deposit insurance systems, development banks, financial inclusion, and financial literacy. She has worked at the Colombian Infrastructure Development Bank, the Colombian Banking Association, and the Colombian Deposit Insurance Corporation. She has also been a professor at Universidad Externado de Colombia.

Michael Brei is a lecturer in Economics at the University of the West Indies, Cave Hill Campus, Barbados. He is also Associate Professor (on leave) at the University Paris Nanterre. His research focuses on the role of banks during financial crises using both theoretical models and empirical analysis. He has also worked on the procyclicality of risk-weighted capital regulation and the procyclicality of bank lending. Michael has recurrently worked on these topics with the Bank for International Settlements.

Lavinia Barros de Castro has taught Economics at IBMEC Faculty since 1999, and on several MBA and MA courses (Coppead/UFRJ, since 2007). She has been an economist at BNDES (since 2001), where she worked in the Risk Management Division for some years (2007–11), and has been a manager in the Planning Division since 2016. She has published several articles on the Brazilian economy and is a co-organizer and co-author of many books, including *Economia Brasileira Contemporânea (1954–2015)*, winner of the Jabuti Prize, 2005, now in its third edition.

Óscar Dancourt is a professor in the Department of Economics of the Pontificia Universidad Catolica del Peru, and was a member of the board of the Central Bank of Peru from 2001 to 2004 and acting president in the period 2004–6. He teaches courses in macroeconomics and has published articles and books on the role of monetary policy, fiscal policy, and external shocks in the aggregate performance of the Peruvian economy.

Renzo Jiménez Sotelo is a professor at Universidad del Pacifico in Peru and has extensive expertise in financial and monetary economy as well as public debt and treasury. Between 1994 and 2011, he held different positions in the credit, market, and structural balance sheet risk departments in a commercial bank, a risk agency, and a development bank. From 2011 to 2016, he served as Analysis and Strategy Director at the Ministry of Economy and Finance. His educational background includes a BA in Economics, an MA in Finance, and an MA in Risk Management. He has taught monetary theory and sovereign asset and liability management.

María Luz Martínez Sola is an economist with a specialization in Development Finance. She has extensive in-country experience working on inclusive finance for strategic financial institutions. She recently advised UNCDF, UN's capital investment agency, whose mandate is to make finance work for poor people. Previously, she was a financial advisor to the Board of Directors at the National Bank of Argentina. In 2013 she received an award from the Argentine Central Bank, for her research on innovation financing.

Mariana Mazzucato is Professor in the Economics of Innovation and Public Value at University College London (UCL) and Director of the Institute for Innovation and Public Purpose. She is author of the highly acclaimed book *The Entrepreneurial State*, debunking public vs private sector myths (Anthem, 2013; Public Affairs, 2015) and winner of the 2014 New Statesman SPERI Prize in Political Economy, the 2015 Hans-Matthöfer-Preis, and the 2018 Leontief Prize. She has advised policymakers around the world on how to deliver 'smart', inclusive, and sustainable growth. In 2013 she was named as one of the 'three most important thinkers about innovation' in the New Republic.

Juan Carlos Moreno-Brid is a professor in the Faculty of Economics at Universidad Nacional Autónoma de México (UNAM). Before joining UNAM he served for many years as Research Coordinator/Associate Director of the UN office in Mexico of the Economic Commission for Latin America and the Caribbean, and from 1995 to 2000 he worked as a Research Associate of the David Rockefeller Center for Latin American Studies at Harvard University. He is a founding member of the World Economic Association. His research interests are mainly focused on economic development and macroeconomic policies with an emphasis on Latin America.

Ulf Moslener is Head of Research at the Frankfurt School/UNEP Collaborating Centre for Climate & Sustainable Energy Finance and Professor of Sustainable Energy Finance at the faculty of Frankfurt School. His research focuses on the economics of climate change, financing sustainable energy systems and climate finance, international climate policy, and the analysis of carbon regulation. Earlier he worked for KfW and at the Centre for European Economic Research (ZEW). He has led a number of research projects, e.g. on behalf of German federal ministries and the European Commission.

Caetano C. R. Penna (PhD) is Adjunct Professor of Industrial Economics and the Economics of Technology and Innovation at the Institute of Economics of the Federal University of Rio de Janeiro (Brazil), where he lectures on the postgraduate programme in Public Policy, Strategy, and Development. He is Associate Fellow at the Science Policy Research Unit (SPRU) of the University of Sussex. His research interests include industrial, technology, and innovation economics and policy, areas in which he also acts as consultant for Brazilian governmental agencies and industry associations.

Esteban Pérez Caldentey is currently Chief of the Financing for Development Unit at the Economic Commission for Latin America and the Caribbean (ECLAC) in Santiago, Chile. He is the coordinator of the ECLAC project 'Promoting Inclusive Finance', which analyses how development banking innovation practices can support social, productive development and structural change with a particular focus on SMEs in Latin American countries. He has published extensively on Latin America and Caribbean development issues.

Javiera Petersen Muga is an economist who has specialized in industrial policy and development economics. Her studies have focused on the industrial policy debate with an emphasis on Chile and Latin America, the economic space available for development strategy and growth perspectives in the region, and the effects of China and other new giant consumers on the trade basket of Latin American countries.

Luma Ramos is a PhD candidate in economics, with a specialization in monetary theory and macroeconomics, at the Federal University of Rio de Janeiro. Her research interests include development banks, financial systems, banking, and monetary economics.

Felipe Carvalho de Rezende is an Associate Professor of Economics and Finance and Director of the Finance programme at Bard College, NY, and a research scholar at the Levy Economics Institute. His research has focused on financial macroeconomics, monetary theory and policy, and finance for development. He previously taught at Hobart and William Smith Colleges from 2010 to 2017 and the University of Missouri–Kansas City in 2009. Rezende has authored more than a dozen book chapters and numerous journal articles, and has testified on a number of occasions in the Brazilian Congress.

Alfredo Schclarek is currently Assistant Professor at the National University of Córdoba, Argentina. In addition, he is Assistant Researcher at the National Scientific and Technical Research Council, Argentina (CONICET) and Academic Director of the Center for Participatory Research in Economic and Social Policies (CIPPES). He worked at the European Central Bank, Germany, the United Nations, Denmark, and the

National Agency for Investment Development, Argentina. He has won several awards including the Economic Research Annual Award 2007, Category: Young Professionals, Central Bank of Argentina.

Rogério Studart is a non-resident Senior Fellow at Brookings Institution, a senior visiting scholar at Boston University, and an international consultant. He was previously an Executive Director to the World Bank Group and Executive Director at the Inter-American Development Bank, an economist at the UN Economic Commission for Latin America and the Caribbean (ECLAC), and an associate professor at the Federal University of Rio de Janeiro. He has written extensively on development issues, macroeconomics, and sustainable finance.

Matthias Thiemann is Assistant Professor of European Public Policy at the Centre des études européennes et de la politique comparée. His work centres around the evolution of financial regulation post-crisis and the concomitant evolution of shadow banking activities (e.g. *The Growth of Shadow Banking*, Cambridge University Press, 2018). Jointly with Daniel Mertens he has published articles on the repositioning of national development banks in the context of the European post-crisis political economy and their increasing engagement with techniques of financial engineering.

Laura Valdez has been Assistant Professor in the Faculty of Economics at Universidad Nacional Autónoma de México (UNAM) and has collaborated in the publication of several papers. She has worked at the Food and Agriculture Organization as an economic advisor. She has acquired experience in Mexico's financial sector at the National Banking and Securities Commission. Currently, she works at the Ministry of Finance and Public Credit as economic advisor to the Under-Secretary, focusing on development banking, economic planning of the public finance, and public accounts.

Peter Volberding is a PhD candidate at Harvard University, currently based at Goethe University in Frankfurt, Germany. His research interests focus on the history of national promotional banks as a tool for economic development. In his dissertation, he explores how Germany's national promotional bank KfW evolved to rely more heavily on market-based financial instruments for the purposes of international economic development. He has also published work relating to public–private partnerships (PPPs), economic development policy, and natural resources in economic development.

Qiyuan Xu has been a member of IWEP (Institute of World Economics and Politics), CASS (Chinese Academy of Social Sciences) since 2008, and a Senior Research Fellow since 2011, and head of the Economic Development Division at IWEP since 2014. In 2012, he also took up the role of advisor to the International Collaboration Department in the Ministry of Finance of the PRC. His interests mainly focus on China's macroeconomic policies, RMB internationalization, and international development financing (related to the Belt & Road initiative). Xu also sits on the work team of CEEM (China's External Economic Environment) in IWEP.

1

The Future of National Development Banks

Stephany Griffith-Jones, José Antonio Ocampo, Felipe Rezende, Alfredo Schclarek, and Michael Brei

1.1 The Role of National Development Banks: A First Look

This chapter presents the framework for Columbia University's Initiative for Policy Dialogue (IPD) research project on national development banks, which has been supported by Brazil's National Economic and Social Development Bank (BNDES) and the Development Bank of Latin America (CAF). The project focuses on development banks, including public sector banks active in project financing for development purposes (for example, in infrastructure), but excludes public sector commercial banks.

The main activity of most development banks is second-tier lending—i.e. partial or full rediscounting of loans provided by other financial intermediaries, particularly commercial or investment banks. However, as is indicated below and is detailed in the case studies for this project, many also do first-tier lending, an activity in which public sector banks active in project financing are also engaged. Several are also involved—and, in fact, increasingly so—in guaranteeing private sector operations rather than lending, and those active in inclusive finance or agricultural lending also run guarantee funds. Equity investments are less common today than in the past, but at least one type of such investments, in equity or debt funds active in sectors of priority of the different banks, has become a growing activity of some of these banks in recent years.

In the wake of the 2007/9 North Atlantic financial crisis, there has been renewed support for these institutions, as the limitations and problems of a purely private financial sector have become more evident to different strands of economic thinking. It became obvious after 2007/9 that the private financial system on its own cannot perform well to support the real economy. It has been procyclical: overlending in boom times but rationing credit during and after crises. In tranquil, but even more in turbulent times, it has also not funded sufficiently long-term investment in innovation and skills, which businesses need to grow and create jobs. Key sectors, like infrastructure, renewable energy, and energy efficiency, have been insufficiently funded. And small and medium enterprises, as well as poor households, get insufficient credit, which is often costly and short-term. The implication of this is that 'irrespective of policy orientation, the failure of private financial markets to deliver adequate long-term finance forces governments to rely on development banking institutions' (Chandrasekhar 2016: 24).

The depth of concern about the financial sector is illustrated by International Monetary Fund (IMF) Managing Director, Christine Lagarde, in her statement: 'We need a financial system that serves society' (Lagarde 2015).

At the same time, as concerns about the limitations of a purely private financial system grew, the positive role that many development banks played during the crisis and its aftermath, especially by providing countercyclical finance, has been increasingly accepted, both in emerging and developing countries—in Brazil, China, and India, to mention just a few cases—where development banks have played key roles, but also increasingly in developed economies. There is, indeed, a growing view amongst many academic economists and policymakers that development banks at different levels—multilateral, regional, and national—have a very positive role to play in development finance in both developing and developed countries.

The growing recognition of their role in relation to developed countries has been reflected in the significant expansion of the role of the European Investment Bank (the largest multilateral development bank in the world) in response to the North Atlantic crisis. It is also evidenced in the recent creation of national development banks (NDBs) in countries like France and Ireland, and the positive evaluation of long-established successful NDBs, like KfW, which is widely seen as having played a positive role in the growth and structural transformation (e.g. to a greener economy) in the most successful European economy, Germany. Furthermore, a number of other developed countries, like Canada and South Korea, have had NDBs for a long time, playing useful roles in their support for funding investment and inclusive financial services.

In emerging and developing countries, NDBs have played a key role in the past, and the recognition of their role was reflected in their strong countercyclical response to the North Atlantic financial crisis. Increasingly, development banks are seen as part of a modern diversified financial system, which includes large as well as small banks, financial intermediaries as well as larger capital markets, and public as well as private institutions. This diversified system allows greater competition and may reduce systemic risk.

The recent creation of two large multilateral development banks, the Asia Infrastructure Investment Bank (AIIB)—that fifty-seven countries, including all major European countries and important emerging economies like Brazil initially joined as members, followed by many more countries that would join later—and the BRICS's New Development Bank (NDB), also seems to reflect the shift in the development finance paradigm towards a more balanced public–private mix for provision of long-term funding.

The basic framework that we used in this project is that development banks can play at least five crucial roles in the development process: (i) counteracting the procyclical behaviour of private financing; (ii) promoting innovation and structural transformation, which are inherent to dynamic economic growth; (iii) enhancing financial inclusion; (iv) supporting the financing of infrastructure investment, which is also crucial for economic growth; and (v) supporting the provision of public goods, particularly combatting climate change, and, more broadly, promoting environmental sustainability and 'green growth'. In several countries, development banks are also active in rural and export financing, as well as in investment of risk capital in specific firms or projects associated with their development mandates.

The key challenge is to make NDBs work as well as possible in fulfilling these roles, and do so as collaboratively as possible with the private financial sector. We therefore examine how NDBs can crowd in long-term private finance and help channel it for societal aims. In the same way, we look at how private finance can best provide essential leverage to limited public resources, through private lending and co-lending and capital market funding. In terms of defining societal priorities, we try to contribute to an understanding of how in a modern market economy the public and private sectors can best collaborate to define national strategies. We also analyse which governance arrangements seem to work best. We do so with detailed in-depth case studies, as well as thematic papers, trying to draw from them both positive and negative lessons.

It is interesting that institutions like the World Bank, which in the past were quite critical of national development banks, drawing on studies such as La Porta, López-de-Silanes, and Shleifer's (2002) paper, have increasingly become supportive of these institutions, especially since the 2007/9 crisis. Thus, drawing on a global survey of national development banks carried out by the World Bank, Luna-Martinez and Vicente conclude that 'DBs with clearly defined mandates, high corporate governance standards, strong risk management capability, proper regulation and supervision, and a strong management team have been successful' (Luna-Martinez and Vicente 2012: 24).

Along similar lines, the London School of Economics' Growth Commission concluded that for the UK: 'An Infrastructure Bank (IB) to facilitate the provision of stable, long-term, predictable, mostly private sector finance for infrastructure is desirable. There are good theoretical reasons for the creation of such a bank . . . There are good practical examples that show the advantages of a bank with this sort of mandate, such as Brazil's BNDES, Germany's KfW, the European Bank for Reconstruction and Development and to some extent the European Investment Bank' (Aghion et al. 2013: 25).

Furthermore, the Addis Ababa Action Agenda (AAAA 2015), approved by all United Nations members in the 2015 Financing for Development Conference, expressed very strong support for NDBs. The Agenda stated, in particular, that NDBs can play a vital role in providing access to financial services, and expressed similar support for using national development banks, in collaboration with private financial institutions and investors, to help fund infrastructure and, more broadly, achieve sustainable development goals.

An important point not frequently made in the literature is that, for emerging and developed economies in particular, a more diversified financial structure than one that is focused mainly on private (often large) banks, may have several advantages, including increased competition and financial stability. Firstly, it may encourage competition between different types of financial institutions, which could lead to reducing the interest rates they charge. Secondly, a more diversified financial system, *especially* if not having interconnected risks, could result in less systemic risk and therefore contribute to financial stability. Thirdly, if different varieties of financial institutions have different strengths, having a more diverse system could make it more likely that the financial sector fulfils the functions needed for inclusive growth.[1]

Many development banks, though having paid-in capital provided by governments, raise their funds on the national and sometimes international private capital markets. Typically, their loans are also co-financed by private agents, helping to prolong the maturities that private finance provides. Leveraging public resources with private ones has been especially valued in contexts of limited fiscal space, such as the European Union in the wake of the Eurozone debt crisis. This has led to important increases in the capital of some banks (e.g. KfW) and to the expansion of the capital of the European Investment Bank (EIB), as well as to the launch of the Juncker Plan, with the EIB at its centre, but with a major role for the private sector.

It is important to underscore that what should be promoted are 'good' development banks. To have 'good' development banks implies having institutions that have clear mandates and are well governed and well run, so they can fulfil their functions well. Their main objective is to maximize their

[1] To include some stylized facts, development banks are good at countercyclical lending and at providing long-term finance for private investment in infrastructure; private banks are good at providing international trade credit as well as financing the needs of large domestic and foreign companies; and low-end institutions are good at giving credit to MSMEs, especially in specific localities.

development impact rather than profits, though assuring at least minimal commercial returns. Their creation and consolidation can thus be understood as part of the effort to build strong state capacities. Indeed, when they fulfil these objectives, they can play a central role in implementing crucial government policies, such as industrial policy, infrastructure investment, and social inclusion. A key challenge is how best to achieve these goals in different categories of countries, which is one of the central themes of this project. Furthermore, 'good' national development banks need to collaborate effectively, both with private financial institutions and investors, as well as with regional and multilateral development banks.

DBs are, of course, political constructs that act in the financial and economic sphere to achieve social goals. There are, therefore, explicit trade-offs that need to be considered: specialized vs universal DBs; scale vs effectiveness; the possibility of crowding out vs crowding in private finance; and, more generally, there are the issues of market vs government failure.

On the first issue we think there are trade-offs between having specialized development banks that know their sectors better, and have fewer asymmetries of information, and universal cross-sectorial DBs that have the benefit of sectorial risk diversification. We will return to this topic in Chapter 13 ('Conclusions'). We think a similar trade-off probably exists for the case of private banks.

There are also trade-offs between the scale of DBs and their effectiveness. A larger scale facilitates greater impact in fulfilling their roles; on the other hand, it increases the risk of mistakes being made, unless careful project evaluation, rigorous monitoring, and other aspects of good governance are implemented. Our policy experience would argue that too large expansion in too rapid a period poses particular challenges and problems for DBs, which may lead to incorrect decisions. Again this seems true for private credit.

As regards crowding out of private lending by DBs, this is clearly a risk, but there is also a potential for crowding in. If private investment in general or for certain activities is low, the case for 'crowding out' is particularly weak. When there are significant under-utilized resources, there is no constraint on the availability of physical or human capital, which would squeeze private investments. On the contrary, under these conditions, public investment, or private investment funded by DBs, is more likely to 'crowd in' private investment. For example, new infrastructure investment, such as in energy, transport, or telecommunications, creates demand in the short term for a wide range of goods and services, and in the medium term stimulates growth through an expanded stock of physical capital and greater efficiency. Furthermore, DBs can take on risks, which improve the risk–reward ratios for private investors. Also many DBs co-finance with private lenders and investors, as well as fund themselves on national and international capital markets. In these three ways, public or DB financing investment may stimulate and complement—rather than compete with—private investment.

In relation to risks, the operation of DBs can help deal with the uncertainties associated with financing long-term and expensive capital projects, such as infrastructure investments and providing funding for innovative enterprises. Governments, sometimes effectively using DBs, often assume the risks associated with such initiatives via guarantees or other mechanisms, as the World Bank has argued (World Bank 2012).

There are preconditions for facilitating better performance by DBs: for example, good macroeconomic policies and well-functioning financial markets. Therefore, the challenge for policymakers is not just to have better DBs, but also good macroeconomic management—as reflected in particular in low inflation, smoother business cycles, and sustainable external accounts—as well as having policies to deepen local financial markets (see also Chapter 13, 'Conclusions').

In section 1.2, we briefly outline key analytical and theoretical analysis underpinning the need for development banks. In section 1.3, we use mainly existing studies to outline key features of national development banks. We will then discuss the main roles that national development banks do and should play in section 1.4. We draw this analysis from thematic papers and key questions posed for the case studies of the project.

1.2 Brief Review of Analytical and Theoretical Literature

Despite their size and importance, little research has been done on the analytical rationale for national development banks.

In the three decades after World War II, NDBs performed and were broadly seen as playing valuable roles in both developing and developed countries. However, policy concerns that the so-called 'financially repressed' systems were inefficient started to emerge. This was the basic argument that encouraged financial liberalization (Gurley and Shaw 1955; McKinnon 1973). In the framework of this efficient financial market school, the existence of public financial institutions, such as development banks, was—almost by definition—seen as negative. As a consequence, development banks were criticized, fairly and unfairly, and their role was reduced sharply in many countries. Some were liquidated.

An alternative theoretical framework that arose as the financial liberalization process was gaining traction emphasized credit rationing, which describes a situation in which, even when agents are willing to pay a higher interest rate to get the funds to finance their investments, private banks may refuse financing. In contrast with the previous school, this framework justifies the existence of development banks, which would supply the necessary credit to investment unavailable in the private financing system. This approach is associated with the theory of market failures in financial markets (Stiglitz and Weiss 1981; Stiglitz 1989). Credit rationing occurs due to a malfunction of the financial markets, caused by imperfect information and information asymmetries that prevent financial markets from functioning efficiently.

Furthermore, in this context, adverse selection and moral hazard accentuate these market imperfections.

Stiglitz (1994) argues that market failures in financial markets are likely to be endemic as those markets are particularly information-intensive, thus making information imperfections and asymmetries as well as incomplete contracts more important and disruptive than in other sectors. Therefore, in this context, market failures tend to be greater than government failures. The benefits of government interventions tend therefore to outweigh their costs. This provides a robust case for a 'visible hand of government', both through effective public development banks and through robust regulation of private financial markets.

Stiglitz and Greenwald (2014) further argue that knowledge and information markets also have huge market imperfections, and that they are basically public goods. As a consequence, governments have a clear role in promoting a learning society, to help achieve increases in productivity. Development banks are an institutional vehicle to help achieve this objective. Besides providing long-term finance, they can offer specific incentives for innovation. Furthermore, because of their long-term perspective, they can help fund, accumulate, and coordinate expertise in specific areas of innovation. Naturally, in this task they need to, and do, collaborate with other actors, both public and private.

Some of these market failures may be dependent on the level of development. Torres and Zeidan (2016) have indeed suggested that 'NDBs are a particularly important institution for channelling long-term credit in less developed financial markets. However, we argue that as countries develop their financial markets, NDBs should share this role with other local banks and specialize their focus, *eventually disappearing altogether*' (Torres and Zeidan 2016, emphasis added).

However, as we argued above, this does not agree with reality, as regional and national DBs continue to play a major role in funding investment and structural transformation in very successful developed and advanced emerging economies, such as Germany, Canada, France, and South Korea, and there have been several initiatives in recent years to create new or strengthen existing DBs in developed countries. Furthermore, the European Investment Bank, the large regional EU multilateral development bank, has been at the centre of efforts to accelerate the EU recovery, via all EU governments initially doubling their paid-in capital, and then making it play a central role in the Junker Plan and its European Fund for Strategic Investment (EFSI), in a major effort to boost private investment in the 2014–20 period.[2]

Furthermore, there are alternative theoretical frameworks to that of Torres and Zeidan. The global crisis has shown that there is no guarantee that developed financial markets promote the capital development of the economy, nor do they promote financial stability, unless properly regulated (see, for example, Wray 2010; Griffith-Jones, Ocampo, and Stiglitz 2010). This has important implications for policymaking, including the existence of 'good' well-governed NDBs, as part of a diversified financial system for countries at all levels of development, including those of high income. Clearly, the nature of NDBs, their aims, and instruments will change, according to the level of economic and financial development, but the need for them seems to remain, whilst market failures persist.

From a complementary theoretical perspective, several commentators (e.g. Wray 2009) argue there is a preference for liquidity amongst investors, as well as banks, which is responsible for the limitations of the supply of credit for investment. Given the uncertainty about the future, depending on the characteristics of the new sectors/projects that require resources, banks often offer no or insufficient credit (especially long-term credit) even if the financial system is fully developed.

The existence of development banks is justified by the existence of key sectors and investment projects that face high uncertainty as to their future success but are essential for structural transformation in different phases of development (Mazzucato 2013). For this reason, they may not be funded by the private financial system, which prefers sectors or investment projects whose expected returns are less uncertain. These are often highly complex and expensive sectors/projects, which require sophisticated expertise in their evaluation, taking account of positive impacts across the economy (positive social externalities, for example, in terms of helping to mitigate climate change via lower carbon emissions). For this reason, Kregel (2015) has argued that historically it has been public banks that have led the way in financing the long-term investment necessary for economic industrialization and transformation. Furthermore, he argues that 'the recent dominance of private financial institutions and the presumption of their efficiency advantage have reduced the availability of long-term finance for development' (Kregel 2015: 1).

Furthermore, a key market imperfection in the operation of financial markets, basically across the board, is the tendency to experience 'boom–bust'

[2] For more details, see a brief description of progress so far under EFSI, written by one of the authors, at <http://www.progressiveeconomy.eu/sites/default/files/EFSI.pdf>.

cycles (Keynes 1936; Minsky 1977; Kindleberger 1978). The procyclical nature of private finance implies the need for public development banks to provide both short-term and especially long-term countercyclical finance, as discussed in section 1.3. Moreover, the 2007/9 financial crisis has shown that there is no guarantee that even developed financial markets promote the capital development of the economy during both non-crisis and crisis periods (Luna-Martinez and Vicente 2012; Wray 2010).

Mussachio and Lazzarini (2014) have taken a more critical line on NDBs, especially with reference to BNDES. Using empirical evidence, based on a relatively short period, they find no evidence of a consistent impact of BNDES lending on firm performance or on greater incentives to invest, other than a reduction in financial expenses due to the effect of government subsidies. Their results also indicate, however, that BNDES is not lending to underperforming firms. Thus Lazzarini et al. (2015) also conclude that 'BNDES does not appear to be systematically picking or bailing out failing firms and its operations are, to some extent, profitable. Thus, our results fail to detect the type of distortion proposed by the political view—that is, that development banks target firms with bad performance.'

It is interesting that other studies take a different view than Lazzarini on the effects of BNDES financing on investment, such as one published by the Central Bank of Brazil which suggests that: 'Firms that are financially restricted in the presence or not of a monetary shock and that have access to BNDES observe on average a smaller decrease in their investment than restricted firms that do not have access to BNDES' (de Oliveira 2014: 24). This paper concludes that there is 'strong empirical evidence that BNDES, Brazil's development bank, is also very important to explain the dynamics of investment' (de Oliveira 2014: 28). See also the discussion of BNDES in Chapter 4 of this volume.

1.3 Key Features of National Development Banks

Several national development banks were created before the end of WWII. However, as Chandrasekhar (2016) points out, most were established in different periods after WWII: 'although almost half of national development banks (49 per cent) were established... between 1946 and 1989, nearly two-fifths (39 per cent) came into existence... between 1990 and 2011' (see also Figure 1.1, for distribution through time, including the pre-WWII period).

One important feature that national development banks share is their large scale. According to Studart and Gallagher (2016), as well as Gallagher and Sklar (2016), the level of total assets of national development banks is very large, reaching approximately US$5 trillion in 2015, which is, for example, far larger

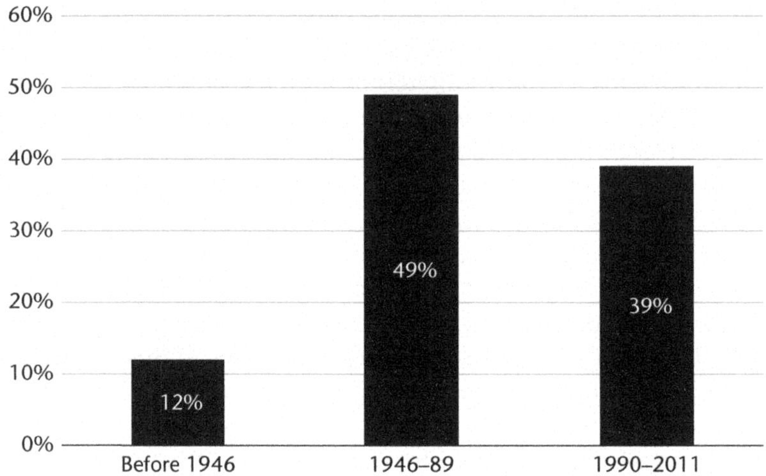

Figure 1.1. NDBs by year of establishment (percentage of DBs)
Source: Luna-Martinez and Vicente (2012: 6)

than the level of loans of the multilateral development banks, which reached around $1 trillion in the same year. It should be mentioned that other estimates for national development banks' assets are somewhat smaller, though in the same order of magnitude.

Besides their large scale, a second important feature is their large number. According to Chandrasekhar (2016), drawing on a 1998 study by Nicholas Bruck, there were 550 development banks worldwide, of which around 520 were national development banks (NDBs). These were located in 185 countries, with developing countries in particular hosting an average of three or more NDBs. Latin America and the Caribbean had the largest number of NDBs (152), followed by Africa (147), Asia and the Pacific (121), Europe (49), and West Asia (47).

The task of analysing and evaluating comparatively different NDBs is rather complex, as they differ according to the following characteristics, as identified in the World Bank study by Luna-Martinez and Vicente (2012):

a. Ownership structure (fully vs partially owned by government)
b. Mandate, targeted sectors, and clients (narrow vs wide focus)
c. Different business (lending) models to carry out their lending operations (first-tier vs second-tier)
d. Credit conditions (subsidized vs market interest rates)
e. Regulation and supervision (special regime vs regime applicable to all banks)
f. Corporate governance (independent vs government-controlled boards)

g. Size (absolute and relative)

h. Loan portfolio and performance indicators.

In section 1.3.1 we summarize what existing studies say about the main characteristics of NDBs listed above. This is complemented by an analysis of key variables of these versus other financial institutions, such as the proportion of loans going to productive lending to corporates by development banks in Latin America and the Caribbean, based on original empirical analysis made by two of the co-authors of this chapter, Michael Brei and Alfredo Schclarek, which is detailed in their own contribution to the project.

1.3.1 *Main Features of National Development Banks According to Existing Studies*

Typically, NDBs 'are institutions owned, administered, and controlled by the government (state), which provides the strategic direction of the DB and appoints their senior management and board members' (Luna-Martinez and Vicente 2012). Almost three-quarters of NDBs surveyed by the World Bank are 100 per cent state-owned, 21 per cent have between 50 and 90 per cent state ownership, and in only 5 per cent do governments have a minority ownership.

According to Luna-Martinez and Vicente (2012: 11–12), '53% of NDBs are "institutions with a narrow and specific mandate, which explicitly refers to the sector(s), type of customers or activities that a NDB is expected to support... [while] 47% of NDBs are institutions with broader legal mandates and are expected to support a broader range of activities and sectors"'.

The advantages and disadvantages of a broad versus narrow mandate are, of course, a central policy issue. Narrow mandates encourage institutions to specialize in their target market. Monitoring and performance evaluation is, therefore, easier for these institutions. In contrast, NDBs with broad mandates require resources to finance a wide range of activities and sectors. This may be valuable as the challenges and needs of the broader economy change, and thus the emphasis required from NDBs.

A good example of the advantages of a broader mandate is the emergence of climate change mitigation and adaptation as a major challenge for governments, and therefore the new priority given for NDBs to play a key role. The strategic role that NDBs play in this new and much-needed frontier of investments is clear: out of total financing, approximately 35 per cent or US$123 billion of investments was financed by development finance institutions, of which about 60 per cent was funded by national development banks (based on estimates provided in Mazzucato and Penna drawing on data from the 2013 Climate Policy Initiative).

Economic sectors targeted by NDBs vary: '86% of NDBs targeted the trade and services sectors, 84% industry and manufacturing, 83% agriculture, 74% construction and housing, 66% energy, and 65% infrastructure. On the other hand, only 48% of the NDBs targeted the health sector, 45% education, and 43% mining' (Luna-Martinez and Vicente 2012). Therefore, there is a smaller emphasis on lending to social sectors. In turn, '92% of DBs responded that they target small and medium enterprises, 60% large private corporations, 55% individuals and households, 54% other state-owned enterprises (SOEs) and 46% private financial intermediaries' (Luna-Martinez and Vicente 2012: 13).

In a more detailed analysis of some of the largest NDBs (CDB, KfW, BNDES, and JFC), three of which have been studied in this project, Ferraz et al. (2016) show that all these large banks lend to MSMEs, for innovation, for the green economy, for internationalization, and for capital market development; three out of four lend to agriculture and to infrastructure.

In terms of business models, again according to Luna-Martinez and Vicente (2012), 52 per cent of NDBs lend through a combination of first- and second-tier operations, while only 12 per cent of NDBs only do second-tier lending. Interestingly, a large number of 'second-tier-only' NDBs are located in Latin America.

In terms of credit conditions, products offered by NDBs are mainly concentrated in 'long-term loans (90%), followed by working capital loans (85%), whereas syndicated loans consisted of 52% of all DBs, and unsecured loans 25%' (Luna-Martinez and Vicente 2012). The maturity of loans that NDBs offer is presented in Table 1.1. It shows that 54 per cent of NDB loans are over ten years' maturity. This is why it is correct to say that NDBs are a major source of so-called patient capital, especially well-suited to fund projects—like in infrastructure—which become profitable only after a long period.

Moreover, 'credit at subsidized interest rates is a practice adopted by 50% of DBs covered in the survey. In this category, 66% of DBs fund these subsidies using transfers from their respective governments.' Finally, '73% of all DBs offer

Table 1.1. Maximum loan term offered by DBs

Maximum loan term	Percentage of DBs
Up to 5 years	16%
6 to 10 years	29%
11 to 15 years	19%
16 to 20 years	22%
21 to 25 years	7%
26 to 30 years	6%
Total	**100%**

Source: Luna-Martinez and Vicente (2012: 16)

loan guarantee products to partially offset the losses faced by a private financial intermediary when a customer defaults' (Luna-Martinez and Vicente 2012).

The World Bank survey shows that '76% of DBs are in fact regulated and supervised by the same institution that supervises private commercial banks in their countries, such as the central bank or the bank supervisory agency... [while] 78% of DBs indicated they are required to comply with the same standards of prudential supervision (minimum capital, minimum capital adequacy requirements, loan classification and provisioning, etc.) as private commercial banks or any other private financial institution' (Luna-Martinez and Vicente 2012).

The fact that the regulatory agencies and principles are the same for NDBs as for other financial institutions poses some questions, which are analysed in detail by Lavinia Barros de Castro in her contribution to this project. The major issue is the treatment of risks of long-term lending and portfolio concentration. As has been widely recognized, existing regulation has biased commercial bank lending towards the short term. This effect must be clearly avoided in the case of NDBs. In turn, in infrastructure lending in particular, portfolio concentration is inevitable, or projects would be inadequately financed. So regulatory norms must be revised to avoid the adverse effects they could have on the activities of NDBs.

As can be seen in Figure 1.2, there is a large range of NDBs, according to the scale of their assets. According to the World Bank survey, 5 per cent of these

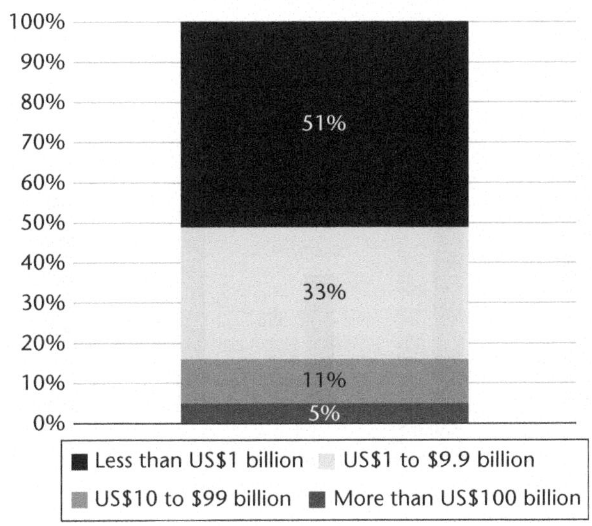

Figure 1.2. NDBs by assets in 2009 (percentage of NDBs)
Source: Luna-Martinez and Vicente (2012: 7)

banks have assets of over $100 billion; at the other extreme, 51 per cent of these NDBs have assets of under $1 billion.

Naturally, the key variable to explore is their scale in proportion to the size of economies, as well as to the size of total credit to the private sector. Figure 1.3 shows these indicators for 2013, for some of the largest development banks. According to this data, the largest loan to gross domestic product (GDP) ratio is that of KfW, fairly closely followed by CDB and BNDES. On the other hand, if total loan portfolio is looked at as a proportion of total credit to the private sector, also for 2013, the highest ratio is for BNDES, followed by KfW and CDB. In both ratios, the other NDBs analysed have significantly lower figures than KfW, BNDES, and CDB.

Even though profit maximization is not the objective of NDBs, the World Bank survey and report shows that 'In 2009, 53% of the surveyed NDBs had a Return on Assets (RoA) exceeding the average of their banking systems. This was up from 42% in 2006 and 2007, and 46% in 2008. In terms of the Return on Equity (RoE), 19% of DBs exceeded the national average in 2009, up from 15% in 2006, 13% in 2007, and 18% in 2008' (Luna-Martinez and Vicente 2012: 18). In turn, 'Non-performing loan (NPL) ratios of all "second-tier-only" DBs fell within the less than 5% bracket' (Luna-Martinez and Vicente 2012: 17).

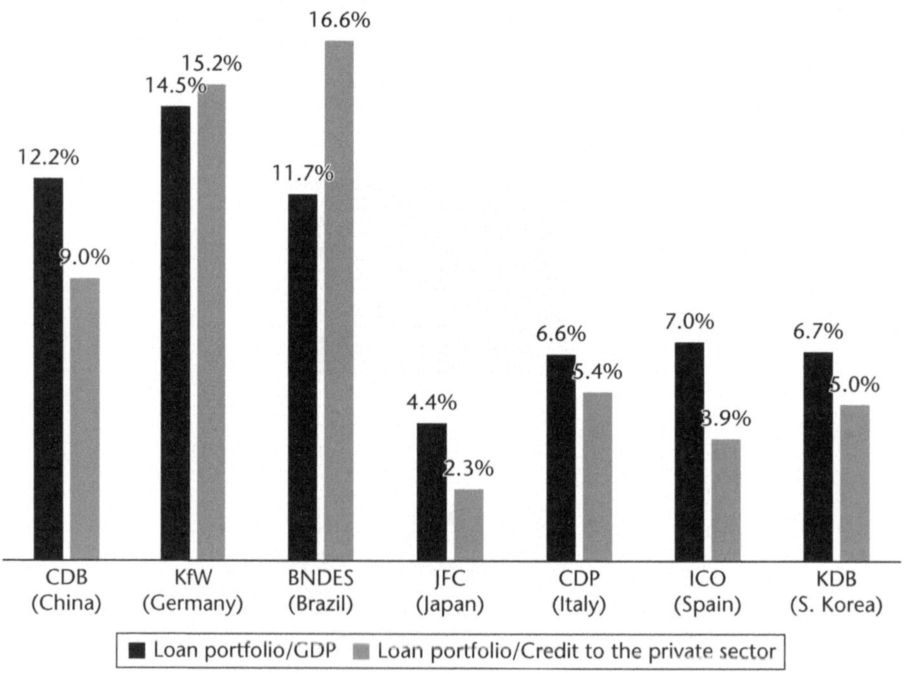

Figure 1.3. NDBs' loan portfolios relative to GDP and private credit, 2013 (percentage)
Source: Além and Madeira (2015: 114)

Table 1.2. Structure and economic and financial performance of selected DFIs, 2013

	CDB	KfW	BNDES	JFC	CDP	CDC	ICO	KDB
	China	Germany	Brazil	Japan	Italy	France	Spain	S. Korea
Assets (US$ billion)	1331.30	619.70	363.40	260.40	242.40	190.70	136.30	131.10
Loan portfolio (US$ billion)	1172.30	528.80	263.50	222.80	137.60	nd	95.00	87.90
Net profit (US$ billion)	13.00	1.17	3.60	(2.90)	3.10	2.50	0.10	(1.30)
Delinquency rate (%)	0.48	0.13	0.01	2.98	0.20	nd	5.30	3.10
Return/assets (%)	1.02	0.27	1.01	(1.13)	1.29	1.33	0.08	(1.01)
Return/equity (%)	15.07	6.21	15.34	(6.84)	14.00	nd	1.76	(8.85)
Number of employees	8468.00	5374.00	2859.00	7361.00	1440.00	nd	310.00	n.d
Year of foundation	**1994**	**1948**	**1952**	**2008**	**1850**	**1816**	**1988**	**1954**

Source: Além and Madeira (2015: 110)

Looking at the some of the largest NDBs, a fairly positive picture also emerges for 2013. As Além and Madeira (2015) point out (see also Table 1.2), delinquency rates on loans are very low, with the highest rates for Spanish Official Credit Institute (ICO) (that was probably worsened significantly by the Eurozone debt crisis) and for Japanese JFC. According to this information, BNDES, KfW, and CDB have the lowest delinquency rates. As regards RoE, the best results according to this source are from BNDES and CDB, whilst the worst are from KDB (Korean) and JFC (Japanese), both of which show actual losses.

A final important feature of NDBs is funding. According to the World Bank survey, 89 per cent of NDBs borrow from other financial institutions or issue debt on local capital markets. This shows the close and positive symbiosis between public development banks and private financial institutions. Forty per cent of these NDBs receive budget transfers from the government and 64 per cent receive government guarantees.[3] It is interesting that 41 per cent of NDBs reportedly take deposits from the general public.

1.3.2 *Lending and Funding Structure of National Development Banks from a Comparative Perspective*

This subsection investigates the lending and funding structure of national development banks and compares it with that of commercial public and

[3] 'It should be noted that receiving direct transfers from the government does not necessarily mean dependence on government funds. Sometimes, DBs—such as KfW in Germany—receive transfers from the government to fund interest rate subsidies to a particular type of borrower' (Luna-Martinez and Vicente 2012: 10–11).

private banks. In addition, it explores the lending and funding rates with which these banks operated. Finally, it examines the lending quality of these banks with a focus on non-performing loans. The data used covers 422 banking institutions (twenty-seven national development banks, thirty-six public banks, and 359 private banks) from thirty-five jurisdictions in Latin America and the Caribbean over the period 2000–14. All values are unweighted averages across banks and countries.[4] A detailed discussion of the underlying data is provided by Brei and Schclarek in Chapter 11 of this book.

The lending activity of NDBs differs remarkably from that of private banks. As can be seen in Figure 1.4a, development banks have focused their activities on lending, as evidenced by an average loan-to-asset ratio of 58.6 per cent over the period 2000–14 (with the rest being composed of assets like securities and liquid assets).[5] This pattern is to some extent similar to commercial public banks, which have invested 52.6 per cent of their assets in customer loans. However, these ratios stand in contrast to those of private banks in the region, which recorded a far lower average loan-to-asset ratio of 43.7 per cent.[6] Interestingly, the lending activity of NDBs has been focused mainly on the provision of productive lending in the form of corporate and commercial loans (see Figure 1.4b).[7] To be more precise, an average of 49.3 per cent of assets have been devoted to the productive lending activity, compared to 31.2 and 20.1 per cent in the cases of public and private banks, respectively. Clearly, national development banks are an important source of productive funding for corporations, reaffirming their role as promoters of economic development.

Over the considered period, public banks have had the highest ratios of holdings of government securities as a proportion of total assets, as can be seen in Figure 1.4c.[8] In the more recent period, however, it appears that NDBs have increased their share of government securities, thereby counteracting the decrease in government securities of their public bank peers. Private banks, on the other hand, have invested much less in government securities. The results might be a sign that national development banks are refocusing their lending activities towards infrastructural lending to the government, an

[4] Our results do not change significantly if we weight for the size of banks.

[5] Total loans include residential mortgage loans, other mortgage loans, other consumer/retail loans, corporate and commercial loans, other loans, and reserve against possible losses on impaired or non-performing loans.

[6] On average, total assets of NDBs are composed of approximately 60 per cent loans, 20 per cent securities (which include any bonds), 10 per cent liquid assets, and 10 per cent interbank positions (may include lending to the central bank). If weighted by total assets, the ratio of loans in total assets increases, which suggests that the large development banks have a heavier focus on lending than smaller development banks.

[7] Corporate and commercial loans include loans and leases to corporate and commercial enterprises.

[8] Government securities include all treasury bills and government securities.

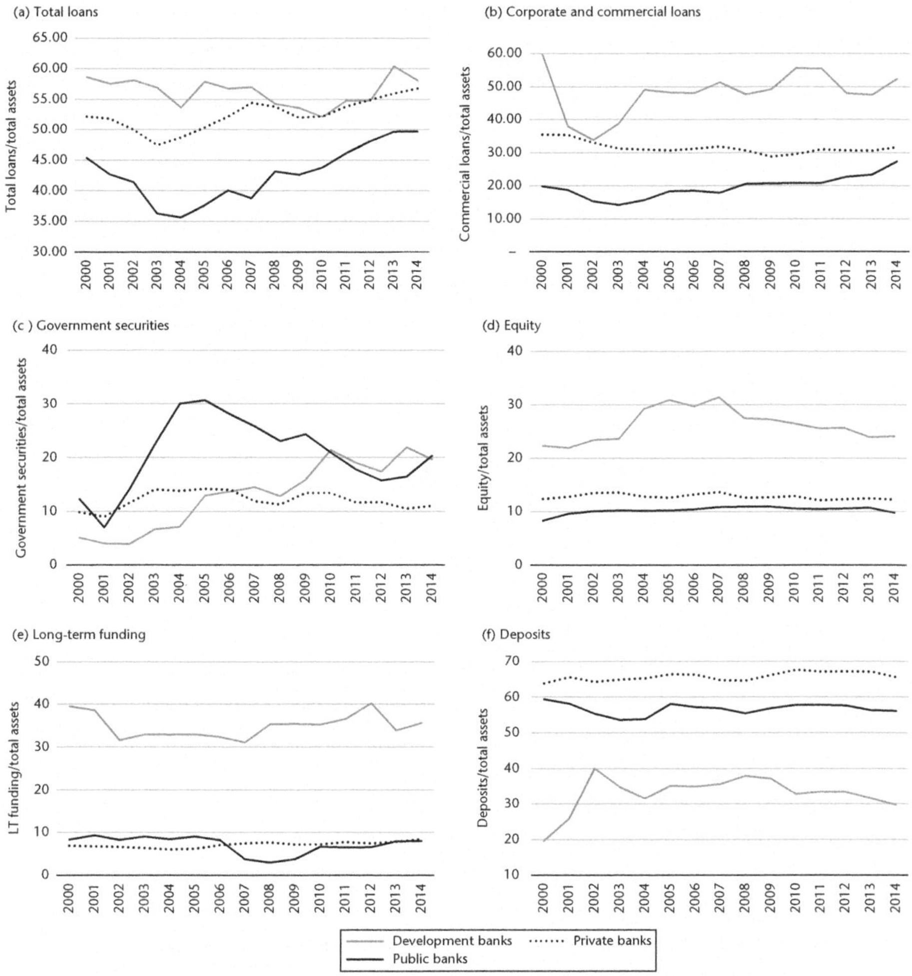

Figure 1.4. Selected indicators on bank balance sheets, 2000–14

Note: The figures are based on 422 banks (27 national development banks, 36 public banks, and 359 private banks) from 35 jurisdictions in Latin America and the Caribbean. Development banks are banks that are state-owned, non-retail deposit-taking, and not foreign- or multilateral-owned development banks. Public banks are majority-owned banks by a government, and private banks are the remaining banks. Government securities include treasury bills and other government securities. Long-term funding includes senior debt maturing after one year, subordinated borrowing, and other long-term funding. All values are unweighted averages across banks and countries.

Sources: Bankscope; Claessens and van Horen (2015); authors' own calculations

important determinant of economic development. However, if the increased holding of government securities were due to increased financing of government current expenses, this would be problematic. Note, however, that from our data it is impossible to assess the exact reason for the holding of government securities or the use of these funds by the government. For example, it could be the case that the government is recapitalizing the bank by granting it government securities. In this case, the increased holding of government securities would not be evidence that the bank is financing the government, but quite the opposite. To get a thorough answer to these questions a detailed case study of funding and lending structures should be carried out for each national development bank, which is not the objective here.

The funding structure of development banks is inherently different from that of public and private banks (see Figure 1.4d and Figure 1.4e). The average figures suggest that development banks have relied on more stable sources of funding, as evidenced by significantly higher equity (bank capital) and long-term funding ratios.[9] More specifically, while development banks recorded on average equity and long-term funding ratios of 25.8 and 35.7 per cent of assets, respectively, these ratios have been much lower for public and private banks. Their long-term funding represented on average 7.4 per cent of assets, while the equity-to-asset ratio averaged 12.5 per cent in the case of private banks and 9.9 per cent in the case of public banks. This difference can be explained by the fact that both private and public banks financed their activities mainly through deposits (see Figure 1.4e), which is not the case for development banks.[10] Evidently, the funding structure of development banks shows that they are better prepared for financing long-term projects without suffering a maturity mismatch.

Regarding real lending rates, NDBs tend to provide their loans at lower interest rates compared to public and private banks in the region (see Figure 1.5a). Across all banks, there has been a declining trend in real lending rates, presumably associated with the increased macroeconomic stability in the region and the reduction in US, European, and Japanese interest rates that came about after the financial crisis. While the real lending rate of private and public banks averaged 13.2 and 9.8 per cent over the period 2000–14, development banks have lent at an average rate of 7.1 per cent. Here again, the evidence shows that national development banks are fulfilling their objective by providing economically more affordable loans to foster economic development. Note that charging a lower real interest rate than other banks does not mean

[9] Equity includes common equity, non-controlling interest, securities revaluation reserves, foreign exchange revaluation reserves, and other revaluation reserves. Long-term funding includes senior debt maturing after one year, subordinated borrowing, and other funding.

[10] Deposits include current, savings, and term deposits by customers.

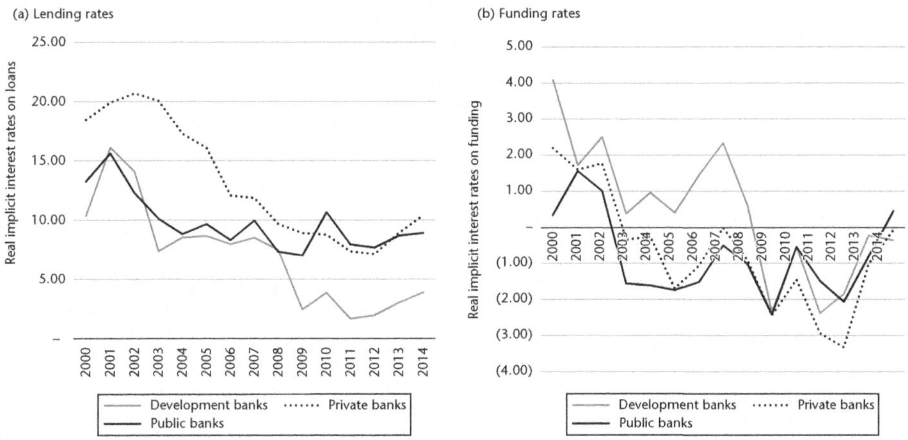

Figure 1.5. Real lending and funding rates, 2000–14

Note: Lending rates are calculated as interest income on loans divided by total loans, while funding rates are calculated as total interest expense divided by total liabilities net of equity. Real rates are calculated using predicted inflation, estimated from a simple autoregressive model. All values are unweighted averages across banks and countries.

Sources: Bankscope; Claessens and van Horen (2015); authors' own calculations

necessarily that development banks are 'subsidizing' lending rates. Although development banks may not be maximizing profits, they still often are making profits at these interest rate levels.

With respect to funding rates (see Figure 1.5b), development banks have consistently had higher costs of external funding prior to 2008. After 2008, real funding rates across banks seem to have converged to levels below zero (after accounting for inflation) with an increasing trend in 2013–14. The lower funding costs are presumably explained by the fact that private and public banks fund themselves mainly in the form of insured deposits, which typically pay lower interest rates than long-term funding in the form of bonds and securities, which is one of the main sources of funding by development banks.

As can be seen in Figure 1.6, the riskiness of the loan portfolios across all bank types has declined significantly over the period 2000–14 for Latin American and Caribbean banks. Presumably associated with the increase in banks' risk aversion, risk management, and macroeconomic stability, non-performing loans have declined to about 5 per cent of loans since 2008. Note also that, currently, development banks have the lowest non-performance of loan ratios among all bank types, which is very positive. Development and private banks faced loan defaults and restructurings in the order of 40 per cent of equity in 2000–1. This pattern can be explained by the various crises that hit the region, including Argentina's and Uruguay's financial crises of 2001

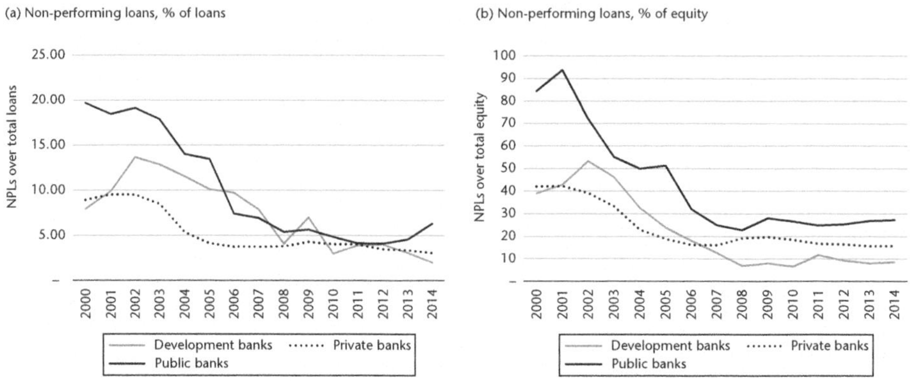

Figure 1.6. Lending quality, 2000–14
Sources: BankScope; Claessens and van Horen (2015); authors' own calculations

and Brazil's confidence crisis of 2002. Since then, banking sector stability has increased significantly. Fostering risk management by banks and macroeconomic stability clearly reinforces the positive working of national development banks.

1.4 The Roles of National Development Banks

As indicated in the introduction to this chapter, development banks play at least five crucial roles in the development process: (i) counteracting the procyclical behaviour of private financing; (ii) promoting innovation and structural transformation; (iii) enhancing financial inclusion; (iv) supporting infrastructure investment; and (v) supporting the provision of public goods, and particularly combatting climate change.

There are other roles that NDBs could or should play. These include helping to develop and deepen financial markets, promoting entrepreneurship, and promoting internationalization of national firms. Indeed, some of these functions may be included in the five on which we concentrate our analysis. This is also true of other areas in which NDBs are active, particularly rural development and export growth, which will also be analysed only in relation to the five crucial functions on which we will focus.

1.4.1 *Countercyclical Lending*

There is growing consensus that a valuable primary function of development banks in general is their countercyclical role when private lending falls sharply or collapses, especially during and in the aftermath of financial crises (Griffith-Jones and Ocampo 2008). This is particularly crucial to help maintain long-term investment, including in infrastructure, thus ensuring the continuity of existing projects and helping new ones start, valuable both for short-term growth and long-term development. It should also help mitigate the business cycle and help prevent financial crises from deepening (Rezende 2015).

The 2007/9 North Atlantic financial crisis showed especially clearly that multilateral, regional, and national development banks of the developed and developing world significantly increased their total lending to developing countries in the years when they were most affected, through the rapid expansion of existing mechanisms, as well as via specially created ones.

Indeed, the multilateral development banks (MDBs) collectively increased their lending commitments to emerging and developing economies by 72 per cent between 2008 and 2009, the year when private capital flows to these countries fell most sharply as a result of the crisis (Griffith Jones and Gottschalk 2012). Their disbursements also grew significantly in the same year by 40 per cent, though at a slower rate than commitments. This represented a major countercyclical response, which helped sustain investment in those countries.

This countercyclical lending by multilateral and regional development banks was complemented by that of NDBs in emerging and developed countries. Furthermore, a group of NDBs (like BNDES and several NDBs in Asia) also contributed to giving continuity to trade finance in cases where private trade lines fell.

Luna-Martinez and Vicente (2012) provide evidence that these banks increased their lending from US$1.16 trillion to US$1.58 trillion between 2007 and 2009. This increase in lending of 36 per cent was larger than the 10 per cent increase in private bank credit in these countries. They also find that development banks increased short- and long-term lending to old and new customers who faced difficulties in refinancing their loans or receiving new lines of credit.

The clear countercyclical role played by the large NDBs can be seen visually in Figure 1.7, which shows that the average growth of their loan portfolio increased from around 10 per cent in the 2005–7 period to almost 25 per cent in 2008, and then declined.

More broadly, the recent literature has emphasized the value of countercyclical lending by NDBs—as well as of countercyclical lending by regional and multilateral banks, including the World Bank. Indeed, the procyclical nature of private banking and financial markets is one of their main market failures. Public development banks compensate for that, which helps maintain economic activity and investment in 'bad times', whilst NDBs' lending should grow less—or even decline—when private lending recovers. As in all other activities, NDBs' lending should fund carefully evaluated

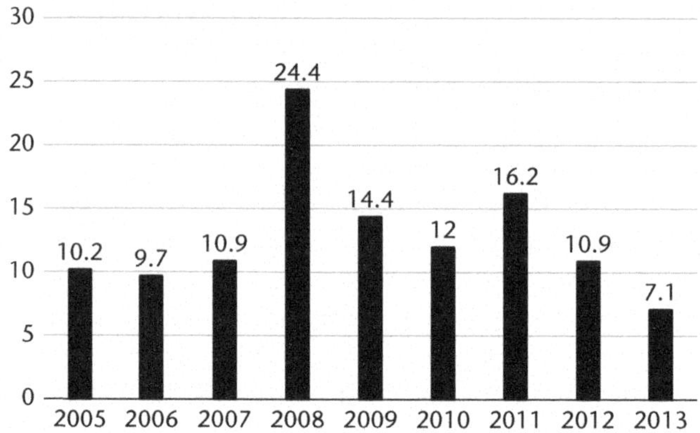

Figure 1.7 Average growth of the loan portfolio of some DFIs from the sample (percentage)

Source: Além and Madeira (2015: 112)

projects or firms, which cannot fund themselves by private banks or markets. Therefore, our focus is on the need for 'good' development banks and the conditions that help make them so.

The countercyclical role of NDBs has been praised internationally, especially since the onset of the North Atlantic financial crisis. For example, Luna-Martinez and Vicente (2012) conclude that: 'During the current financial crisis, most development banks in Latin America, followed by Asia, Africa, and Europe, have assumed a counter-cyclical role by scaling up their lending operations exactly when private banks experienced temporary difficulties in granting credit to the private sector'.

There is also a small but growing body of detailed empirical evidence that national public banks provide countercyclical finance. Brei and Schclarek (2013 and 2015) compare the lending responses to financial crises across national public and private banks, using balance sheet information for about 560 major banks from fifty-two countries during the period 1994 to 2009. They find evidence that the growth rate of lending during normal times is higher for the average private bank compared to the average public sector bank. During financial crises, however, private banks' growth rate of lending decreases while that of public banks increases. These results indicate that public banks have played a countercyclical role in their banking systems, while private banks behaved procyclically.

They offer three explanations for this. First, the objective of state-owned banks, in contrast to their private peers, is not only to maximize profits given risks, but also to stabilize and promote the recovery of the economy. There is a similar argument made by Rudolph (2010), who argues that state financial institutions have less volatile risk aversion and therefore provide a more stable source of financing. Second, public banks may suffer fewer deposit withdrawals or avoid a bank run in a severe crisis, because of the implicit guarantee of the state; the securities issued by these institutions also have a preference in the market during crises. Finally, in crisis conditions, public sector banks may be more easily capitalized by governments than private banks, which may have difficulties raising the additional equity funds in the market.

In addition, Mazzucato and Penna (2016), as well as Turner (2015), argue that the procyclical behaviour of private banks is further increased by the fact that these banks have become increasingly focused over the past decades on short-term profits, meaning that they target low-risk, short-term gains through the trade of securities and other investments, being less interested in financing long-term productive and innovative projects.

Other papers reach similar conclusions. Thus, Micco and Panizza (2006) use bank-level data for 119 countries for the period 1995–2002 and find that lending by government-owned banks is less sensitive to business cycle fluctuations than that of private banks. They find that this differential behaviour is due to an explicit objective to stabilize credit. Bertay et al. (2015) find that lending by state banks varies less with the economic cycle, and even rises during a banking crisis. The empirical analysis is based on an international sample of 1633 banks from 111 countries for the period 1999–2010.

The findings may be important in policy terms. It seems key to have fairly large public sector development banks (as a proportion of the total banking sector) so they can play a more significant role in generating countercyclical finance, and can thus contribute more to economic recovery in times of crisis or slowdown. A significant scale of development banks may be also important for other reasons, which we elaborate in sections 1.4.2 to 1.4.5: helping to ensure enough long-term finance for key sectors, like sustainable infrastructure and innovation, where profitability tends to be long-term, as well as supporting structural transformation to a sustainable and inclusive development path, and helping to channel sufficient and sufficiently low-cost credit to small and medium enterprises and others.

1.4.2 *Promoting Innovation and Structural Transformation*

There is a growing consensus that NDBs have to prioritize their role in fostering innovation and structural transformation in national economies (Gutierrez et al. 2011; Mazzucato and Penna 2016; de Olloqui 2013). Moreover, all of the eight NDBs surveyed by Além and Madeira (2015) foster innovation. In terms of fostering industry or sector diversification as objectives for NDBs, the recent literature is relatively limited, Mazzucato and Penna (2016), as well as the authors of this chapter, being among recent exceptions. This objective is easy to justify when considering, as Hidalgo et al. (2007) and

Ocampo et al. (2009) show, that fostering product and sector diversification is an important determinant of innovation and economic development. Moreover, as Schclarek and Navarrete (2016) argue, industry or sector diversification, by lowering aggregate credit risk, is also an important factor in fostering financial development.

The greater need for instruments to implement more long-term national development strategies for structural transformation and innovation, and in particular NDBs, has been increasingly recognized in general terms. This coincides with the acceptance of the value of a modern 'industrial policy' and the importance of an 'entrepreneurial and development state', which, working closely with the private sector, helps give a dynamic push for private innovation and structural transformation (Rodrik 2004; Mazzucato 2013). This builds on the success stories of the past, for example in East Asia, as well as more recently in China and India. Mazzucato (2013) also shows that key innovations in the US, the most free-market of economies, were spearheaded by public funding for innovation, though implemented by the private sector.

However, there is an important new element, which we discuss in more detail in section 1.4.5 on public goods. There is an urgent need for a major structural transformation in the development model, to make it compatible with the needs of the planet. This implies the urgency of major investment in green development. Renewable energy, partly financed by public development banks, is a key instrument for this.

In a complementary perspective, Stiglitz and Greenwald (2014) argue that successful and sustained growth requires the creation of a learning society and a knowledge economy to increase productivity. NDBs are an important institutional vehicle to support this aim. Indeed, development banks can help overcome market failures in both financial and knowledge markets simultaneously.

The role of NDBs related to innovation is particularly important for two reasons. First, technologies need significant financing for research and development (R&D), where investment is high risk due to factors such as failure of some projects in the search for successful solutions, and lengthy project time frames with limited interim financial returns. These factors constrain private investment in these areas. Such research requires special financing by the state, but NDBs could help finance the private component of that task. Second, as new technologies become increasingly operational and their implementation gathers speed and scale, financing is needed for large-scale and long-term investment. In this area, NDBs need to be involved in financing the required large-scale infrastructure (e.g. funding of green grids) that has important positive externalities. This will enable full-scale execution, for example, of clean energy projects which otherwise may be less attractive to the private sector due to their scale or time length, and because social benefits may outweigh private benefits.

More broadly, in terms of the capacities that NDBs already possess, which make them especially suited for providing financing to innovation as well as creation and development of new sectors or industries, Mazzucato and Penna (2016) make the point that:

> Because these are banking institutions, NDBs already have the capability and knowledge to access the economic feasibility of projects. Moreover, NDBs have traditionally supplied long-term funding (for capital-intensive projects, for example), and patient long-term committed capital is crucial for making new mission-oriented projects economically feasible. These institutions are also well positioned to coordinate stakeholders, as part of the development banking process is to coordinate stakeholders, to establish relationships, and to build up a network with an array of actors (from government officials to corporate actors to consumers). The fact that NDBs have a vast portfolio of funding tools (equity, loans, grants, etc.) will likely enable them to match the most appropriate tool to the project, whether it is incremental or radical (for example, equity or risk contracts for radical innovation, loans to incremental innovation projects, and grants to blue sky R&D). Finally, NDBs have traditionally executed their roles in coordination with governmental policies . . . and new missions could potentially build on this important node in the governmental network.

The last point is perhaps particularly important. NDBs should not be seen in isolation. Their success also depends on coordination among national economic policy agents to foster development and its funding. The latter would usually be provided in part by NDBs, which also play a key role in catalysing private finance for key societal aims (Rezende 2015). A good example of this is German KfW, which has played a key role in starting up renewable energy in Germany, by funding initially all private investment in solar energy; this was done in the clear frame of government policies designed to encourage such private investment. The coordination of both elements led to an important success in this field (Griffith-Jones 2016).

An important aspect to underscore here is the need for close collaboration and consultation between the government and the private sector to help design the best strategy, to define the right targets for structural transformation, and to achieve them most effectively. Amongst the issues that we will explore in more depth in the different case studies is, therefore: what is the role of development banks in public–private articulation to identify and select enterprises, sectors, chains, and regions?

When evaluating which sectors and sub-sectors to foster, governments and development banks should put more emphasis on maximizing development returns, not just financial returns. Development banks should also take the long view, prioritizing sectors that yield the highest development returns over the longer term. After sectors have been selected on this basis, projects within prioritized sectors need to be scrutinized for both potential development impact and their ability to generate positive financial returns (Griffith-Jones et al. 2016).

1.4.3 *Enhancing Financial Inclusion*

There is much agreement about the important role that NDBs should and do play in providing access to financing for SMEs and microenterprises (including family agriculture), especially, but not only, long-term credit (Gutierrez et al. 2011; de Olloqui 2013; UN-DESA 2005; World Bank 2012). This relates firstly to NDBs playing an important role in assisting implementation of national development strategies, which is helping to improve financial inclusion in those sectors traditionally excluded from the formal financial sector, such as the rural sector. Financial inclusion for SMEs is a prerequisite for productive development, innovation, and higher productivity. In turn, financing microenterprises is critical for poverty reduction and for improving the low-quality standards that characterize self-employment in developing countries. In non-inclusive financial systems, it is normally small firms and poor individuals that do not have access to finance. This, in turn, is a mechanism that reinforces inequalities. In many emerging economies, and even in some developed ones, access to finance both by individuals and small firms is still an issue that needs major policy action, especially but not only during and after financial crises or downturns. In general, financial systems in developing countries exhibit problems of segmentation and exclude broad segments of the productive sector such as micro, small, and medium-sized firms.

SMEs play a crucial role in most market-based economies as providers of employment and income opportunities and as vehicles of innovation and growth. On average, SMEs account for 45 and 67 per cent of total formal employment in the manufacturing sector of high-income countries and developing countries respectively, as well as contributing to sizable shares of GDP (G20 Financial Inclusion Experts Group 2010).

SMEs consistently report having met severe obstacles in their access to finance in comparison to larger firms, which limit their ability to grow. In turn, the greater financing obstacles are reflected in their financing pattern, as they tend to use significantly less external funding than larger firms for both working capital and fixed-asset investment, and tend to finance the latter with a very large component of short-term financing.

Cross-country evidence shows that the gap in access to financial credit between SMEs and large firms is much smaller in higher-income countries than in emerging ones. Nevertheless, the Eurozone debt crisis has reduced access to private credit for SMEs, especially in crisis countries, showing that even developed economies are not immune to cyclical downturns of such credit, requiring compensating actions by public development banks.

The problems faced by microenterprises, including family agriculture, are even more severe than those of SMEs, and tend to make these agents highly dependent on informal channels of financing. In this regard, it is important that a broad view of financial inclusion be taken, embracing old and new agents active in small-scale financing—credit unions and microfinance institutions, for example—but also the mainstream financial sector (both private and public).

When access to external funding is limited, the production capacity of firms and their ability to grow and prosper is constrained, as they have to rely on their own resources to operate. This creates a vicious cycle that maintains smaller production units in a permanent state of vulnerability and low growth with large social consequences in terms of poverty and inequality.

However, it is important to emphasize that credit to micro and SMEs should meet the standards of creditworthiness, and thus the capacity of these enterprises to pay back. There is broad evidence that this is quite frequently the case, and can be enhanced by the design of appropriate guarantee funds for these firms. In broader terms, services to these agents must be provided responsibly, sustainably, and in a well-regulated environment.

A common rationale for development banks and similar institutions in industrial and developing countries alike is, therefore, to provide financing for micro and SMEs. Many of these firms can be viable institutions, and in the case of microenterprises move from subsistence to competitive firms. Furthermore, many SME start-ups do not survive very long, yet they can generate benefits going beyond their lifespan. Private markets will thus tend to underinvest in all these enterprises. Public development banks, or special mechanisms that focus on lending to micro and SMEs, are created to overcome this market failure by designing their lending and other facilities to meet the particular needs of their small business clients, including providing technical support.

Not all NDBs are necessarily well positioned to meet the financial needs of small businesses. In this context, other kinds of intermediaries such as credit unions and community-based banks may offer valuable insights into as well as channels for meeting the financial needs of micro and SMEs. So, the access these agents have to rediscounting as well as direct lending from NDBs is crucial. On the recipient side, it is important that different forms of association of producers be used as agents of inclusion, as they may be the appropriate mechanisms to reach the poorest producers.

Furthermore, according to Mazzucato and Penna (2016), there is an additional challenge to detect, finance, and follow up on those SMEs with the highest growth and innovation potential. Perhaps a combination of criteria is desirable here: fund SMEs that seem commercially viable and generate sustainable jobs, but give priority to SMEs that seem more likely to grow and innovate. For these companies, providing risk capital (in the form of venture capital, for example) is as important as providing them with social capital (in form of support for networking and co-management, for example). Furthermore, for NDBs, one of the main challenges when investing in innovation projects is how to cope with not knowing the chances of success—fundamental uncertainty. As Griffith-Jones et al. (2016) argue, the best response to these possible financial losses is to finance portfolios of SMEs in order to diversify idiosyncratic risks.

Regarding the evidence on the prevalence of SME financing by NDBs, Além and Madeira (2015) show that all eight reviewed banks provide lending to SMEs. Furthermore, the EIB and many NDBs put special focus on SME lending when they implemented countercyclical policies in the aftermath of the 2007/9 crisis. In the case of the EIB, not only did they increase lending via private banks to SMEs, but they also increased the available funds to the European Investment Fund (EIF), which is a specialized fund of funds dedicated exclusively to SMEs within the EIB group.

Despite the growing consensus on the important role played by NDBs in financing SMEs and their effective involvement in this financing, there is scarce econometric evidence on the differential behaviour of private banks and state-owned banks regarding SME financing. A notable exception is the work by Behr et al. (2013), which focuses on small state-owned commercial banks in Germany and finds that SMEs are less financially constrained when they have access to these types of banks in comparison to private commercial banks. Furthermore, they find evidence that these state-owned banks neither underperform commercially nor do they take more risks than other banks. In addition, Behr et al. (2017) find that SME lending by these small state-owned commercial banks is less cyclical than lending by cooperative banks.

1.4.4 *Infrastructure*

NDBs are especially well suited for infrastructure financing, as they can provide the long-term financing needed for infrastructure investment to become profitable, given the large scale of the initial investment and the long period of time for amortization. Furthermore, NDBs can finance at relatively low cost, as they often have very high credit ratings (typically as high as their governments) so they can borrow relatively cheaply on capital markets and pass on that cost advantage to their borrowers (Griffith-Jones and Kollatz 2015).

There is a broader case for NDBs to play an important role in financing infrastructure investment. In this regard, Studart and Gallagher (2016) argue that: 'National development banks can play leading roles in reducing costs and identifying risks of projects, leveraging global and local finance, and in governance and leadership on projects and project goals. At their best, national development banks can impart confidence, reduce risks, bring relevant instruments and encourage participation of other sources of financing both at the initial phase and once a project reaches maturity. As honest brokers they can help bring together governments, the private sector, investors and civil society and help establish replicable and scalable models.' They also note a few challenges faced by NDBs as regards financing infrastructure. A major one is their size relative to countries' investment needs. This goes beyond a simple balance sheet constraint but, with a small size, limits the 'capacity to engage in an efficient manner with project identification, design, and beyond'.

Before the 2007/9 North Atlantic financial crisis, private investors financed a fairly high volume of infrastructure in emerging economies. Banks and other private investors granted loans with long maturities, which were refinanced by them with shorter tenors on the capital markets. When the crisis emerged, the maturity mismatch turned out to be one of the reasons for rapid contagion, because refinancing was far more difficult. Following the crisis, banks have reduced the maturity mismatch and new regulation seems to be forcing them to do so even further. Though this is good for financial stability, it will reduce the supply of long-term private financing for infrastructure projects, especially in the short to medium term. This accentuates the 'good-time' problems facing pure private infrastructure finance in emerging, and sometimes even in developed, countries, such as 'long maturities' and 'big tickets', particularly in certain sectors with high perceived risks.

This limitation of private lending, combined with the massive need for infrastructure in the emerging and developed world, strengthens the case for enhanced financing by NDBs and their close collaboration with the private sector to achieve valuable leverage, as well as with MDBs, including regional development banks (like CAF, which has played a major role in infrastructure in Latin America). The creation of new MDBs, such as the NDB and the AIIB, initially devoted mainly to infrastructure, shows the importance attached, for example in Asia and among the BRICS, to the area of infrastructure. Similarly, the European Union has launched major initiatives to enhance the role of the EIB and NDBs in financing infrastructure.

NDBs face some restrictions in their ability to provide support to infrastructure but nonetheless have numerous advantages regarding financial terms, information, and ability to cope with risk, which implies that they can play a significant catalytic role. This will particularly be the case if NDBs continue to move towards developing an appropriate mix of traditional long-term loans with other financial instruments to achieve project closure, such as equity investments, guarantees, or partnerships. NDBs have unexploited potential to ramp up the use of instruments that can leverage greater volumes of private sector lending. However, the risks of non-traditional financial instruments are significant, so caution is needed in their application, to avoid excessive contingent liabilities (for further discussion of these issues, see Griffith-Jones and Kollatz 2015).

A key issue in infrastructure finance is the design of instruments such as guarantees, which involve NDBs assuming enough risk to make the investment attractive for private lenders and investors, but do not imply excessive future risk for the NDB or the government, via contingent liabilities. This can be complemented by attempting to design instruments that help the NDBs and the government 'capture the upside' for those projects that become more profitable than expected.

In infrastructure, the type of risks varies throughout the cycle of the project, and therefore NDB mechanisms may need to vary with the stage of the project, including in the crucial preparation stage. As discussed in Bhattacharya, Oppenheim, and Stern (2015), there are different stages of infrastructure projects and the risks and financing considerations involved vary for each stage.

Two parameters—maturity and scale—are simultaneously crucial for the development of infrastructure, as the investment is normally high up front, the construction period can be very long, and the amortization time usually required is also long. Therefore, financing by public banks and/or governments may be needed to overcome market gaps or imperfections, such as lack of large-scale long-term finance. In some cases, especially in green infrastructure (see section 1.4.5), NDBs and governments are better to deal with externalities, where social costs and benefits differ from private ones. This is also true for strategically important infrastructure, for example linking several countries, which implies large benefits, but may impose additional risks due to different regulations in different countries.

In the past, a high share of infrastructure was financed by public budgets. But the demand for infrastructure cannot be served by budgets alone. On the contrary, since the 2007/9 North Atlantic financial crisis, constraints (real and perceived) on budgets in many countries across the globe have led to reduction in investments financed by public budgets, with negative effects on output, private investment, increased unemployment, and future growth, as IMF (2015) and many others have pointed out. Furthermore, existing MDBs, whilst playing a valuable role in funding infrastructure, can only finance a part of the vast needs for infrastructure financing of developing and emerging economies. NDBs can play a key role in general in helping to fund infrastructure, and thus complementing public and private investment in infrastructure, but also especially in fiscally difficult times; they can do this well, particularly in cases where they have previous accumulated expertise and access to long-term funding.

According to Bhattacharya and Holt (2015), there are vast unmet infrastructure needs in both emerging and developing economies, which will constrain these countries' growth if not met soon and on a sufficient scale. They estimate the gap between current and required investment in infrastructure in those countries to reach between US$1 trillion and US$1.5 trillion per year for the core infrastructure sectors only between 2014 and 2030. Other estimates are even higher. For example, Studart and Gallagher (2016) estimate up to $3.5–4.0 trillion for infrastructure investment needs each year for the next fifteen years in emerging market and developing countries. As current levels are about $1 trillion per year, this implies unmet needs of $2.5–$3.0 trillion per year. The magnitude of the unmet needs provides a clear rationale for NDB activity to help, together with other actors, fill this massive unmet gap in infrastructure financing that currently exists.

1.4.5 *Financing the Provision of Global Public Goods*

A final and extremely important area of engagement for the NDBs in the coming decades relates to combatting climate change, perhaps the most crucial 'global public good' of our time.

The international community has defined preventing and adapting to climate change as a major new priority, given the great urgency of the subject. Indeed, the aim of 'sustainable' growth makes environment issues central to development strategies, so as to balance climate and environmental needs with economic growth.

Because the NDBs bring the advantages of accumulated expertise, administrative efficiencies, and convening power, they can play an important role. They can help mobilize additional funding, design the necessary policy frameworks, and implement effective projects that can showcase the viability of certain green investment, as in renewable energy (see Spratt, Griffith-Jones, and Ocampo 2013). Above all they can help ensure that a sustainable climate policy is wholly compatible with, and indeed facilitates the achievement of the post-2015 global development goals and the Paris agreement. Given these advantages, some elements for a strategy for the NDBs to combat climate change could include:

(i) *Mainstreaming climate change into current policies and operations.* To begin with, in conformity with the Hippocratic principle, the NDBs should 'do no harm'. This is more than a platitude when it comes to otherwise meritorious development projects that nonetheless lead to, or do not try to limit, greenhouse gas emissions. The NDBs are in a key position to pursue low-carbon options that also support poverty reduction and other development objectives. In this sense, the traditional financing role of the NDBs should be adapted to incorporate environmental externalities and to facilitate the introduction of required technologies—e.g. for renewable energy, even when this is less commercially attractive in the short term. Of particular relevance to emerging economies, in relation to externalities, is the opportunity to 'leapfrog' by immediate adoption of post-carbon technologies. Not only will this contribute to the adaption to and mitigation of climate change globally, but it will also avoid the transition costs that are being incurred by developed nations today and that would be required to be incurred where carbon-based technologies are adopted instead.

(ii) *Green initiatives by NDBs.* It seems especially valuable when NDBs, jointly with the government, which designs the policy framework, and with the private sector, which plays a large role in financing and implementing, take major, mission-oriented initiatives in the field of green finance, such as building green grids, helping to introduce new forms of renewable energy, etc.

An interesting and positive example is the key role that KfW played in the initial phase of introduction of solar PV to Germany. In fact, KfW funded *all* the investment in solar PV during 2007–9 in Germany, when solar PV began to be introduced on a major scale in the country (see Griffith-Jones 2016). It then played a diminishing role as other, basically private, funding sources stepped in.

Such a catalytic role is precisely what a development bank should do to kick-start a major structural transformation by funding and showcasing new technologies and sectors. Thus, KfW Germany successfully crowded-in private financing: from 2010, at least half of the new investment in solar PV came from private or other non-KfW sources.

(iii) *Adaptation.* According to recent estimates on the uses to which the current flow of climate finance is put, $93 billion of the $97 billion total is allocated to mitigation, and only $4 billion to adaptation (Buchner et al. 2011). An emphasis on mitigation initiatives is understandable—it seems more sensible to allocate resources to tackling the problem at its source, rather than to helping victims of climate change. More mitigation today could mean less need for adaptation in the future. But this misunderstands the crucial importance of adaptation today (Culpeper et al. 2016).

First, much of the worst devastation caused by climate change will be visited upon the poorest people, who are largely blameless for climate change. Second, 'adaptation' is best considered as 'building resilience' against climate change, that is, as a strategy to reduce risk, which is essential for all developing countries.

These considerations point to the key role that NDBs (in cooperation with the private sector and MDBs) increasingly need to play in spearheading climate change prevention and adaptation projects. Mitigation has the characteristics of a global public good, the benefits of which would be universally felt, while adaptation has fewer aspects of a global public good and is more consistent with traditional support for development. But both are crucially necessary, and since the bulk is presently flowing into mitigation, more funding is crucially needed for adaptation (Ghosh 2010).

References

AAAA (Addis Ababa Action Agenda). 2015. 'Addis Ababa Action Agenda of the Third International Conference on Financing for Development'. New York: United Nations. Available at <www.un.org/esa/ffd/wp-content/uploads/2015/08/AAAA_Outcome.pdf>, accessed November 2016.

Aghion, P., T. Besley, J. Browne, F. Caselli, R. Lambert, R. Lomax, C. Pissarides, N. Stern, and J. Van Reenen. 2013. *Investing for Prosperity: Skills, Infrastructure and Innovation.* London: Report of the LSE Growth Commission.

Além, A. and R. Madeira. 2015. 'Public Development Financial Institutions and Long-Term Financing', in L. Burlamaqui, S. Rogério, and M. Trotta (eds), *The Present and the Future of Development Financial Institutions: Theory and History*, 91–122. Rio de Janeiro: Multidisciplinary Institute for Development and Strategy (MINDS).

Behr, P., D. Foos, and L. Norden. 2017. 'Cyclicality of SME Lending and Government Involvement in Banks', *Journal of Banking & Finance* 77: 64–77.

Behr, P., L. Norden, and F. Noth. 2013. 'Financial Constraints of Private Firms and Bank Lending Behavior', *Journal of Banking & Finance* 37: 3472–85.

Bertay, A., A. Demirgüç-Kunt, and H. Huizinga. 2015. 'Bank Ownership and Credit over the Business Cycle: Is Lending by State Banks Less Procyclical?', *Journal of Banking & Finance* 50: 326–39.

Bhattacharya, A. and R. Holt. 2015. *Assessing the Changing Infrastructure Needs in Emerging Markets and Developing Countries.* G24/GGGI Paper Series. Washington, DC: Global Green Growth Institute and G24.

Bhattacharya, A., J. Oppenheim, and N. Stern. 2015. 'Driving Sustainable Development through Better Infrastructure'. Brookings Global Economy and Development, Working Paper 91. Washington, DC: Brookings Institute. Available at <www.brookings.edu/series/global-working-papers/>, accessed November 2016.

Brei, M. and A. Schclarek. 2013. 'Public Bank Lending in Times of Crisis', *Journal of Financial Stability* 9(4): 820–30.

Brei, M. and A. Schclarek. 2015. 'A Theoretical Model of Bank Lending: Does Ownership Matter in Times of Crisis?', *Journal of Banking & Finance* 50: 298–307.

Buchner, B., A. Falconer, M. Hervé-Mignucci, C. Trabacchi, and M. Brinkman. 2011. *The Landscape of Climate Finance.* Climate Policy Initiative (CPI). Available at <climatepolicyinitiative.org/europe/publication/the-landscape-of-climate-finance/>, accessed November 2016.

Chandrasekhar, C. 2016. National Development Banks in a Comparative Perspective', in A. Calcagno, S. Dullien, A. Marquez-Velasquez, N. Maystre, and J. Priewe (eds), *Rethinking Development Strategies after the Financial Crisis, Volume II: Country Studies and International Comparisons*, 21–30. New York and Geneva: UNCTAD.

Claessens, S. and N. van Horen. 2015. 'The Impact of the Global Financial Crisis on Banking Globalization', *IMF Economic Review* 63(4): 868–918.

Culpeper, R., S. Griffith-Jones, and D. Titelmann. 2016. 'Multilateral Development Banks', in J. Alonso, and J. Ocampo (eds), *Global Governance and Development*, 168–90. Oxford: Oxford University Press.

Ferraz, J. C., A. Além, and R. Madeira. 2016. *Development Banks Contribution to Long Term Financing*. Rio de Janeiro: BNDES.

G20 Financial Inclusion Experts Group. 2010. *Innovative Financial Inclusion*. Available at <https://www.gpfi.org/sites/default/files/documents/Principles%20and%20Report%20on%20Innovative%20Financial%20Inclusion_0.pdf>, accessed January 2018.

Gallagher, K. and S. Sklar. 2016. *Nationalizing Development Finance: Putting National Development Banks in Context*. Boston University Global Economic Governance Initiative Working Paper.

Ghosh, A. 2010. *Harnessing the Power Shift: Clean Technologies, Innovative Finance, and the Challenge for Climate Governance*. Paper presented at the Oxford–Princeton Global Leaders Fellowship Colloquium, Princeton University. Available at <www.princeton.edu/~pcglobal/conferences/GLF/ghosh_glf.pdf>, accessed November 2016.

Griffith-Jones, S. 2016. *National Development Banks and the Case of Sustainable Infrastructure: The Case of KfW*. GEGI Policy Brief 007, Boston University. Available at <www.bu.edu/pardeeschool/files/2016/08/Infrastructure.Sustainable.Final_1.pdf>, accessed November 2016.

Griffith-Jones, S. and R. Gottschalk. 2012. *Exogenous Shocks—Dealing with the Only Certainty: Uncertainty*. Paper prepared for the Commonwealth Secretariat, London. Available at <http://policydialogue.org/publications/policy-briefs/exogenous-shocks-dealing-with-the-only-certainty-uncertainty/>, accessed 30 April 2018.

Griffith-Jones, S. and M. Kollatz. 2015. *Infrastructure Finance in the Developing World—Multilateral Lending Instruments for Infrastructure Financing*. G24/GGGI Paper Series. Washington, DC: Global Green Growth Institute and G24. Available at <www.g24.org/wp-content/uploads/2016/05/MARGGK-WP09.pdf>, accessed November 2016.

Griffith-Jones, S. and J. A. Ocampo. 2008. 'A Counter-Cyclical Framework for a Development-Friendly IFA', in J. Fanelli (ed.), *Macroeconomic Volatility, Institutions and Financial Architectures: The Developing World Experience*, 25–44. New York: Palgrave Macmillan.

Griffith-Jones, S., J. A. Ocampo, and J. E. Stiglitz. 2010. *Time for a Visible Hand: Lessons from the 2008 World Financial Crisis*. New York. Oxford University Press.

Griffith-Jones, S., L. Xiaoyun, and S. Spratt. 2016. *The Asian Infrastructure Investment Bank: What Can It Learn from, and Perhaps Teach to, the Multilateral Development Banks?* Institute of Development Studies Evidence Report 179.

Gurley, J. G. and E. Shaw. 1955. 'Financial Aspects of Economic Development', *The American Economic Review* 45(4): 515–38.

Gutierrez, E., H. Rudolph, T. Homa, and E. Beneit. 2011. *Development Banks: Role and Mechanisms to Increase their Efficiency*. World Bank Policy Research Working Paper, WPS 5729. Washington, DC: World Bank.

Hidalgo, C., B. Klinger, A. Barabasi, and R. Hausmann. 2007. 'The Product Space Conditions the Development of Nations', *Science Journal* 317(5837): 482–7.

International Monetary Fund (IMF). 2015. *World Economic Outlook: Uneven Growth. Short- and Long-Term Factors*. Washington, DC: IMF.

Keynes, J. M. 1936. *The General Theory of Employment, Interest And Money*. London: Macmillan.

Kindleberger, C. P. 1978. *Manias, Panics, and Crashes: A History of Financial Crises*, 5th edn. London: Macmillan.

Kregel, J. 2015. 'Public Financial Institutions after the Crisis: A New Financial Deal in the Making?', in L. Burlamaqui, R. Sobreira, and M. Vianna (eds), *MINDS Conference on the Present and Future of Development Financial Institutions—Rio de Janeiro, July 28–29, 2014*. Rio de Janeiro: Multidisciplinary Institute for Development and Strategy (MINDS). Available at <http://www.minds.org.br/media/papers/kregel-minds-bndes-financial-i53d557d967047.pdf>, accessed 5 April 2018.

La Porta, R., F. López-de-Silanes, and A. Shleifer. 2002. 'Government Ownership of Banks', *The Journal of Finance* 57: 265–301.

Lagarde, C. 2015. 'Ethics and Finance—Aligning Financial Incentives with Societal Objectives'. Speech delivered at 'A Conversation with Janet Yellen, Chair of the Board of Governors of the Federal Reserve System', Washington, DC. Available at <www.imf.org/external/np/speeches/2015/050615.htm>, accessed April 2017.

Lazzarini, S. G., A. Musacchio, R. Bandeira-de-Mello, and R. Marcon. 2015. 'What Do State-Owned Development Banks Do? Evidence from BNDES, 2002–09', *World Development* 66: 237–53.

Luna-Martinez, J. de and C. Vicente. 2012. *Global Survey of Development Banks*. World Bank Policy Research Working Paper, No. WPS 5969. Washington, DC: World Bank.

Mazzucato, M. 2013. *The Entrepreneurial State: Debunking Public vs. Private Sector Myths*. London: Anthem Press.

Mazzucato, M. and C. Penna. 2016. 'Beyond Market Failures: The Market Creating and Shaping Roles of State Investment Banks', *Journal of Economic Policy Reform* 19(4): 305–26.

McKinnon, R. 1973. *Money and Capital in Economic Development*. Washington, DC: Brookings Institution Press.

Micco, A. and U. Panizza. 2006. 'Bank Ownership and Lending Behavior', *Economics Letters* 93(2): 248–54.

Minsky, H. P. 1977. *A Theory of Systemic Fragility*. Hyman P. Minsky Archive Paper 231. Available at <http://digitalcommons.bard.edu/hm_archive/231>, accessed 5 April 2018.

Mussachio, A. and S. Lazzarini. 2014. *Reinventing State Capitalism: Leviathan in Business, Brazil and Beyond*. Cambridge, MA: Harvard University Press.

Ocampo, J., C. Rada, and L. Taylor. 2009. *Growth and Policy in Developing Countries: A Structuralist Approach*. New York: Columbia University Press.

Olloqui, F. N. de. 2013. *Public Development Banks: Toward a New Paradigm?* Washington, DC: Inter-American Development Bank.

Oliveira, F. N. de. 2014. 'Investment of Firms in Brazil: Do Financial Restrictions, Unexpected Monetary Shocks and BNDES Play Important Roles?'. Brasilia: Central Bank of Brazil.

Rezende, F. 2015. 'Why Does Brazil's Banking Sector Need Public Banks? What Should BNDES Do?', *PSL Quarterly Review* 68(274): 239–75.

Rodrik, D. 2004. *Industrial Policy for the Twenty-First Century*. CEPR Discussion Papers, No. 4767. London: Centre for Economic Policy Research.

Rudolph, H. 2010. 'State Financial Institutions: Can They Be Relied on to Kick-Start Lending?'. Crisis Response Note 12. Washington, DC: World Bank.

Schclarek, A. and J. Navarrete. 2016. *Industry Diversification and Financial Development*. Working paper. Department of Economics, National University of Córdoba.

Spratt, S., S. Griffith-Jones, and J. Ocampo. 2013. *Mobilizing Investment for Inclusive Green Growth in Low-Income Countries*. German Federal Ministry for Economic Cooperation and Development (BMZ).

Stiglitz, J. 1989. 'Financial Markets and Development', *Oxford Review of Economic Policy* 5(4): 55–68.

Stiglitz, J. 1994. *The Role of the State in Financial Markets*. Washington, DC: World Bank.

Stiglitz, J. and B. Greenwald. 2014. *Creating a Learning Society: A New Approach to Growth, Development, and Social Progress*. New York: Columbia University Press.

Stiglitz, J. and A. Weiss. 1981. 'Credit Rationing in Markets with Imperfect Information', *The American Economic Review* 71(3): 393–410.

Studart, R. and K. Gallagher. 2016. *Infrastructure for Sustainable Development: The Role of National Development Banks*. GEGI Policy Brief 007. Available at <http://www.bu.edu/pardeeschool/files/2016/08/Infrastructure.Sustainable.Final_1.pdf>, accessed 5 April 2018.

Torres, E. and R. Zeidan. 2016. 'The Life-Cycle of NDBs: The Experience of Brazil's BNDES', *Quarterly Review of Economy and Finance* 62: 97–104.

Turner, A. 2015. *Between Debt and the Devil: Money, Credit, and Fixing Global Finance*. Princeton, NJ: Princeton University Press.

UN-DESA. 2005. *Rethinking the Role of National Development Banks*. UN-DESA Financing for Development Office. Available at <www.un.org/esa/ffd/msc/ndb/NDBs-DOCUMENT-REV-E-020606.pdf>, accessed April 2017.

World Bank. 2012. *Global Financial Development Report 2013: Rethinking the Role of the State in Finance*. Washington, DC: World Bank.

Wray, L. 2009. *An Alternative View of Finance, Saving, Deficits, and Liquidity*. Levy Economics Institute of Bard College Working Paper 580.

Wray, L. 2010. *What Do Banks Do? What Should Banks Do?* Levy Economics Institute of Bard College Working Paper 612.

Part I

Case Studies

2

China Development Bank

Born Bankrupt, Born Shaper

Qiyuan Xu

Established in 1994, China Development Bank (CDB) was soon on the verge of bankruptcy in the late 1990s, but then it miraculously recovered in the early 2000s. Now with total assets of USD 1.85 trillion, CDB ranks as one of the largest and most dynamic national development banks in the world. What happened to CDB? What contributions has CDB made to China's rapid development? This chapter will explore in detail CDB's role in light of China's transition economy. CDB is a key contributor to the establishment of an accommodative local government credit system and a facilitator for infrastructure construction. Therefore, CDB's role goes beyond financing tangible infrastructure. It is above all a shaper of the government credit system, and one of the starting points for understanding China's economy.

2.1 Introduction

In China, there are three policy banks: CDB, the Export-Import Bank of China (EIBC), and the Agricultural Development Bank of China (ADBC). CDB is the largest and most influential of the three. This chapter will explain how CDB underwent a transformation from born bankrupt in 1990s to born shaper in 2000s. China's economy has been in transition over last four decades, and viewed against this background CDB's story can enhance our understanding of the development that China has undergone.

Established on 17 March 1994, CDB was born with the key markers of a planned economy and its inherent disadvantages. Affected by the shocks from the Asian financial crisis in 1998, CDB suffered an NPL (non-performing loan) ratio of 42.7 per cent, and came to the verge of bankruptcy. Both China and CDB desperately needed to change. But as a developing and transition economy, what was China's priority in 1990s?

2.1.1 *Born in a Transition Economy*

China set out to reform and open its economy at the end of the 1970s, when the focus was mainly the real sector, instead of the financial one. Up until 1992, China explicitly defined the reform target as establishing a market economy (Jiang 1992). In the 1992 framework, the financial system was at the top of the list.

Since the end of the 1970s, the reform and opening-up policies have resulted in a great change in the national income distribution among the central government, local government, and private sector. By the early 1990s, the central government's fiscal resources were substantially weakened, and being crowded out by the disordered expansion of local government fiscal capacity. The proportion of local government revenue to the total revenue rose from 59.5 per cent in 1984 to 78.0 per cent in 1993; at the same time, the proportion of central government revenue decreased from 40.5 per cent to 22 per cent.

In early 1994, China's first budget law was published and came into effect at the beginning of 1995. This law redefined the framework of the fiscal system, and redistributed the financial resources between local and central government. More tax revenues were transferred to the central government, and local government was even forbidden to run a deficit.[1] This was the situation in China's fiscal system when CDB was born in 1994. We will explain later how CDB played a role in rebalancing the fiscal capacity between central and local government.

Before 1994, one of the many functions that Chinese commercial banks served in financial markets was also to play the part of policy bank.[2] At that time, the Agricultural Bank of China (ABC) was also heavily involved in national agricultural policies. China Construction Bank's (CCB) business also covered infrastructure policy financing. Therefore, commercial business and policy responsibilities were mixed. In 1994, the central government decided to establish CDB and the other two policy banks, the EIBC and ADBC. ADBC took over the agricultural policy business mainly from ABC

[1] Budget Law of the People's Republic of China (Beijing: Law Press, 1994).

[2] In 1993, the four largest state-owned commercial banks, ICBC, BOC, CBC, and ABC, were the leaders with 80.4 per cent market share in terms of total assets. The remaining market share was taken by joint-equity commercial banks controlled by the local or the central government. In 2014, the four largest banks' market share decreased to 40 per cent, leading to a more diversified banking system.

(Bai and Li 2005), while CDB took over the policy finance business from CCB and six state investment corporations (see section 2.2) (Gao and Chen 2007). These arrangements aimed to separate policy finance from commercial banking.

From then on, commercial banks became more market-oriented. Finally, in 1995 China's Commercial Bank Law was published. At that time, the role of commercial banks was clarified by Article 4 of the law: commercial banks should work under the principles of efficiency, safety, and liquidity with full autonomy and full responsibility for their own risks, profits and losses, and self-restraint. Stripped of their policy financing functions, commercial banks could move forward with fewer burdens. However, these burdens were transferred to the policy banks, rather than addressed.

In addition, in late 1990s, China suffered from two external shocks: the Asian financial crisis in 1998 and the internal impact of SOE reforms. A policy bank like CDB, on the verge of bankruptcy, could hardly support the projects assigned by central government, and it became an extra burden itself. At the same time, resolving financial risks became the priority of the central government (Literature Research Division of the Central Committee of CPC 2011). With the new priority of the central government and the recent appointment of a powerful president, Yuan Chen, to lead the bank, CDB was willing to make every possible effort.

2.1.2 *CDB Helps to Reconstruct the Credit System*

For China, it was critical to build a sound credit system for the market economy. As a transition economy, China has encountered bottlenecks both in public and private credit systems. According to Adam Smith, division of labour and specialization are the source of productivity and economic growth. But a poor credit system hinders labour division and specialization and undermines economic development.

China's World Trade Organization (WTO) entry in 2001 led to an improvement in the private credit system. The tradable sector was forced to reconstruct its credit system in order to do international business. Foreign direct investment companies also facilitated a sound credit system in some cities. On the other hand, the emergence of third-party e-commerce payment platforms, such as Alibaba, Taobao, Tencent, and Jingdong Mall, helped to boost the private credit system. All these positive influences spread throughout the whole of China's economy and significantly improved the domestic private credit systems.

Yet the underdeveloped local government credit system hindered the provision of local public goods and infrastructure projects, the latter being both capital-intensive and government-credit-intensive. From 1998 to 2003, CDB carried out a series of significant reforms, to ensure, on the one hand, the sustainability of its own business, and, on the other, to promote the rebalancing of the central–local government credit system and improve its adaptability. Prior to 1998, CDB had been operating in strict accordance with the instructions of the central government. Its lack of independence and its nature as an extension of the central fiscal system, which was viewed by local government as a quasi-central fiscal system, pushed CDB's operations to the brink of bankruptcy. Chen, who proved to be a powerful president, came to the helm of CDB just at that time. He restructured the framework of the policy bank and repositioned CDB as a shaper: 'Our mission is not merely to support social and economic development, but to drive the formation of sound markets and institutions that underpin such development' (Chen 2013).

Outsiders trying to understand China's transition economy often encounter many phenomena: mismatch of fiscal capacity between local and central government, mounting local government debt, controversial land finance, investment-driven growth, and rapidly developing infrastructure, when in fact a study of CDB would offer a special perspective to better comprehend them.

The rest of the chapter is organized as follows. Section 2.2 reviews the crisis faced by CDB at its birth in the 1990s, which caused its bankruptcy and presents a sharp contrast with CDB's achievements in 2000s. These achievements will be described in section 2.3. Section 2.4 explores CDB's substantial self-reforms. Then in section 2.5, we observe CDB as a shaper of China's financial system. Section 2.6 concludes the chapter.

2.2 Born Bankrupt in the 1990s

In March 1995, one year after CDB's foundation, when he met with the director of the Industrial Bank of Japan, then prime minister Zhu Rongji explained to his guest that CDB benefited from a mixture of two kinds of talent: people from the financial sector, familiar with financial business, and the rest from central government, ministries, with a good knowledge of the macroeconomy (Editorial Board 2013). These two advantages combined would allow CDB to excel. Nevertheless, CDB's early operations failed to live up to expectations.

2.2.1 *CDB: A Born-Bankrupt Bank*

In its early days in the late 1990s, CDB struggled, not to grow but to survive. By the end of 1997, CDB's total assets amounted to RMB 381 billion, and its NPL ratio reached 42.65 per cent (RMB 162.5 billion).[3] At that very moment, the total volume of mid- and long-term loans was RMB 365.6 billion, of which RMB 155.9 billion were non-performing loans. Among them, the coal industry was the hardest hit. By June 1998, the amount of CDB loans to the coal industry was RMB 64.2 billion, of which 48.3 billion were non-performing. The NPL ratio for this single industry reached 75 per cent (Editorial Board 2013). Theoretically, NPLs on such a scale would bankrupt CDB many times over. Indeed, CDB was on the verge of bankruptcy.

When the state investment corporations were established in 1988,[4] they suffered from chaotic internal governance due to the absence of corporate law or banking law, because China had just begun its market-oriented reforms. Meanwhile, the task of the managers of the six corporations was described as ferrying money to various projects (Guo 2006). So, when CDB took in the policy investment finance from the six state investment corporations in 1994, it planted the seeds for the later NPL crisis, which became CDB's historic burden.

The six state investment corporations were set up to finance policy projects, all of which were featured as having significant positive spillovers. Although these projects were supposed to be socially bankable, they were not economically bankable. Consequently, the quality of the loans, which were transferred from the six corporations to CDB in 1994, was worrying. Except for the NPL problem, in terms of lending volume, CDB accounted for 2 per cent of the total lending system with RMB 81.9 billion. It was a second-tier bank.[5]

The six corporations were based in Beijing and had no subsidiaries in other cities; CDB therefore inherited no branches in 1994. Thus, other commercial banks that had local branches played the role of CDB's local loan agents. By 1998, 88.6 per cent of CDB's loans had been lent through the commercial banks' network (Editorial Board 2013). However, because of insufficient incentives and supervision mechanisms, it was difficult for CDB to monitor the ultimate borrowers through the commercial banks, and the losses were solely borne by CDB.

[3] For the whole banking system, the People's Bank of China (PBoC) estimates that at the end of 1997, around 20–25 per cent of total bank loans, or about RMB 1,500 billion (US$ 180 billion), were non-performing. See Y. K. Mo, *A Review of Recent Banking Reform in China. Strengthening the Banking System in China: Issues and Experience*. BIS Policy Papers, No. 7 (1999), 90.

[4] In 1988, learning from the Temasek model in Singapore, China's central government established six state investment corporations to take the financing functions from the ministries. These six corporations provided financing to agriculture, forestry, energy, transportation, raw materials, and mechanical and electronic textiles, taking the national perspective into consideration. For example, the Three Gorges Dam, the largest hydropower project in the world, was financed by the six corporations and then by CDB.

[5] In 2015, this ratio increased to 10 per cent, according to CDB's annual report published in 2016.

Chen, the former president of CDB, remembers that when he joined CDB in 1998, a foreign media report described CDB as a bank that had 'nearly exhausted' its initial capital, 'sits on a mountain of bad debt', and 'toes the line' in lending to government projects (Chen 2013).

2.2.2 *Local Government with Poor Capacity to Finance Infrastructure*

From the late 1980s to the beginning of the 1990s, when CDB was about to be founded, many local governments had issued too many municipal bonds to finance local infrastructure projects. Some even went beyond the local governments' capacity and could only be sold through forced administrative measures. For instance, in some cities, staff were forced to purchase apportioned bonds issued by the local governments and their affiliates. In other cases, instead of cash, the staff got part of their wages in the form of local government bonds, with zero interest rates (Wang 2006).

The over-indebted local governments had not only crowded out central government financing resources, but also pushed up the fiscal risks. To counteract this, the central government issued a new budget law in 1994[6] and centralized the most lucrative tax sources, including value added tax (VAT), resource tax, and personal and enterprise income tax. Meanwhile, local governments were prohibited from having a budget deficit and from issuing local government bonds (Lu and Sun 2013).[7]

Consequently, local governments' financing capacity to support infrastructure projects was significantly weakened. As shown in Figure 2.1, the mismatch between local government revenue and expenditure appeared suddenly in 1994, and still remains.[8]

To balance fiscal revenue and expenditure, and make use of market resources, many local governments have established city investment companies (CICs) since the beginning of the 1990s. The first CIC was launched by the Shanghai municipal government in 1992. Then many CICs emerged in other cities. But the city investment companies faced challenges in at least two ways.

First, the CICs' financing model was project-oriented: that is, each project was individually financed by a borrowing arrangement. However, infrastructure projects, which have positive spillovers, long-term funding requirements,

[6] Before 1994, the fiscal relations between central and local government were similar to those between a parent company and subsidiaries. Roughly, a local government that ran a surplus would submit its 'profits', according to a given ratio, while if it ran a deficit, it would get transfers from the central government.

[7] In 2015, in the wake of the updated budget law, local governments legally started to have a deficit and they resumed issuing bonds.

[8] After 1994, there was no possibility for local government to run a deficit, and transfers from the central government were far from adequate. This large fiscal gap was closed by CDB's innovations in LGFV and land finance. We will elaborate on this in section 2.5 in this chapter.

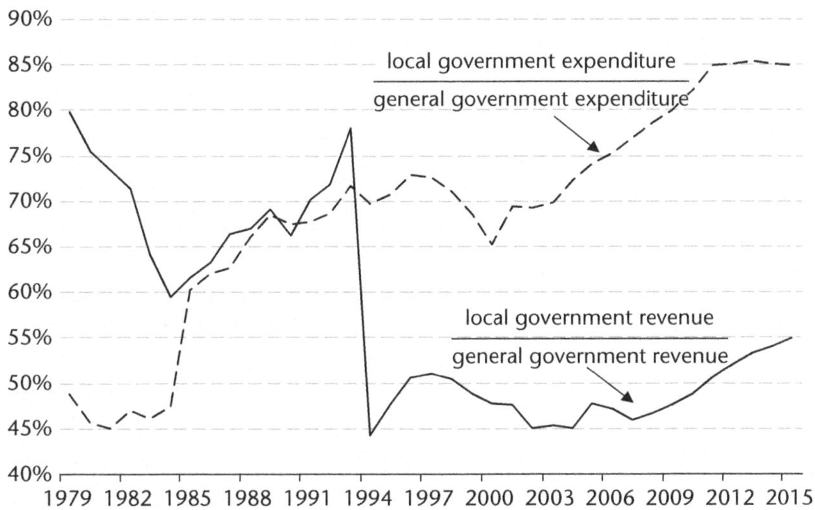

Figure 2.1. The mismatch between local government revenue and expenditure
Sources: National Bureau of Statistics of China and WIND Data, 2017

and capital-intensive features, can only be unevenly financed, due to their diversified and heterogeneous natures. Projects like water utility and environment protection are hardly going to be bankable in economic terms, even if they could profoundly enhance overall social welfare; other schemes like highways and power stations are relatively more profitable and therefore bankable. Consequently, although such projects have significant positive spillovers, they could not attract abundant capital in the financial market (Shen 1999).

Second, in the early and mid-1990s, CICs found it difficult to finance capital-intensive infrastructure projects, because they only had limited self-owned capital. To enhance the CICs' financial capacity, it was natural for the local government to become their guarantor. With the direct endorsement of the local government, CICs got more loans with favourable interest rates.

The Law of Guarantee, issued in 1995, banned local governments from acting as guarantors, including local government provision of guarantees for CICs or any infrastructure projects.[9] This new law cut off the guarantee relations between the CICs and the local governments, without which the CICs' high leverage (debt/asset ratio) became unsustainable. Consequently,

[9] There was an exception: if the local government provided on-lending loans extended by foreign governments or international financial institutions, then it could play the role of guarantor. But the volume of such kinds of loans was very limited. For details, see the third article of the second chapter, in the Guarantee Law (Beijing: Law Press of China, 1995).

the CIC model was on the verge of collapse. Again, local governments were faced with a difficult fiscal situation.

2.2.3 *Central Government: Excessive Intervention in CDB*

From the perspective of liabilities in CDB's balance sheet, since CDB was founded in 1994, the People's Bank of China (PBoC) had forced CDB bonds onto other Chinese financial institutions via administrative command. With such rules of play, when CDB attempted to expand its business, it inevitably brought more pressure for the other commercial banks to buy more CDB bonds. Besides, CDB bonds had no liquidity in the secondary market at that time. With growing assets and large NPLs on CDB's balance sheet, the commercial banks complained and opposed such compulsive arrangement (United Study Groups 2007). Correspondingly, the commercial banks demanded a higher yield rate premium to purchase CDB bonds. CDB's financial costs, in turn, increased. CDB was thus caught in a vicious circle.

From the perspective of assets in CDB's balance sheet, when CDB was established, it had followed the lead of the State Planning Commission (SPC), which was the predecessor to the National Development and Reform Commission (NDRC) (Chen 2013). In the early years of CDB, most of its investment projects were decided by the SPC and the state, which meant that the central government had absolute control over the project selection. The main concern of the central government and the SPC was long-term social development, but not necessarily being economically bankable. Consequently, CDB's responsibility was solely to provide funds for preselected projects. In this way, CDB acted almost as an 'ATM machine'. Many borrowers used to view CDB as the second ministry of finance. Yuan Chen, the president from 1998 to 2012, said, 'They feel like it's a free lunch. You can borrow and you don't have to pay back' (Sanderson and Forsythe 2013).

But the relations between the government and the 'ATM machine' were not always harmonious. Excessive intervention from the central government had derailed CDB's operations, which went from market-driven to politically driven. The borrowers, usually state-owned enterprises (SOEs) or 'joint stock' firms controlled by the state, considered CDB as a de facto extension of the treasury, and they also regarded CDB loans as zero-cost fiscal appropriation. Consequently, this aggravated the massive NPL problem.

In 1997, a full three years after CDB was set up, the East Asian financial crisis struck China, causing deterioration in the country's economy and financial market. Overcapacity emerged as a problem in many of China's industries, and CDB's loans to the designated pillar industries suffered. In the same year, CDB's NPL ratio rose to 42.65 per cent (Editorial Board 2013).

2.3 An Amazing Turnaround

CDB was born bankrupt. Indeed, CDB's high NPL ratio back then would instantly have caused the bank to go bankrupt, according to the Basel Accord III.[10] Nonetheless, CDB survived into the late 1990s, and developed at a breathtaking pace thereafter, playing a significant role in both China's infrastructure construction and the improvement of people's living standards. How did CDB managed to survive and change? We will examine the reforms undertaken by CDB in section 2.4, and how CDB has played a role as shaper of the fiscal and financial system in section 2.5. But first, we will focus in detail on the outcomes of this amazing turnaround.

At the end of 1990s, CDB survived the NPL crisis and East Asia financial crisis.[11] From then on, CDB speeded up its development. In 1994, CDB's total assets amounted to USD 11 billion, equal to 1.9 per cent of China's GDP. They rocketed up to USD 1,849 billion and 18.6 per cent of China's GDP in 2015.[12] Meanwhile, CDB has played a critical 'crowd-in' role of drawing capital from commercial banks and other financial institutions (Y. Wang 2016).

The high NPL ratio was a fatal issue for CDB in late 1990s. After Chen took the office of president of CDB in 1998, he primarily restructured CDB's internal governance, so as to decrease the NPL ratio. We will review the basket of measures he introduced in section 2.4. The trajectory of the NPL ratio declined substantially from 42.7 per cent in 1997 to 1.8 per cent in 2002; and then, for the first time, CDB's NPL ratio fell below 1 per cent in 2005. Since then, the NPL ratio has been kept at or below 1 per cent for eleven years. Even during the global financial crisis, CDB's NPL ratio did not exceed 1 per cent. From 2012 to 2015, it experienced a moderate growth from 0.3 per cent to 0.8 per cent.[13]

CDB's capital adequacy ratio and CDB's return on assets (ROA) have not shown a continuous increase. In 2006, the former declined to just above 8 per cent. It was not due to write-off and equity capital losses, but because of the rapid expansion of total assets. Corresponding to the relatively low capital adequacy ratio in 2006, CDB's ROA reached a peak of 1.32 per cent in the same year. Since 2007, the capital adequacy ratio has been maintained at around 11 per cent to 12 per cent.[14]

[10] According to the Basel Accord III, the capital adequacy ratio of a bank should not be lower than 8 per cent.

[11] For details of how CDB proved resilient at the end of the 1990s, see section 2.4.

[12] Source: The data for 1994 are drawn from the editorial board of *The History of China Development Bank* (2013). The data for 2015 are from the annual report of CDB in 2016.

[13] Source: The data before 2013 are from the editorial board of *The History of China Development Bank* (2013). The data starting from 2013 are from CDB's annual reports in 2013, 2014, and 2015.

[14] Source: The data before 2013 are from the editorial board of *The History of China Development Bank* (2013). The data starting from 2013 are from CDB's annual reports in 2013, 2014, and 2015.

CDB's ROA received a shock from the global financial crisis, decreasing to 0.62 per cent in 2008. It rose moderately to 0.9 per cent in 2015, but never came back to the peak level it held in 2006, partly because CDB took the initiative to operate at lower leverage and be more prudent about financial risks.

Because CDB's balance sheet became sounder and more sustainable, CDB bonds gained popularity in the bond market. Generally speaking, the over-subscription rate in the issuance market for CDB bonds is around three times. The last CDB bond issue of 2016 was on 20 December, when three CDB bonds with three-year, five-year, and seven-year maturities were issued on the same day. The oversubscription rate in the issuance market was above three times for all of them. For the three-year bond, it was even close to five times (J. Wang 2016). The central government no longer forces CDB bonds onto other commercial banks. With favourable market conditions, CDB's annual bond issuance has expanded from RMB 0.2 trillion in1998[15] to RMB 1.48 trillion in 2016.[16]

When CDB expanded its business rapidly, it funded large investments in railway, public highways, electric power, water resources, petroleum and petrochemicals, public infrastructure, and strategic emerging industries. In addition to these core businesses, CDB also provided financing to improve people's livelihoods. By 2015, CDB's loans outstanding in education had accumulated to RMB 56.2 billion, in rural development RMB 855.7 billion, poverty alleviation RMB 962.3 billion, small and medium enterprises RMB 1,120 billion, transformation of shantytowns RMB 1,310 billion, and green credit RMB 1,570 billion.

2.4 CDB as a Self-Shaper

Before CDB could play its role as a shaper of China's financial system, it first had to reshape itself. As mentioned in sections 2.2 and 2.3, CDB was born bankrupt and then turned prosperous. How did CDB achieve such an amazing turnaround?

2.4.1 *Improving Internal Governance*

Disposing of NPLs. In 1999, China set up four Asset Management Corporations—Great Wall, Cinda, Huarong, and Dongfang—to strip toxic assets

[15] The editorial board, *The History of China Development Bank*, Beijing: China Financial Publishing House, 2013.

[16] Wind Data, 2017.

from Chinese national banks. In that round, the NPLs of the four largest national commercial banks, which amounted to RMB 1.4 trillion, were stripped. At the same time, Cinda Corporation acquired CDB's bad assets for RMB 100 billion. In 1999, CDB launched a debt-to-equity swap plan for qualified enterprises. At last, thirty-six enterprises were included, and the debt-to-equity swap amounted to RMB 44 billion. In this way, CDB's NPLs decreased by RMB 18.8 billion (Editorial Board 2013).

In 1997, the stock of NPLs in CDB was RMB 162.5 billion. In 1999, the NPL problem was largely solved when 100 billion toxic assets were stripped and 18.8 billion NPLs were solved through a debt-to-equity swap plan. Because of these measures, CDB's NPL ratio decreased from 42.6 per cent in 1997 to 18.7 per cent at the end of 1999.

Additionally, to resolve NPLs whose borrowers were local governments and SOEs, CDB kept in close communication with the higher authorities responsible for these issues, and collaborated with them.[17] In the imperfect financial market of 1990s China, CDB and its president had to resort to the higher authorities to exert pressure on the borrowers in order to recover the loans. The strong position of CDB, and especially of its president, was critical in this process.

Building up the national network of branches. In section 2.2, we mentioned that CDB heavily depended on the other commercial banks as local loan agents. But there was a serious principal–agent problem. It was difficult for CDB to operate interbank supervision. This was also one of the explanations for the NPL surges. Up until 1998, CDB had only one branch in Wuhan city and three offices in Chendu, Xi'an, and Shenzhen (Editorial Board 2013). To internalize principal–agent relations and ensure smooth coordination between head office and local agents, CDB needed to set up a national network of branches and subsidiaries.

At the end of 1998, CDB took over China Investment Bank and restructured the bank. By the end of 1999, CDB had a national network of twenty subsidiaries on the mainland and one office in Hong Kong. In April 2002, the mainland network increased to twenty-nine subsidiaries and two offices. After the branch banking system was established, CDB transferred nearly 3000 loan projects and 16,000 correspondent banking accounts to the local branches (Editorial Board 2013). Since then, the local branches have entirely

[17] As the Chinese administrative system is relatively centralized, provincial leaders are appointed by the central government and municipal leaders are appointed by provincial leaders. At the same time, CDB is based in Beijing and has a close relationship with the central government and the local government. With this background, CDB kept in close communication with the higher authorities, to use their influence on the debtor (a provincial or a municipal government).

replaced the external loan agents; meanwhile, internal governance has replaced the interbank principal–agent coordination.

Reforming the loans approval process. In this respect, CDB introduced a firewall mechanism (in 1999) and an independent review committee (in 2002 and 2004) to control potential risks. The firewall framework consists of three new departments: a market and industry analysis division, a financial analysis division, and an evaluation and review division. A local branch will first submit a project plan to the head office in Beijing. Then, the above-mentioned three departments will review the project respectively in terms of market future, repayment capacity, and compliance. Next, the evaluation and review division will report all the information to an independent review committee, which will vote to make the decision.

When the evaluation and review division reports to the independent committee,[18] the prospective borrower for the project will also hold a roadshow through electronic means. This way, the commissioners get more information from the borrower but they do not meet the borrower face to face. The anonymity provided by the electronic roadshow affords the commissioners sufficient protection.

Each time, member selection for the independent committee is generated randomly from a candidate pool, and commissioners vote in an anonymous way. The mechanism is designed to enhance the weight of objections. A project will be rejected if 30 per cent or more of the commissioners are against it. In the first year after the firewall was built, of the 308 projects submitted, nearly 200 projects, or 65 per cent, required substantial revisions or were rejected (Editorial Board 2013; Chen 2013).

Following this step, the approved projects are submitted to the committee at head office, and finally to the president. In this way, the president cannot approve a project from the beginning, and only has the power to veto at the end.

2.4.2 *Becoming Independent of Central Government Intervention*

As mentioned in section 2.2, CDB got 'excessive support' or too much intervention on both sides of the balance sheet from central government in the 1990s. On the credit side, since CDB was founded in 1994, PBoC had forced CDB bonds onto other Chinese financial institutions through administrative command. Because CDB bonds have no liquidity in the secondary market, the investors, usually commercial banks, demanded a higher yield rate premium.

[18] The members of the independent committee consist of internal specialists, external lawyers, accountants, and economists.

The central bank designed an administrative issuing rate with a trade-off between CDB and other investors.

But in 1998, because China's economy continued to face downward pressure, PBoC lowered interest rates five times in one year to the lowest level in history. Given this situation, CDB faced a much narrower spread between lending interest rates and financing costs (the bond issuing rate). Every time the primary interest rate was lowered, CDB required a reduction of the bond-issuing rate, but the commercial banks insisted on the given rate. The conflict of interest between CDB and commercial banks was clear (Editorial Board 2013).

Finally, a consensus was built to develop a bond market, where bonds would be priced by the market instead of the government. Meanwhile, it was also necessary to foster the liquidity of CDB bonds. But in the late 1990s, the bond market was not mature enough to sustain such liquidity.

On 2 September 1998, CDB issued RMB 5 billion bonds for the first time as a step towards marketization. Beforehand, PBoC gave three assurances: (1) CDB bonds would have liquidity in the interbank market, (2) a guarantee to buy back through open market operations, (3) a two to three-year transition period. Meanwhile, CDB bonds would be issued through a dual-track system, with traditional administrative pricing and a market pricing system (United Study Groups 2007).

The above measures amounted to an endorsement of the market liquidity for CDB bonds, and ensured the confidence on the part of investors. On 2 September 1998, the oversubscription rate for CDB's first bond issuance was 3.73 times. The coupon rate was 5.19 per cent, relatively lower than the administrative rate of 6.12 per cent, and even lower than PBoC's relending rate of 5.58 per cent (Editorial Board 2013). By 2004, the Ministry of Finance of the PRC, the Export-Import Bank of China, and the Agricultural Development Bank of China, in succession, also realized marketization issuance for their bonds. With the development of China's bond market, CDB also gained the independence to decide when to issue bonds and how many to issue. Meanwhile, the bond market developed quickly, and PBoC had more instruments for open market operations.

On the debit side, before 1998 the central government identified and selected the projects for CDB, while CDB played the role of a 'cash machine'. As mentioned in section 2.4.1, CDB has restructured the loans approval process since then, introducing three firewalls and an independent review committee, so that the loans approval system has been able to reject project applications not only from local government, but also from the powerful SPC. The loans approval system decentralized the decision-making power from the president, releasing the president from external pressures, which has kept CDB more independent. In 1998, CDB launched 437 new projects on its own initiative, which accounted for 30.5 per cent of the total amount that year. In 1999, it even exceeded 60 per cent (Editorial Board 2013).

Unlike commercial banks that select profitable projects from applications, CDB is to actively provide development financing for potential or so-called pipeline projects. One effective way to nurture such projects is 'planning first' (Chen 2013). CDB is actively involved in the five-year plan at the national level, regional planning, and industrial planning in many provinces and cities, and it has sometimes even led the development of certain programmes. In this way, CDB has nurtured a pipeline project pool by taking into consideration global development tendencies, national economic growth strategies, and regional and industrial plans. As a result, CDB has not only gradually gained independence from over-intervention by central government, but has also bridged the gap between central government plans and regional and local plans.

2.5 CDB as a Shaper of the Financial System

CDB positions itself as a development bank. In this case, development means not only directly developing the economy or the related public infrastructure, but also developing sound markets and institutions.

CDB plays its role as a key shaper of the financial market and the credit system in the following ways: it reshapes the local government credit system through a local government financial vehicle (LGFV) model, helps to construct the primary interest rate in the bonds market, and acts as a tool of monetary policy to guide long-term interest rates.

2.5.1 *Local Government Funding Vehicle Model Launched in Wuhu City*

As mentioned in section 2.2.2, with the constraints of the updated Budget Law introduced in 1994 and the Guarantee Law issued in 1995, China's local government encountered financial bottlenecks for infrastructure projects.

In cooperation with CDB, in early 1998, the municipal government of Wuhu, a port city alongside the Yangtze River, set aside its quality assets to establish the Wuhu Urban Construction Investment Co. Ltd (WUCI). Authorized by the local government, WUCI was mandated to raise funds for the city's infrastructure. It marked the start of the LGFV, which leverages government credit (Sanderson and Forsythe 2013).

The first feature of the Wuhu model was the legal person status of WUCI, which was registered as a local state-owned enterprise (Chen 2013). WUCI's borrowing behaviour was not restricted by the Budget Law of 1994. Meanwhile, the local government also issued a promise with a stamped document, though not a guarantee,[19] to CDB. As a specific form of promise, the local government injected its quality assets into the company. If the infrastructure asset, such as a highway or power station, was profitable, WUCI could take the future profits as collateral and borrow from CDB. To enhance the credibility of the promise, there were more innovations such as the build–operate–transfer (BOT) model.[20] In addition, CDB kept informal but close relations with its superior government, Anhui province in the Wuhu case. Even without a guarantee from the local government, the close relations between CDB and the superior government forced the local government to keep their promise. These implicit arrangements avoided the explicit constraints of the Guarantee Law published in 1995. As a bottom line, CDB had an internal credit rating system for the local government and its officials. If a loan became non-performing and could not be resolved, the local government and its officials would be recorded in the credit rating system (Figure 2.2) (Chen 2013).

The second characteristic was bundled loans (Liebman and Milhaupt 2015). Urban infrastructure projects are highly diversified and heterogeneous. In late

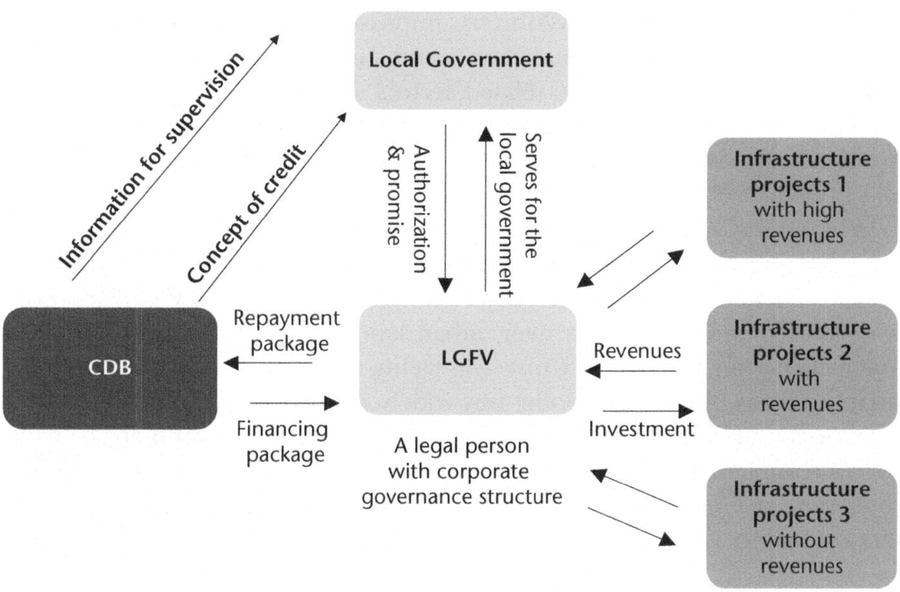

Figure 2.2. Wuhu model: The start of LGFV
Source: Summarized by the author

[19] Because the Guarantee Law of 1995 forbids local government to do so.

[20] In the BOT framework, the local government delegates to another entity to *build* infrastructure and to *operate* this facility for a certain period. During this period, the private party has the responsibility to raise the finance for the project, is entitled to retain all revenues generated by the project, and is the owner of the facility. The facility will be then freely *transferred* to the public administration after the period.

1998, CDB signed an agreement with Wuhu municipal government, which promoted the latter to designate WUCI to raise and repay funds for various projects in a basket (Figure 2.2). This way, WUCI got financing from CDB for six infrastructure projects to supply highways, water utility services, waste disposal, and landfill. Consequently, socially bankable infrastructure projects were financially supported by economically bankable ones. And conversely, economically bankable projects also benefited significantly from the positive spillovers of socially bankable infrastructure projects.

The third feature was land finance. In 2002, the Wuhu model was upgraded with an innovation. That August, CDB signed a new Financial Collaboration Agreement with WUCI, based on which CDB agreed to provide an additional lending of RMB 1.095 billion. Correspondingly, the municipal government authorized WUCI, the LGFV of Wuhu municipal government, to bid and auction its land to get land transfer revenue, which would at the same time guarantee the repayment to CDB (Editorial Board 2013; Chen 2013). This marked the origin of China's land finance model.

As a result of the above innovation and collaboration by CDB and WUCI, since 1998, infrastructure in Wuhu has improved remarkably, and the overall business and investment climate has become more attractive. In the wake of fully equipped infrastructure, related sectors such as construction, building materials, real estate, tourism, and car manufacture have boomed as pillar industries. In last two decades, the per capita GDP of Wuhu has risen from US$1,000 in 1998 to US$10,000 in 2015.[21]

In 2003, the Wuhu model was applied to Tianjin city, one of China's four municipalities. In this case, Tianjin city got financing from CDB to support a basket of urban infrastructure projects: highway and subway construction, watershed management of a river, urban landscaping, and land acquisition and reclamation. In 2009, as China was facing the external shock of the global financial crisis, the Wuhu model was widely replicated and applied to other provinces and cities. At that time, all the other Chinese commercial banks were encouraged to follow the LGFV model.[22] As a comparison, in 2007, the total debt of China's local government amounted to RMB 13.9 trillion; by 2014, it had rocketed up to RMB 30.3 trillion (Li et al. 2015).[23] Meanwhile, the

[21] Source: National Bureau of Statistics of China, 2016.

[22] This was not the case in 2006, since central government was not in favour of LGFV at that time. But in 2009, it changed its stance dramatically to stimulate the economy.

[23] For the same criterion, in 2007, China's local government assets totalled RMB 49.9 trillion, then in 2014, RMB 108.2 trillion, which was much larger than the debt in the corresponding year. This criterion for debt includes the most comprehensive items, such as contingent debt, like a guarantee, and indirect/implicit debt incurred by local SOEs. If the implicit debt (by SOEs) is excluded, then the total debt of local government (including the contingent debt) would be RMB 3.0 trillion in 2007 and RMB 16.8 trillion in 2014 respectively.

explosive local government debt posed more potential risks in real terms.[24] As an increasing number of banks began to cooperate with local government, they were unaware that some local governments were making promisess to several banks at once, backed by the same asset. Given this situation, in the event of a default, even promises that looked solid could prove to be very weak, leading to a potential banking crisis, not to mention moral hazard.

In spite of this, the main problem for China's local government debt is not the stock, but the explosive growth. In 2013, the total debts of local government, including all of the contingent liabilities, accounted for only 30 per cent of GDP (or RMB 17.9 trillion). If we combine central and local government debt, the general government debt, including all contingent liabilities, accounted for 50.9 per cent of GDP in 2013. Compared with other countries in the world, it was a fairly moderate ratio. From this point on, the low level of central government debt offset the explosion of debt in local government.

The burden of local government debt rocketed up from RMB 3.0 trillion in 2007 to RMB 17.9 trillion in 2013, and it seemed that LGFV had opened a Pandora's box in early 2010s. Many economists and decision makers were afraid that local government debt would get out of control, and the LGFV model had already made the financial supervision ineffective (Wei 2010; Liu and Zhang 2010). Consequently, after a fierce debate, China's finance ministry published *Measures for Screening Outstanding Debts of Local Governments and Including Them in Budget Management*, which was launched to reorganize and suppress LGFVs. As a substitute for LGFVs, local government now needs new funding to meet the financing demand for infrastructure. The central government introduced some supporting measures, as follows: a new budget law was issued at the very beginning of 2015, which formally allowed local government to run a deficit and issue bonds. In addition, the central government promotes the Public–Private Partnership (PPP) financing mode as well. Nowadays, different financing modes continue to be explored as China moves forward in the course of its development.

China has learned many lessons from the explosion of local government debt, and is still facing trouble to some extent. But it is undoubtedly the case that China's economy has significantly benefited from well-developed infrastructure networks. The LGFV model is set to exit the stage of history, but it

[24] As described above, the LGFV was registered as a local state-owned enterprise. Meanwhile, the local government gave promises to LGFV, but not guarantees. This arrangement was a way to bypass the constraints of the 1994 Budget Law and 1995 Guarantee Law. As a result, LGFV debts became contingent liabilities of the local government. But this does not mean the LGFV model has no other value than bypassing constraints. Land finance and bundled loans are forms of development finance practised in China. Land finance enhances the credibility of LGFV, so LGFV can attract more loans. With bundled loans, projects with and without profits are bundled together to get finance in such a way that the socially bankable infrastructure projects are financially supported by economically bankable ones.

did substantially free local government from budget constraints and facilitate infrastructure construction. From the perspective of institutional evolution, although LGFV was a temporary innovation, it finally forced and accelerated national fiscal reforms from top to bottom. In some emerging markets, such as Ethiopia, land financing, bundled loans, and 'planning first', the kind of approaches applied by CDB, have achieved rapid development.

2.5.2 *CDB as a Key Player in the Monetary Policy Framework*

China's central government remains conservative about running a large deficit and issuing a big volume of government bonds. Insufficient government bonds and consequently liquidity are the key reasons why China's bond market has lacked a developed benchmark for yield curve for decades. To some extent, CDB has filled in the gaps. CDB is the second largest bond issuer in China, after the Ministry of Finance. For most years in the last decade, the issuance of CDB bonds has generally accounted for about 20 per cent of the whole bond market (Figure 2.3).

In addition to its large scale, (1) CDB covers all bond maturities, (2) its bonds are issued regularly and traded with a high liquidity in the secondary market, and (3) CDB's credit rating is as high as China's sovereign credit rating. Under these conditions, CDB bonds contribute to developing the yield curve of a benchmark interest rate.

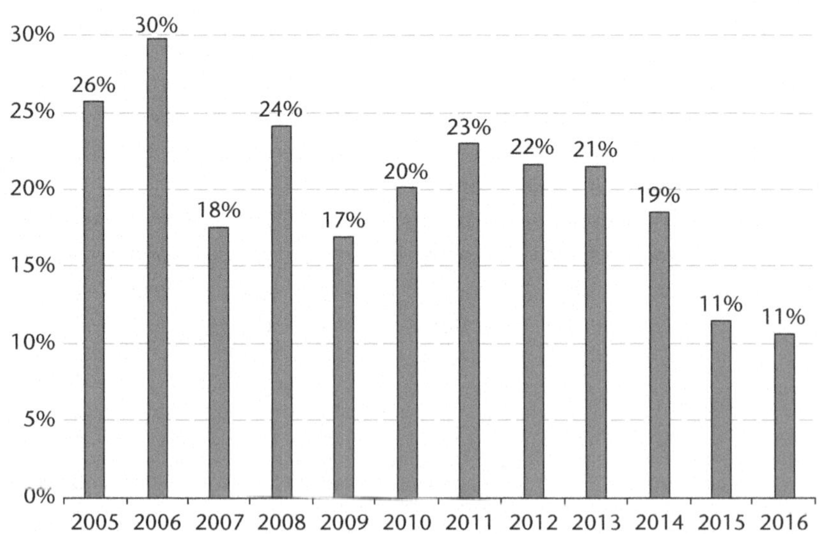

Figure 2.3. CDB bonds issuance accounts for a key portion of the market
Source: WIND Data, 2017

On 24 April 2015, Guangxi Yuchai Machinery Group issued the first bond taking the CDB bond rate as a benchmark (Gao 2015). Since then, the CDB bond rate itself has behaved as a kind of benchmark in the market. On 30 June 2016, China Securities Index Co., Ltd released the price index for ten-year CDB bonds to set up new benchmarks and references for investors.[25] By the end of August 2016, the trading volume for bonds of China's three policy banks, among which CDB plays the leading role, amounted to 53 trillion yuan, with a ratio of 46 per cent of the total volume.[26] In China's secondary market, CDB bonds are the most liquid asset with the most active quotations and the minimum spread. Consequently, many financial tools, such as bond index funds, are created based on CDB bonds.

Since the end of 2014, the pledged supplementary lending (PSL) tool has been introduced as a new channel to inject liquidity into the market. This new type of supplementary lending instrument for targeting injections of funding into the market is backed by collateral that includes high-credit-rating bond assets and high-quality credit assets.

As the programme used to provide direct and effective funding support for infrastructure and shantytown renovation, PSL distributes major resources to CDB. At the very beginning of PSL in 2014, CDB got a quota of RMB 1 trillion for PSL from PBoC. CDB has become the dominant borrower in PSL. On the other hand, PBoC designed and created this monetary policy tool to lower medium and long-term funding costs. By the end of 2016, the outstanding balance of PSL had accumulated to RMB 2.1 trillion.

2.6 Concluding Remarks

CDB was born in 1994 in an economy undergoing transition, which still bore the features of central planning in both the macroeconomic system and CDB's internal governance. CDB's revival can be attributed to: (1) the reconstruction of its internal governance, (2) the restructuring of the domestic credit system and financial market, which was motivated by CDB's reform efforts, and (3) corrections to the excessively strict 1994 fiscal reform. This refers in particular to rebalancing the fiscal capacity between local and central government within the constraints of the 1994 Budget Law. In addition to the carrying out reconstructions and corrections, (4) CDB works as a coordinator between

[25] CSI Ten-Year CDB Bond Index is composed of CDB bonds of which the term to maturity is between 6.5 and 10.25 years. For more information, see China Securities Index Co., Ltd at <http://www.csindex.com.cn/zh-CN/indices/index?class_1=1&class_11=11&is_custom_0=1>.

[26] For the first time, a (7–10 year) CDB Bond Index Fund was issued on 22 September 2016, <http://www.cdb.com.cn/English/xwzx_715/khdt/201610/t20161013_3702.html>.

the central government's macroeconomic plans and local government's fiscal capacity.

In macroeconomic textbooks, there is consensus on the need for an independent central bank. CDB's history in the 1990s proved an independent development bank is also necessary. Otherwise, with excessive support or administrative interventions, CDB could easily have ended up as a second ministry of finance and gone bankrupt. In the late 1990s, CDB was lucky to have a powerful president. The accumulated failure of centralized control, weakened macroeconomic situation, and high NPL ratio gave CDB a valuable opportunity to make substantial reforms.

But independence does not mean a development bank should cut off all relations with the central government. On the contrary, CDB should work closely with the state on national plans. CDB is actively involved in the state five-year plan and the national industry plan, and should closely cooperate with the related ministries to integrate their ideas into the provincial and municipal plans.

Last but not least, CDB grows against a special background, which does not necessarily apply to other countries. One special characteristic is that China's economy took off again in the early 2000s. CDB's expansion is also closely linked to interactions with the macroeconomy. Another special aspect is that China's local government is in possession of massive resources, such as local state-owned enterprises and land-transferred revenues, which directly enhance local government credit.

Appendix: CDB's Role as Countercyclical Lender

Most development banks play a role as countercyclical lenders. CDB is no exception. We focus on its role in this appendix.

CDB's shareholders include the Ministry of Finance of China (36.54 per cent), Central Huijin Investment Ltd (34.68 per cent), Buttonwood Investment Holding Co., Ltd[27] (27.19 per cent), and the National Council for Social Security Fund (1.59 per cent).[28] MoF of China and PBoC are two major direct shareholders of CDB. Thus, CDB was not only established for sustainable development, but also to facilitate fiscal or monetary policy for countercyclical purposes. CDB's assets business reflects its countercyclical role. On the assets side, CDB invests through lending and capital injection, which both play a role in quasi-fiscal policy (Figure 2.4).

As for the fiscal system, CDB is a crucial policy vehicle to provide funding to quasi-fiscal projects. Through credit support and capital injection, CDB leverages more capital

[27] Buttonwood Investment Holding Co., Ltd is an investment corporation solely invested by SAFE (State Administration of Foreign Exchange). And SAFE is also directly affiliated to PBoC.

[28] Source: CDB's annual report of 2015, p. 27.

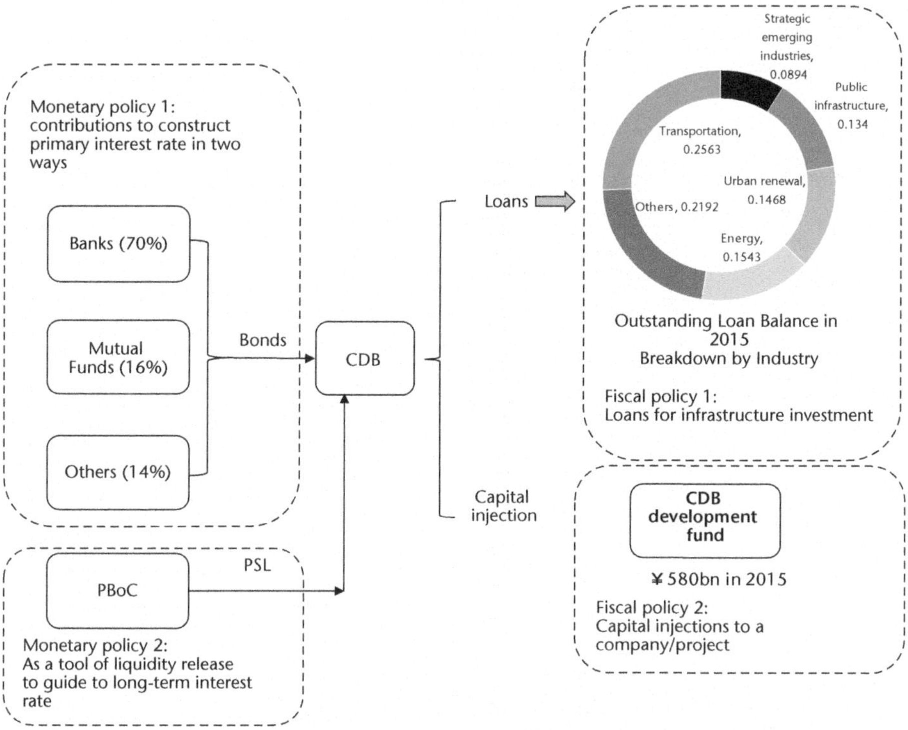

Figure 2.4. An overview of DCB's countercyclical role

Note: This circle diagram describes CDB's outstanding loan balance, which is broken down by industry.

Sources: Goldman Sachs' Global Research (2016), CDB's annual report, and the author

from the commercial system. By the end of 2015, the composition of CDB's outstanding loan balance in different industries was: strategic emerging industries 9 per cent, public infrastructure 13 per cent, urban renewal 15 per cent, energy 15 per cent, transportation 26 per cent, and others at 22 per cent (Figure 2.4).

On 25 August 2015, CDB Development Fund (CDF) was established to support domestic investment in key fields. Different from the traditional loan business, CDF supports the projects as a shareholder by means of capital injection, equity investment, and loans to a project.

It is possible that some projects, which are not qualified to get loans according to the standard of risk control, are initiated with a high leverage. But among these projects, some are potentially profitable and featured as having positive external effects. If a project is identified and qualified by CDF, then CDF can directly inject capital into the project to become a shareholder. At the same time, the debt/asset ratio will be expected to decline to a desired level because of the capital injection. Thus, the project will also be qualified and enabled to borrow more from CDB, commercial banks, or the bond market. In the process, CDF (including CDB) can obtain interest rate subsidies from MoF of China, and dividends and interest on loan from the project. These activities lead

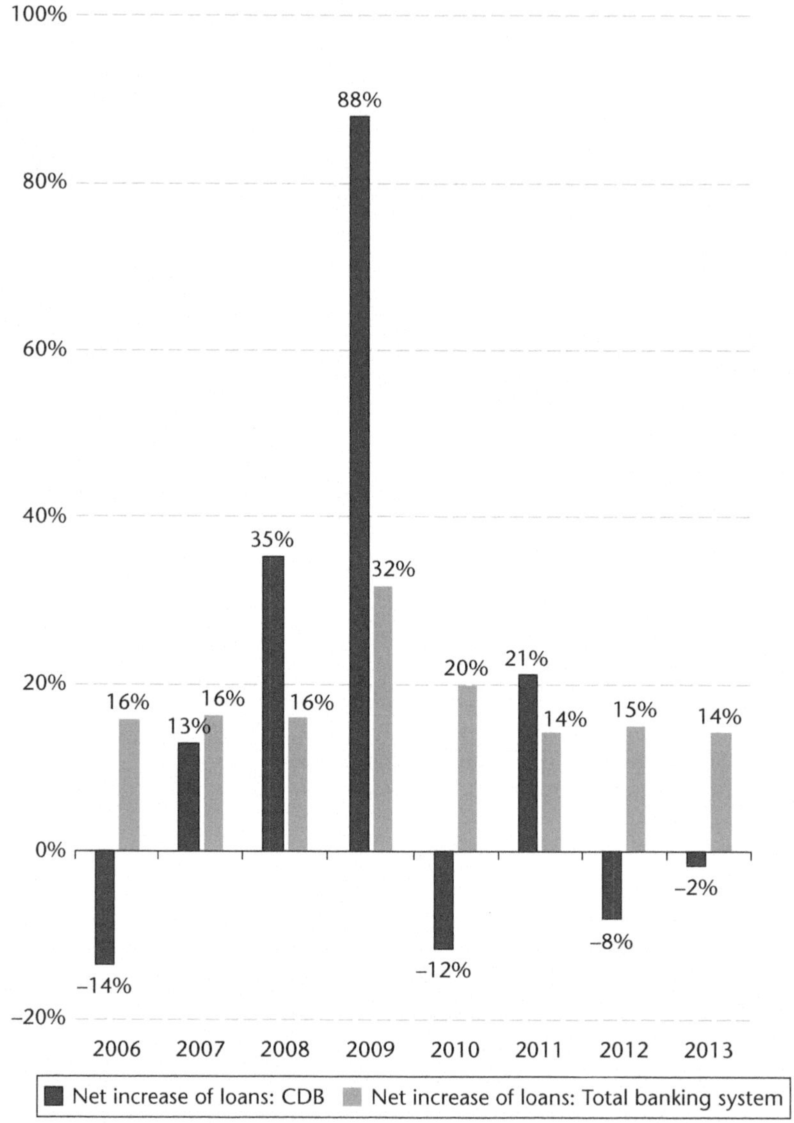

Figure 2.5. CDB's countercyclical role: Net increase of loans

to a sustainable business. Besides CDF, CDB Capital[29] and China's Investment Fund of Integrate Circuit Industry[30] also operate equity investments.

As a fiscal policy vehicle, CDB's loan business is characterized as countercyclical. As shown in Figure 2.5, at the end of 2008 and throughout 2009, just after the global

[29] CDB's wholly owned subsidiary, established in 2009.
[30] Initiated by CDB and other institutions, established in 2014.

financial crisis, CDB's loans for investment projects rocketed. In 2009, to deal with the shock of the global financial crisis, the growth rate of CDB loans was a striking 88 per cent. In 2010, by contrast, facing an overheated economy, CDB loans grew at a speed of −12 per cent.

References

Bai, Qinxian and Jun Li. 2005. 'The Legislation of China's Policy Finance and its Related Issues', *Shanghai Finance* [in Chinese] 26(11): 4–7.

CDB. 2016. *Annual Report of CDB*, Volumes of 2013, 2014, and 2015. Available at <www.cdb.com.cn/English/gykh_512/ndbg_jx/ndbg2015/>, accessed 29 December 2017.

Chen, Yuan. 2013. *Aligning State and Market: China's Approach to Development Finance.* Beijing: Foreign Language Press.

Editorial Board. 2013. *The History of China Development Bank* [in Chinese]. Beijing: China Financial Publishing House.

Gao, Guohua. 2015. 'CDB's Bonds Started to Be the Benchmark of the Floating Rate Bonds', *China's Financial Times* [in Chinese], April.

Gao, Hui and Chun Chen. 2007. 'China Development Bank: Move Ahead with an Embarrassment', *The Chinese Banker* [in Chinese] 15(12): 23–7.

Guo, Dapeng. 2006. 'The Past Life of State Development and Investment Corporation', *Journal of State-Owned Enterprises* [in Chinese] 6(2): 12–18.

Jiang, Zemin. 1992. 'Promote Reform and Opening Up Process, Speed Up Socialist Modernization, Construct Socialism with Chinese Characteristics', in Jiang Zemin (ed.), *Selected Works of Jiang Zemin*, 224–40. Beijing: People's Publishing House.

Li, Yang, Xiaojing Zhang, and Xin Chang. 2015. *China's National Balance Sheet: 2015.* Beijing: China Social Sciences Publishing House.

Liebman, Benjamin L. and Curtis J. Milhaupt. 2015. *Regulating the Visible Hand? The Institutional Implications of Chinese State Capitalism.* Oxford: Oxford University Press.

Literature Research Division of the Central Committee of the Communist Party of China. 2011. *Selected Important Literatures since the 15th National Congress of the CPC* [in Chinese]. Beijing: Central Party Literature Press.

Liu, Yuhui and Juchen Zhang. 2010. 'A Study of Local Government Financial Vehicle', *The Chinese Banker* [in Chinese] 17(6): 48–52.

Lu, Yinqiu and Tao Sun. 2013. *Local Government Financing Platforms in China: A Fortune or Misfortune?* IMF Working Paper, WP/13/243. Washington, DC: IMF.

Sanderson, H. and Michael Forsythe. 2013. *China's Superbank: Debt, Oil and Influence—How China Development Bank is Rewriting the Rules of Finance.* Singapore: John Wiley & Sons.

Shen, Min. 1999. 'Reforms of the Investment and Financing Systems for Municipal Infrastructure', *Shanghai Journal of Economics* 19(1): 50–2.

United Study Groups of China Development Bank and Renmin University of China. 2007. *Development Finance: Bond Market Innovation in China* [in Chinese]. Beijing: China Renmin University Press.

Wang, Jiao. 2016. 'The Demand for CDB's Bonds Is Strong', *China Securities* [in Chinese], September.

Wang, Lianshan. 2006. *Research on Fiscal Security and Risk in China*. Dalian: Dongbei University of Finance and Economics.

Wang, Yongzhong. 2016. *The Sustainable Infrastructure Finance of China Development Bank: Composition, Experience and Policy Implications*. Global Economic Governance Initiative, GEGI Working Paper No. 5. Boston University.

Wei, Jianing. 2010. 'The Risks of Local Government Financial Vehicle', *China Finance* [in Chinese] 61(16): 16–18.

3

National Development Banks as Active Financiers

The Case of KfW

Ulf Moslener, Matthias Thiemann, and Peter Volberding

3.1 Introduction

National development banks (NDBs)[1] were originally hailed as critical institutions to rebuild war-torn Europe and ameliorate economic bottlenecks, but by the early 1980s interest in them had waned significantly (Verdier 2000). The spread of the neoliberal school of thought and the lack of financial firepower severely curtailed both their abilities and influence. Yet beginning in the late 1990s, and accelerating after the 2008 global financial crisis, national development banks were once again in vogue across Europe. Armed with both expanded mandates and larger balance sheets, supporters argued that NDBs could intervene in the domestic economy when private actors were unwilling or unable to do so. More recently, support for NDBs grew after the European Commission highlighted the critical role that NDBs could play in catalysing long-term finance, countering the procyclicality of the macroeconomy, promoting the green economy, and fostering innovation (European Commission 2015). In particular, this growth of interest in NDBs has elevated the profile of Germany's KfW, the largest NDB in Europe. With a total balance sheet of EUR 500 billion and new yearly loan issuances of EUR 80 billion, KfW serves as one of Germany's largest financial institutions. KfW has participated in financing numerous domestic economic programmes ranging from SMEs

[1] In Europe, these institutions are often called national promotional banks (NPBs), yet they are functionally equivalent to an NDB.

to housing efficiency projects to student loans, and has been a key player in the retooling of the German economy for innovation and green technology. As such, KfW operates as a classic NDB, supplying financing to important projects that may be underinvested in by private actors.

While the activities of KfW have been well documented, less scholarly attention has focused on *why* KfW has grown to strategic importance. We contend that KfW's status as a state institution is central to understanding its influence. On the one hand, KfW is tasked with implementing policy objectives of the German government. In order to do so, KfW receives the full financial backing of the federal government, which allows it to borrow cheaply on capital markets and follow social, economic, and environmental goals rather than purely commercial ones. In this way KfW aims at ameliorating market failures and compensating for the under-provision of private capital. On the other hand, the operations of KfW are largely conducted according to market principles; KfW creates a spectrum of investment support instruments, takes advantage of its easy access to the capital market, and cooperates extensively with the commercial banking sector. This chapter aims to explore one important aspect of its unique position. In particular, how is KfW able to bridge the objectives of the public and private sector? More importantly, how does this position at the nexus between the public and private impact the ways in which KfW can contribute to policy creation and implementation?

We argue that the key to understanding the role of KfW in the German economy extends beyond its official tasks of ameliorating market failures or providing countercyclical financing. Rather, KfW's importance rests on its active participation within the domestic policy cycle, ranging from project proposal to evaluation. Since KfW is able to engage with the German government at all stages of policy, KfW can profoundly impact *how* these policies are determined, designed, implemented, and evaluated. KfW derives this legitimacy as an important policy actor through three characteristics: (1) it acts on the financial market with the government's backing to pursue economic—rather than purely commercial—objectives; (2) as a government agency, KfW has privileged access to officials and regulators; and (3) it has extensive technical and engineering expertise. Consequently, KfW has advantages that other institutions—both public and private—do not. For one, KfW's stronger financial position can be leveraged to pursue investments in public goods. In addition, KfW exists within a protected space in which it serves as an expert actor, allowing it to coordinate with government policy and impact the commercial and regulatory environment in which it operates. KfW has a role in developing these policies, such as providing technical advice or collaborating in the programme design. In this way, KfW can create and expand the policy space in which it operates. This potent dynamic results in KfW being an active and effectual economic institution, provided that none of these channels is systematically abused by either the government or the public bank. This close operational relationship allows KfW and the German government to achieve policy synergy, where regulation and financing can be coordinated within the domestic economy.

It is important to note that this chapter focuses on the process by which KfW engages with policy creation and implementation, and does not endeavour to evaluate the overall economic efficiency of a development bank intervention. In the (many) cases, where the market imperfection to be addressed is not a capital market imperfection (e.g. if an emissions externality is to be addressed), the approach through investment support tends to be of a second-best nature (first-best would be to put a price on emissions). As a consequence, first-best solutions are, in general, not achievable anymore. In practice, the design of an intervention through investment support is additionally complicated by the fact that an intervention is often targeted at multiple market imperfections simultaneously (e.g. emissions externality, innovation externality, etc.). Further, there may be additional policy goals.

It is not the goal of this chapter to evaluate how close implementation through KfW comes to a hypothetical first-best option. An efficiency perspective on investment support is provided by Kempa and Moslener (2017), while Bulow and Rogoff (2005) critically discuss the instrument choice of development banks. Rather, we leverage the example of KfW as a window into the process by which a development bank can shape policy formation and implementation.

The chapter proceeds as follows. First, we examine the particularities of the relationship between KfW and the German government within the policy cycle. We highlight how the three aforementioned characteristics profoundly impact the ability of KfW to operate and implement programmes from project proposal to implementation. Next, we examine this dynamic through the lens of two cases studies, the structural change towards a low-carbon economy and the financial sector after the 2008 global financial crisis. Finally, we conclude with thoughts on the replicability of KfW's institutional model to other countries, noting both the advantages and limitations of such an approach.

3.2 The Nexus between Private and Public: KfW, the German Government, and the Policy Cycle

NDBs are unique entities because they are institutions that link the private sphere and government, allowing them privileged access to both policy-makers and the commercial market. As opposed to the government, which typically limits its engagement to macroeconomic policy and regulatory spheres, a national development bank engages as a modified market participant: it plays by the rules, but does not behave entirely with commercial motivations. As Europe's largest NDB, KfW has served this function since the end of WWII. Yet while the particular programmes have changed, KfW has persisted as one of the most important domestic German financial institutions, and has consistently served to finance policy priorities. As such, KfW has also served an important role throughout the policy cycle.

3.2.1 *KfW in Historical Context*

KfW was originally established in 1949 to expedite the reconstruction of postwar Germany. KfW received its initial capitalization through the European Recovery Program (ERP), colloquially known as the Marshall Plan, and channelled American funds for investment in the housing, agricultural, power, and heavy industrial sectors (Grünbacher 2004). By the end of the 1950s, as the *Wirtschaftswunder* took hold in Germany, there existed less need for a purely reconstruction credit agency. Yet rather than eliminating KfW, the objectives of KfW adapted to the new challenges facing the German economy. Beginning in the 1960s, KfW assumed more global responsibilities, and began providing financing for foreign investments to secure primary commodities for German manufacturers as well as for international development aid projects. Domestically, KfW began emphasizing SME financing, vocational training, and more advanced industrial projects. From an early stage, KfW emphasized prudent investment over subsidization. Rather than providing a one-time grant to a specific project, KfW would instead extend a loan or provide a guarantee that did not erode its capital base. Any earned profits would be used to expand the capital base and reinvested to support new promotional programmes. Over the next few decades, the particular emphasis of KfW vacillated between domestically and internationally oriented projects, yet KfW's mission of promoting economic development via targeted financing remained largely unchanged. The reunification with East Germany and the fall of the Soviet Union ushered in a greater role for KfW in the early 1990s, when it became more active in SME financing, technical assistance, and governance and transparency initiatives (Harries 1998). Ultimately, KfW was critical in financing German reunification.

Today, KfW is one of Germany's largest financial institutions and one of Europe's largest bond issuers. In 2016, KfW had total assets worth EUR 503 billion and issued EUR 81 billion in new development activities, of which EUR 55 billion was targeted domestically (KfW 2017). SME financing still accounts for a substantial portion of KfW's domestic activities; in 2016, EUR 21.4 billion was committed to SME promotion and development. Significant expenditures were also recorded in housing investment (EUR 20.8 billion), education and

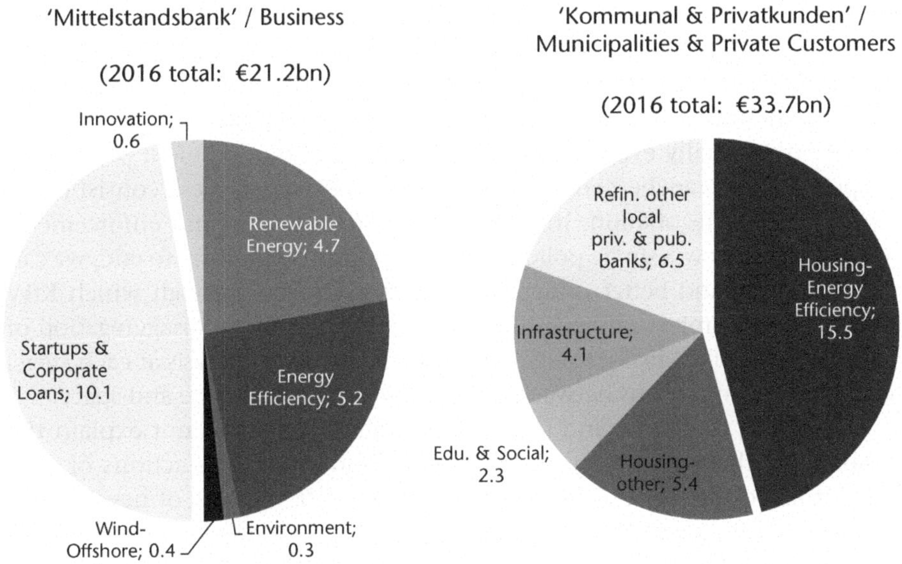

Figure 3.1. Commitments of KfW in 2016 made by the two major national parts: 'Mittelstandsbank' and 'Kommunal & Privatkundenbank'
Source: KfW (2017)

social development (2.3 billion), infrastructure (4 billion), and state promotional banks (4.4 billion). Outside the domestic promotion bank, KfW also has 24.9 billion in international activities, with the majority (16.1 billion) directed towards German export promotion. KfW's Development Bank and DEG or Deutsche Investitions- und Entwicklungsgesellschaft, which promotes private enterprise globally, account for a relatively small portion of total activities, comprising only 8.9 billion in 2016. In the past few years, KfW has also earned EUR 2 billion in consolidated profits in 2016.[2] As Figure 3.1 illustrates, the climate and energy-related part of the promotional activities dominate the portfolio. Note that within other areas, e.g. start-ups and corporate lending or infrastructure, the criteria for concessional lending has to have an environmental component, too.

3.2.2 *KfW within the Policy Cycle*

As one of the largest economic institutions in Germany, KfW has certainly impacted how the German government implements domestic economic

[2] KfW (2017). See also KfW, 'Nachhaltigkeitsbericht—Fakten-Update 2017', 7 December 2017. Available at <https://www.kfw.de/PDF/Download-Center/Konzernthemen/Nachhaltigkeit/Faktenupdate-Nachhaltigkeit-2017.pdf>.

priorities. In order to gain analytical traction into this dynamic, we examine the relationship between the German government and KfW using the heuristic of the policy cycle (Blum and Schubert 2009). The policy cycle identifies how a particular policy is created from initial conception, through implementation, to finally evaluation. According to Abbott and Snidal (2009: 46), the policy cycle can be conceptualized as a five-stage process consisting of agenda setting, negotiation, implementation, monitoring, and enforcement. By focusing on how a single policy is developed from beginning to end, we can limit the scope and better understand the mechanisms through which KfW affects policies, project implementation, and outcomes. The disaggregation of the process into five distinct stages also allows a detailed analysis at each stage, and permits comparisons between different policies across time and space.

Yet defining the scope and steps of the policy cycle does not explain the dynamics of this process. In order to better understand the actions of KfW within this policy cycle, we utilize the theoretical framework of new institutionalism within organizational sociology (DiMaggio and Powell 1983; Powell and DiMaggio 1991), combining it with resource dependency theories that assign a greater degree of agency to organizations in shaping their environment (Pfeffer and Salancik 1978; Oliver 1991; Wry et al. 2013). Essentially, we make two assumptions. First, we assign institutional agency to KfW—that is, we expect KfW to be not merely a passive actor in the policy cycle, but rather to be cognizant of its preferences and environmental limitations and, critically, to operate strategically to achieve these desired outcomes. Moreover, as resource dependency theories posit, we can expect the institution to attempt to shape the environment within which it operates. Second, and a key assumption of new institutionalism, we assume that organizations seek legitimacy within their environment. As such, they will adopt scripts and behaviour that will raise their legitimacy vis-à-vis their peers, independent of economic efficiency or rational-choice considerations. Consequently, we expect that KfW will act strategically within the policy cycle in order to achieve legitimacy within its operating environment and pursue its interests, broadly defined.

A cursory examination of KfW's actions in the policy cycle bears this out. Rather than passively serving as the German government's financing agency, KfW has instead actively participated in affecting the outcomes of policy at each of the five stages. As will be detailed in the two case studies, KfW has routinely assisted the government in selecting targeted policy areas, designing projects and programmes, implementing and financing them, monitoring the progress, and finally adjudicating the results that then inform the next iteration of the programme. Throughout the process, KfW is keenly aware of its institutional objectives. It is careful to create programmes that do not strain its resources, that allow it to better use available, but possibly unused, resources, and that allow it to expand its business operations in a fiscally responsible manner. Moreover, KfW has demonstrated an understanding of its limitations. Since it engages actively with both the German government and financial markets, in particular bond markets and rating agencies, KfW must constantly adjudicate between the competing pressures of the public and the private.[3] On the one hand, the Ministries of Finance, Economy, Environment, and Economic Cooperation seek to guide KfW towards a public mission; on the other hand, KfW also relies on financial markets and rating agencies to raise funds. Navigating these various demands can be challenging, as KfW must therefore balance technical government requests while maintaining high-quality standards in its credit decisions that allow it to operate on a commercial basis. The necessity of obtaining consent from the Ministry of Finance as a prerequisite to fund disbursement adds to these challenges.

Yet KfW's status as a public institution bridging the public and private spheres also affords it significantly more flexibility than other institutions, both public and private. For instance, KfW often has an information advantage. As a consequence of its proximity to policymakers, KfW may know more about policy trends and government priorities than its commercial peers. Due to its nature as a bank, it also better understands how commercial investment and financing decisions are undertaken than most government ministries. Additionally, KfW is acutely aware of the demands of the rating agencies, as well as the technical limitations of policy objectives. This information arbitrage assists KfW in navigating between the public and private spaces. More specifically, we identify three reasons as to why KfW is able to so successfully pursue its objectives within the policy cycle: a broad economic objective with government financing, proximity to both policymakers and regulators, and extensive technical expertise.

1. **A Financial Market Actor with an Economic Objective and Government Financing:** KfW's objectives are to compensate for market failures and promote socially or environmentally beneficial projects. These projects tend to carry aspects of public good provision or of other positive externalities which are typically not reflected in commercial rates of return. Projects range across a broad spectrum, including innovation, clean energy through renewable energy or housing energy efficiency programmes, technical and financial support for SMEs, revitalizing post-industrial economies, and student loans. KfW is able to support these underfunded projects largely because of its government financial backing. In exchange for implementing the government's policy objectives, the

[3] There is an argument to be made that commercial banks also play an important role, but because of space constraints will not be addressed here.

German government also effectively guarantees the institution. As a consequence, KfW receives the same (AAA) credit rating as the government, and can borrow more cheaply than its commercial banking counterparts. The indirectly subsidized financing (via government guarantees) allows KfW to undertake financial projects that the commercial sector deems insufficiently profitable. In order to prevent KfW from undercutting the commercial banks,[4] KfW typically does not directly lend to businesses or consumers. Instead, it relies on the network of commercial banks to assess risk, distribute the loans, and monitor repayment. Finally, even though KfW receives both its mandate and its financing advantage from the government, the German government gives KfW a remarkable amount of flexibility in project implementation. This allows KfW to more quickly adapt to funding needs and respond to market conditions. Perhaps more critically, since it is able to retain any profit it earns, KfW has an incentive to prudently invest.

2. **Proximity to Policymakers and Regulators:** By virtue of its institutional structure as a government agency, KfW has close ties with multiple German ministries. In fact, the Federal Minister of Economic Affairs and Energy and the Federal Minister of Finance are the Chairman and Deputy Chairman of KfW's Board of Supervisory Directors, respectively. Numerous members of the Bundestag, state parliaments, and trade unions similarly serve on the supervisory board. KfW regularly communicates with the parliament, and also has direct relationships with the Federal Ministry for the Environment, the Federal Ministry for Economic Cooperation and Development (BMZ), and its implementing agency, the Deutsche Gesellschaft für Internationale Zusammenarbeit (GIZ), and many other ministries (Bernau 2015). These relationships distinguish KfW from its commercial banking counterparts. On the one hand, the proximity to policymakers can increase the amount of pressure they exert on KfW to implement new policies. This means that KfW may in fact be required to implement policies it would otherwise have little interest in independently supporting. KfW is frequently called upon to provide its expertise on potential policy programmes and, as a trusted independent voice, has a substantial amount of influence. Perhaps more importantly, KfW and the government can coordinate policy, usually in a carrot and stick dynamic. For example, the federal government may increase the stringency of environmental regulations (the stick), but KfW will simultaneously provide a new subsidized financing instrument (the

[4] The challenge to avoid crowding out commercial financing by public financing institutions is, however, omnipresent and an issue of constant concern for an NDB and its government.

carrot). This institutional dynamic creates policy synergy, and allows the economy to respond more quickly to policy directives.

3. **Technical Expertise:** A substantial portion of KfW is also dedicated to technical expertise beyond what is required for a technical credit decision. As a primarily financial institution, it is unsurprising that a lot of these specialists examine the financial sector. These experts have profound knowledge of capital markets, risk assessment, bond issuance, and even financial securitization. They assist KfW's in-house operations as a financial institution as well as its investments in the domestic economy or, on occasion, in an exchange with other public institutions and authorities. However, KfW additionally employs experts with specific—often engineering-type—sector knowledge in agriculture, energy, transport, water, natural resources, and civil engineering, to name but a few. This substantively distinguishes KfW from the commercial banking sector. It allows KfW to base its investment decisions on a broader set of criteria from internal employees rather than relying on the market generally or external actors, such as consulting firms. This deeper understanding of sectors and the related markets is also essential not only to identify market imperfections, but also to anticipate the consequences of the respective interventions and programmes. Such knowledge further increases the likelihood that a particular project will be more successful from a socioeconomic as well as a commercial perspective. Technical expertise further allows KfW to serve as an important conduit between its investments in the private sector and government policy, adding to its information advantage. Finally, KfW's stamp of approval can effectively signal to other private investors that the project is viable.

These three characteristics ultimately allow KfW more latitude to operate within the policy cycle. As such, the implications of this active participation in the policy cycle are dual. First, it gives KfW greater control over implementing policy in line with its stated social objectives by coordinating its capabilities with government policy. With a staff of technical experts on hand, KfW can provide recommendations to the government on the best strategy to achieve those desired policy outcomes, whether it be in the project design phase or the project evaluation phase. Moreover, KfW can coordinate with the government to achieve policy synergy. It can also signal to the government if the demands are too strenuous. For example, KfW has directly requested additional funds or risk guarantees from the government in order to implement their desired policies in case these are assessed to be not directly economically viable. Elsewhere, it is often argued that 'credit agencies [...] are having a substantial and negative impact on the ability of MDBs to undertake their development mission' (Humphrey 2016). Second, and more critically,

KfW can also serve to influence those policies. KfW will frequently advise the government on the different possibilities for the implementation of projects. Both their technical and on-the-ground knowledge is useful for policymakers, and this provides opportunities for KfW to guide the creation and implementation of the policy. Possessing the ability to establish the parameters of the policy that the same institution implements is a substantial advantage.

Taken together, KfW's active engagement in the policy cycle ultimately assists in its pursuit of promoting the German economy, particularly with regard to structural transformation, critical infrastructure projects, and programmes such as small- and medium-sized enterprise (SME) financing. More recently, KfW has played a strong role supporting Germany's economic transformation to a green economy, both in terms of supply (through the support of green technology firms) and demand (through the financing of solar and wind power) (cf. Griffith-Jones 2016). While it is difficult to determine how far this is from a hypothetical first-best implementation in a context of multiple market imperfections combined with distributive policy goals, we argue that KfW's active engagement has enhanced its capabilities as a national development bank to support the policy process, though, as will be addressed later, that may not be entirely reproducible in other economic contexts. Moreover, this does not imply that KfW's policies are more economically efficient or produce better outcomes, but rather only that KfW as an institution has a broader set of tools to impact the policy process.

We use the heuristics of the policy cycle to describe how NDBs may work and shape the policy process. In practice, the policy process is also infinitely more complex, and it should not blind the analysis to the fact that anticipation of problems with respect to, for example, monitoring and enforcement does not already shape the behaviour of KfW at the agenda-setting or negotiation phase. However, we maintain that by using the framework of the policy cycle, we can achieve a better understanding of the complex process by which policy is created with the presence of an NDB. The next two case studies explore these policy cycle dynamics, detailing how KfW's unique role as a government institution cum commercial bank has shaped investment and policy in the structural change towards a low-carbon economy and in the financial sector after the 2008 global financial crisis.

3.3 Greening the Economy

One prominent aspect of KfW's domestic promotional mandate is the support of the structural change towards a low-carbon economy. While this particular shift has acquired added urgency due to the German government's recent *Energiewende* programme, this transition towards supporting environmentally sustainable practices on a comprehensive scale has its roots decades earlier. As such, KfW has had an active and important role throughout numerous iterations of the policy cycle. This is particularly evident in two areas: energy-efficient housing for consumers, and energy saving and renewable energy promotion for businesses.

Housing quickly became an economic and sociopolitical priority in post-war Germany, if for no other reason than to neuter potential social tensions that would lead to increased support for radical political parties (Harries 1998). In 1949, KfW allotted DM 34 million to building homes; in 1950 that figure grew to DM 400 million, and continued to rise in the subsequent years. While KfW unwaveringly supported housing, it was not until 1990 that energy efficiency became an important component within KfW's housing policy. In particular, the German government faced the daunting task of reunification; increasing energy efficiency was seen as a positive step forward for both businesses and East German residents alike, particularly with regard to the installation of modern heating systems. KfW had a natural role in shaping this phase of agenda setting and negotiation as it already had decades of experience in housing finance. The first step in implementation seemed almost business as usual. A scalable programme was designed that managed to modernize about 3.2 million flats by the end of 1997; some estimate that this was half the housing stock in the German Democratic Republic (GDR) before reunification (Harries 1998). However, a closer look reveals another role that KfW played in the monitoring and enforcement phase. Despite the government providing funds to reduce the interest rate by 3 per cent relative to the market, the programme was insufficiently attractive to induce modernization of the prefabricated, low-quality apartment complexes ('Plattenbauten'). KfW identified that owners (often municipal cooperatives) were not even able to pay interest on their old pre-unification loans after the West German currency was introduced. Consequently, the government and the governments of the 'new' states absorbed approximately DM 29 billion (EUR 14 billion) as *old debt assistance* ('Altschuldenhilfe'). The federal government and the states then asked KfW to completely administer the corresponding liquidation process. After a controversial discussion within the KfW board, it was decided that KfW would—as a bank—take on this purely administrative task which would normally be the task of a government agency (Harries 1998).[5] Following this

[5] In 1993, a law was passed that defined this 'old debt' and at the same time created an interest subsidy which fully covered interest payments for about two years at first. In the years to follow, a significant part of this debt would be paid for by a newly created public fund ('Erblasten Tilgungsfonds') if the housing cooperatives (or private owners) who applied for the relief agreed to sell or privatize 15 per cent of the flats over the coming years. See <https://www.kfw.de/KfW-Konzern/%C3%9Cber-die-KfW/Auftrag/Sonderaufgaben/Altschuldenhilfe-f%C3%BCr-ostdeutsche-Wohnungsunternehmen/>, accessed 15 May 2017.

change in 1993, the pace of apartment complex modernization accelerated (KfW n.d.). Those who received the relief invested EUR 45 billion to modernize their flats until the end of 1999.

The policy cycle in energy efficiency took another turn in 2010, when the government decided to substantially increase its efforts in reducing the energy consumption of buildings. KfW, armed with long-term experience and established connections with related research institutions, contributed to the design of the strategy put forward by the Ministry for the Economy ('Energieeffizienzstrategie Gebäude'). The strategy as published by the government emphasized the parallel approach through 'Informing, Promoting and Challenging'. It explicitly referred to the KfW programme 'Energy-Efficient Building and Renovating' as an important pillar of implementing the strategy. During the negotiation phase of this new policy, KfW—with the help of its internal technical/engineering expertise in energy efficiency in buildings—played a critical role by defining the standards for an energy-efficient house. This standard referred to the baseline as defined by the government in the building code (minimum standard in the so-called EnEV). For a new building, this indicates how much energy it will take to heat the house; a KfW Efficiency House 55, for example, means that the house can be expected to only need 55 per cent of what is required by the building code. If the building code changes, this relative standard changes accordingly. In addition, the Efficiency House standard determined the level of financial support offered by KfW. As of January 2017, all loans within the programme are offered at slightly below-market rates, 0.75 per cent, yet as a result of the low-interest environment the level of support is reflected in a parallel grant support that is expressed as a fraction of the loan size. Highest grant support (27.5 per cent of the loan) is offered if the effort to be financed leads to the building consuming less than 55 per cent of what the building code mandates. Though 12 per cent (of the loan volume) is granted if a renovation leads to the building consuming less than 115 per cent of what would be required for new buildings.[6] On top of determining the support level, the standard is established on the real estate markets as a quality signal and typically part of the basic description of the house.[7]

Additionally, KfW has routinely engaged in the monitoring and evaluation of its housing energy efficiency programmes. Typically on an annual basis,

[6] This is more than 100 per cent. Note that this support targets the renovation of already existing buildings. Energy efficiency requirements for new buildings in the building code show strongly increasing ambition over time. Therefore, bringing the efficiency of an old building even close to what is required from a new one (e.g. 115 per cent) is considered to qualify for some support.

[7] 'Was ist ein KfW-Effizienzhaus?', <https://www.kfw.de/inlandsfoerderung/Privatpersonen/Bestandsimmobilie/Energieeffizient-Sanieren/Das-KfW-Effizienzhaus/>, accessed 10 April 2018.

KfW's internal department for research commissions a monitoring report of the building efficiency programmes.[8] The monitoring exercise tracks loans, the number of flats, expected CO_2 emission savings, as well as quantitative estimates of employment effects of the programme. Less frequently, KfW asks research institutions to examine specific topics looking beyond the programme itself. One recent example of this evaluative research has been an empirical analysis of the most relevant drivers of the decision whether to engage in an energy efficiency investment in buildings or not.[9] In this case, the scope included surveying households that had decided against energy efficiency investments. The objective was to identify the reasons why these households did not participate in the programme, and subsequently provide recommendations as to how to improve future programmes.

Similar to the area of energy-efficient housing, improving energy savings and the use of renewables by businesses has its origins in policy initiatives from decades ago. In the late 1970s, after having faced two oil crises, the German government asked KfW to support its economic stimulus policies. As part of the request, KfW was involved in two ways. First, it executed programmes on behalf of the government where the full volume of the loans that were provided came from the government budget rather than from KfW's own funds. Second, KfW expanded its 'own' so-called M-Programme, which supported SMEs via funds that KfW itself raised on the capital market. Those were lent at below-market interest rates. When KfW decided to keep the artificially low interest rate in 1981, despite the rising market interest rate, the institution recorded very low profit margins while strengthening its ties to German policymakers. More importantly, these events established the pattern of cooperation between the German government and KfW, whereby KfW would raise funds on the capital market and then would combine them with government funds to subsidize interest rates.

Unlike the 1970s and 1980s, when energy efficiency promotion was a consequence of a global petroleum shock, in recent years the promotion of SMEs using clean energy has been strongly driven by climate concerns. One important programme targeting SMEs demonstrates how KfW engages in all stages of the policy cycle, ultimately leading to an improved programme design. The programme 'Renewable Energy (Standard)' began in 2009. As

[8] 'Monitoring der KfW-Programme "Energieeffizient Sanieren" und "Energieeffizient Bauen"', 2015, <https://www.kfw.de/PDF/Download-Center/Konzernthemen/Research/PDF-Dokumente-alle-Evaluationen/Monitoringbericht_EBS_2015.pdf>, accessed 26 January 2017.

[9] 'Einflussfaktoren auf die Sanierung im deutschen Wohngebäudebestand: Ergebnisse einer qualitativen Studie zu Sanierungsanreizen und -hemmnissen privater und institutioneller Eigentümer', June 2016, <http://www.iwu.de/fileadmin/user_upload/dateien/wohnen/2016/IWU_2016_6363_1603_KfW_Einflussfaktoren_Sanierung_Abschlussbericht.pdf>, accessed 10 April 2018.

the programme is implemented via on-lending through commercial banks, in accordance with normal guidance, those institutions are responsible for finding customers and selecting the projects that are supported. The commercial banks have contact points at KfW, with whom they regularly discuss the programmes and provide market feedback. From 2010, KfW received increased feedback that customers were expressing demand for financing the storage attached to photovoltaic (PV) installations—something that was not possible to finance under the current programme. KfW then entered into discussions with relevant government agencies such as the grid regulator and the Ministry for the Economy, which was also independently interested in potentially promoting storage. KfW suggested a change in the programme, leading to further discussion with the ministry, which approved the new version in 2016.

Finally, there are examples where excess institutional capacity has prompted KfW to seek expansions of existing environmental programmes. This example has its origins in a programme that substantially differs from traditional on-lending programmes such as the 'Renewable Energy (Standard)'. In the aftermath of the 2007 global financial crisis, KfW operated an economic stimulus programme to mitigate the negative economic consequences (see section 3.4). During the implementation of the stimulus package, KfW had to quickly act in building up expertise in direct lending to medium, but also larger, corporations. Unlike the practice of on-lending through commercial banks (where the commercial bank takes the loan risk), in this case, the loan went to corporations directly, involving the corresponding risk. The goal of KfW's intervention was not to provide an interest rate subsidy, but rather to engage in countercyclical lending which would offer strategic finance that the commercial banks were reluctant to provide. The end of that stimulus package coincided with the emergence of the *Energiewende* as a policy priority, which had gained bipartisan momentum. During the lengthy exchanges between KfW and the government regarding the investment side of the *Energiewende* and what KfW could contribute, KfW initiated a discussion about programmes that would in a broader way support companies driving the structural change forward. This initiative would have the added benefit of utilizing the direct corporate-lending expertise that had just been built up in context with the stimulus package. Discussions with the government shaped the programme further, and the new promotional programme 'Financing Initiative Energiewende', later renamed 'Konsortialkredite Energie und Umwelt' (Consortium Loans for Energy and Environment), was then designed and implemented. The programme was designed so as to keep KfW in the role of a catalyser rather than a driver 'picking' companies or technologies. The programme offers only joint finance with other banks, and KfW will not finance more than 50 per cent of any one deal. Neither does it offer conditions more favourable than other commercial co-financiers. Correspondingly, it is not using funds from the government budget and KfW is actually taking investment risk.

These cases illustrate that the full promotional effect of KfW can only be achieved through positive interactions of NDBs with the national policy and domestic financial sector throughout the policy cycle. Through this relationship, NDBs can serve an important role as technical experts that can aid both policy creation and investments from the financial sector.

3.4 Financial Crisis and the Aftermath

The involvement of KfW in the turmoil of the financial crisis and its aftermath shows both the advantages and challenges of having KfW as the intermediary between the government and the commercial banks. Before the crisis, KfW actively supported the installation of a (synthetic) securitization market in Germany, engaging in substantial purchases of loans bundled in asset-backed securities. These purchases were undertaken with clear industrial policy goals, seeking to increase the provision of both SME loans and housing loans to German SMEs and households respectively while mitigating declining profitability across the banking sector (Asmussen 2006; Mertens 2017). In particular, the upcoming Basel II regulations and their feared negative impact on SME loan provision were an important element in these considerations (Krämer-Eis 2000). Due to regulatory and taxation issues, KfW in the beginning mostly engaged in synthetic securitization, selling CDS to banks for specific loan portfolios, bundling the revenues of these CDS in turn, and selling credit-linked notes based on these revenues through a special-purpose vehicle.

In order to strengthen this synthetic form of securitization, KfW established the Promise Platform in December 2000 and the Provide Platform for mortgage-related loans in 2001. Up until the summer of 2007, credit risk for more than EUR 100 billion was transferred to financial markets, freeing up banks' balance sheets to expand lending. Due to its promotional duties, KfW passed any gains to be had from this business onto the banks originating the loans, thereby assuring the approval of commercial banks regarding this activity.[10] KfW had already been active in this policy initiative, at the agenda-setting stage, seeking a role in the upcoming business of securitization (Krämer-Eis et al. 2001). Engaging in synthetic securitization in the 2000s was an attractive role for KfW, signalling its prowess as a modern commercial bank. Its engagement in capital markets exposed KfW to these trends and made it keen to apply them to the German market. In the negotiation phase

[10] More than two-thirds of the loans insured by KfW were mortgage-related loans, indicating that the mortgage-related Provide Platform was more successful than the insurance of SME loans.

with the government as well as the banks, KfW secured a certain amount of fee business to compensate for manpower and risks taken, arguing for a cautious stance with respect to the evaluation of credit default risks of SMEs without hindering the take-off of the market (interview, March 2015). Implementation and monitoring were carried out by experts based in the capital markets division, who were actively learning about the techniques and were vital in disseminating knowledge on the new form of financing and its advantages (cf. Ranne 2005). Nevertheless, such expertise could not prevent the well-known problems of SME loan securitization, in conjunction with the financial crisis and structural constraints in the German financial system, from leading to a termination of both of the platforms KfW had installed (interview with KfW, March 2015; Mertens 2017). As part of the push of the German government for more true-sale securitization,[11] KfW became the central player in a consortium of fourteen private and public commercial banks which set up the True Sale Initiative in 2004 (Boston Consulting Group 2004). The True Sale Initiative acted and still acts as a catalyst for securitization in Germany, providing knowledge and platforms for securitization as well as a true-sale certificate, reducing transaction costs for engaged commercial banks.

Yet the most illustrative engagement of KfW with securitization occurred through a quasi-subsidiary of KfW, the IKB. The IKB was a medium-sized SME lender that was to become infamous during the financial crisis due to its off-balance-sheet engagement in the Asset-Backed Commercial Paper market. In the 2000s it became a major player in the issuance of SME-related securitization, a direction it had taken under the supervision of the KfW and the Ministry of Finance. KfW had become the major shareholder of that bank in 2001, when two large German insurers were selling their stakes in the bank. Thereby, the independence of IKB came into question as foreign banks were interested in taking over the lender. Through its relationship with the German government, KfW was advised to acquire the shares (interview with KfW official, March 2015). In line with the policy of creating and shaping the market for asset-backed securitization for SMEs in Germany, a goal KfW had pursued since 1999, IKB also began to set up large Asset-Backed Commercial Paper programmes with the aim of securitizing portfolios of SME loans through this vehicle. Approved by both the Ministry of Finance and KfW, IKB, in order to build up the size of its ABCP programme, began to acquire billions of US RMBS, which led to large losses once the crisis erupted in 2007. As the majority shareholder, KfW had the task of stabilizing IKB during the

[11] True sale refers to the actual transfer of assets from banks' balance sheets. The initiative was begun by the Ministry of Finance in 2003, when it assigned to the Boston Consulting Group the task of investigating the optimal conditions for such a true sale in Germany.

financial crisis, and eventually became liable for losses of several billion euros.[12] The government guarantee, which continued to secure cheap financing and the equity capital accumulated during the years of successful business up to then, provided the cushion to deal with this particular aspect of the crisis.

Once the crisis reached the real economy in the fall of 2008, however, the advantages of having a large national development bank became fully apparent. KfW acted as the primary countercyclical lender, expanding its on-balance sheet loans in 2008, and most dramatically in 2009, despite a substantial reduction in securitization activities. As a consequence, its balance sheet, which made up EUR 340 billion in 2005, reached EUR 441 billion in 2010 (KfW 2010; see Figure 3.2).

Furthermore, KfW programmes became a major policy tool for the German government when implementing government economic stimulus packages (KfW 2008). In particular, KfW played a central role in administering the Deutschlandfonds, a programme which had a maximum size of EUR 115 billion backed by government guarantees and risk capital (Welt 2010). The latter allowed KfW to expand direct lending to SMEs, as well as indirect lending programmes through large commercial banks and state guarantees, by EUR 7.2 billion in 2009. Overall, the programme helped 11,000 enterprises: 94 per cent of the number of loans went to SMEs and about half of the overall volume (Welt 2010; *Augsburger Allgemeine* 2010). For this programme, the capacity of the KfW to quickly implement and properly monitor these loan

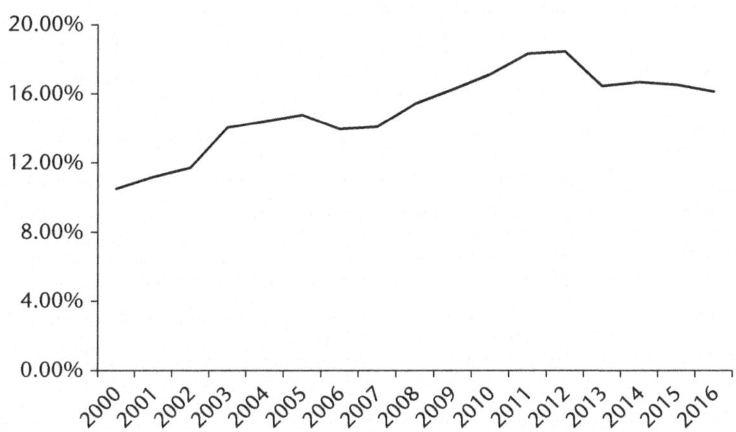

Figure 3.2. Balance sheet size of KfW, 2001–13, as a percentage share of GDP
Source: KfW Annual Reports

[12] In addition to its protracted efforts to rescue IKB, KfW had its fair share of criticism when in 2008 it sent about EUR 300 million in payment to Lehman Brothers the day after it declared bankruptcy, earning it the title of 'the dumbest bank in Germany'.

programmes was of great advantage to the German government. One need only compare the positive effects of this programme with the failure of the British government to achieve similar results by incentivizing private British banks to increase lending during the slump (Macartney 2014). Without a public development bank and with no capacity to force private banks to expand lending, the British government failed to implement anti-cyclical policies and SME lending basically remained flat.

These programmes by the KfW were also designed to address the liquidity needs of SMEs during the financial crisis, whose liquidity lines through commercial banks had shrunk and whose existence was thus put into peril. Indeed, this part of the programme made up the majority of the 3700 applications, with more than EUR 7.4 billion of credit granted to SMEs, thereby comprising the majority of the volume of the entire programme (Pichler 2010). The task of providing liquidity to these companies during a financial crisis highlighted the problems of information asymmetries and adverse selection as several of the companies which had applied for continued credit were excluded from refinancing for business reasons. Separating insolvent companies from healthy ones that were merely suffering from the reduced lending capacity of the private sector due to the fallout of the financial crisis was a particularly difficult issue which KfW had to face. Nevertheless, it can be conducive to overall welfare if losses caused by the closure of otherwise viable companies and the destruction of human and physical capital it entails can be avoided. Countering the volatility of the financial system in order to provide the social benefits of liquidity assistance requires a risk absorption capacity that private, profit-making activity could not provide. Luckily for the German government, the KfW had already begun to engage in this task by 2003 on a much smaller scale (BBP 2003: 152). Hence, when the need arose, the government could rely on an existing programme and scale it up in order to deal with the problem of market disruptions. In the negotiation process with the government, KfW sought to make sure it was not forced to take excessive losses, seeking to protect its triple A credit rating which was seen as the foundation of the business model. For that reason, KfW requested budgetary assistance from the government in order to bear the losses it would undoubtedly accrue when expanding its programme, a subsidy of several hundred million which it received (interview with KfW official 24 May 2016). Its financial expertise allowed KfW to assess the problem of separating insolvent firms from illiquid ones better than a simple government agency could have done, and it was able to avoid using the entire subsidy granted (same interview).[13]

[13] An important aspect here was also the quickly ameliorating economic situation in Germany, which itself was partially caused by the quick intervention of the German government.

These measures undoubtedly helped the German economy to absorb the shock of the financial crisis. Based on its financial expertise, KfW was thus able to stabilize the provision of capital from a financial system which has become ever more unstable. KfW officials further supported government efforts to cost-effectively ameliorate the financial crisis when they were assigned to the bad bank FMS, which the German government founded in 2010, to determine how to deal with the 'toxic loans' accumulated before the crisis.[14]

Since then, KfW has continued its engagement in ABS transactions, purchasing more than EUR 1 billion of high grade ABS in 2015, thereby stabilizing the ABS market during the downturn (KfW 2015). Furthermore, it has collaborated with the European Investment Fund (EIF) of the EIB and engaged in InnovFin and other European platforms for the securitization of SME loans. In 2016, it founded in conjunction with the EIF the European National Securitization Initiative (ENSI), a platform for European SME loans, taking the idea of Promise onto the European level. Expanding this platform allows KfW to pursue its promotional mandate itself on a continental level, seeking to relieve the balance sheets of banks to allow for more SME financing. While limited in size, this activity (like several others) points to the growing role of the KfW as a policy entrepreneur, expanding its function on the European level in the wake of the crisis (Mertens and Thiemann 2016).[15] Overall, at the moment of crisis, the KfW did not only offer the German government a capable bureaucratic apparatus that executed anti-cyclical policies, but also provided it with an infrastructure of already existing and tested programmes (such as the liquidity assistance for SMEs), which could be scaled upwards to meet the challenges of the crisis.

3.5 The Case for Replication: Prospects and Limitations

KfW's unique role between the public and private sectors has allowed it to have substantial influence on the promotion of the domestic German economy. As the two case studies illustrate, KfW has played an integral part in the support of development and use of green technology and the financial sector precisely because of a combination of its general economic mandate, its hybrid financing structure, its technical expertise, and its participation in national policymaking. Consequently, KfW's large impact has also attracted attention elsewhere in Europe, especially following the financial crisis when

[14] Arguably, government action could have been more forceful. Using the expertise of KfW officials, the restructuring of newly partially state-owned banks such as the Commerzbank could have been more extensive.

[15] Such as the issuance of loans of more than EUR 1 billion to the Spanish promotional bank ICO during the crisis.

governments sought to increase the amount of countercyclical financing for SMEs and the private sector. KfW has served an advisory role in the establishment of other NDBs, including the Portuguese Development Financial Institution, the Strategic Banking Corporation of Ireland (SBCI), and the UK's Green Investment Bank. KfW has also partnered with the European Investment Bank (EIB) to promote innovative financing schemes across Europe. These include some of the traditional domains of NDB financing, such as financing for underprovided sectors, as well as more recent goals, such as encouraging Europe's structural transformation to a green and innovative economy. Thus far, billions of euros have been raised through various investments funds. Whether or not NDBs provide a more efficient allocation of resources or achieve better outcomes than a fully public or private institution, however, is beyond the scope of this chapter.

Nevertheless, while by most accounts KfW has greatly assisted the German government's economic and social policies, this does not mean the results are easily replicable in other contexts. A few cautionary notes are warranted. First, KfW's institutional model largely functions because of a strong legal framework. With such close proximity between business and government, there is a significant risk that investment decisions ultimately become determined by political interests rather than societal objectives. This can lead to a slow siphoning off of funding from other investments that reduces the positive impact that the NDB is designed to engender. At its extreme, NDBs can serve as an extra-budgetary balance sheet that can channel funds to lavish political projects, and can likewise become fertile grounds for corrupt transactions. Therefore, even though KfW may be a government-owned institution, it requires operational autonomy that is legally protected. Moreover, this separation allows the NDB to function in conjunction with financial markets, a move that, at least in theory, engenders market discipline.

Second, NDBs require a relatively well-functioning domestic financial system to achieve optimal results. Even though in KfW's fledgling days the German economy was in ruins, there was still an underlying commercial banking sector with significant technical expertise that could be revived. Modern financial instruments also require deeper financial markets than before. Today, KfW both leverages its own funds on the domestic capital markets and distributes loans through the commercial banking sector. Without the private financial sector, these operations would not be possible. It is therefore necessary for the government to establish a well-functioning financial system as a precondition for an NDB, as the purpose of NDBs is to exploit the financial markets for the objectives of government policy, not to create these financial markets *de novo*. In this regard, NDBs are not substitutes for a functioning financial market. Moreover, this also means that NDBs may not be the most effective instruments in countries with shallow financial markets or weak economic protections, or, the KfW is at least not immediately replicable in other institutional and macroeconomic contexts.

Finally, enormous technical capacity is required to achieve positive economic outcomes. The operations of KfW are inherently difficult because it is not always apparent a priori whether a particular instance of an under-provision of financing constitutes a market failure. There is an inherent risk that NDBs will artificially prolong investment in a project that is either economically inefficient or socially unbeneficial. In order to mitigate these risks, NDBs must have extensive knowledge in capital markets, banking, regulation, and, most importantly, the individual sectors which it is supporting. NDBs cannot wholly rely on the financial market to allocate these resources and therefore must possess the technical capacity to do so independently. Relatedly, it requires policy clarity on the part of the government. Policymakers must implement clear guidelines on what the priority of the NDB should be and, moreover, have faith in the NDB to independently implement these goals.

Despite the limitations to exact replicability across the developing world, KfW serves as an important example of how a national development bank can bridge the public–private divide when creating policy. If developing countries are determined to use KfW as a model for how an NDB can operate, then the case study provides important lessons. For instance, developing-country governments should ensure that NDBs are incorporated into the policymaking process, yet also operate independently in domestic financial markets. Resources should be provided to NDBs so they can develop in-house technical capacity. Perhaps most importantly, NDBs should be promoted as part of a broader and more coordinated strategy of policy change, enabling a synergy to develop between NDBs, policy, and regulation. Under these conditions, NDBs can serve as an important tool to compensate for market failures, promote economic sectors, and encourage structural transformation of the economy.

References

Abbott, K. W. and D. Snidal. 2009. 'The Governance Triangle: Regulatory Standards Institutions and the Shadow of the State', in Walter Mattli and Ngaire Woods (eds), *The Politics of Global Regulation*, 44–88. Princeton: Princeton University Press.

Asmussen, Jörg. 2006. 'Verbriefungen aus Sicht des Bundesfinanzministeriums'. *Zeitschrift für das gesamte Kreditwesen*, No. 12, 10–12. Frankfurt.

Augsburger Allgemeine. 2010. '10 Milliarden aus "Deutschlandfonds"', *Augsburger Allgemeine*, 5 January. Available at <www.augsburger-allgemeine.de/wirtschaft/10-Milliarden-aus-Deutschlandfonds-id7105086.html>, accessed 10 April 2018.

Bernau, Patrick. 2015. 'Der Staat als größter Lobbyist', *Frankfurter Allgemeine Zeitung*, 29 November. Available at <http://www.faz.net/aktuell/wirtschaft/wirtschaftspolitik/lobbyisten-liste-des-bundestags-kfw-und-gkv-spitzenverband-vorne-13939161.html>, accessed 10 April 2018.

Betriebswirtschaft im Blickpunkt (BBP). 2003. 'Das KfW-Mittelstandsprogramm-Liquiditätshilfe für KMU'. *Betriebswirtschaftliche Mandantenbetreuung*, no. 6: 152. Available at <www.iww.de/bbp/archiv/liquiditaetshilfe-das-kfw-mittelstandsprogramm-liquiditaetshilfe-fuer-kmu-f34209>, accessed 10 April 2018.

Blum, Sonja and Klaus Schubert. 2009. 'Prozesse—Der Policy-Cycle', in *Politikfeldanalyse*, 101–40. Wiesbaden: Springer.

Boston Consulting Group. 2004. *Optimale Staatliche Rahmenbedingungen fuer einen Kreditrisikomarkt/Verbreifungsmarkt fuer Kreditforderungen und -risiken in Deutschland.* Gutachten im Auftrag des Bundesministeriums der Finanzen, Projektnummer 16/03, Abschlussbericht.

Bulow, Jeremy and Kenneth Rogoff. 2005. 'Grants versus Loans for Development Banks', *American Economic Review* 95(2): 393–7.

DiMaggio, Paul J. and Walter W. Powell. 1983. 'The Iron Cage Revisited: Institutional Isomorphism and Collective Rationality in Organizational Fields', *American Sociological Review* 48(2): 147–60.

European Commission. 2015. *Working Together for Jobs and Growth: The Role of National Promotional Banks (NPBs) in Supporting the Investment Plan for Europe.* COM/2015/0361. Brussels.

Griffith-Jones, Stephany. 2016. *National Development Banks and Sustainable Infrastructure: The Case of KfW*. Global Economic Governance Initiative Working Paper 006. Boston University.

Grünbacher, Armin. 2004. *Reconstruction and Cold War in Germany: The Kreditanstalt für Wiederaufbau (1948–1961)*. Aldershot: Ashgate Publishing.

Harries, Heinrich. 1998. *Financing the Future: KfW, the German Bank with a Public Mission*. Frankfurt: KfW.

Humphrey, Chris. 2016. *The Principal in the Shadows: Credit Rating Agencies and Multilateral Development Banks*. Working Paper for the Intergovernmental Group of Twenty-Four on International Monetary Affairs and Development (G24).

Kempa, Karol and Ulf Moslener. 2017. 'Climate Policy with the Chequebook: An Economic Analysis of Climate Investment Support', *Economics of Energy & Environmental Policy* 6(1): 111–29.

Krämer-Eis, Helmut. 2000. 'Ratings, Basel II und die Finanzierungskosten von KMU'. KfW-Beiträge zur Mittelstands- und Strukturpolitik 16, 21–30.

Krämer-Eis, Helmut, Claudia Schneider, and Christoph Tiskens (2001). 'Die Verbriefung von Mittelstandskrediten durch die KfW'. KfW-Beiträge zur Mittelstands- und Strukturpolitik 21, 24–30.

KfW. 2008. *Annual Report 2010*. Frankfurt: KfW.

KfW. 2010. *Annual Report 2010*. Frankfurt: KfW.

KfW. 2015. *Annual Report 2015*. Frankfurt: KfW.

KfW. 2017. 'Förderzahlen per 31. Dezember 2016'. Press Release. Available at <www.kfw.de/Presse-Newsroom/Pressematerial/PDF-Dateien-Pr%C3%A4sentationen/

PDF-Dokumente-2016/LAY_KfW_Geschaefts_Foerdertabellen_2017_f_Jahreskonferenz_DE_170130_03-2.pdf>, accessed 2 December 2017.

KfW. n.d. 'Altschuldenhilfe für ostdeutsche Wohnungsunternehmen'. Available at <https://www.kfw.de/KfW-Konzern/%C3%9Cber-die-KfW/Auftrag/Sonderaufgaben/Altschuldenhilfe-f%C3%BCr-ostdeutsche-Wohnungsunternehmen/>, accessed 10 April 2018.

Macartney, Huw. 2014. 'From Merlin to Oz: The Strange Case of Failed Lending Targets in the UK', *Review of International Political Economy* 21(4): 820–46.

Mertens, Daniel. 2017. 'Putting "Merchants of Debt" in their Place: The Political Economy of Retail Banking and Credit-Based Financialisation in Germany', *New Political Economy* 22(1): 12–30.

Mertens, Daniel and Matthias Thiemann. 2016. *Towards a European Investment State?* Unpublished manuscript.

Oliver, C. 1991. 'Strategic Responses to Institutional Process', *Academy of Management Review* 16: 145–79.

Pfeffer, J. and G. R. Salancik. 1978. *The External Control of Organizations: A Resource Dependence Perspective*. New York: Harper and Row.

Pichler, Roland. 2010. 'Hilfsfonds läuft aus'. *Stuttgarter Zeitung*, 1 June. Available at <www.stuttgarter-zeitung.de/inhalt.staatshilfen-fuer-unternehmen-hilfsfonds-laeuft-aus.722cbc44-9397-4901-b4e3-52e6b841e437.html>, accessed 10 April 2018.

Powell, Walter W. and Paul J. DiMaggio. 1991. *The New Institutionalism in Organizational Analysis*. Chicago: University of Chicago Press.

Ranne, Omar. 2005. 'Securitisation and Access to Finance for European SMEs'. *KfW Research Economic Observer* 8 (September): 9–15. Available at <https://www.kfw.de/Download-Center/Konzernthemen/Research/PDF-Dokumente-WirtschaftsObserver/Englisch/WirtschaftsObserver_08_e.pdf>, accessed 10 April 2018.

Verdier, Daniel. 2000. 'The Rise and Fall of State Banking in OECD Countries', *Comparative Political Studies* 34: 227–62.

Welt. 2010. 'Deutschlandfonds hat 11.000 Unternehmen geholfen', 8 March. Available at <www.welt.de/wirtschaft/article6692874/Deutschlandfonds-hat-11-000-Unternehmen-geholfen.html>, accessed 10 April 2018.

Wry, T., J. A. Cobb, and H. Aldrich. 2013. 'More than a Metaphor: Assessing the Historical Legacy of Resource Dependence and its Contemporary Promise as a Theory of Environmental Complexity', *Academy of Management Annuals* 7: 429–86.

4

The Future of Development Banks

The Case of Brazil's BNDES

Rogério Studart and Luma Ramos

4.1 Introduction

Infrastructure and logistics (I&L) in Brazil fall short of the demand for basic needs, are a drag on national productivity and competitiveness, and may be inappropriate to address the challenges imposed by climate change. In a country facing one of the most significant recessions of its history, this chapter claims that increasing investments in *sustainable I&L* may, in turn, offer a golden opportunity to raise growth and to achieve sustained, inclusive, and environmentally compatible development. It is Brazil's necessary step out of its current middle-income trap.

The challenge of boosting I&L investment seems enormous at a moment when (i) national and subnational governments face severe fiscal constraints; (ii) private sources of long-term funding continue to be scarce and the cost of capital too high; and (iii) project development capabilities, particularly for more complex and innovative projects, are limited. Recent studies, including Gallagher and Studart 2016, indicate that national development banks may be critical to promote projects, and leverage and crowd-in private capital to transformational investments—such as sustainable I&L. Brazil's national development bank, we argue, should be no exception.

Founded in 1952, the Brazilian Economic and Social Development Bank (BNDES) has had a catalytic role in promoting *transformational investments* in different phases of Brazil's socioeconomic development. From 2002 to 2015, the bank increased its support for badly needed I&L projects, and its lending level hiked exponentially. BNDES became a financial giant, but in this process, it paid a high price: the political and economic turmoil that engulfed the nation placed it under strong public scrutiny. An abrupt change of economic orientation by the federal government since 2015, and particularly in 2016, led to a 'change of heart' about the role it should play in Brazil's future development path.

This chapter analyses the potential role of BNDES in promoting transformational changes needed for Brazil now—which in our view must come from, but not solely, a wave of sustainable infrastructure and logistics investments. The chapter argues that BNDES could, and should, play a critical role in developing a much-needed I&L investment financing architecture—through its potential in fostering project development capacities, and financing, leveraging, and crowding-in private resources for the sector.

It is organized as follows. Section 4.2 assesses the I&L gaps and their consequences for Brazil's growth, and discusses why raising *sustainable* I&L presents an opportunity to help overcome the current crisis, setting a new and promising path of socioeconomic development. Section 4.3 reviews the history, financial performance, and funding of BNDES. Section 4.4 presents a preliminary analysis of more recent changes of its orientation and operational policies, and their likely effects on I&L financing. Section 4.5 summarizes our findings and offers our main conclusions.

4.2 An Economic Giant Trapped by I&L Gaps

Brazil's growth in the past three decades has been characterized as a typical case of 'middle-income trap'.[1] Indeed, Brazil's per capita gross domestic product (GDP) trajectory, which had been quite robust in the 1970s, was almost nil during the whole of the 1980s, and extremely low in the 1990s. Only in the 2000s did this performance improve. More recently, though, the country has entered an economic recession which is producing a reversal of such achievements. In our view, much of Brazil's 'middle-income trap' results from the significant decline in public and private investments during the so-called lost decade, the 1980s. This deterioration may have affected at least three pillars of economic development: education and knowledge, innovation, and I&L. The lag in I&L investments, in particular, has created enduring challenges for

[1] Kharas and Kohli (2011) define 'middle-income trap' as follows: 'In a steadily growing economy, per capita Gross Domestic Product (GDP) rises continuously over time (growth) toward higher income levels. That has been the experience of the Republic of Korea. But many middle-income countries do not follow this pattern. Instead, they have bursts of growth followed by periods of stagnation or even decline, or are stuck at low growth rates. Instead of steadily moving up over time, their GDP per capita simply gyrates up and down. They are caught in the Middle-Income Trap—unable to compete with low-income, low-wage economies in manufactured exports and unable to compete with advanced economies in high-skill innovations. South Africa and, until recently, Brazil are examples of this phenomenon.'

Brazil's capacity to remain on a sustainable and inclusive path, which was chosen for itself after its return to democracy in the 1990s.

4.2.1 *The Double Legacy of a 'Lost Decade'*

Brazilian early industrialization was a result of the closure of international trade during the First World War, which allowed the country to pursue import substitution (ISI) starting at the beginning of the twentieth century initially (Furtado 1959). The post-war period was characterized by a government-sponsored import substitution strategy, accompanied by rapid urbanization and the emergence of an incipient middle class, particularly in industrial cities, such as Sao Paulo. These changes to class structure had social, political, and economic consequences, as the pace of growth in demand generated constant mismatches of aggregate supply and demand for goods and services. Not surprisingly, the experience of post-war growth was followed by macro-economic imbalances, inflation, or balance of payments difficulties, and increased social and political tensions.

The dramatic political turmoil of the early 1960s resulted in a military coup in 1964 and twenty-five years of dictatorship. Following several years of stagnation, paradoxically with policies focused on macroeconomic adjustment and reforms, the military regime resumed import substitution industrialization, anchored in the development of intermediary goods—including chemical complexes. Brazil reached the end of the 1970s with a diversified, internationally competitive manufacturing sector, but also with one of the highest poverty and inequality levels on the planet. An additional vulnerability inherited by Brazil's high growth period in the 1970s was linked to its balance of payments. Indeed, the international interest rate shock of 1979 transformed a relatively small external debt situation into a full-fledged debt crisis.

This was the beginning of the 'lost decade' characterized by structural adjustment, economic stagnation, and rampant price hikes that led to hyper-inflation. These years were also distinguished by processes that had a direct impact on the infrastructure challenges faced by Brazil until now: the rapid decline of private and public investments, particularly in I&L, and deterioration of the state's capacity to develop, implement, and monitor large investment undertakings (Figure 4.1). Finally, it was a period of rising inequality and poverty, which together with the infrastructure gaps became the two main heritages for governments after 1990, when Brazil entered a democratic and inclusive course.

This heritage only began to change with the successful stabilization programme in 1994, and the establishment after 1999 of a macroeconomic model anchored on a 'tripod'—based on its fiscal responsibility law, central bank

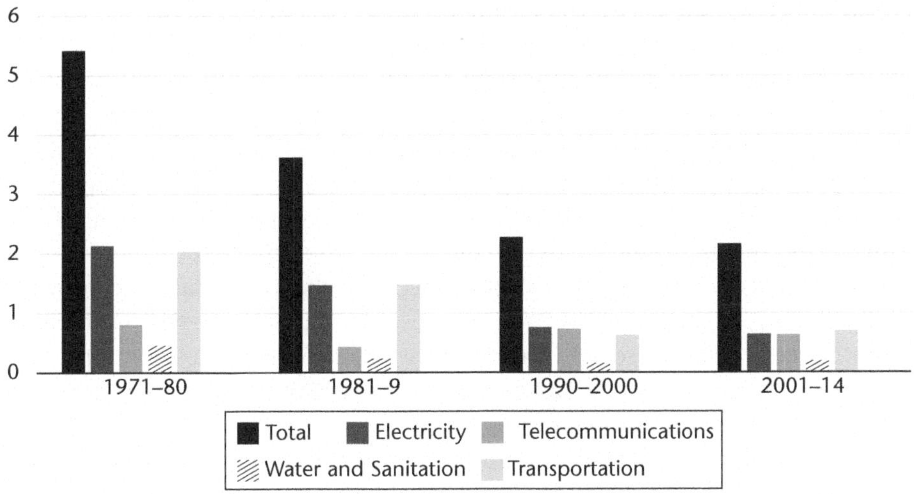

Figure 4.1. Brazil: Investments in infrastructure (percentage of GDP)
Source: CNI (2016)

autonomy, and flexible (dirty floating) exchange rate regime. Even though inequality fell as a one-off consequence of price stabilization in 1994, the achievement of macroeconomic stability opened the possibility of addressing the social debt through, for instance, the enhancement of social programmes and real-wage growth policy. Poverty and inequality fell significantly, while GDP per capita had the highest advances since the 1990s. In this process, a new middle class emerged and access to credit expanded significantly, which led to a boom in consumption of goods and services.

Notwithstanding these socioeconomic advances, the I&L investments needed to increase the provision of public goods and services did not follow. Widening I&L gaps contributed to the increasing pressure put on infrastructure in general, but particularly in the urban areas where 85 per cent of Brazil's population live. This is what we shall see next.

4.2.2 *I&L Gaps as Constraints to Sustained Inclusive Development*

It seems to be a consensus among analysts and policymakers that I&L gaps have become a true constraint on Brazil's growth and particularly on its prospects for a future of sustainable development (e.g. Castelar Pinheiro and Frischtak 2014). Whatever measure is applied, these gaps are extremely large and their negative externalities in Brazil's recent socioeconomic history cannot be understated. For instance, the 2010 World Bank Enterprise Survey pointed out that 28 per cent of firms considered transportation to be a major constraint, compared to 23 per cent in Latin America and the Caribbean (Garcia-Escribino, Goes, and Karpowicz 2015).

Other evidence that I&L gaps represent a drag on the national business environment and competitiveness is that Brazil ranks 120 out of 144 countries surveyed in the 2014 World Economic Forum overall infrastructure quality. Only in electricity and telecommunication is Brazil in a better ranking than some competitors, areas in which it has invested comparably more in recent years—with greater interest and participation of the private sector.

Poor I&L also create significant bottlenecks in Brazil's social development and, arguably, political 'ceilings' for a process of inclusive growth. In this vein, despite recent hikes in social infrastructure investments, access to improved sanitation was still denied to 12.0 per cent of the urban population and almost 50 per cent of the rural population.

Other indicators also paint a grim picture of the obstacles created by I&L gaps for the new needs generated by inclusive growth and rapid urbanization. For instance, even though the national fleet of cars and trucks has almost doubled in the last ten years, less than 15 per cent of Brazil's roads are paved (including municipal roads) and multi-lane roads are still relatively rare, although they have doubled over the past half-decade. This makes traffic jams a major concern in any of its largest urban centres.

Finally, when it comes to environmental sustainability most I&L are not climate-smart, both when it comes to mitigation and adaptation, even though the effects of climate change are already being felt. Building I&L that help the country follow a path of low-carbon, climate-resilient, and inclusive growth simultaneously may be the challenge in the next decades for Brazil.

Overcoming the existing I&L financing gaps will not be easy, as it requires investments estimated to be as high as R$1.1 trillion, the equivalent of one-fourth of Brazil's 2012 GDP (Wagner et al. 2015). This will demand a simultaneous increase in public and private investment, at a moment when the national and subnational government faces tremendous budgetary challenges, and long-term private financing—traditionally very limited—is scarcer than ever. BNDES could play an important role in achieving these goals. This is the topic of section 4.3.

4.3 BNDES: History, Business Model, and Funding Challenges

BNDES's history is profoundly connected with Brazil's post-war development. In the early years, its main role was to finance economic infrastructure projects and develop the steel industry that were critical for industrialization-based consumer durables (Studart 1995). Already in the 1960s, it helped finance the development of the consumer goods industry. BNDES played a fundamental role in 1970s import substitution programmes that strengthened several industrial input-producing sectors (e.g. petrochemical industry) and capital goods, and even created completely new ones (e.g. information technology and microelectronics). Indeed, BNDES helped shape what is now the most diversified industrial sector in Latin America (Castro and Souza 1985).

During the 1980s, in addition to its other mandates, BNDES promoted the expansion of energy exports and agriculture and promoted social integration. In the 1990s, it was a critical part of the federal privatization programme, by assisting in the sale of large state-owned Brazilian companies. From 2002 to 2015, besides all its other activities, BNDES increased its support for large I&L projects and for their global presence. In the last decade, its lending level increased exponentially, until it fell dramatically in the past year; and despite its attempts to leverage and crowd-in private capital, its dependency on transfers made from the National Treasury for its funding also rose. BNDES became a financial giant, and a centrepiece of Brazil's social and economic development.

Since the early 2000s, BNDES has become an even more critical player in major government infrastructure investment programmes. Its business model and funding strategy were adapted to facilitate private participation in infrastructure (PPI) and other government programmes, but also became a source of political exposure. This vulnerability partly explains some of the more recent changes in its orientation and operational policies, and will be discussed in detail in the next section.

4.3.1 *Business Model, Performance, and Funding*

The overall financial performance of BNDES has been impressive in the past decade. Disbursements have been multiplied by more than four times (in average US dollars), whereas profits almost quadrupled (Figure 4.2). This performance is partly due to BNDES's role in supporting the two large government-sponsored investment programmes, the Growth Acceleration Programme (PAC in its Portuguese acronym) and the Logistics Investments Programme (PIL), and the countercyclical role it played in the aftermath of the 2009 crisis.

PAC was launched in early 2007, still under the Lula da Silva administration. It consisted of a set of economic policies and investment projects with the objective of eliminating the I&L bottlenecks and easing growth in Brazil. The programme had a budget of RS$503.9 billion between 2007 and 2010, and soon after the 2009 global financial crisis became one of Brazil's main countercyclical efforts. The Rousseff administration (2010–15) continued the programme under the name PAC-2. The Logistics Investment Programme (PIL) was launched in 2012 to promote concessions of 7500 kilometres of highways

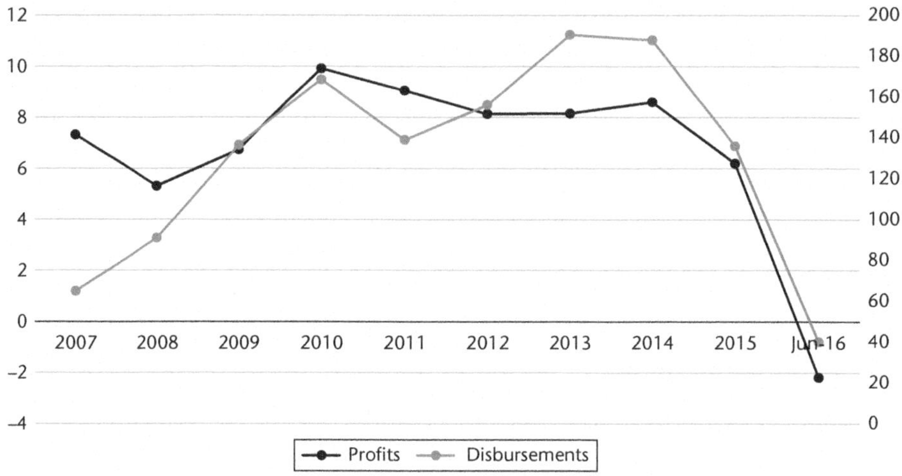

Figure 4.2. BNDES: Disbursements (left axis) and profits (R$ billion)
Source: BNDES

and 10,000 kilometres of railroads. The total planned investment over twenty-five years was to reach R$133 billion (R$42 billion for highways and R$91 billion on railroads), with R$79.5 billion to be invested in the first five years.

BNDES became one of the largest financial institutions in Brazil—in addition to becoming one of the five largest development banks (be it national, regional, or multilateral) in the world. This market position did not come without challenges. And one of them became increasingly controversial in Brazil: its funding strategy. Indeed, until very recently the main sources of funding to BNDES were provided by investments of 'quasi-public' funds associated with social insurance and workers' safety nets—PIS (Social Integration Programme), PASEP (Public Servant Pension Fund), and FAT (Labour Redundancy Programme)—returns of its outstanding loans and equity investments, bond issuance, and/or borrowing from multilateral institutions (Figure 4.3). This has changed since 2009, when BNDES stepped in to fill the vacuum created by the retrenchment of private financing in the aftermath of the 2008 crisis. Incapable of tapping the market at a pace compatible with the expansion of its loan portfolio, BNDES's funding became highly dependent on transfers from the National Treasury and the volume of resources coming from it increased substantially, becoming higher than 50 per cent of the total.

This extraordinary growth of transfers from the National Treasury revived an old controversy on the societal costs of promoting industrial policies, and therefore on the validity of BNDES's funding strategy. The problem lies in the fact that Brazil does not have a developed term-structure interest rate curve (or yield curve), because most private debt instruments have short maturities.

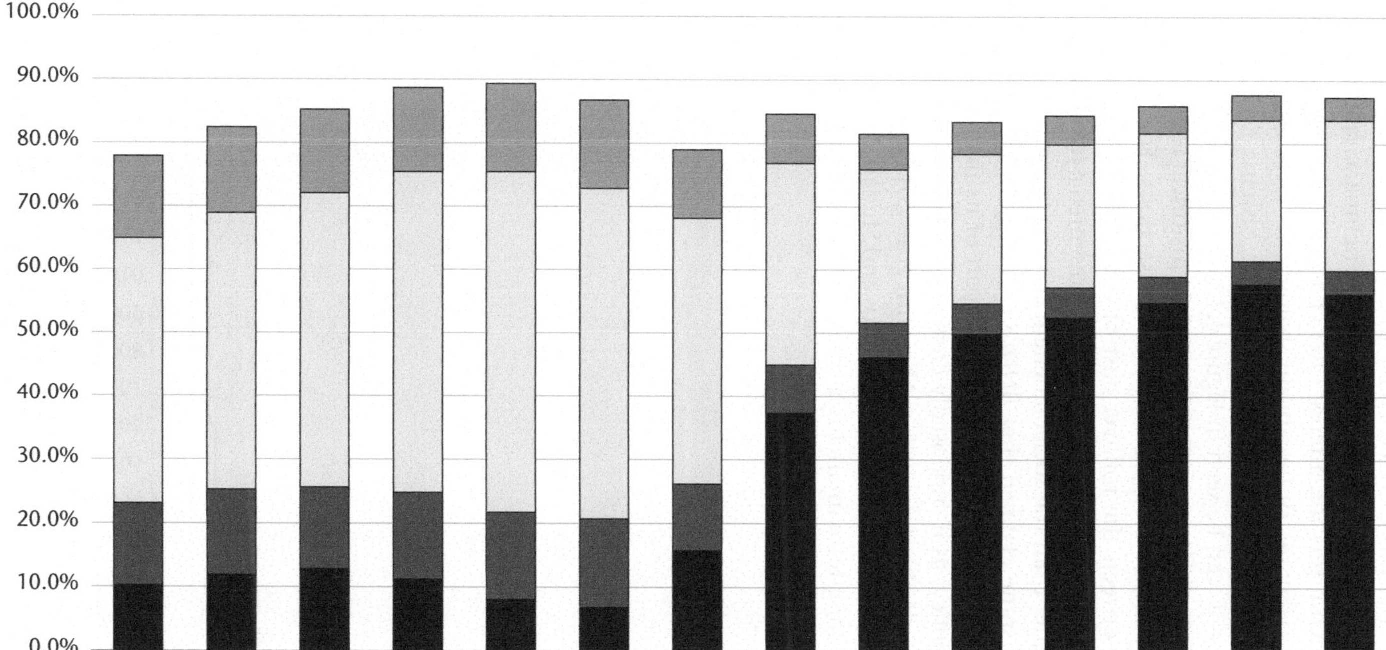

	2002	2003	2004	2005	2006	2007	2008	2009	2010	2011	2012	2013	2014	2015
External Funding	0.129254495	0.134396056	0.131295019	0.1352255	0.137404987	0.137708979	0.106457406	0.077704179	0.05615096	0.050705235	0.045838004	0.04300781	0.038322243	0.036248517
FAT	0.418275282	0.435562859	0.463384139	0.505603914	0.535879451	0.522777964	0.420376928	0.316830172	0.240907435	0.234088796	0.226217264	0.225308295	0.222817791	0.237127328
PIS-PASEP	0.129254495	0.134396056	0.131295019	0.1352255	0.137404987	0.137708979	0.106457406	0.077704179	0.05615096	0.050705235	0.045838004	0.04300781	0.038322243	0.036248517
National Treasury	0.101597795	0.118711586	0.125500887	0.112146862	0.080485398	0.068570752	0.15581657	0.372997132	0.460926742	0.497376074	0.525566808	0.547492213	0.577067984	0.562809486

Figure 4.3. BNDES's funding structure (percentage of total liabilities)

Source: BNDES

For that reason, BNDES uses the so-called TJLP ('taxa de juros de longo prazo', meaning the long-term interest rate), which is the benchmark rate created by BNDES, around which it sets the interest rates charged on its loans. Since its creation, TJLP has been set systematically below the Treasury interest rates, even the rate on their most liquid bonds (SELIC, Sistema Especial de Liquidação e Custodia)—as can be seen in Figure 4.4.

As the granting of Treasury loans to BNDES reached historical levels, critics raised concerns about the fiscal impact of such transactions. For many of them, the difference between the rollover cost of the national public debt and the long-term interest rate charged by BNDES represented a fiscal burden, 'handouts' that are higher than the societal benefit coming from the projects financed. In addition, some claimed that BNDES's strategy to lend to large companies and/or exporters should not have been part of its mandate as an instrument of public policy, as it supposedly created unnecessary distortions in the macroeconomic supply of credit (e.g. Lazzarini et al. 2011).

Others, like the authors of this chapter (e.g. Ramos and Studart 2016), argue that the lack of private long-term financing and high short-term interest rates

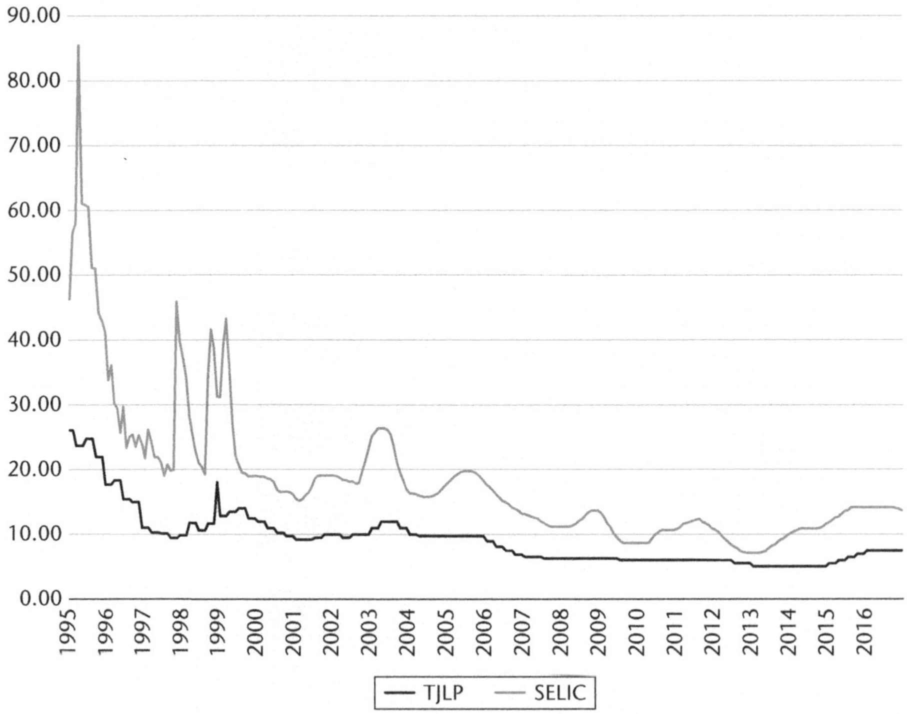

Figure 4.4. TJLP and SELIC (per cent)
Source: Central Bank of Brazil database

makes it necessary for BNDES to set an interest rate that is less volatile than Treasury rates and compatible with the maturity structure of the projects and investments it supports. In addition, we directed attention to the important role that BNDES loans play in directing investment as part of a broader industrial policy, and their externalities and multiplier effects (on production, employment, and competitiveness). It is important to note that there has been a convergence of TJLP towards Treasury interest rates, including SELIC, over the years, particularly in the years when they declined and/or became less volatile (Figure 4.5).

This debate is not easily settled and would deserve an essay of its own. For our purposes here, however, we emphasize that the increasing dependency on semi-fiscal sources of funding creates challenges for the bank model. Not surprisingly, well before 2015, BNDES had come under pressure to adjust its pricing (and reduce the differential with Treasury bond rates), to widen the co-financing of larger projects and to simply downsize.

Therefore, for financial and political reasons, this model needs to evolve if BNDES wants to expand its relevance in addressing the significant challenges faced by Brazil—particularly those related to the improvement of existing infrastructure and logistics. This evolution could, and perhaps should, build on the long-standing experience of BNDES in leveraging and crowding-in private financing resources. This is the topic of section 4.3.2.

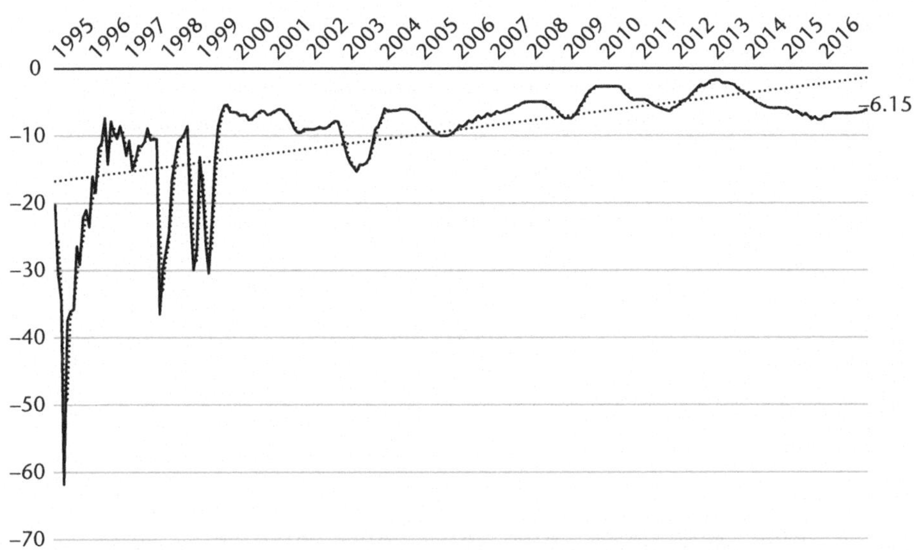

Figure 4.5. TJLP-SELIC differentials (per cent and trend line)
Source: Author's calculations based on data from Central Bank of Brazil

4.3.2 *Leveraging and Crowding-In Private Capital for Infrastructure*

BNDES has a history of policies and instruments to leverage its own resources. This includes lowering the final loan cost through co-financing projects; risk mitigation through its Tier-2 (indirect) lending operations; and risk sharing though its project finance platform and guarantee funds. It has also started a programme to crowd-in private capital, by fostering the issuance of infrastructure bonds that goes beyond the traditional risk-sharing initiatives. The latter efforts started in 2012, and were particularly intensified in 2015.

Co-financing and indirect lending have been part of BNDES's model for a long while. Indeed, indirect operations through a network of public and private banking agents constitute approximately half of its credit operations (Figure 4.6). The partner banks conduct project analyses and take on the credit risk behind loans. The returns of financial intermediaries come directly from project financing, but also from having access to BNDES resources with longer maturities, which allows them to increase the customer base with which they can intensify their business relationship—including management of cash flow, structuring of new operations, absorption of employees' salary accounts, and sales of direct services. In a way, BNDES indirect operations do more than just reduce loan costs: once private banks become more acquainted with certain types of clients, sectors, and investments, they can better analyse the credit risk and directly finance the best clients. On some occasions, this has led private banks to take the lead in consortia to finance long-term undertakings. This partnership also gives capillarity to BNDES's financial products, once the network reaches commercial banks in most of the 5570 Brazilian municipalities.

Yet another example of risk sharing is the evolution of a very 'peculiar' type of project finance operation carried out by BNDES since 2003. Project finance

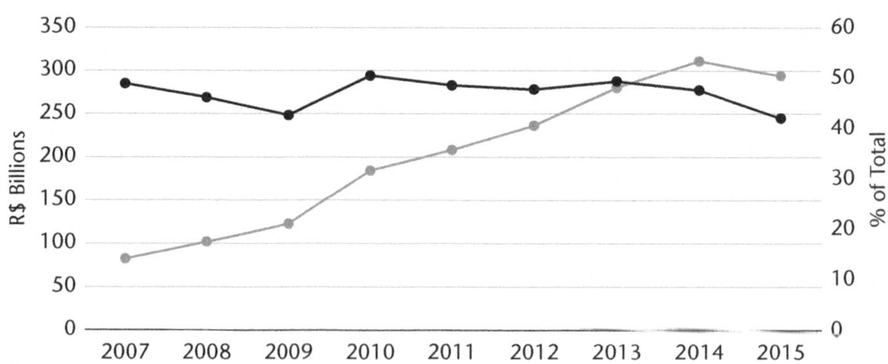

Figure 4.6. BNDES: Evolution of indirect lending (R$ billion and percentage of total)
Source: BNDES

is knowingly backed by the projected cash flows of the project rather than the balance sheets of its sponsors. But in the case of those sponsored by BNDES, corporate or banking guarantees are required from the companies participating in a concession consortium. Despite the limitations of this 'sponsored' project finance, by introducing this innovation, BNDES does share risks by inducing private players, both developers and their private bankers, to increase their participation in infrastructure financing. Indeed, in the past, private financial institutions increased their participation in such projects—by providing equity and advisory services, offering collateral, guarantees, and insurance, and by leading loan consortia.

Risk sharing through guarantees became part of BNDES's attempt to leverage private financing. The increased funding constraints on BNDES led to the creation of guarantee funds to reduce the uncertainty of certain projects and to leverage private sector financing in sectors previously funded only by public institutions. Two were built to support small and microenterprises in securing credit with financial intermediaries: the Investment Guarantor Fund (IGF) and Guarantee Fund of Free Investment Credit (FGI—free credit).

BNDES's role as a financier of I&L was enhanced further as it became a critical financial player in the government commitment to address I&L gaps though extremely large programmes—the Programme for Growth Acceleration (PAC and PAC2) and the Logistics Investment Programme (PIL). PAC was a strategic investment programme that combined management initiatives and public works. In its first phase, launched in 2007, the programme called for investments of US$349 billion (R$638 billion).

Similarly, PAC2 focused on investments in the areas of logistics, energy, and social development, organized under six major initiatives: urban infrastructure and particularly mobility; safety and social inclusion; popular housing; sanitation and access to electricity; renewable energy, oil and gas; and transportation (highways, railways, airports). PIL, in turn, was aimed at increasing investments in infrastructure, enhancing the competitiveness of the economy, and improving transportation conditions (Table 4.1).

In both programmes, BNDES had a critical role in helping to build a financing structure for the concessionaires that won the auctions for specific projects. That is why there is a significant correlation between overall infrastructure investments and BNDES disbursements to the sector (Figure 4.7). PAC and PIL aimed to expand access and improve infrastructure services for the emerging middle class. Therefore, in addition to guaranteeing the feasibility of higher-risk and more complex projects, the explicit goal of BNDES intervention was to allow lower tariffs to be charged once the project became operational.

BNDES's financing model traditionally included fixed- and variable-income products with very favourable financing conditions—both in term of maturities and cost. BNDES, through its subsidiary BNDES Participações S.A. (BNDESPAR),

Table 4.1. I&L investments as share of GDP

	PAC				PAC2			
Segment	2007	2008	2009	2010	2011	2012	2013	2014
Electric Energy	0.56	0.61	0.63	0.69	0.72	0.70	0.70	0.66
Telecommunications	0.46	0.80	0.56	0.41	0.49	0.50	0.42	0.52
Sewage	0.14	0.22	0.24	0.21	0.17	0.19	0.20	0.19
Transportation	0.62	0.74	0.90	0.96	0.84	0.84	0.96	0.92
Roads	0.35	0.40	0.55	0.57	0.48	0.39	0.47	0.44
Railroads	0.11	0.16	0.11	0.14	0.14	0.13	0.14	0.16
Urban mobility	0.05	0.10	0.17	0.10	0.08	0.10	0.15	0.16
Airports	0.03	0.02	0.01	0.02	0.03	0.06	0.11	0.09
Ports	0.07	0.04	0.03	0.10	0.09	0.15	0.08	0.06
Hydroways	0.01	0.02	0.03	0.03	0.02	0.01	0.01	0.01
Total	1.78	2.37	2.33	2.27	2.22	2.23	2.28	2.29

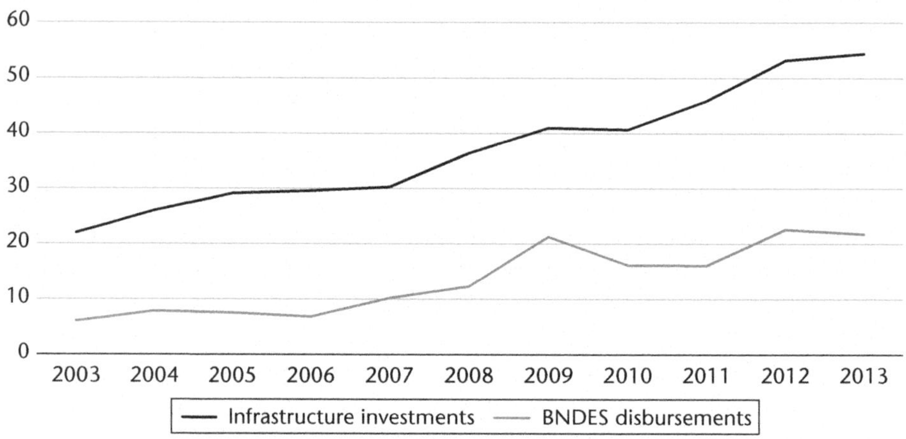

Figure 4.7. Infrastructure investments and BNDES disbursements
Source: Coutinho (2015)

has also bought stakes in companies that could prospect for new business in the sector. For that reason, BNDES ended up assisting the federal and state governments' structure concessions for the private sector and public–private partnerships (PPP).

In the 2000s, BNDES's 'coverage' of I&L sectors widened in scope and in commitments as large volumes of its investments went to energy production, transmission, distribution, and efficiency. BNDES also financed large logistics projects, such as highways, railways, airports, navigation, and ports. Urban mobility projects grew in number and volume, amounting to R$92 billion in 2014. Investments in high- and medium-capacity transport systems financed by BNDES became part of a larger block of investment headed by the federal government PAC programmes dedicated to mobility in the states.

The financial arrangements around the concessions issued by the federal government always involved BNDES directly as financier. This involvement had positive and negative consequences. First, BNDES's support increased the share of I&L investment in Brazil's GDP, and private participation in the concessions of the I&L investment programmes (PAC and PIL). In fact, according to the World Bank in 2014, Brazil was a leader among developing countries in private participation in I&L projects, with 44 per cent participation—a situation that only reversed in 2015 as the federal government promoted a fiscal retrenchment, mainly through cuts in government expenditure on I&L projects (MFB 2015).

Secondly, though, this arrangement created significant fragility for BNDES, as its loans were used as 'adjustment variables' to make infrastructure projects viable. Indeed, the federal government was determined to maintain at low levels the tariffs charged by concessionary I&L projects, even though private cost of capital remained extraordinarily high. To lower the overall cost of capital for those projects, BNDES had to offer lending rates below its own funding and operating costs. Not surprisingly, it had to receive significant support from the National Treasury to expand its operations. This funding strategy significantly increased BNDES dependency on Treasury transfers, and was already becoming a source of concern for the government and BNDES management. That is why they introduced initiatives to attract and crowd-in private sources to finance I&L, as was the case with its programme to sponsor the infrastructure bond markets.

4.3.3 *Fostering the Market for Infrastructure Bonds*

In 2011, the federal government launched an initiative to build a market of infrastructure bonds, and BNDES became an important part of this development. The government created several tax benefits for investments in market instruments to channel funds to finance I&L investment. These incentives included a tax exemption on incomes generated by bonds acquired by domestic and foreign investors. BNDES in turn expanded guarantee-sharing clauses in its financing contracts, equalizing the level of seniority of bondholder to loans co-financed by BNDES. Lastly, in some projects, BNDES relaxed financial requirements in its credit operations in case there was issuance of bonds.[2]

These efforts were only intensified in 2015, for two reasons: (i) under a severe fiscal adjustment agenda, the government could no longer commit to

[2] The first was to reduce the coverage ratio of debt services, increasing the maximum leverage of the projects, which improved profitability and reduced the capital requirement of the projects. The second was to change the amortization schedule for the issuance of bond infrastructure to allow the cost of capital to be redistributed to later phases in the investment cycles.

the increased volume of public investment—as it had done in the last twelve years; and (ii) by setting the reduction of gross debt as a policy goal, the government decided not to increase the funding for BNDES with Treasury resources.[3] BNDES responded to this new challenge by enhancing its infrastructure bond issuance programme to include additional de-risking engineering and pricing incentives.

The efforts paid off. From 2012 to 2016, total issuances have reached R$11 billion in fifty-five issuances. This may seem to be a significant amount. However, it is significantly smaller than the total investment needed. Only in 2013, according to the Brazilian Association of Infrastructure and Basic Industry (ABDIB), the annual infrastructure investments, excluding the oil and gas sector, amounted to R$125 billion.

Such modest results should not be taken as a failure of the government's attempt to foster the market for infrastructure bonds, for at least two reasons. First, as pointed out by Wajnberg (2014), there is a learning curve needed for both potential issuers and potential bondholders to start operating with such instruments. Second, there are high costs involved in this learning process—such as hiring banks, lawyers, rating agencies, auditors, and costs related to documentation and offer record-keeping. Therefore, only issuances that exceed a certain critical value manage to reach the market. Third, and perhaps most importantly, the macroeconomic environment was not friendly, as the launch of the bond instrument coincided with the years of greatest economic turmoil and a steep rise in Treasury interest rates. Finally, the level of corporate debt has increased substantially since 2012.

Despite the results, BNDES followed the correct guidelines in helping to build a market for infrastructure bonds, fostering their issuance and stimulating their secondary market. It is quite possible that in a more stable political and economic environment, with declining interest rates, these efforts will bear fruit. That is, they may contribute to the development of a market for securities, particularly those backed by infrastructure.

However, no matter what incentives are created to promote the issuance of infrastructure-backed assets, developing an infrastructure bond market will depend on the capacity and interest of institutional investors to acquire them. In other words, it will require 'building bridges' between potential demanders of long-term funds for I&L projects and those institutions that have a need to acquire such types of assets. In Brazil, the potential is there.

[3] As mentioned above, from 2009 to 2014, total Treasury funds to BNDES amounted to about US$430 billion. The way to reconcile the growth of investments in infrastructure, which is one of the guidelines for moving the Brazilian economy towards a new growth cycle, is to promote private participation, not only as an investor in concession projects, but in long-term financing as well.

The pension fund segment in Brazil, for instance, is relatively large, and has been growing strongly. The total amount of its investments in September 2016 was R$750 billion. There is plenty of room for infrastructure bonds in their portfolio—indeed, little more than 2 per cent of Brazilian pension fund assets are currently invested in infrastructure. However, there remain difficulties in placing infrastructure bonds with pension funds.

The first one is intrinsic to infrastructure projects: uncertainty about the funded project's ability to generate sufficient resources for the payment of interest, especially in the first years of operation. Second, infrastructure projects have a high degree of indivisibility—that is, most of the investment is done prior to cash generation. Thus, it is not possible to adapt it to the growing demand, and if the desired degree of use is not achieved during the planned period, cash flows will be insufficient for the payment of financial obligations. Third, pension funds in Brazil are used to allocate their resources to fixed-rate investments in government bonds and public companies that have low-risk profiles and relatively high returns. They lack the incentives and capabilities to diversify their portfolio towards long-term riskier assets, particularly companies that are not listed.

Finally, the development of an I&L bond market depends on the existence of a pipeline of projects that in turn requires public and private project development capabilities. This is a critical issue that deserves a section of its own (section 4.3.4).

4.3.4 *Project Development Capacity*

One of the greatest challenges to boost sustainable infrastructure is to create a pipeline of projects that are simultaneously technically solid, environmentally smart, and financially sustainable. Infrastructure projects are not exactly 'plain vanilla' investments, and their 'risks' depend on how well they are developed. As pointed out in Beckers et al. (2013):

> The long-term character of such projects requires a strategy that appropriately reflects the uncertainty and huge variety of risks they are exposed to over their life cycles. Infrastructure projects also involve many different stakeholders entering the project life cycle at different stages with different roles, responsibilities, risk-management capabilities and risk-bearing capacities, and often conflicting interests. While the complexity of these projects requires division of roles and responsibilities among highly specialized players (such as contractors and operators), this leads to significant interface risks among the various stakeholders that materialize throughout the life cycle of the project, and these must be anticipated and managed from the outset.

Despite the sophistication of domestic players, the country faces project development constraints, for reasons already mentioned. Indeed, from the

1980s until the 2000s, there had been a deterioration in the state's capacity to plan, develop, implement, and monitor large investment undertakings. There were at least three consequences of this process.

The first one is straightforward: the government's capacity to plan and develop large-scale infrastructure projects shrank, which naturally created problems in project development and implementation as a result—particularly at subnational levels. The problem became more evident in the 2000s, due to the push given by the PAC and PIL programmes, including public–private partnerships (PPPs) and concessions as part of the Brazilian federal government's effort to boost infrastructure investments, which demanded far more than the existing budgetary and other public financial resources. Not surprisingly, a strong effort was made in the 2000s to promote the recovery of such capabilities, some of which directly involved BNDES, such as the creation of the Brazilian Project Development Company—Estruturadora Brasileira de Projetos S.A. (EBP)—in 2008.

Second, project development was transferred to private actors, but the financing of such projects often involved governments' budgets and/or financing from public institutions. This transfer made it very difficult for governments to evaluate and monitor projects independently, and may *partly* explain excessive delays in their construction and governance problems that became obvious in the recent corruption investigations.

A third characteristic is indirectly related to the bankability of projects. Indeed, it is quite possible that a significant number of the infrastructure concessions could have been developed with a view to using private sources from their outset. That is, if the projects were structured from the outset in such a way as to mitigate the risks throughout their life cycle, many of them could have had access to private financing, at least from international capital markets. However, if the public entities possess limited project development capabilities, their capacity to propose alternative financial modelling for the projects brought to them is constrained. This creates a 'catch-22' situation, where the dependency on public financing is perpetuated.

Despite this effort in capacity building, most project development capabilities remain in the hands of very large private developers and consulting firms. Smaller companies have been thriving in new types of infrastructure projects—such as those in sustainable infrastructure—but are even less prepared to produce projects that are simultaneously technically sound, environmentally smart, and bankable from the outset. This may create important challenges for attracting the interest of private investors, even in a friendlier macroeconomic environment of steady growth and low and stable interest rates.

BNDES may play a role in capability building, sponsoring the development of an investment financing architecture. This has been the case with its support for sustainable infrastructure projects and particularly for renewable energy ones. It is worth then describing this interesting experience briefly. This is the topic of section 4.3.5.

4.3.5 *BNDES and Sustainable Infrastructure: A Chapter on its Own*

BNDES is an important player in the current financing architecture sponsoring sustainable infrastructure projects in Brazil. This is associated with a history of promoting internal project development capability and expertise in sustainable energy since the early 2000s. Like other national development banks in the world, BNDES has not only implemented government directives towards 'greening the economy', but has also had a role in drafting and improving them (Gallagher and Studart 2016). Indeed, when assessing direct and indirect non-automatic operations, it not only checks if they comply with its own environmental standards, but also assesses the environmental risks, and promotes environmentally related improvements in investment and company management.

Additionally, BNDES has for a while offered products and instruments to other sectors, with special financial conditions that depend on sustainability standards. It also manages three dedicated 'green funds': Amazon Fund, BNDES's Atlantic Forest Initiative, and the Climate Fund. Indeed, BNDES disbursements increased almost six times from 2004 levels (R$4.7 billion) to 2014 (R$27.8 billion). Despite this increase, the proportion of green investments has never exceeded 15 per cent of total lending, still a small portion of loans outstanding.

The potential role of BNDES as a promoter of sustainable I&L, although already substantial, is still far from being fully tapped. First, a significant part of BNDES's 'green' pipeline still consists of hydroelectric power plants, but the case for diversification into other sources of renewable energy is there. For instance, in the past ten years, the Brazilian energy matrix has not been able to cope with the fast increase of demand, which has forced the more intensive use of costlier and environmentally damaging coal-generated energy. These mismatches of supply and demand are due not only to a rise in demand, but also to the increased intensity of droughts, a probable consequence of climate change, and can only be mitigated through expansion towards renewable energy. Because of the privileged climate conditions in Brazil, there is significant scope for other alternative, cleaner sources of energy—such as solar energy and wave power—and, definitively, for more energy efficiency.

Further, freight and transportation systems in Brazil are still highly geared towards automobiles and trucks, which explains why almost 40 per cent of its energy is produced by oil and derivatives. The actual roads are in a poor state and unfit to address the current demand, which is the main reason for traffic congestion in urban areas and inefficiency in the freight transportation system. Developing alternative, 'green' transportation systems would not only reduce transportation costs for consumers and producers, but also improve urban mobility.

Finally, BNDES can be a key player in financing, leveraging, and crowding-in private capital to I&L—*sine qua non* condition for a sounder and more stable financing of the sector in the future. The Climate Bonds Initiative indicated that despite the macroeconomic and political uncertainties, the outstanding volume of bonds in Brazil in 2016 was US$2.4 billion (Climate Bonds Initiative 2016). Of those, 54 per cent were transportation projects and 23 per cent were associated with clean energy. The potential expansion of this market is significant, particularly if it develops an appropriate *architecture* (of regulation, institutions, risk management tools, and instruments), that can build the bridge between final demanders and suppliers of such bonds.

BNDES's efforts in boosting such investments show its comparative advantages as a central point in establishing this architecture—a role, as we have insisted elsewhere, that has been successfully been played by other national development banks. These efforts have been undermined by many external factors—particularly the limited pipeline of technically sound and 'finance-able' projects and the constraining macroeconomic environment.

With the change of government in July 2015, a new leadership has been put in place with the clear mandate to change the focus and business model of the institution—including a greater focus on sustainability and on crowding-in private capital for green investments. An analysis of these changes can only be preliminary. But given the importance of the institution to Brazil's development, it cannot be avoided. In section 4.4, we present some of the main features of these changes and speculate about their possible consequences.

4.4 BNDES: New Directions

After the impeachment of former president Dilma Rousseff in July 2016, a coalition government led by former vice-president Michel Temer came to power. With it, a new economic team was appointed and a replacement of leadership in BNDES followed, along with significant changes of orientation.

The first one was associated with the pressure put on BNDES to make an anticipated repayment of its debt to the National Treasury, starting with R$100 billion (US$30 billion) in December 2016. This transfer, comprised of RS$40 billion in securities and RS$60 billion in cash, was justified by the need to reduce overall federal debt (corresponding to 70 per cent GDP). The early payment is the equivalent of nearly 19 per cent of the total debt that BNDES holds with the Treasury, and over 120 per cent of the disbursements in 2016, but it would only lead to a fall of 1.6 per cent of the debt-over-GDP ratio.

Another important change was very recently announced by BNDES senior management concerning the pricing system method and the creation of the long-term interest rate (TLP). Even though the acronym for the new rate seems like the earlier one (TJLP), this change has important governance and operational consequences.

Concerning the governance of this policy instrument, the TJLP was set quarterly by the National Monetary Council, which included representatives from the Ministries of Finance and Planning, as well as from the central bank. This composition allowed the final decision to be determined by the overall development strategy set by the executive branch, but also influenced by the monetary policy objectives. The new TLP will be determined solely by the central bank, which is guided by targeting price stability (Table 4.2).

The announcement of the changes has brought about an even greater emphasis on environmental sustainability. Indeed, BNDES stopped financing coal-fired power plants, and, as pointed out by its new president, will now focus even more on green technologies. Given the current levels of subsidization of other sectors, it is significant that BNDES is prepared to contribute up to 80 per cent of the financing needs of 'green projects' supported.

Also, even though BNDES already has its own monitoring and evaluation procedures, the current leadership created a department that will be responsible for implementing the new policies and for producing a 'results matrix', in

Table 4.2. TJLP and TLP: A summary

	TJLP	TJP
Frequency	Set on a quarterly basis by the National Monetary Council (CMN, comprising the Central Bank Governor and the Ministers of Finance and Planning)	Announced monthly by the Central Bank, based on a pre-defined formula
Formula	TJLP = international interest rate in real terms + country risk + inflation, all evaluated from a long-term perspective	TLP = 5-year sovereign inflation linker (NTN-B) yield x smoothing factor + 12-month IPCA
Nature of BNDES loans	Fully floating rate—loans benchmarked on TJLP will have their cost oscillating according to changes in TJLP over the duration of the loan	Hybrid rate—loans benchmarked on TLP will have their cost defined by two components: a real rate component (fixed for the duration of the loan at the level prevailing when the loan was granted), brought to nominal terms according to accumulated inflation over the lifetime of the loan
Validity	All life of loans granted by BNDES up to 31 December 2017	All loans granted by BNDES from 1 January 2018 onwards

Source: Santander (2017)

which goals will be defined per project. This is very similar to what is already in place in multilateral development banks, such as the World Bank—which is reported to have been a source of advice in creating the new system for BNDES. And, to address the criticisms that have targeted BNDES in the past two years, the actual board has placed emphasis on efficiency, and processes are being reviewed, with more use of technology to speed up loan applications and improve operations.

Finally, BNDES is moving towards a 'transversal' approach in its interventions. The bank seemingly will cease to promote 'sectors' and large firms and/or exports of services. It is introducing the use of external auditing firms for large-scale infrastructure projects with more than R$1 billion in financing and more than R$500 million in financing for other sectors. BNDES's participation will be limited to 80 per cent of the cost of projects. As is currently proposed, the bank will focus on six categories of investment with differentiated financial conditions: education, health, innovation, export promotion, MSMEs, and infrastructure projects are priorities.

It is still very early to draw conclusions about these changes. But it is worth discussing some possible consequences.

First, the focus on sustainability seems to be a correct strategic decision. Sponsoring sustainable I&L may have significant positive externalities for overcoming the current crisis and promoting long-term inclusive sustainable growth. In addition, BNDES already has significant experience in supporting green and climate-smart projects and, building on this experience, can promote project development, leverage and crowding-in private capital to a critical area. Finally, BNDES can also benefit from the potentialities of the green bond market, both in Brazil and abroad, to significantly open its funding basis.

The second possible consequence is related to the transfer of resources back to the National Treasury. Given the significant fall in the demand for its resources in the past two years, BNDES is experiencing a moment of high liquidity. According to its capital position, it is unlikely that BNDES will have any difficulties in maintaining its current lending—which is, as mentioned earlier, at its lowest level since 2008. However, when investment demand increases, the institution is likely to be under pressure to expand its lending, and will have little capacity to do so.

The third question refers to its new pricing policy. It remains to be seen how this directive will be implemented, but some observations should be made. First, TJLP is already set taking several variables into consideration, including Treasury bonds. Changes in this rate were implemented with a certain delay and a significant amount of discretion. The lag was necessary to avoid volatility in TJLP, which would make it inconsistent as a rate guiding long-term undertakings, such as infrastructure projects. And the discretionary approach

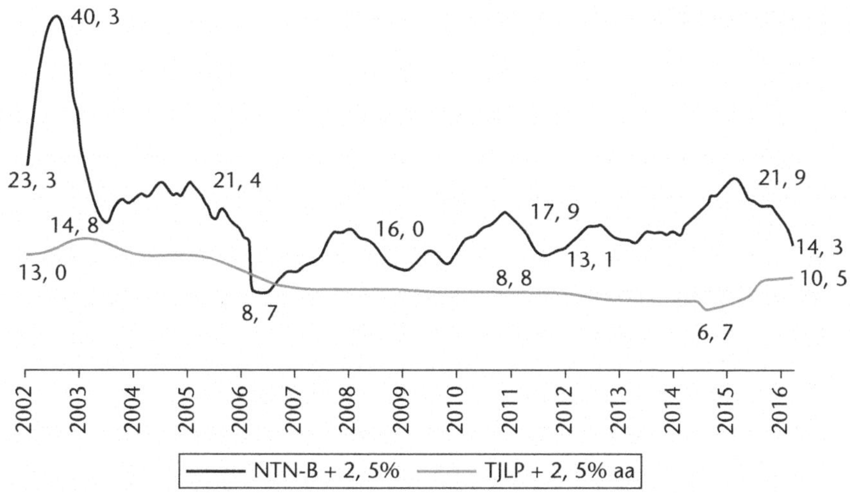

Figure 4.8. Final cost of BNDES loans using NTN-B and TJLP
Source: Torres (2017)

was meant to avoid TJLP ending up being procyclical—a role of development banks since the 2009 crisis, which has been supported by the G20, multilateral institutions, and think tanks.

In addition, the new TLP will be set monthly and will peg a rate that for the past decade has not only been very volatile, but significantly higher than TJLP (Figure 4.8). Indeed, according to several recent reports, including Santander (2017) and Torres (2017), if the TLP had been used as a reference rate on BNDES loans, except for 2006, it would be systematically higher than TJLP—which has in turn already been one of the highest interest rates in the world for the past decade. When adopted, the TLP may end up being too high to be relevant in financing long-term investment, and BNDES may cease to be a potential instrument for countercyclical policies, when needed. Indeed, it may even turn procyclical, given that in the past Treasury rates have behaved that way.

Finally, there remain some question marks around the change of orientation of BNDES operational policies towards a horizontal support for investments. Until now, it has been unclear how this new guidance will be able to handle the fact that BNDES has traditionally been an industrial policy instrument, providing support to specific government programmes and initiatives that usually target sectors—rather than tackling cross-sector issues. How this problem will be dealt with will evidently be fundamental to defining the future of this institution, including the role that BNDES may have in the structural changes that Brazil requires. With that, we can move to the conclusions of the chapter.

4.5 Summing-Up and Concluding Remarks

Low public and private investment levels have generated a sizable overall infrastructure gap in most nations, but particularly in developing ones, that creates strict 'ceilings' on potential socially inclusive and environmentally sustainable paths. Brazil would appear to be an extraordinary case of such a phenomenon, where the gaps have been structural impediments in overcoming its 'middle-income' trap. Indeed, despite the recent socioeconomic achievements, this nation now faces daunting new challenges related to its outdated, and to a certain degree dysfunctional and 'climate-dumb', infrastructure. If Brazil aims to achieve sustained inclusive growth in the future, it must find ways to fill its significant sustainable I&L gaps.

This will not be an easy task, for many reasons. An important one is related to the capacity of governments, in different spheres (federal, state, and municipal), to expand their required investments in a very delicate (to say the least) fiscal situation. Another constraint is the peculiar Brazilian financial landscape. Indeed, for the past two decades, Brazil's financial system has undergone significant transformations that have increased its sophistication and linkage with international markets. However, one feature has not changed: private capital continues to be allocated to short-term assets and its securities markets are relatively shallow. This has led to a 'catch-22' situation, whereby the financing of long-term and/or riskier undertakings was left mainly to public financial institutions.

The main conclusions that we have reached in this chapter are:

1. Promoting transformational investments are a *sine qua non* condition for Brazil to overcome the trap of low productivity and competitiveness, required for guaranteeing an inclusive and environmentally sustainable path. Part of such efforts should come from addressing its significant social and economic infrastructure gaps by promoting sustainable I&L.
2. To raise such investments will require an effort to expand the pipeline of technically solid and financially smart projects, and leverage public finance and crowd in private capital to finance them. In our view, policy is required to achieve these goals—particularly in the case of I&L, where investing in greenfield projects or during the construction phase means financing assets with long time maturities and highly uncertain returns.
3. Such architecture needs an appropriate macro- and microeconomic environment, incentives (embedded, for instance, in a carbon-pricing system), and policies. However, the right policy to address this challenge is to sponsor the development of an *I&L financing architecture*—with specific incentives, an appropriate regulatory framework, new players, innovative instruments, and markets. It is also to expand the pipeline of

projects, improve the efficiency of public money dedicated to them, and bridge the gaps between ultimate borrowers and large institutional investors. It will require 'institutional leadership' to speed up a process that in many economies took decades to be built. This is where a national development bank, such as BNDES, is fundamental.

4. With the experience achieved throughout its history, BNDES is perhaps one of the few institutions in Brazil that can play that leadership role, by (i) investing more in project development, particularly in support of developers in building a pipeline of technically sound and bankable projects—either by increasing in-house capabilities and expertise in project development or by developing an 'origination' fund that can be used to outsource it; and by (ii) fostering the development of new instruments that can leverage additional resources from private banks and create a bridge between infrastructure developers and institutional investors.

Finally, this chapter has discussed the potential impacts of the new operational policies of BNDES launched in January 2017. Obviously, any analysis of these changes now can only be preliminary. Here are some of them.

1. Focus on sustainability seems to be a 'spot-on' strategic decision. Sponsored sustainable I&L is not only a moral imperative to warrant a better future for all, but contributes to overcoming the current crisis and promoting long-term inclusive growth.
2. In view of the shortages and the important role we ascribe to BNDES in supporting I&L investment, we have raised concerns about whether the recent return of National Treasury resources could impact in BNDES's balance sheet and long-term lending capacity. In addition, the change of pricing methodology by the new TLP seems to rest on an optimistic view about the perspective for the rapid development of a private long-term corporate debt market. If such expectations are not met, access to long-term financing will be even more limited than it already is.
3. Finally, we are puzzled by the changes from vertical to horizontal orientation of its operational policies. At a moment when Brazil needs significant transformation investments, particularly those related to sustainable I&L, this shift may be incompatible with BNDES acting as a government policy instrument in this task.

The future of BNDES will evidently depend on these policies, and they are very uncertain now. However, it is certain that BNDES is one of the few institutions that can help promote transformational changes that will allow Brazil to aspire to a future of inclusive and sustainable growth—a future its citizens set for themselves almost three decades ago, when, after years of dictatorship, they were finally given a chance to decide it.

References

Beckers, F., N. Chiara, A. Flesch, J. Maly, E. Silva, and U. Stegemann. 2013. *A Risk-Management Approach to a Successful Infrastructure Project: Initiation, Financing, and Execution*. McKinsey Working Papers on Risk No. 52, November.

BNDES. 2012. *BNDES: A Bank with a History and a Future*. Available at <https://goo.gl/b5Vak3>, accessed 12 April 2018.

BNDES. 2014. *Perspectivas do Investimento 2015–2018 e Panoramas Setoriais*. Available at <https://web.bndes.gov.br/bib/jspui/bitstream/1408/2842/5/Perspectivas%20do%20investimento%202015-2018%20e%20panoramas%20setoriais_atualizado_BD.pdf>, accessed 12 April 2018.

Brazilian Association of Infrastructure and Basic Industry (ABDIB). Available at <http://www.abdib.org.br>, accessed 12 April 2018.

Castelar Pinheiro, A. and R. Frischtak. 2014. *Gargalos e soluções na infraestrutura de transportes*. São Paulo: FGV Editora.

Castro, A. and F. Souza. 1985. *A economia brasileira em marcha forçada*. Rio de Janeiro: Paz e Terra.

Climate Bonds Initiative. 2016. *Bonds and Climate Change: State of the Market in 2016*. Climate Change Initiative, July.

Confederação Nacional da Indústria (CNI). 2016. *O financiamento do investimento em infraestrutura no Brasil: Uma agenda para sua expansão sustentada*. July, 2016.

Coutinho, L. 2015. *Financing Infrastructure in Brazil*. A BNDES presentation given in New York, 29 June 2015. Available at <https://goo.gl/qKy45l>, accessed on 12 April 2018.

Furtado, C. 1959. *Formação Econômica do Brasil*, 30th edn. São Paulo: Companhia Editora Nacional, 2001.

Gallagher, K. and R. Studart. 2016. *Infrastructure for Sustainable Development: The Role of National Development Banks*. GEGI Policy Brief 007, October.

Garcia-Escribano, M., C. Goes, and I. Karpowicz. 2015. *Filling the Gap: Infrastructure Investment in Brazil*. IMF Working Paper No. 15/180. Washington, DC: IMF. Available at <https://goo.gl/UbAIeM>, accessed 12 April 2018.

Kharas, H. and H. Kohli. 2011. 'What Is the Middle-Income Trap, Why Do Countries Fall into It, and How Can It Be Avoided?', *Global Journal of Emerging Market Economies* 3(3): 281–9.

Lazzarini, S., A. Musacchio, R. Bandeira de Mello, and R. Marcon 2011. *What Do Development Banks Do? Evidence from BNDES, 2002–2009*. Brazil: Social Science Research Network (SSRN).

Ministry of Finance of Brazil (MFB). 2015. *Informativo Mensal de Infraestrutura*. Secretary of Economic Monitoring, June. Available at <https://bit.ly/2HNhYS1>, accessed 2 May 2018.

Ramos, L. and R. Studart. 2016. *Financing Infrastructure in the Americas*. Global Economic Governance Initiative Working Paper 07. Available at <https://goo.gl/b8vkyq>, accessed 12 April 2018.

Santander. 2017. 'Brazil—Monetary Policy. "De-Jaboticabizing" Brazil, Part I: End of TJLP is a First Step toward More Rational Credit Market' by Adriana Dupita.

Studart, R. 1995. *Investment Finance in Economic Development*. London: Routledge.
Torres, E. 2017. 'A extinção da TJLP: Um salto no escuro'. Mimeo.
Wagner, M., G. Bertol, and A. Murphy. 2015. *Enhancing Private Infrastructure Investment in Brazil*. Oliver Wyman Report.
Wajnberg, D. 2014. 'Debêntures de infraestrutura: Emissões realizadas e perspectivas', *Revista do BNDES*, 41. Available at <http://goo.gl/U8W2BR>, accessed 12 April 2018.
World Bank. 2010. *Enterprise Survey*. Washington, DC: World Bank.
World Bank. n.d. *World Development Indicators*. Washington, DC: World Bank. Available at <http://goo.gl/nMKAT9>, accessed 13 April 2018.
World Economic Forum. 2014. *Brazil—The Global Competitiveness Report 2014–2015*. World Economic Forum.

5

Changing Challenges in the Modernization of Nacional Financiera

Mexico's Key Development Bank

Juan Carlos Moreno-Brid, Esteban Pérez Caldentey, and Laura Valdez

5.1 Introduction: NAFINSA and the History of Development Banking in Mexico

Mexico has a long tradition in development banking that dates back to the mid-1920s and early 1930s when the state put in place the pillars of its monetary, banking, and financial intermediation systems. Fundamental to this was the creation in 1925 of the Central Bank, with exclusive rights to issue notes and control their circulation, as well as to set nominal interest rates and the exchange rate. It was also empowered to directly fund the government, through an open line of credit of up to 10 per cent of the bank's capital.

Development banks were created and designed to be the leading actors in the provision of long-term credit for infrastructure and for major investment projects aimed at boosting the fixed capital stock necessary for Mexico's long-term economic expansion and social progress. They also had significant political leverage given their discretionary power to grant preferential access to long-term finance, which could be exerted to favour selected business interests and groups.

A landmark in this institutional building process was the creation of Nacional Financiera (NAFINSA) in 1934, which soon became the most powerful policy bank and a key instrument in Mexico's political consolidation and economic reconstruction in the aftermath of the Revolution (1910–21). Three more development banks were then created: Banco de

Crédito Agrícola (1926), Banco Nacional Hipotecario y de Obras Públicas (1933), and Crédito Hotelero (1937). Each of them was in charge of promoting one specific sector of economic activity (see Table 5.1). The first one explicitly targeted its financial resources to assist small farmers and members of the Ejido (Mexico's ancestral form of communal land in the rural areas). The second one focused on road building and irrigation systems. The last one provided finance to private firms for hotel construction and renovation.

The main priority of NAFINSA at the time of its establishment was to manage the productive and financial assets of a number of then recently nationalized banks. This task included the design and implementation of a programme for public land redistribution, a responsibility that was later shifted to Banco de Crédito Agricola. Most importantly, NAFINSA was designated as the main financial agent for the government and, in addition, given two major tasks: developing Mexico's stock exchange and building up an active open market for government bonds.

In 1940, NAFINSA's Organic Law was modified, turning it into a fully fledged development bank. The change in its legal status reflected two fundamental concerns of the government. The first concern was to promote industrialization, manufacturing, earmarked by planners as the economy's future, and most dynamic engine of growth. The second one was to have a strong financial institution, not only with significant capital resources, but also technical, managerial capacities, and lending instruments to promote investment in infrastructure, as well as in selected activities. These concerns reflected, on the one hand, the state of the global economic situation resulting from World War II, and on the other, the Mexican government's commitment to have a direct role in the allocation of resources to bring about a major structural transformation and modernization of Mexico and thus become an industrialized economy.

The New Organic Law defined NAFINSA's following functions: (i) monitor and regulate the stock market and supervise the evolution of long-term credit; (ii) promote investment and help to strengthen and modernize private firms, a task that also covered possible mergers and acquisitions; (iii) operate as a financial intermediary to carry out investment projects by different firms through direct credits as well as provision of guarantees; (iv) act directly as a financial and investment institution; (v) operate as a financial agent for the government and public entities; and (vi) act as a savings institution.[1]

[1] Órgano del Gobierno Constitucional de los Estados Unidos Mexicanos, Diario Oficial, 31 December 1940, p. 6.

Table 5.1. Development banks in Mexico, date of creation and mandate

Bank	Date of creation	Mandate and functions
Banco Nacional de Obras y Servicios Públicos (BANOBRAS)	Feb. 1933	Provide direct and induced credit Promote participation of commercial banks in financing of infrastructure Attract resources of institutional investors to finance infrastructure projects Promote the financial and institutional strengthening of federal entities, municipalities, and their agencies Promote financial inclusion of municipalities not served by commercial banks, with emphasis on those in the National Crusade against Hunger and the National Programme for the Social Prevention of Violence and Delinquency
Nacional Financiera (NAFINSA)	Apr. 1934	Expand access to finance in preferential conditions Provide finance for long-term projects in priority and high-impact sectors Foster regional and sectorial development Contribute to the development of financial markets Aim to maximize the impact on economic development, with a flexible and innovative management structure to ensure a results-oriented administration.
Banco de Comercio Exterior (BANCOMEXT)	Jul. 1937	Promote finance for foreign trade and for the expansion of productive capacity of exporting companies. Help internationalize selected firms by providing quality services, credit, guarantees and other specialized financial services
Banco Nacional del Ejército, Fuerza Aérea y la Armada (BANJERCITO)	Jul. 1947	Provide credit to Army, Air Force, and Navy staff, and the general public
Banco del Ahorro Nacional y Servicios Financieros (BANSEFI)	Dec. 1949	Boost saving and financial inclusion Help consolidate and streamline social programmes Act as the main instrument for financial inclusion policies
Sociedad Hipotecaria Federal	Apr. 1963	Promote the development of housing markets through guarantees and other financial instruments for construction, acquisition, and residential improvement.
Financiera Nacional de Desarrollo Agropecuario, Rural, Forestal y Pesquero (FND)[1]	1926	Provide financial resources, directly and indirectly as 'second floor' intermediary, to foster economic activities by the rural population in locations of less than 50 thousand inhabitants.

Notes: [1] FND was created with the financial reform of 2014, by consolidating a number of financial entities dealing with rural development. It performs the functions of 'Financiera Rural', the development bank for the agricultural sector, which in 2002 replaced the 'Banco Nacional de Crédito Rural', that in turn incorporated the three institutions that preceded it until 1965: 'Banco Nacional de Crédito Ejidal', 'Banco Nacional Agropecuari', and 'Banco Nacional de Crédito Agrícola'. Of these institutions, the last one is the oldest and dates back to 1926.

Source: Authors' own elaboration based on official information

5.2 NAFINSA and State-Led Industrialization

During the period of state-led industrialization (1940–82) NAFINSA responded to the view that a major, concerted effort between the public and the private sectors to boost fixed capital accumulation was a *sine qua non* for Mexico's long-term economic development. This view presupposed that 'market forces', by themselves, would be incapable of creating a robust and competitive industrial sector, and thus lift the Mexican economy out of its low-development trap. Consequently, development banks were given a prominent role in state-led industrialization that went beyond funding fixed capital accumulation, and also included a commitment to expand and modernize infrastructure and engage in strategic planning to jump-start and finance strategic sectors linked to the production of machinery and equipment or technologically advanced activities. Helping to reduce regional disparities in Mexico's economic development was also one of its concerns.

As shown in Figure 5.1, between 1940 and 1954, infrastructure accounted on average for 49.8 per cent of the total financial resources provided by NAFINSA for sectorial development, increasing to 67.8 per cent during 1963–70. In the 1940s, the predominant public works projects backed by NAFINSA mainly consisted of irrigation and the development of roads and bridges. Between 1948 and 1954, the areas of electricity and transport became the main beneficiaries.

Basic industry absorbed on average between 13 per cent and 15 per cent of NAFINSA's financial intermediation from 1940 until the early 1960s, declining

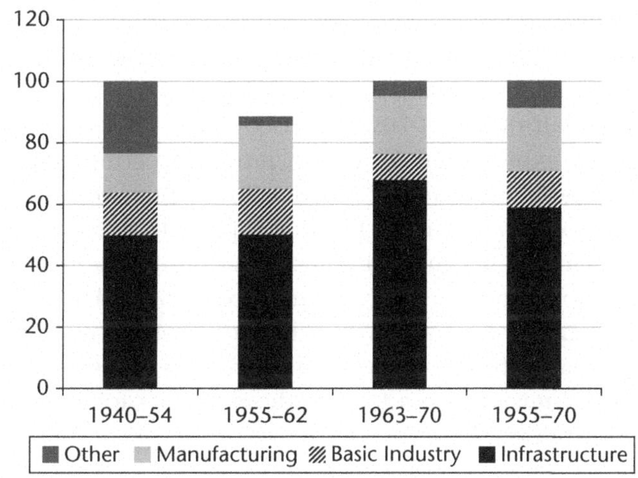

Figure 5.1. Sectorial destination of NAFINSA's resources, 1940–70 (percentage of the total)

Source: Authors' own elaboration based on official figures

to 8.3 per cent during 1963–70. For its part, manufacturing represented 12.9 per cent of NAFINSA's total resources for the 1940–54 period, rapidly expanding to reach an average of roughly 20 per cent thereafter. In practice, this support was provided through various instruments, including direct credits at preferential subsidized rates, or as part of specific development-cum-investment projects on selected activities. In addition, NAFINSA's role went far beyond that of fund provider, and covered planning, operations management, and technical support or upgrading as required.

In the mid-1950s Mexico entered the most successful phase in its long-term development, marked by high and sustained growth of output and employment, low inflation, and financial stability. However, in the early 1970s, adverse shocks in the international oil market and in the world monetary order affected Mexico's economic performance. Important to note, during this period a fixed exchange rate regime prevailed. Indeed, after the drastic devaluations of the early 1950s, the nominal exchange rate remained unaltered until 1976 when the peso was acutely depreciated in the midst of Mexico's first major balance-of-payments crisis in decades. This event signalled the end of the economy's golden era, locally known as 'Stabilizing Development', characterized by high and persistent expansion of economic activity coupled with low inflation, and significant advances in key indicators of social development. During this time, NAFINSA maintained its status as the key policy bank to selectively and preferentially provide long-term funds to boost fixed capital formation in key activities, mainly industrial ones. One of its mechanisms to achieve these goals was by obtaining resources from abroad (in US dollars) and channelling them to private companies (in Mexican pesos). In this way, it absorbed the exchange rate risk and made funds available at rather preferential rates. It also played a key role directly managing a number of large firms with the aim of promoting industrialization.

In the second half of the 1970s, the discovery of vast oil reserves in the country and their exploitation for export purposes permitted an ambitious industrialization programme to be funded. With oil prices forecasted to rise in real terms in the foreseeable future, this developmental agenda was enhanced further, and public investment, manufacture, and oil became the pillars of a new phase of rapid and strong economic expansion. The López Portillo administration launched an ambitious industrialization strategy to deepen Mexico's import substitution strategy and extend it to heavy industry. The plan was to use oil revenues as a fund to develop the capital equipment and machinery industries in Mexico.

Thus, Mexico's state-led industrialization strategy received a second and highly significant boost. NAFINSA, with a revision of its Organic Law, was granted more attributions to participate directly in the management and even have full ownership of public enterprises. Associated with this shift, there was a major rise in the share of total financing granted by NAFINSA to the industrial sector, largely linked to the expansion of heavy, capital intensive industries.

The end of the oil boom in the world markets, the rise in US interest rates, and the slowdown of the US economy in 1981–2, coupled with Mexico's mishandled fiscal policy, dramatically terminated the era of high expansion. In August 1982, Mexico declared a moratorium on external debt service payments. In the aftermath of this crisis, the exchange rate sharply depreciated, and the government nationalized the banking system and implemented fully fledged foreign capital and exchange rate controls, as well as standard contractionary monetary and fiscal measures. In this scenario the new administration of President De la Madrid decided to launch a new agenda for development, moving away from the traditional one of state-led industrialization and trade protection and towards prioritizing economic stability, understood as low inflation and negligible fiscal deficits and at the same time, opening the domestic goods and financial markets, as well as drastically reducing state intervention in the allocation of resources.

5.3 Market Reforms: A New Dawn for NAFINSA and Development Banks

The new neoliberal agenda placed the private sector as the pivotal agent for capital accumulation through the interplay of market forces, in a macroeconomic context marked by low inflation and moderate fiscal deficits.

This agenda had a major impact on development banks' functions and their scope of action. Essentially, with the phasing out of the state-led industrialization strategy, the new administration saw no rationale for policy banks or for state-owned enterprises (SOEs) to have any leading role in investment for a structural transformation of the economy. This responsibility was shifted to the private sector—businesses, banks, and other financial intermediaries—with as little intervention as possible from the public sector. Market reformers portrayed Mexico's traditional development banks and SOEs as bureaucratic, inefficient institutions that distorted market mechanisms and induced a rent-seeking behaviour that undermined the very foundations for growth and development (see Table 5.2 for a comparison of the functions and responsibilities of development banks in Mexico before and after the market reforms).

In the neoliberal era, policymakers justified the need for development banks only to the extent that they could help to solve the major imperfections in Mexico's financial markets that in their view caused credit rationing and thus insufficient and far from optimal capital accumulation by the private sector.

Table 5.2. Mexico's traditional structuralist view and post-market reform view of development banks

	Traditional perspective (pre-mid-1980s)	Market reform view (post-early 1990s)
Perspective and criteria	Industrialization, market creation. Long-term development	Services, commerce, industry; open and liberalized markets
Priorities	Key industries set by policy, infrastructure and regions	Preserve bank's capital, do not endanger or pressure fiscal balances, financial inclusion
Tools	Preferred loans/credit, direct intervention in capital formation with SOEs	Financial instruments of a second-tier intermediary, to help support private commercial bank lending to SMEs
Target population	Mega projects and large firms, mainly SOEs	Mainly SMEs. Support and modernize them, ease access to new technologies. Mainly private firms, as the number and scope of SOEs acutely shrunk with the neoliberal agenda and market reforms
Marketing	Supply driven by bank's promotion of development policy	Demand driven by investment projects of private firms, including need for working capital
Fund allocation	Direct/first tier	Indirect/second tier
Relative competitiveness	Subsidized interest rates, ease of access, total funds	Products, advisory service, serve as support to facilitate loans of commercial banks to SMEs
Resources	Federal funds as well as deposits of the private sector	Private and external/foreign funds

Source: Authors' own work based on various sources

In this context, a main concern is the effect of information asymmetry on the performance of financial markets. This difference in the information held by lenders and by borrowers regarding specific investment projects gives rise to two undesirable effects—adverse selection and moral hazard—that, in turn, translate into credit rationing by the private sector. This rationing distorts fund allocation among the whole set of investment initiatives. Thus, at market interest rates, numerous very good projects end up blocked due to lack of finance, while other not-so-good investment proposals, riskier and more likely to end in default, receive funding and begin to be executed.

How does the specialized financial literature tackle the problem of asymmetric information? Let's assume the case of a potential entrepreneur who needs bank financing for a number of investment projects. Assume too, a unique probability distribution—known by the entrepreneur but not by the banker—of success of each one of those investment projects. The bank may be aware of the average return on similar projects but is not able to assess the degree of risk involved and probability of failure of each specific venture. Increases in the bank's active interest rate may not help to select the best projects. Instead it may attract riskier ventures, due to problems of adverse selection and moral hazard. These possibilities reduce the bank's expected earnings, as they will be severely affected if the borrower can't pay the loan or interest. Attempts by the bank to effectively discriminate among projects/borrowers according to their risk or probability of default fail, due to the existence of asymmetric information. In this situation, the preferred route of action for the bank, given the objective to maximize profits, leads to credit rationing; i.e. at the prevailing market interest rate, the demand for loans from the private sector exceeds the supply of them by the banking system (see, inter alia, Jaffee and Stiglitz 1990).

Another approach to tackle the issue of information asymmetry in financial markets, somewhat more associated with a macroeconomic view, allows for banks to have the capacities to reduce adverse selection and moral hazard (Ball 2009). Under this vision, banks do have the power to gather and process relevant information, to evaluate projects, discriminate among borrowers assessing their associated risk, and adequately monitor them if they are granted a loan. According to this view, development banks become potentially useful tools to overcome the difficulties and market failures associated with credit rationing if and only if they act as complements and subordinates of commercial banks. They are seen as well positioned to provide funding to the segment of micro-, small, and medium-sized enterprises (MSMEs) whose credit needs, due to structural obstacles such as market failures, are simply unmet by the private commercial banking and financial system.

In practice, the responsibilities inherent in the development banks' new ancillary role included offering long-term loans, working capital loans, syndicated loans, and unsecured loans.[2] They also began promoting a series of products tailored to meet the funding needs of MSMEs. The former included loan guarantees, leasing and factoring services, microcredits, seed capital, and financial support to entrepreneurship, as well as education, health, and insurance services. The latter comprised advisory services, capacity building, and training programmes on various key areas.

To a certain extent, development banks kept partial responsibility for contributing to the development of the financial sector and capital markets. In theory, development banks could still be allowed to mobilize savings, especially in a period of high liquidity, for public or private projects in strategic economic, social, and environmental areas. However, in practice this is a

[2] A recent survey of development banks across the world shows that 90 per cent of banks offer long-term loans and that 85 per cent, 74 per cent, and 52 per cent of the banks offer loans for working capital, short-term loans, and syndicated loans. Less than 50 per cent of the institutions surveyed offered loans for a new product and unsecured loans (Luna-Martínez and Vicente 2012).

relatively minor role compared to the provision of credit to micro-, small, and medium-sized firms and the task of strengthening Mexico's domestic capital markets. This latter responsibility was simply stripped away from development banks in Mexico with the market reforms of the 1990s.[3]

The neoliberal agenda brought a new and formidably binding constraint on development banks: preservation of the financial capital—i.e. financial sustainability—was set as their top concern in their lending operations! Thus, first and foremost, development banks had to avoid generating any pressure on the fiscal budget as the main guideline for their lending practices. Preserving fiscal soundness took precedence over promoting structural change for development. In practice, such financial sustainability implied: (i) maintaining real capital constant; (ii) achieving a rate of return no lower than the government's long-term borrowing cost; (iii) setting an explicit rate of return on capital (ranging from 7–11 per cent).[4]

In full accordance with the new paradigm, NAFINSA's mandate was radically changed. First of all, it had to preserve its capital and ensure its financial sustainability. Second, it had to promote financial inclusion. Most importantly, it now had to act exclusively as a second-tier financial intermediary. Moreover, its target population was set to be general MSMEs in commerce and service activities. The (small) size of the firms became the key variable to be considered in NAFINSA's lending operations, rather than their specific activity or place in global value chains. The share of funds oriented to industry declined from 100 per cent in 1989 to 41 per cent in just five years. Contrarily, commerce and services, which did not receive any funding in 1989, captured 32 per cent and 26.6 per cent of the total by 1994.

In addition, NAFINSA was subjected to additional and multiple regulatory and supervision constraints. They included compliance with each and every regulation that applied to private commercial banks, even those set in Basle III standards. In line with its new mandate NAFINSA sold or divested its industrial firms, and cancelled its key role as promoter of industrialization. The trust funds it had devoted to such objectives were dwarfed, merged, or eliminated. The New Organic Law limited its activities, in particular stating that it could engage directly in investment projects only as minority partner (up to 15 per cent) and only for a maximum of three years.

[3] In the case of Latin America and the Caribbean, this role has been taken on by regional development banks, including the Central American Bank for Economic Integration (BCIE), the Latin American Development Bank (CAF) and the Caribbean Development Bank. With the exception of the national development bank of Brazil (BNDES), national development banks in Latin America remain committed basically to providing financing for micro-, small, and medium-sized firms with a few initiatives to develop the financial and capital markets.

[4] Luna-Martinez and Vicente (2012).

5.4 NAFINSA: New Objectives, Instruments, and Target Population

NAFINSA's current mission is: 'To contribute to economic development through facilitating access to financial resources to micro, small and medium-sized enterprises (MSMEs) and priority investment projects, as well as financing business development services and contributing to the formation of financial markets and acting as trustee and financial agent of the Federal Government, in order to foster innovation, improve productivity, competitiveness, job creation and regional growth' (NAFINSA 2016).

In relative terms, and taking only into account the credit directly granted as a first-tier or second-tier financial intermediary, NAFINSA is now second only to Banco Nacional de Obras (BANOBRAS). This latter institution is dedicated to providing finance to investment projects in infrastructure or in public services. BANCOMEXT has grown very rapidly, providing financial support to export and import activities (Table 5.3).

In line with the revised mandate set by Mexico's market reforms of the 1990s, NAFINSA's financial support is granted entirely to the private sector. The new regulatory framework radically transformed it to operate as a second-tier intermediary that, essentially, meets short-term and working capital needs of micro-, small, and medium-sized private firms, mainly in the service sector. Since 2005, or even earlier, it stopped directly financing the government or state-owned enterprises. Moreover, in full accordance with its mandate to preserve its capital, it has not received any resources from the fiscal authorities and has obtaining its funds from other sources. As an example, in 2015 NAFINSA's funding came from money market operations (16 per cent), bank bonds (2 per cent), interbank loans and international organizations (42 per cent), as well as, in a very small proportion, share capital (7 per cent).

Table 5.3. Mexico development banks, credit directly granted as first- and second-tier intermediary 2013–16 (constant prices, INPC 2013=100)

Banobras	272693	295059.7928	315379.7963	321402.7137
NAFINSA	120,608.00	143,980.65	159,754.49	173,951.67
Bancomext	82,789.00	109,713.41	141,473.66	161,643.39
SHF	70,612.00	69,491.48	67,908.36	65,613.74
Banjército	20,245.00	23,971.07	28,293.06	32,203.37
Bansefi	498.00	1,924.54	2,323.25	2,014.97
Development banks (A)	567,445.00	644,140.95	715,132.62	756,829.86
Commercial Banks (B)	3,033,539.00	3,206,226.11	3,575,575.62	3,917,176.88
Share (A/(B+A)), %	0.16	0.17	0.17	0.16
NAFINSA's share in total (commercial and development banks)	3.35%	3.74%	3.72%	3.72%

Moreover, in many recent years, it has become NAFINSA's regular practice to have part of its operating profits retained or transferred—defined as the item *aprovechamientos* in the fiscal budget—to the Ministry of Finance to engross public revenues. Given this change in mandate, its financial support to the private sector rapidly expanded, through diverse tools tailored to meet the needs of MSMEs, its new target business population.

Notwithstanding, NAFINSA's share in the aggregate flow of credit to the private sector is very small: less than 4 per cent of the total. In fact, the overall share of development banks is 16 per cent (see Table 5.3). To better grasp the situation, in Mexico, total financing to the non-financial private sector reached the equivalent of 36 per cent of gross domestic product (GDP) in 2014, way below the average of the OECD (146 per cent) and the figures of Chile (109 per cent) and Brazil (69 per cent).[5] Moreover, at that time in Mexico, total financing provided by all development banks to the non-financial private sector reached the equivalent of 3.9 per cent of GDP: 1.7 per cent of GDP in the form of guarantees for the commercial banks and 2.2 per cent of GDP as direct credit. This low participation of development banks in providing resources to the non-financial private sector prevails today, notwithstanding that a financial reform, implemented in 2014–16, gave them more leeway in their day-to-day operations and, in particular, liberated them from the mandate set by the neoliberal reforms of the 1990s that made preservation of their capital a top priority. Two additional queries arise immediately concerning development banks' impact on Mexico's economic growth potential. First of all, their funds are targeted at MSMEs—and not at specific industries or regions as is the case with major development banks elsewhere—regardless of their capacity to innovate, export, or augment capital formation. Second, with regard to NAFINSA's guarantees, the consensus is that such programmes do not significantly expand credit to sectors, groups, or activities traditionally excluded from formal finance. Guarantees do not correct for that market failure, but merely allow commercial banks an ampler management of their credit portfolio with their usual clients. In fact, the main beneficiaries and users of NAFINSA's guarantees programmes are large retailers and commercial businesses whose impact on innovation and on fixed capital formation on plants, machinery, and equipment is weak.

Mexico's development banks'—in particular NAFINSA's—current credit portfolio is limited partly by the regulatory framework, partly by the lack of an active industrial policy, and also by the deterioration in the investment perspectives of the private sector. Indeed, Mexico's business sector has become much less concerned with the expansion and modernization of its capital

[5] See Instituto Belisario Domínguez (2016).

equipment than with just having short-term finance to maintain its day-to-day operations. A similar discussion is currently taking place in Mexico concerning the extremely low figure of commercial banks' lending to the private entrepreneurial sector. Banks' surveys tend to indicate that there is a lack of demand for long-term credit for investment from trustworthy, sound creditors. Also, the commercial banks tend to complain that the existing legal and judicial framework makes it very difficult for them to 'execute' guarantees in case of creditors' default on loans. On the other hand, surveys among private users of the banking system picture a totally different situation, fully consistent with the view of a severely credit-rationed financial market in Mexico.

Between 2000 and 2013, NAFINSA's total financing to the public and much more to the private sectors grew more than tenfold, rising from 86.8 to 631.9 billion constant pesos. Although it decreased slightly in the next couple of years, by 2015 it still stood at 500.4 billion constant pesos, as shown in Table 5.4. This spectacular expansion was accompanied by a major sectorial shift in its public/private composition. In 2000, more than 50 per cent of its direct and indirect funding went to the public sector. Soon, virtually all its financial support was directed to the private sector. By 2005, more than 90 per cent of its funding was channelled to the private sector, a percentage that kept on climbing to reach 99 per cent. In fact, NAFINSA has virtually

Table 5.4. NAFINSA's total financing by programme, 2000–15 (in billions of pesos and as a percentage of the total)

Financing programmes	2000	2002	2005	2010	2012	2013	2014	2015
Productive Chains		24.5	102.2	250.3	230.2	208.9	197.0	178.1
Fixed-asset financing		16.1	13.8	4.1	4.3	24.2		
Micro-businesses		1.4	4.3	11.3	17.0	18.7	28.9	16.6
Traditional programmes	34.0	37.6	24.7	32.0	29.5	33.4	53.9	57.7
Second-tier credit	**34.0**	**79.6**	**145.0**	**297.7**	**281.1**	**285.1**	**279.9**	**252.3**
First-tier credit	2.4	1.8	0.9	7.1	3.5	6.6	0.0	18.0
Total private sector credit	**36.4**	**81.4**	**145.9**	**304.8**	**284.6**	**291.7**	**279.9**	**270.3**
Guarantees and induced credit	3.0	7.1	33.5	200.0	315.3	339.8	255.9	227.1
Total private sector financing	**39.5**	**88.5**	**179.4**	**504.8**	**599.9**	**631.5**	**535.8**	**497.5**
Public sector financing	19.2	65.0	14.4	0.4	1.8	0.5	3.9	2.9
Other	28.1	10.9	0.5					
Total financing	86.8	164.4	194.4	505.2	601.7	631.9	539.7	500.4
Productive Chains	0.0	27.7	56.9	49.6	38.4	33.1	36.8	35.8
Fixed-asset financing	0.0	18.2	7.7	0.8	0.7	3.8	0.0	0.0
Micro-businesses	0.0	1.6	2.4	2.2	2.8	3.0	5.4	3.3
Traditional programmes	86.2	42.5	13.8	6.3	4.9	5.3	10.1	11.6
Second-tier credit	86.2	90.0	80.8	59.0	46.9	45.2	52.2	50.7
First-tier credit	6.2	2.0	0.5	1.4	0.6	1.0	0.0	3.6
Total private sector credit	92.3	92.0	81.3	60.4	47.4	46.2	52.2	54.3
Guarantees and induced credit	7.7	8.0	18.7	39.6	52.6	53.8	47.8	45.7
Total private sector financing	45.5	53.8	92.3	99.9	99.7	99.9	99.3	99.4
Public sector financing	22.1	39.5	7.4	0.1	0.3	0.1	0.7	0.6

stopped funding the public sector; from 65 billion constant pesos granted to it in 2002, it channelled only 2.9 billion constant pesos in 2015.

NAFINSA's funding to the private sector had an interesting transformation in terms of its composition between, on the one hand, credit directly granted essentially as a second-tier bank and, on the other hand, financial support given indirectly through guarantees and induced credit. In 2000, the first component totalled 36.4 billion constant pesos and the second, ten times less. By 2015, their magnitudes were much more similar: $270.3 vs 227.1 billion constant pesos respectively. NAFINSA's financing by sector of economic activity during 2008–15 shows that the majority of its funding is targeted at commerce, distribution, and other services (54 per cent), while industrial activities receive only 13 per cent of the total.[6] This sectorial composition is rather incidental and does not reflect any policy intention on the part of NAFINSA to promote a particular change in the productive structure. It is more a byproduct of its focus on financing MSMEs.

In 2000, MSMEs accounted for 49 per cent of NAFINSA's portfolio, 78 per cent in 2003, and 82 per cent by 2005. It has remained around that percentage thereafter. In line with this policy trend, the number of firms supported by NAFINSA has grown exponentially. Available evidence shows that in 2000, it provided financial resources to 12,185 firms. By 2005, the cumulative number of beneficiary firms had expanded to 743,295 and by 2012, to nearly two million (1,949,223). The impact of such financial support for each firm has yet to be measured. In 2015, the number of recipients of some direct or indirect financial support from NAFINSA was 534,270. Approximately one-third of them (176,979) were firms and the other two-thirds (357,291) were microcredits given in their entirety to very low income entrepreneurs to cover the following credit needs: personal loans, insurance, and housing. Interestingly, 53 per cent of the overall recipients were first-time users of some kind of financial support from NAFINSA (NAFINSA 2016). However, when measured in relative terms, NAFINSA's coverage is rather limited. Indeed, measured as a percentage of the total universe of firms in Mexico, NAFINSA provides direct or indirect financing to only to 15 per cent of large firms and 14 per cent of micro firms (NAFINSA 2016).[7]

The limited coverage is explained, in part, by firms' self-exclusion from financial markets. Indeed, available evidence shows that vast numbers of entrepreneurs claim not to need financial support or credit. One of the most

[6] The latest available figures for 2016 show a 48 per cent share of commerce and distribution in NAFINSA's total financing, with 29 per cent going to industry and 22 per cent to services (see NAFINSA 2016).

[7] According to the National Institute of Statistics and Geography (INEGI), firm size is determined by the number of employees as follows: micro firm (1–10 employees); small firm (11–50 employees); medium-sized firm (51–250 employees); and large firm (more than 250 employees).

recent surveys by INEGI (2014) revealed that 54, 74, 75, and 82 per cent respectively of micro, small, medium-sized, and large firms do not need financial support to carry their activities. This is consistent with the well-known stylized fact that firms tend to finance their operations with retained earnings or by deferred payment to suppliers. On average, Mexican firms finance more than 70 per cent of their investment in fixed and circulating capital with retained earnings (Pérez and González 2016).[8] And what is particularly worrying, is that the main source of credit for day-to-day operations for a majority of firms, especially MSMEs, is deferred payment to suppliers.

Obviously, there are other reasons for the absence of credit demand, including high interest rates. According to the same survey quoted above, 33 per cent, 15.3 per cent, 10.5 per cent, and 6.8 per cent of micro, small, medium-sized, and large firms surveyed cited high interest rates as a significant obstacle to access credit.[9] In the case of NAFINSA, financial support for MSMEs is provided basically through induced credit and second-tier operations. In line with the supply-side view emphasized, NAFINSA provides finance through a series of instruments: mainly second-tier credit, guarantees, and induced credit. Among NAFINSA's second-tier credit programmes, the one that has drawn major attention is Productive Chains, but it also has others such as fixed-asset finance, micro-business, and traditional programmes. In 2015, it started a programme specifically targeted at young first-time entrepreneurs, which is still in its infancy.

The intermediaries through which NAFINSA operates include commercial banks and specialized financial institutions, as well as micro-financing institutions. Currently, it works with roughly 150 financial intermediaries (NAFINSA 2016). In practice, NAFINSA's financial support is channelled through different credit instruments and intermediaries to reach different segments of MSMEs. This novel financial strategy is denominated in NAFINSA as 'segment–product channel'. On the one hand, second-tier credit and guarantees are channelled through three types of financial intermediaries: commercial banks, specialized financial entities, and micro-financing institutions. On the other hand, the credit provided through productive chains uses commercial banks and specialized financial institutions. In turn, commercial banks attend to all types of firms, including large, medium, small, and micro firms. For their

[8] The literature argues that firms prefer different sources of finance for capital formation in the following order: retained earnings, bank credit, and funds through the capital market. See Leary and Roberts (2010). This ranking did not consider suppliers' credit, in Mexico fundamentally associated with current operations' credit practices.

[9] Another reason that prevents firms' access to formal bank credit is lack of collateral. According to the World Bank (2016), the average value of the collateral for a loan in Mexico is among the highest in the region: 179 per cent of the value of the loan for large firms and 243 per cent for small ones.

part, specialized financial institutions work with small and medium-sized firms. Finally, micro financial institutions focus only on micro firms.

NAFINSA has several programmes of microcredit: (i) Entrepreneurs; (ii) Financing Programme; (iii) Supporting Women Micro-Entrepreneurs; (iv) Comprehensive Modernization Microenterprise; and (v) Fiscally Compliant Business (*Adheridos*). This last programme aims at strengthening the 'formalization' of SMEs, i.e. to increase the number of firms complying with fiscal obligations and registering their employees in the social security system. None of these programmes involves large amounts of funding. They seem to be pilot studies to be operated in the future on a larger scale.

Productive Chains has become, without doubt, the most important second-tier credit programme in Mexico, far surpassing the others. Credit granted through it by NAFINSA reached 13.9 billion pesos in 2002 and expanded exponentially thereafter to reach 250 billion pesos by 2010, though declining to 211.8 billion pesos by 2015. Currently, in relative terms, Productive Chains accounts for 71 per cent of NAFINSA's total of second-tier credit granted, and for 35.8 per cent of its total finance to the private sector. One of the key traits explaining the success of the Productive Chains programme is innovative reliance on an electronic platform, extremely user-friendly for potential borrowers to rediscount their bills. It is precisely through this reverse factoring scheme—i.e. rediscount of unpaid bills before maturity—that the programme helps suppliers to keep operating smoothly as a link of the productive chains. As mentioned above, given the shallowness of Mexico's financial market, supplier credit is one of the main sources of credit for private firms to finance their current operations. In this regard, Productive Chains most successfully tackles a key weakness of the financial system in Mexico. It has achieved great effectiveness and efficiency. It has been praised and recently imitated by other intermediaries for its great administrative and marketing dynamics. The number of incorporated companies and the amounts financed give solid proof of its role in strengthening local supply chains.

Large companies as well as government entities participate in the Productive Chains programme. By doing so they may invite their suppliers (whether MSMEs or individual entrepreneurs) to form part of a productive chain of suppliers. For each of these chains, a website is developed that becomes an e-marketplace, where information, products, and services can be shared. Membership in a productive chain opens attractive financing options to its participants. Perhaps the key instrument in this set, as mentioned above, is the innovative technological platform for immediate electronic factoring. Through very simple and transparent procedures, it allows MSME suppliers in any such designated productive chain to rapidly obtain finance through a rediscount mechanism of accounts receivable by electronic billing before their expiration date.

This so-called reverse factoring scheme differs from that of traditional factoring because it targets a select group of MSMEs associated with the supply chain of large companies of renowned strength and solvency. In the case of reverse factoring, the participating companies are chosen on the basis of high standards in terms of business strength and risk in order to reduce and practically eliminate credit risk. In NAFINSA's Productive Chains programme, the participants are large companies of the highest level and also their suppliers. In addition to substantially reducing risk, in this reverse factoring operation by NAFINSA, all transactions are carried out electronically, which helps to reduce costs and transaction time.

The financial resources for such factoring are provided by NAFINSA, in its role as an intermediary with other banking and non-banking institutions. The funds can be granted in local currency or in dollars, with a maximum amount of 3.26 million Investment Units (IDUs, which are adjusted daily per the variation of the consumer price index). The financing term is between thirty and 120 days. It operates with an interest rate determined in relation to the overnight commercial bank interest rate, and with no extra commissions being charged.

NAFINSA's Productive Chains programme had a market share of only 2 per cent in 2001, which climbed to 60 per cent by 2004. In 2009, the Production Chains programme comprised about 700 large buyers—36 per cent of which were public sector entities and the remaining 64 per cent private firms—and a gamut of financial agents including banks, factoring companies, and non-bank intermediaries. By then, a daily average of 10,000 transactions were made, providing financial support to approximately 27,000 SMEs in the year. The number of operations accumulated since its launch in the early 2000s until 2013 stands at 24 billion, mostly concentrated in the commercial sector, followed by industry and services (with shares of 41, 35, and 14 per cent of the total respectively). The Productive Chains programme has somewhat lost in presence in recent years. The main reason behind this is that an important number of so-called First-Order Companies (large private firms)—with a very high frequency of daily operations—have left the programme. According to various analysts, a key reason for their withdrawal has been the surge of similar programmes for microfinance from commercial banks, also based on electronic factoring. This negative effect was partly offset by an increased outlay of resources to providers of public agencies and entities within the Federal Procurement Programme of Government, specifically created for SMEs. In recent years, 40 per cent of the Production Chains funds operated in this way.

In addition to second-tier credit, NAFINSA provides financial support through the Guarantees programme, which, jointly with the Productive Chains programme, constitutes the hallmark of NAFINSA's operations. This programme was established in 1997 as a countercyclical instrument to offset the credit contraction that the Mexican economy suffered following the 1995 'Tequila Crisis', and the adjustment policies designed to confront it. Thereafter, the Guarantees programme focused mainly on financial inclusion though still maintaining, to a certain extent, a countercyclical role as shown for example by its response to the global financial crisis (2008–9).[10]

The current objectives of the Guarantees programme are to expand access to credit, improve the conditions under which loans are granted (lower rates and principals), and increase the overall supply of credit. In this regard the offering of guarantees is a tool that aims to overcome some of the problems of asymmetric information and moral hazard that bring about credit rationing in Mexico. In other words, Guarantees are a form of financial coverage through which NAFINSA shares the credit risk with commercial banks, with the aim of facilitating access to financial resources to private firms. Its beneficiaries include micro, small, or medium-sized firms in the industrial, commercial, and service sectors. The resources thus channelled serve multiple purposes, such as financing investment in fixed capital, complementing working capital, and funding projects of technological development or even improvement of the environment. The programme also seeks to boost the commercial financial sector's capacity or willingness to grant credit to firms or micro-entrepreneurs, which, for a number of reasons, are credit-constrained by the formal financial system. It also serves to put in place an institutional mechanism to diversify risk and thus provide support for some federal entities, SOEs, or public agencies as well.

The Guarantees programme works through the creation of trust funds by the government, through the Ministry of Economic Affairs (*Secretaría de Economía*) of the Federal Government, managed and administered by NAFINSA in its financial operations. These trust funds work with a selected group of financial intermediaries through legal contracts, so that the fiduciary guarantee is granted on a virtually automatic basis once the financial intermediary has approved the request for a loan from a given firm.[11] In order to participate in the Guarantees programme, a financial intermediary must have or design credit products specifically tailored to small and medium-sized firms. In addition, NAFINSA has the responsibility to evaluate, approve, and authorize the

[10] The importance of financial inclusion is reflected in NAFINSA's 2013–18 institutional programme where its states that its number one objective is to widen financial access under better conditions (more credit and lower interest rates) and other entrepreneurial services to MSMEs with a focus on improving their productivity.

[11] A financial guarantee is defined as 'a contract under which a guarantor agrees to become responsible for the obligations of a principal debtor to a third-party creditor'. In this case the guarantor is NAFINSA, the principal debtor is the firm, and the third-party creditor is the financial institution. Guarantees create a legally enforceable obligation on the part of the guarantor to pay the debt. See DBRS (2010).

loan products so designed by banks, in accordance with the regulations of the *Secretaría de Economía*. The guarantees scheme has two modalities: *pari passu* and first loss. The *pari passu* modality means that, in case of a loan default, NAFINSA and the financial institution must respond simultaneously and in equal measure (or in the proportions convened). The portfolio coverage is 50 per cent for working capital, 70 per cent for fixed assets, 80 per cent for sectors, and 100 per cent for emergencies (ALIDE 2016). NAFINSA fixes the price of the *pari passu* guarantees and these contain an implicit subsidy (Peña and Ríos 2013).

The first-loss modality establishes that NAFINSA covers the first portfolio losses up to an amount not exceeding 10 per cent of its losses. Accordingly, through this modality, if a bank acquires a guarantee it covers 10 per cent of its first losses. The first-loss modality is implemented through an auction process convened by NAFINSA where banks make offers by credit batches with given characteristics and compete for a predefined guarantee coverage.

It is interesting to note that, given the way the programme is designed, participant firms do not directly apply for a guarantee, and neither are they aware of the benefit of having such guarantees by NAFINSA. Commercial banks do not inform firms that their credits are covered by a guarantee, in order to avoid a moral hazard problem (Peña and Ríos 2013). Credit granted by NAFINSA through the Guarantees programme shows a steady increase until 2007. The impact of the global financial crisis, felt in 2008 but especially in 2009, gave additional impetus to the programme and it expanded significantly. Indeed, from 2000 to 2007, the volume of credit channelled through guarantees rose from 3 to 55 billion constant pesos representing 7.7 and 17.4 per cent of the institution's total credit to the private sector. In 2008 and 2009, guarantees rose to reach 128.7 and 265.2 billion constant pesos (29 and 39 per cent of the total). The countercyclical role played by the Guarantees programme in these two years can be illustrated by the difference between the programmed finance and the actual finance provided by it. Figure 5.2 plots the difference between both for the years 2007 to 2012. The difference between programme finance and actual finance was negative for 2007 (12,974 million constant pesos) and increased significantly in 2008 to 39,846 million constant pesos to reach a maximum of 84,597 million constant pesos in 2009. In 2010, the difference went the opposite way, then rose in 2011 and declined thereafter.

As the Productive Chains' credit stalled in 2010–12 and eventually began to decline in 2013–15, guarantees became the most important instrument of NAFINSA to grant credit to MSMEs. Subsequently, the credit granted through guarantees represented more than 50 per cent of its total financing to the private sector.

Besides the Productive Chains and the Guarantees programmes, NAFINSA has taken additional initiatives to further develop and strengthen Mexico's

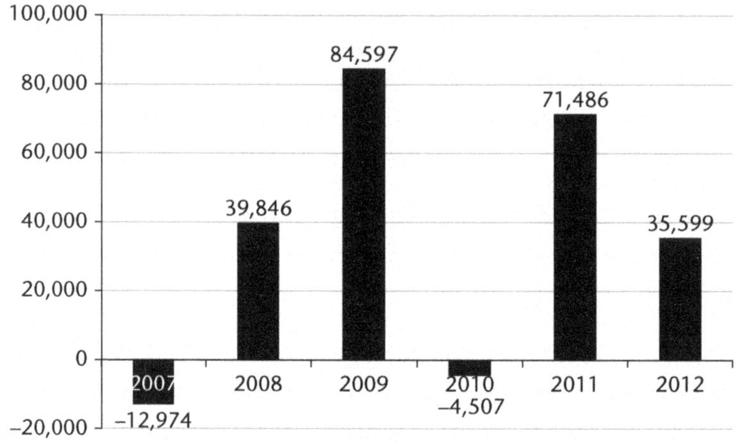

Figure 5.2. Mexico: Difference between the programmed and actual financial support provided by the guarantees programme for 2007–12 (in million constant 2010 pesos)
Source: Authors' own calculations on the basis of NAFINSA's annual reports 2007–12

financial markets through the provision of venture capital. The first risk capital fund was established in 2004, and it was an important basis for the creation of forty-three companies with technological projects. Furthermore, NAFINSA, in collaboration with other local development banks, created another promotion fund in 2006. In 2010, with the Ministry of Economic Affairs, they created the fund called Mexico Ventures, whose main purpose is to invest in projects of Mexican entrepreneurs. In 2012, both institutions launched the *Fondo de Capital Semilla* (Seed Capital Fund) and in 2013 they considerably augmented its capital. That same year, the Mexican Government inaugurated the Entrepreneur Institute (*Instituto del Emprendedor*). As a partial result of these initiatives, capital financing to SMEs almost doubled between 2007 and 2012, but its share is tiny compared to similar capital available to large companies.

NAFINSA's *Programa Nacional de Franquicias* (National Franchise Programme) allows larger SMEs to participate in a franchise with an interest-free loan through a financial institution that covers up to 50 per cent of the costs, to be reimbursed in thirty-six months. Between 2007 and 2011, the programme supported 1627 franchise outlets (CNBV 2015). For its part, the *Red Mexicana de Inversionistas Ángeles* (Mexican Network of 'Angel' Investors), which are associations of investors looking for potential projects to invest their capital, expanded to thirteen in 2011, thanks to government support. An additional investment guarantee was established, over a period of three to five years, specifically directed at innovation-oriented SMEs or exporters of products with high value-added. In 2011, the Ministry of Economic Affairs launched the *Programa de deuda* (Debt Programme) in partnership with the Stock Exchange of Mexico and AMEXCAP, a financial intermediary, to help companies issue bonds.

However, despite all these very successful initiatives, in Mexico, funds for venture capital are far from achieving a significant scale. In practice, this channel of finance is at best irrelevant and at worst non-existent for most MSMEs and even large firms in Mexico. Many obstacles remain, including Mexico's particular corporate culture, the relative absence of truly competitive practices in many markets, and the inadequacy of legal frameworks coupled with the absence of a culture of long-term planning for structural change within the Federal Government.[12]

5.5 NAFINSA: Strengths, Weaknesses, and Future Challenges

From a strictly and acutely microeconomic perspective, NAFINSA has been a successful story of institutional transformation in the face of drastic changes in the nation's development agenda. As an individual bank, NAFINSA positively adapted to the changing situation. It has become a profitable entity, in particular creating innovative Factoring and Guarantees schemes. From systematically relying on fiscal resources—sometimes in an urgent way—it is now a self-sustained, solvent financial institution capable of regularly transferring part of its profits to strengthen fiscal revenues. A fundamental constraint has been that until the recent financial reform of 2014–16, capital preservation and sustainability were set as NAFINSA's key priorities in order to avoid putting pressure on the Federal Budget. NAFINSA has been able to preserve and even augment its capital. Within the narrow perspective set decades ago by the market reforms and still in vogue, the challenges for NAFINSA to meet its additional key objective—of strengthening the financial inclusion of MSMEs—are far from overwhelming. Essentially, they boil down to having larger capital and much more independence or leeway in selecting and hiring its body of human resources at the top level. Some of its intermediation programmes should be revised and perhaps eliminated, given the scant number of their beneficiaries or even duplication with other schemes.

However, from a macroeconomic perspective, the conclusion on NAFINSA's role in helping to overcome key obstacles on financing Mexico's development points in a very different direction. In its current operations as a second-tier

[12] NAFINSA has also been a key financial agent in securing funds from international financial organizations and donors in the external capital markets. Recently it floated a Green Bond signalling its return to world markets, for the first time in eighteen years.

intermediary focusing on SMEs, NAFINSA's direct and indirect contribution—and for that matter that of virtually all development banks in Mexico—to alleviate credit restrictions is very limited. Moreover, it is highly questionable whether its stellar financial instrument of Guarantees significantly expands the commercial banks' credit supply or merely helps such private institutions manage more profitably and in a less risky way essentially the same portfolio of clients and activities, with virtually no additional exploration of new, innovative ventures put forward by traditionally tightly credit-constrained private firms. Given its design, the major beneficiaries of the Factoring programme are large, well-consolidated corporations—many of them in the service and retail sectors—which thus avoid paying their suppliers in time. In addition, in its operations to support commercial banks' loans to private SMEs, scant or no consideration is paid to the beneficiary firm's activity, the strength of its forward and backward linkages, its innovation or export potential, or even its prospects for employment creation.

For decades, the Mexican economy has been stuck in a trap of scant growth, aggravated by an increasing incidence of poverty that now affects more than 50 per cent of the population. Its productive structure is marked by an acute dualism, with on the one hand a few very dynamic, large manufacturing firms, which are extremely successful global players and, on the other hand, the vast majority of firms, which are excluded from the international, modern circuits of technical innovation, export markets, and financial flows. Moreover, for decades Mexico's extraordinarily dynamic manufacturing export sector has failed to generate enough local value added, and therefore has been unable to be the much-promised engine of growth for the rest of the economy. Experts concur that finance has been and continues to be a constraint on the Mexican economy's long-term growth potential. As we mentioned above, in Mexico, bank lending to the private sector is extremely low in any relevant international comparison. Moreover, the gap between financial saving and banks' lending to the non-financial private sector is also very wide in Mexico.

Most importantly, in Mexico, the provision of long-term finance for private fixed capital formation is more an exception than a norm. Indeed, among Latin American countries, Mexico has one of the lowest ratios, as a proportion of GDP, of banking loans to private activities. The small magnitude of the ratio is even more worrying if the focus is placed instead on formal finance for private investment. Its domestic financial market is very shallow, highly concentrated, and characterized by an acute exclusion of micro, small, and medium-sized firms, marked by informality, and with an urgent need to modernize capital equipment and machinery, and update its technology. According to survey data, more than 90 per cent of private firms in Mexico have no access to loans from the commercial banking system, including the development banks sector. Without access to finance, there is simply no way to have sufficient investment and, ultimately, to move away from the trap of scant economic growth and underdevelopment for the vast majority of the Mexican population.

The context has darkened since the election of Trump in the United States, given his promise to cancel NAFTA, impose large tariffs, adopt a border tax system, cut down imports, and reverse American FDI in Mexico. Thus, fascinating and daunting challenges are open for NAFINSA to become a relevant instrument: a policy bank to channel financial intermediation for fixed capital formation with a developmental vision to promote a structural transformation of the Mexican economy. This means the goal for NAFINSA must be to recover some of its functions, prerogatives, and responsibilities as a policy bank, but without the alleged excesses of the past, some of them true and others exaggerated due to its association with the black legend of import substitution and state-led industrialization (Suárez Dávila 2017).

The Financial Reform of 2014–16 opened the door, in principle, for NAFINSA to become once again a major policy instrument for such structural transformation. In particular, it eliminated the preservation of capital as a key priority in development banks' operations. It is too soon to give a final assessment of its impact. But there is consensus that it has yet to make an impact on significantly increasing credit access among the population and reducing its cost. Whether it will do so in the future is uncertain, but the possibility for change is open.

NAFINSA's challenge is to have a new role not limited to compensating for market failures and the absence of markets, and to act as a significant financial agent of the Federal Government. This means that its practices must still be adjusted to favour open markets but also, and this is a huge assumption given the current views of the Mexican government, that there should be a significant return to state intervention in economic matters. Not on the same scale as in the 1970s, by any means, but it can't remain as absent as it was from the 1990s until the years before the 2008–9 international financial crisis and even today. Expanding its mandate to authorize it to engage significantly again in first-tier, direct credit operations is necessary to alleviate the credit constraint faced by the non-financial private sector, especially in certain less developed regions, as well as in long-term, capital-intensive ventures in innovative areas. In addition, the prevailing insistence on full compliance of development banks—NAFINSA, in particular—with Basel III norms and regulations significantly hinders their intervention in sectors like infrastructure and heavy capital equipment, which tend to be heavily concentrated. Given their distinctive mandate to fund the creation of markets, to promote innovation and discovery of new ways and activities to push forward structural transformation, development banks can't be subject to the same regulation and supervision criteria as commercial banks. Standard methods based on profit lines, capital requirements, and exposure should not be the only or main guideline for the assessment of their contribution to development. Alternative criteria should be explored.

Sensible state intervention in the Mexican case has been and continues to be badly needed. It has now become urgent in two main areas in particular. The first one is in building and modernizing Mexico's infrastructure. For the last seven years, public investment has been declining in real terms to a point where today, its ratio as a proportion of GDP is less than 4 per cent, the lowest in Mexico's history since the 1950s, and one of the lowest in the region. This decline in public investment runs very much against improving Mexico's infrastructure, and undermines its economic growth potential. The second one is in the implementation of a modern industrial policy. On January 2013, President Peña Nieto said in his inaugural speech: 'the effort of the government through the implementation of an industrial policy will lead the Mexican economy to higher rates of expansion' (Peña Nieto 2013). Moreover, the National Development Plan 2013–18, which the former government unveiled in June 2013, explicitly considered industrial policy as a tool for development. It argued for the implementation of a set of policies in which the state's role in promoting strategic sectors—among which it specifically includes the industrial one—also aims to create stronger forward and backward linkages between exports and the rest of productive activities to boost Mexico's economic growth and its internal market, in addition to removing obstacles and correcting market failures. Most importantly, in those arguments, the President gave room to the option of using industrial policies to go beyond consolidating static comparative advantages and advance to creating or discovering new advantages by fostering nascent industries and innovation. Unfortunately, this discourse has not been put into practice; thus an active industrial policy has yet to be designed and implemented.

Frankly, for the above to happen, a key condition—way beyond NAFINSA's sphere of action—is that the Mexican government should commit itself to a new development agenda, different from the current one centred on maintaining so-called 'macroeconomic fundamentals'—i.e. low and stable inflation, moderate fiscal deficits, and minimal state intervention in the economy—as necessary and sufficient conditions for economic growth. Whether the Mexican government will finally be lucid and bold enough to do so is uncertain. But this road is more and more likely to be travelled soon, given the long-time failure of the current market reform agenda and the major challenges that the Trump administration poses to Mexico's financial and fiscal stability as well as to the possibility of export-led growth as a viable option. Very soon, time must and will tell.

References

ALIDE. 2016. Available at <http://www.alide.org.pe/alide/>, accessed 14 April 2018.

Ball, L. M. 2009. *Money, Banking, and Financial Markets*. New York: Worth Publishers.

CNBV (Comisión Nacional Bancaria y de Valores). 2015. *Estudios Económicos*, vol. 3.

DBRS. 2010. Rating Report.

INEGI. 2014. *Censos económicos 2014: Micro, pequeña, mediana y gran empresa.*

Instituto Belisario Dominguez. 2016. Available at <www.ibd.senado.gob.mx/>, accessed 14 April 2018.

Jaffee, D. and J. Stiglitz. 1990. 'Credit Rationing', in B. Friedman and H. Frank (eds), *Handbook of Monetary Economics*, vol. 2, 837–88. New York: Elsevier Science Publishers.

Leary, M. T. and M. R. Roberts. 2010. 'The Pecking Order, Debt Capacity and Information Asymmetry', *Journal of Financial Economics* 95(3): 332–55.

Luna-Martinez, J. de and C. L. Vicente. 2012. *Global Survey of Development Banks*. World Bank Policy Research Working Paper 5969.

NAFINSA. 1994. *Nacional Financiera ante el siglo XXI: El pensamiento de sus directores generales*. Mexico City: Nacional Financiera, S.N.C.

NAFINSA. 2007–16. Annual Reports.

NAFINSA. 2016. Mission Statement. Available at <www.nafin.com/portalnf/content/sobre-nafin/nuestra-estrategia/mision.html>, accessed 14 April 2018.

Peña, P. and I. Ríos. 2013. 'Incidencia de las garantías gubernamentales sobre las condiciones de crédito a las empresas'. In *Estudios Económicos*, vol. 2, 105–36. CNBV.

Peña Nieto, E. 2013. *Discurso de toma de posesión, Oficina de la Presidencia de la República*. México.

Pérez Caldentey, E. and A. González. 2016. 'Inversión, financiamiento y la paradoja de la deuda en Minsky: Un análisis microeconométrico aplicado a América Latina', *Ensayos Económicos* 73: 58–90.

Suárez Dávila, F. 2017. 'BANCOMEXT: Creación, auge, supervivencia y ¿renacimiento?', *Comercio Exterior* 11: 94–101. Banco Nacional de Comercio Exterior. México.

World Bank. 2016. *Enterprise Surveys*. Washington, DC: World Bank Group.

6

The Role of CORFO in Chile's Development

Achievements and Challenges

Stephany Griffith-Jones, María Luz Martínez Sola, and Javiera Petersen Muga[1]

6.1 Introduction

CORFO (Corporación de Fomento de la Producción or Production Development Corporation) was created in 1939. In the initial period, it was an overarching and powerful institution that participated in the funding of over 30 per cent of Chilean investment in equipment and machinery and 25 per cent of public investment (Durán and Fermandois 2011). Through many instruments, it played a key role in the process of Chilean economic development, including the creation of many crucial enterprises that it also helped to run.

In later years, its relative scale diminished significantly, both in terms of the part it plays in promoting development, and the share that its operations have in relation to total credit to the private sector. In 2015, the financial support deployed by CORFO (through grants, credits, and guarantees; see Table 6.1) amounted to USD 2,863 million, which represents only 1 per cent of Chile's gross domestic product (GDP). As will be discussed, guarantees granted by CORFO now play a much larger role than loans made by CORFO to banks, which on-lend to the private sector. It is noteworthy that CORFO's credit to the private sector is not just far smaller than it was in earlier periods in Chile,

[1] We thank BNDES and CAF for their financial and intellectual support; we are especially grateful to Lavinia Barros de Castro, Vinicius Carrasco and Pablo Sanguinetti, for their valuable comments on the initial draft, and Lavinia for her valuable comments on the second draft. We are very grateful to all colleagues interviewed, who gave their valuable time and knowledge; these included the current Executive Vice President of CORFO, Eduardo Bitran, and two former Vice Presidents, Carlos Alvarez and Gonzalo Rivas; a full list of people interviewed and who provided information is provided at the end of the paper.

but is also significantly smaller in scale, compared to the size of the Chilean economy (as a proportion of GDP) and to total domestic credit to the private sector, than is the case with national development banks in other countries, such as KfW in Germany, with a ratio of loan portfolio to GDP of 14.5 per cent and to domestic private sector loans of 15.2 per cent; the National Development Bank of Brazil (BNDES) with 11.7 per cent and 16.6 per cent respectively; or the China Development Bank (CDB) with 12.2 per cent and 9 per cent respectively.

An important question to ask is whether the relatively small scale of resources that CORFO provides at present is sufficient at a time when Chile urgently needs to undertake a major structural transformation of its economy, for 'smart' and higher productivity diversification, so as to achieve more dynamic, inclusive, and sustainable growth. The urgency of the challenge is clearer at a time when the sharp fall in the copper price in recent years has contributed to a major slowdown of Chile's economic growth, which shows the vulnerability of a model based on exports, mainly of primary commodities. There are more long-term structural challenges for future growth based on natural resources, which also make structural transformation urgent. These are linked to the physical and environmental limits for further natural resource development in Chile; they relate for example to scarcity of water (to produce one glass of wine requires an input of 100 litres of water!), limits of land available to expand forestry, for wood, as well as paper and cellulose, and resource limits to the production of salmon. Furthermore, very slow productivity growth in Chile makes it crucial to accelerate investment aimed at enhancing productivity growth and thus increase the competitiveness of the Chilean economy.

While the fairly deep Chilean banking and capital markets may have been relatively efficient in financing established enterprises and sectors at a relatively low cost, they may not be able or willing to take on the risk of financing the new enterprises in new sectors that the current and future circumstances of Chile demand, especially at sufficient maturities. Thus, funding *'mission-oriented investments'* that could catalyse transformational impacts in the economy is essential and requires the action of public financial institutions, such as CORFO, capable of channelling sufficient resources to strategic sectors with large positive externalities, such as renewable energy (see section 6.9) (Mazzucato and Penna 2015). Such channelling of public resources would help raise additional private resources, which would co-finance such investments. Thinking of the new industrial revolution worldwide, Chile needs more and better investment in high-speed connectivity, such as a network of fibre optics; it also requires the digitalization of agriculture to improve productivity. It may require large and lumpy finance for major projects that are socially profitable; an example is a potential major investment in Chile's smelting copper capacity, which could help the country move up the value chain in copper exports. Often such activities are not profitable in the short term, as they involve major economic or environmental externalities; also large-scale investment, even if profitable in the long term, may be difficult to fund purely with private finance.

An institution like CORFO could help provide and catalyse funding necessary for such initiatives. In this sense, it seems important both to expand the scale of CORFO and make sure that the instruments it uses are appropriate for the current stage of Chilean development.

Fiscal resources are currently fairly constrained, and perceived to be constrained in Chile (like in many other Latin American countries), as growth has slowed down, and tighter fiscal policies have been adopted. At the same time, there has been greater emphasis in Chile on prioritizing the use of these limited fiscal resources to meet social needs (especially in education), with long-term development benefits. This, however, limits the scale of CORFO, which currently relies mainly on fiscal resources for funding, as there are (or are perceived to be) relatively less fiscal resources available to finance structural transformation, such as support for research and development (R&D), financing innovation in new companies and new sectors.

R&D is particularly key for natural-resource-based economies, which reportedly need to invest more in relation to GDP than other economies to be successful; furthermore, R&D spending is fairly low in Chile, so support by institutions like CORFO, in collaboration with other public and private institutions, is very relevant.

It would therefore seem desirable to use CORFO to help fund and catalyse further private funding towards such key activities. Given Chile's deep domestic capital markets and favourable access to international capital markets, as well as the fact that it has investment grade credit rating, an interesting funding alternative for CORFO would be getting authorization from the Finance Ministry to raise funds on the local capital markets. This is the most regular source of funding for many other national development banks, such as KfW in Germany, the Business Development Corporation (BDC) in Canada, and others. Indeed, according to Luna-Martinez and Vicente (2012), 89 per cent of national development banks borrow from other financial institutions or issue debt on local capital markets; it would therefore seem appropriate for CORFO to do so as well.

This would mean public resources could be significantly leveraged, as the enlarged activities would be financed from the private capital market, and any public contribution would be related to relatively small increases of CORFO's capital, to comply with Basel capital requirements; the latter would be the only part which would go into calculations of the fiscal deficit, as is the case, reportedly, for KfW, for example. Therefore, there would be very limited impact on the fiscal deficit, and CORFO could benefit from a potentially very large expansion, with resources raised on the capital markets to increase its credits and guarantees.

Reportedly, in the late 2000s, the then vice-president of CORFO suggested that CORFO could issue bonds for USD 500 million to fund new credit lines for SMEs (interview). However, the Finance Ministry preferred to increase the fiscal contribution to CORFO. As the precedent for such a proposal exists, and CORFO is authorized to raise funding in this way once the Finance Ministry approves it, this should make it easy for CORFO to raise funds on capital markets.

Besides raising funds in national and international capital markets, CORFO could further increase its scale through additional funding from other development banks. It already successfully taps institutions like the Andean Development Corporation, the Inter-American Development Bank (IADB), and KfW, and could do more; this could be further expanded to include institutions like the CDB, especially given the strong trade and investment links that Chile has with China and the European Investment Bank (EIB).

As will be detailed here, CORFO has been innovative in deploying a number of activities (such as supporting entrepreneurship through innovative programmes like *Start-Up Chile*), and supporting a variety of sectors. However, within the range of instruments it has used, it has given a decreasing role to credit and an increased role to grants and, especially, guarantees. Though this may be a fairly common trend in some Latin American development banks (e.g. Nacional Financiera (NAFINSA) in Mexico), it is different from the instruments used by highly successful banks like German KfW, which continue to use credits, mainly channelled through financial intermediaries, as a major instrument, especially for new sectors (such as renewable energy) and for small and medium enterprises (SMEs); this is the case even though German capital and banking markets are more developed than their Chilean counterparts.

Helping to promote Chilean exports in new sectors, as well as helping Chilean companies to invest abroad, is another key challenge that CORFO should address more to boost Chile's long-term international competitiveness (going beyond sectors where Chilean firms have already successfully expanded abroad, such as retail and paper). This is an important new function of public development banks, carried out by institutions like the CDB and BNDES.

Particularly in this new phase of Chilean development, which urgently requires economic diversification into new sectors, but faces initial risks and uncertainty that may be far higher than in the past, it seems crucial that CORFO should swiftly deploy a full battery of instruments. These should include credits especially, to support more innovative enterprises and sectors that generate a high proportion of employment in the Chilean economy—as well as SMEs more generally—especially for loans of longer maturities, which private banks are less likely to grant. This will allow these companies to obtain enough credit, at sufficiently long maturities and at reasonable cost. Naturally, such an expansion of credit should be combined with the continued use of currently deployed instruments, such as guarantees, grants, and contributions to risk capital. The above-mentioned expansion of the scale of CORFO's resources would thus facilitate not just an increase in the level of activity of the institution, but also allow the deployment of a more complete mix of instruments required to finance private enterprises and support structural diversification.

The chapter is structured as follows: first, in section 6.2, we briefly analyse the history of CORFO, then linking it to the needs of Chile's development model in section 6.3. Section 6.4 outlines CORFO's objectives within the national strategy, while section 6.5 describes the main features of CORFO today, with particular emphasis on its countercyclical role in section 6.6. Then, in sections 6.7 and 6.8 we explain and analyse the main programmes and activities that CORFO pursues currently. This is not easy, as CORFO has developed a large number of instruments and activities; as we will argue, there may be a case for streamlining some of these instruments, making access to them simpler for users, as well as possibly putting greater focus on fewer priority sectors. We then, in section 6.9, examine in some detail the role of CORFO in the development of solar energy in Chile. Finally, we conclude and draw policy implications.

6.2 Brief History of CORFO

Since 1939, CORFO, seen overall by governments of different persuasions as an efficient instrument to serve their development objectives and strategies, has played very varied roles (Muñoz Goma 2009).

Its launch in 1939 made CORFO one of the first national development banks in Latin America, after México's Nafin, established in 1934. At the time, the needs of import substitution industrialization (ISI), blended with the catastrophic consequences of the 1939 Chillán earthquake, set the stage for CORFO's creation. In the initial period, it was a large and influential institution that participated in the funding of over 30 per cent of investments in equipment and machinery and 18 per cent of gross capital formation. (Durán and Fermandois 2011). Furthermore, CORFO created and played an important role in many of the key public enterprises central to Chile's development. In the initial years, these included the enterprise for electricity distribution (ENDESA), steel (CAP), sugar beet processing (IANSA), oil (ENAP), and national airline (LAN). In the 1960s, it continued creating key enterprises, in sectors like telecommunications (ENTEL) and public TV (TVN) (Rivas 2012). CORFO also supported the transition to a more export-oriented model: for example, by providing financial backing to the forestry sector, which helped develop the paper and cellulose industry (interview).

During the Popular Unity government, CORFO played an important role in nationalizing enterprises, whereas under the military government, it did the reverse and was involved in the privatization of many companies. Also under the military government, CORFO was forbidden from owning or creating state enterprises; it is interesting that other national development banks, like KfW, still own shares in public enterprises today. During the 1982/3 debt and banking crisis (which hit the Chilean economy especially hard), as well as more recently during the 2008/9 financial crisis, CORFO played an important countercyclical role by significantly increasing its credit to private enterprises and guarantees for such credit to banks.

When democracy returned, CORFO was in a very weak financial position, with USD 1.6 billion of liabilities linked to the privatization process and over USD 700 million of impaired loans. Some voices then raised the possibility of dissolving CORFO, but the view prevailed that the institution should continue to play a key role in supporting private investment to achieve productive development. CORFO managed to improve its financial position and focus on its new tasks. Furthermore, its credibility was enhanced by a series of independent evaluations of impact, as well as the Ministry of Economy setting clear guidelines for CORFO and identifying challenges (Rivas 2012).

Following suggestions made by the World Bank, CORFO switched from giving credit directly to becoming a second-tier institution providing credit and, increasingly, guarantees through financial intermediaries. The shift towards reducing the role of credit, while increasing the role of guarantees and targeted grants, has accelerated since the Pinera government came in.

Currently, CORFO implements long-term strategic goals determined by the National Council for Innovation and Competitiveness (CNIC), which advises the executive and legislative branches of government. Several ministers sit on the board of CORFO. Thus CORFO is closely linked to the development aims of the government, while having a close dialogue with the private sector.

6.3 Development Strategy in Chile and the Role of CORFO

The legacy of privatization during the military regime and of unpaid debts to the institution relegated CORFO mostly to tasks related to financial management in the early 1990s. The difficult financial situation that CORFO inherited required efforts directed towards a solution. Thus, for a time, CORFO's historical role was pushed into the background of its activities.

With the return of democracy, a debate started on the appropriateness of keeping CORFO. Within the political and academic sphere, questioning the very idea of economic intervention through industrial policies had become quite widespread. However, the prevailing stance suggested that even within a market economy, there are important market imperfections and failures, which can undermine productivity and overall growth. These market failures and imperfections, as well as some (then weak) concerns about the need for a structural diversification of the Chilean economy, justified policy interventions that looked to correct market imperfections.

The most decisive step towards official confirmation that a policy agenda for productive development was needed was the design of new CORFO instruments, as well as evaluations to assess their impact, which were especially important to justifying them to the Finance Ministry.

Subsequently, with the creation of the National Council of Innovation and Competitiveness, more ambitious progress was achieved in terms of the need to direct efforts at the sectorial level. A study by the Boston Consulting Group proposed ten sectors as priority: aquaculture, functional foods, fruit farming, mining, pig and poultry farming, global services, special-interest tourism, logistics and transportation, wideband, and financial services. A committee of ministers chose five clusters, to propose a policy design that would boost each industry.

In recent times, CORFO and the Ministry of Economy have launched the Strategic Programme of Smart Specialization (SPSS) or *Transform Programme*: 'The Transform Programme aims to improve the competitiveness of our economy through the development of eleven strategic sectors.' This statement set out a commitment to the implementation of productive development policies. Chile had already embarked on this path with the proposal made earlier by the National Council of Innovation and Competitiveness.

'Chile needs to change its productive structure—with the production and export of goods based not only on natural resources—and advance towards a more sophisticated, specialized, diverse, and innovative economy, which will enable it to create a new national productive baseline' (Chile Transforma 2017). Productive sectors chosen for the SPSS are high-grade mining, tourism, health foods, building industry, fishing and aquaculture, solar industry, logistics for exports, smart industries, creative economy, advanced manufacture and technologies, and health services.

In 2014, the Productivity, Innovation, and Growth Agenda was launched, which aims to overcome obstacles preventing the increase of economic productivity. A Fund for Strategic Investments (FSI) was created to finance initiatives aimed at improving productivity and productive diversification. Among the funded projects is the SPSS or the Transform Programme (Fondo de Inversión Estratégica 2017).

Priority sectors for the FSI are fishing and sustainable aquaculture, sustainable tourism, solar industry, logistics, sustainable building industry, advanced manufacturing, smart industry, creative industry, services and health technologies, high-grade mining, and healthy food.

The previous paragraphs show clearly which sectors Chile is looking to promote; the Chilean productive development strategy is thus set. However, different government entities play a role in the productive transformation of the country, often with their own policy agendas, and there is not full coordination between them, nor with the private sector. It is important for them to coordinate better, and develop and implement a productive development approach in a strategic way at an institutional level.

6.4 CORFO and its Institutional Relationship with the Government

CORFO is attached to the Ministry of Economy, and is led by a governing board chaired by the Minister. The Vice-President of the board and the Executive Vice-President of CORFO are appointed by the President of the Republic. Moreover, this board includes the Ministers of Foreign Affairs, Finance, Social Development, and Agriculture.

Until 2006, the relationship between CORFO and the government was focused on the composition of its board and the reach of its instruments and programmes, involving the participation of other ministries. The creation of the National Innovation and Competitiveness Council established a new institutional design to support the proposed national strategy (Rivas 2012). Within this strategy, CORFO has a defined role, and it is therefore possible to identify its relations with other government institutions more clearly.

The objective of the National Council of Innovation and Competitiveness, apart from setting long-term strategic guidelines for the policy, is to propose ideas for the use of the Innovation and Competitiveness Fund (ICF), funded by income from the royalties paid by the mining sector. ICF works as a financial implementation entity for CORFO and Comisión Nacional de Investigación Científica y Technológica (CONICYT); the latter, as a branch of the Ministry of Education, specializes in tasks related to science, technology, and production of human capital.

There is also the Committee of Ministers for Innovation, whose executive secretariat is headed by the Ministry of Economy. The Innovation Department of the Ministry of Economy is in charge of coordinating several public entities related to the programmes defined by the innovation policy and strategy.

In addition to the innovation strategy, there is the Productivity Agenda for Innovation and Growth, which has a more short- and medium-term scope of action. CORFO and the Agenda are related through the Strategic Inversion Fund, which finances CORFO programmes that are aligned with the objectives proposed for the Agenda.

Furthermore, CORFO is committed to policies and instruments that go beyond the national system of innovation. A big percentage of their programmes are own-initiatives funded mainly by the allocated public budget.

The national system of innovation establishes networks that only respond to one part of the productive development policy of the country. The institutional organization needs to be expanded to all the spheres of action of public policies working on productive transformation, search for innovation, and promotion of competitiveness, with the aim of coordinating all efforts and available resources efficiently to maximize the impact on the economy.

6.5 CORFO Today

In 2015, CORFO had total assets worth USD 6,272 million, which represent 2.6 per cent of Chile's GDP. When analysing their composition, we can note that in 2015, the financial support deployed by CORFO (through grants, credits, and guarantees; see Table 6.1) amounted to USD 2,863 million, which represents only 1.2 per cent of Chile's GDP. This makes CORFO significantly smaller in scale than national development banks in other countries, such as KfW, CDB, and BNDES.

As pointed out, CORFO's main financial support to the private sector in recent years has not been through loans, which only amounted to USD 74 million in 2016, but through loan guarantees to financial institutions. By 2016, the guarantee stock level was USD 2,467 million. Indeed, in GDP terms, CORFO's guarantees are among the highest granted by a public institution in Latin America. Given the importance of guarantees in CORFO's current activities, we focus more on this instrument in section 6.8.

It seems useful to point out here, that there is a perception among many observers and users of CORFO's resources, that the institution has too many

Table 6.1. CORFO's financial support

Financial Support (million USD)	2010	2011	2012	2013	2014	2015	2016
Subsidies	194.54	181.89	194.68	199.61	304.96	332.94	332.17
Guarantees	1,219.59	2,277.88	2,541.56	3,414.83	2,729.42	2,360.37	2,457.36
Loans	508.34	192.97	166.41	104.08	80.13	61.07	74.35
TOTAL	*1,922.47*	*2,652.74*	*2,902.65*	*3,718.52*	*3,114.50*	*2,754.38*	*2,863.88*

priority sectors and too many instruments. As one observer commented, 'for every problem, there is a separate instrument' (interview). Reportedly, users also find procedures for application for resources in some programmes unclear and cumbersome, and sometimes requiring major transaction costs, which prospective applicants can find discouraging. There are exceptions, and users report that some programmes—including guarantees—operate in a fairly agile way. Streamlining priority sectors and instruments, and working on the simplification and transparency of application procedures, may be a valuable and high priority task to increase CORFO effectiveness.

6.6 CORFO's Countercyclical Role

The role that governments should play in the financial system has been much debated. Some authors had negative views about the role of public development banks as growth catalysers, basing their critique on the risk of political favouritism and corruption, as well as arguing for the efficiency of private financial markets (La Porta et al. 2002; Sapienza 2004). During the 1980s and 1990s, public banks were severely criticized by neo-classical economists, who argued that what they called 'financial repression' was inefficient. Thus, regions such as Latin America, where 65 per cent of the banks were publicly owned during the 1970s, went through massive privatizations in the 1990s, and by the mid-1990s only 40 per cent remained state-owned (Micco and Panizza 2005). Nonetheless, in the aftermath of the 2008/9 financial crisis, the previous trend was reversed in many emerging and developed economies (Culpeper 2012). In European economies, national development banks were expanded or even created, and the regional development bank, the European Investment Bank, has been given a far greater role since the 2008/9 crisis as well (Griffith-Jones and Cozzi 2016).

In many Latin American economies, public banks' operations surged due to the countercyclical lending they deployed after the crisis, while private banks' lending shrunk (Figure 6.1). Empirical evidence has been collected by authors such as Bertay, Demirgüç-Kunt, and Huizinga, who studied more than 1600 banks in both emerging and developed economies and found that 'state banks can play a useful role in stabilizing credit over the business cycle as well as during periods of financial instability' (2015: 327). Furthermore, Brei and Schclarek in Chapter 11 of this volume, provide empirical evidence that shows how countercyclical public development banks have been.

In the case of Chile, Banco del Estado, the public bank that lends directly to small businesses, increased its loans sharply, while private loans plummeted. Ribeiro de Mendonça, Ana Rosa, and Sibin (2008) show how Banco del Estado

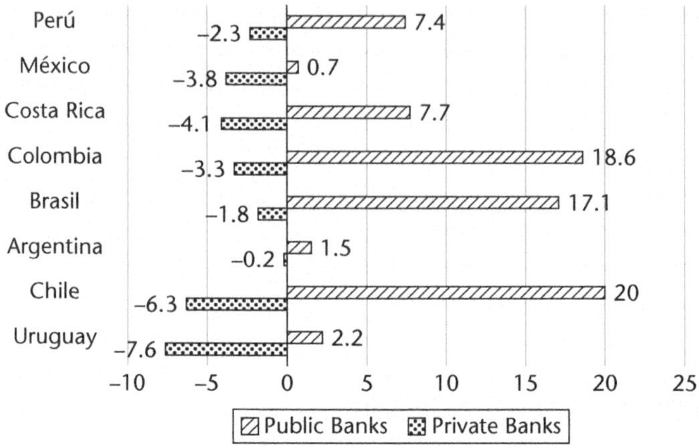

Figure 6.1. Loans made by private and public banks (percentage variation 2008–9)
Source: Own elaboration based on ALIDE (2009)

increased its corporate loans by 32 per cent in 2009, while others shrunk more than 7 per cent. At the time, Banco del Estado also encouraged the construction sector by reducing mortgage interest rates. This was part of a more general anti-cyclical policy encouraged by the national government, which, in the wake of the international financial crisis, increased its fiscal expenditure by 15 per cent in a clear countercyclical move.

Chile's previous adoption of the so-called Cyclically Adjusted Balance (CAB) rule compels the government to follow spending targets that enable the deployment of general countercyclical fiscal policies, which is very positive. However, authors such as Ffrench-Davis (2010) argue that it was only during the 2008/9 global financial crisis that the fiscal rule operated in a really countercyclical manner, whereas this should become the case generally. Instead, he regards the general Chilean rule as more 'cyclically-neutral' and not sufficiently countercyclical, though superior to the procyclical nature of private finance, both domestically and internationally.

It is important to stress, in the context of this chapter, that CORFO, whose funding sources are to an important extent provided by the Chilean Finance Ministry, also expanded its programmes countercyclically. This is clearly evident when examining CORFO's annual budgets, which almost doubled from 2008 to 2009. CORFO provided liquidity to the financial market by injecting an additional USD 850 million in 2008, intended to leverage USD 1,800 million. Out of this figure, most of the money was targeted at long-term investments (USD 500 million), but short-term lending was also supported. Ensuring solid payment chains across the different sectors is of the utmost importance in crisis settings. Thus, CORFO tendered USD 300 million to support working capital through the banking system and used factoring mechanisms that could target the usually unattended smaller firms.

Apart from providing liquidity to the financial system, CORFO also made most of its guarantee scheme's requirements more flexible and increased its limits to expand its reach (Alide 2009). Overall, between 2007 and 2011, CORFO increased its guarantees for SMEs seven times (Hermann 2014). This partly reflected the shift of preference for the guarantee instrument, but also had an important countercyclical aim.

Along with the general countercyclical stimulus implemented by national governments in Latin America, national development banks had a crucial role in supporting the economy, when private lending fell (Alide 2009; Griffith-Jones et al. in Chapter 1 of this volume). It is also important to notice that the countercyclical role of national development banks is complemented by the important countercyclical role that regional and multilateral development banks play; this was very clear in the case of CAF and Inter-American Development Bank lending to Latin American countries in the wake of the 2008/9 crisis.

6.7 Areas of Activity

In terms of areas of activity, CORFO has three focal areas: productive diversification, support to innovation and entrepreneurship, and foreign and national investment promotion (Bitran 2016).

6.7.1 *Structural Transformation and Economic Diversification*

The total factor productivity (TFP) growth rate in Chile dropped from an average of 2.4 per cent in the 1990s to 0.5 per cent in the 2000s, a situation that becomes even gloomier when considering manufacturing TFP. In addition, the export sophistication index significantly decreased in the last years of the 2000s (Bitran 2016). These figures illustrate that Chile needs to develop dynamic competitive advantages and achieve structural transformation, through greater and 'smarter' diversification. The need for such a strategy has received increased support in the last few years, especially from the Bachelet government; the urgency of both increasing productivity and diversifying the Chilean economy was made clear by the sharp fall in copper prices and the apparent end of the 'commodities super-cycle'.

CORFO is seen by the Chilean government as a valuable policy instrument, which should play a key role in the coordination of private companies, channelling appropriate finance for them, and identifying market gaps as well as opportunities. Furthermore, far higher priority than in the past is given to the task of diversifying the Chilean economy, and especially exports. In this context, in 2014 the Chilean government launched the Transform Programme, which makes CORFO responsible for thirty-seven 'Strategic Schemes of Intelligent Specialization' and grants support, including subsidies to ten sectors, selected as engines for development.

The main goal of this tool is to try to diversify Chile's productive structure, moving from an economy exclusively based on natural resources to one that is more complex, knowledge-intensive, and competitive. For example, in 2013 CORFO launched a financial programme called 'Engineering 2030' to help Chile's economy diversify and become more knowledge-intensive. The scheme consists of subsidies to Chilean universities, which aspire to transform their educational programme in engineering, focusing on key areas (health and sustainability) that could boost international competitiveness across several productive sectors (interview). With the same developmental purpose, complementary subsidy lines are given to 'strategic nodes', which aim to promote engagement among entrepreneurs and SMEs in order to foster collaboration in areas of mutual interest. The type of nodes covered are related to public and private coordination failures and include market information, quality control, or the improvement of standards for suppliers; the project is presented by an intermediary consultant, who deploys the programme. An important difficulty of using nodes is the risk of capture by consultants, which can be minimized by filtering demands by companies requiring these services (interview).

Also, initiatives such as Programa de Proyectos Asociativos de Fomento (PROFO) aim to enhance firms' associativity and grouping for common tasks to gain competitiveness in both internal and external markets. This programme was inspired by similar initiatives supporting clusters in Spain and Italy; its success is illustrated by the example of small winemakers, who used to sell to larger producers, but decided to team up and improve market access by constituting their own brand (Rivas 2012). In a similar way, the Programa de Desarrollo de Proveedores (PDP) scheme provides subsidies to stimulate local value chains and co-finance the development and improved quality of local providers. Overall, financial support to encourage competitiveness, given through these different programmes to 24,963 beneficiaries involved in 1473 projects, amounted to USD 60.2 million in 2015.

6.7.2 *Innovation and Entrepreneurship*

Leapfrogging into higher value-added activities in Chile entails taking full advantage of previous productive capabilities and enhancing them through the creation and diffusion of new technological opportunities. However, a reverse trend seems to have unfolded in Chile in the last decade, when the percentage of innovative firms plummeted from 37.9 per cent in 2004 to 16.6 per cent in 2014 and expenditure in R&D lagged behind many countries, at only 0.39 per cent of GDP (Bitran 2016). To tackle this obstacle, and in consideration of the constraints faced by uncertain innovative projects and start-ups with no track record, a significant number of CORFO's programmes rightly focus on this area, where externalities and high-risk investment play such an important role.

According to the Global Entrepreneurship Index, Chile is positioned among the top twenty entrepreneurship ecosystems in the world and first in Latin America, creating more than 200 new dynamic firms per year. The main CORFO programmes to support entrepreneurs are 'Seed Capital', which had applications from over 5200 firms and granted over USD 4 million to 118 of them in 2015; 'Start-Up Chile', further detailed in section 6.8.2; and the 'Scheme for Regional Entrepreneurship and Innovation', with more than 250 applicants and over USD 2.5 million granted to eighty projects. The budget for financial support to innovation exceeded USD 60 million in 2015, which entailed a 98 per cent increase compared to the average in 2010–13. These programmes include interesting instruments, such as tax exemptions for R&D given to private companies. A significant 80 per cent of the 680 approved projects were from SMEs. Also, CORFO stimulated the creation of technology centres and technology transfer programmes, which received support for over USD 33 million in 2015. The above-mentioned schemes, in large part, provide funds given as subsidies, granted through public tenders. Subsidies disbursed by CORFO in 2016 totalled over USD 330 million (Table 6.1).

Part of the rationale for a structure of instruments that gives priority to guarantees and grants is that, overall, there is plenty of funding available in Chilean private markets for established companies, allegedly for relatively long maturities at relatively low costs. Loans by CORFO to commercial banks for on-lending are apparently seen as less necessary than in other Latin American countries. This seems, however, not to be the case for innovative enterprises and start-ups, due to uncertainty—a situation typical for new activities and enterprises, which often do not have tangible guarantees; nor is it clear that long-maturity loans are available for SME projects.

The fact that such high priority is given to sectorial diversification, which implies going into new sectors where uncertainty and externalities are higher, as well as to the need for Chilean companies to invest abroad in new sectors, implies private banks and capital markets may not be up to the task on their own, especially of providing long-term finance to new sectors, as well as to new enterprises and start-ups.

Acknowledging this funding gap, CORFO, since 1999, has been providing long-term resources to expand the role of risk capital funds, which aim to support innovative firms, both during their early and growth stages. Up to 2016, the historical investments amounted to USD 630 million, provided to forty-three funds and 194 beneficiaries, the vast majority of which were SMEs in the information, technology, and communications (ICT) sector (interview).

Furthermore, there are gaps in Chilean non-banking financial intermediaries, such as for cooperative financial institutions, leasing, and factoring companies; CORFO is developing initiatives to support the development of these institutions. Often the issue with the funding that these institutions are able to provide relates not so much to the amounts granted, but to the conditions (of cost and especially maturity). Furthermore, these financial institutions need both financial support and technical assistance, which CORFO is providing with its new initiative, funded by KfW. Also, the banking system is fairly concentrated in Chile, which can lead to excessive spreads on borrowing, and very high return on equity of banks (interview). CORFO and other institutions are designing measures to deal with these market gaps and imperfections.

6.7.3 *Foreign and National Investment Promotion*

CORFO works in cooperation with Chile's Foreign Investment Committee to attract foreign capital to the Chilean market. Also, CORFO encourages local investments by granting loan guarantees, financing Reciprocal Guarantee Institutions (IGR), and operating through financial institutions.

The guarantee mechanism consists of ten different programmes. The main three are FOGAIN, by far the largest scheme, which represented 93 per cent of CORFO's guarantees transactions in 2016, and covers long-term investments and working capital; the other interesting programmes are COBEX, which covers export operations and PROINVESTMENT, a new programme that represents only 3 per cent of the guarantee portfolio and encourages the long-term investments of larger firms. In addition, CORFO also provides financial support to Chilean Institutions of Mutual Guarantee, namely IGRs.

The IGR system was born in Europe and diffused into some Latin American countries in the 1990s. In Chile, the IGR fund was established in 2007 and its norms have been designed by CORFO, which can leverage private investments up to ten times. However, its size has always been modest, covering only 2 per cent of the guarantees issued between 2010 and 2016.

CORFO's main area of intervention is now guarantees. However, this focus has only been stressed since March 2010, when the FOGAIN and IGR systems were reformulated by CORFO. Originally, public guarantees were mainly issued by Fondo de Garantía para el Pequeño Empresario (FOGAPE), a government fund launched in 1982. Until 2011, FOGAPE was still the main protagonist in the public guarantee landscape, far ahead of the IGR system and CORFO. For instance, in 2010 the number of its transactions reached 76,171, while IGR and CORFO only recorded 1522 and 4484 transactions respectively. However, by 2013, FOGAPE's activities had dropped by 36 per cent while CORFO's surged by almost 2000 per cent, to more than 93,000 guarantees. It is noticeable, though, that apart from taking the lead in the guarantee system, CORFO's intervention also enabled a general increase of support to a wider range of beneficiaries. This is because, unlike FOGAPE, which only supported small and microenterprises, CORFO reached medium-sized firms (Hermann 2014).

It is also noteworthy that, at the same time, in 2011, the credit lines managed by CORFO fell sharply, dropping 62 per cent in only one year. In the period between 2010 and 2014, the value of loans fell even more dramatically by 84 per cent, with some fairly minor recovery in 2016 (Table 6.1). In 2011 and in the following years, many medium- and long-term credit lines for SMEs ceased to exist, which partly explains the sharp fall in the level of loans (interview). This structural shift in CORFO, away from the loans that were granted during President Piñera's government, is attributed by some observers to the belief that public financial institutions should not crowd out private banking, but instead cover the private banking sector's risks, by guaranteeing its loans.

6.8 CORFO Programmes Relevant Today

6.8.1 *Impact of Guarantee Programmes*

An interesting question is why CORFO has used guarantees far more than credits in recent years, a trend that became particularly marked during President Piñera's 2010–14 government, even if it continued in later years. Though guarantees are clearly a valuable instrument, especially for providing access to companies without sufficient physical assets to offer as collateral (e.g. those who have mainly intangible assets, like an innovative idea), and they allow for additional leverage of CORFO's capital, guarantees often need to be complemented by other instruments, such as credits and subsidies.

The emphasis on guarantees seems based on the idea that banking and capital markets are well developed in Chile, which is true. However, this line would also argue that guarantees are sufficient to encourage additional private finance to previously excluded SMEs and that credit granted by institutions like CORFO may 'crowd out' private finance. This is certainly not true for financing in sectors where there is much uncertainty, where economic, social, and environmental externalities are not privately internalized, and where there is a need for patient capital (e.g. new strategic sectors that demand high initial investments, innovative companies, etc.) and in sectors or activities in which private finance is unwilling to take the risks, especially on its own.

Furthermore, the problem with guarantees is that, although profits from the loans will go to the private financiers, the risks or at least those portions covered by the guarantees, will be assumed by the public sector. This asymmetry may be problematic, as it may result in large contingent liabilities for CORFO. In this sense, it is important that enough provisions are made upfront; CORFO seems to have been prudent in this respect by restricting the scale of its leverage well below the limits established in its regulations. It is a source of some concern that CORFO's guarantee programmes, which have been scaled up so much, have only partly been evaluated; however, the evaluation of FOGAIN, which represents the largest guarantee mechanism, has shown positive results, especially in terms of broadening financial inclusion.

Indeed, the FOGAIN scheme was evaluated in 2013 through qualitative interviews, in which 84 per cent of respondents declared they had experienced a positive impact from using the scheme, 40 per cent in terms of productivity, 16 per cent in terms of increased sales, 13 per cent in terms of profit, and 5 per cent regarding employees. Furthermore, the scheme enabled the financial inclusion of previously excluded companies, which amounted to 15 per cent of the total.

The impact of guarantee granting is allegedly large, as the funds are allowed to extend collateral for up to eight times its value, implying high leverage. The lack of adequate collateral is one of the most severe limitations to financing long-term projects in Chile. In many cases, traditional banks demand real assets that duplicate the value of the loan, to cover any potential unpaid interests or associated expenses. Thus, many firms, especially SMEs, that intend to pursue investments to increase their productive capabilities or efficiency, cannot access such funding, unless it is provided with guarantees, an area where CORFO plays a key role. Though the guarantee instruments have been successful in helping to leverage additional credit, they have reportedly been less successful in lowering its cost (interview).

6.8.2 *Start-Up Chile*

The main aim of the National Innovation Policy, designed by the Innovation Department of the Ministry of Economy, is the promotion of entrepreneurship and innovation to achieve the objectives of the productive development strategy. The plan placed great importance on the establishment of an 'innovation and entrepreneurship ecosystem', creating the Start-Up programme, a competition for global entrepreneurs that offers rewards to entrepreneurial initiatives with high potential in Chile.

Participants in the programme have to develop their projects with minimal financial resources (bootstrap) within a six-month deadline. The grants reached up to USD 40,000 for seed capital and a one-year work visa. The pilot plan, carried out by Innova Chile with twenty-two start-up projects, was successfully completed during the testing phase. The programme was then officially implemented.

Since mid-2011, more than ten generations, with around a hundred projects, have gone through Start-Up. Over the years, modifications have been made to the benefits and requirements. Currently, Start-Up offers 90 per cent of total programme cost funding, with a maximum of USD 40,000 per project. Beneficiaries should contribute 10 per cent of the expenses. There is an additional prize of USD 20,000 for carrying out the projects in regions outside the capital and for Chilean repatriated students with postgraduate degrees obtained in the best 150 universities around the world. Finally, successfully completed projects can apply for a second stage of funding, which can reach up to USD 120,000.

Within the institutional framework of the national system of innovation, the impact evaluation of the instruments and programmes is a key element. In 2015, the Ministry of Economy hired an outside consultant to evaluate Start-Up. The main objective was to evaluate specific results from the programme, as well as assess the aggregate impact on the economy.

For the evaluation, four objectives of the programme were identified: (i) world class entrepreneurs develop companies with global potential in Chile (attraction/retention); (ii) local entrepreneurs develop knowledge, skills, and networks; (iii) other participants in the Chilean entrepreneur ecosystem improve their access to information and become more entrepreneurial and open to innovation; and (iv) the international community improves its perception of the Chilean innovation and entrepreneurship ecosystem (Verde 2016).

The first nine generations of beneficiaries, involving 785 projects, were evaluated. The methodology included surveys of project leaders and interviews of participants from the national entrepreneurship ecosystem, considering intermediate and final variables. Results showed that the programme had a positive impact on raising capital and the amount of capital raised. However, the programme did not have a statistically meaningful impact for the projects in terms of continuity of the start-up, sales (total value and growth), profits, exports, level of employment, later support from business incubators and accelerators, and number of subsequent entrepreneurial ventures launched by the project leader.

Finally, the evaluation made a series of suggestions, including defining as the main purpose that world-level entrepreneurs have to develop start-ups with high global potential in Chile (a recommendation that has started to be implemented), as well as prioritizing criteria related to the entrepreneurship potential and its permanence in the country, and the incorporation of specialization alternatives for the programme, by market or technology.

The evaluation carried out by Verde clearly has value regarding the understanding of the impact of Start-Up on the economy. However, while having evaluation reports is key to testing the effectiveness of instruments, the results have to be interpreted within the context of the limitations of the methodology used, in order to determine the value of the evaluation and its limits.

The high reputation of the Start-Up Chile project is evident and acknowledged in the national and international press as well as in publications by important international organizations, such as the Organization for Economic Cooperation and Development (OECD) Development Centre, which concluded that the Start-Up programmes reveal a different, more dynamic side to the Latin American region, and to Chile, specifically (OECD 2016). According to the OECD (2016), 'Start-Up Chile media impact has helped make Chile a talking point around the world and inspired young people to become entrepreneurs.' Besides, Start-Up Chile has been a model for the creation of similar initiatives aimed at establishing favourable environments for start-ups in other countries of the region (www.startupchile.org). Engineering projects, 3D educational projects, applications to facilitate communication with suppliers, and schemes that offer digital books to children represent the range of entrepreneurship projects that have successfully gone through the programme.

At the end of 2015, the family of start-ups in Chile included one unicorn (start-up of at least USD 1 billion), four centaurs (with a valuation between USD 100 million and USD 1 billion), and thirty-one little ponies (with a valuation between USD 10 and USD 100 million). This is one of the most positive situations in the Latin American region, and is even comparable in scale to Singapore, one of the vanguard countries in terms of entrepreneurship, which has generated two unicorns, twelve centaurs, and twenty-seven little ponies (OECD 2016).

General perceptions of Start-Up within the Chilean innovation ecosystem are positive, particularly due to the way the programme is conceived, with identification and project selection, and the resulting international positioning of Chile within the start-up field (Rivas 2012). Assessing the overall impact of the programme from a broader economic point of view (value generation, quality employment, productive diversification, and sophistication) is complex, but there have been positive individual results from the projects, and perceptions of the programme show a favourable picture regarding its impact in Chile. Specific problems, such as excessive concentration in the capital city, are seemingly being corrected, with special emphasis on encouraging start-ups in different regions.

One of the benefits of the CORFO Start-Up programme, which has its own dedicated division in CORFO, is that it has encouraged the modernization, improvement, and broadening of the policy mix to support these companies in Chile. For example, relevant regulations have been simplified, with a new law that allows people to start a new business in a single day. Furthermore, available financing has been expanded to support different phases of the projects. CORFO, the rest of the government, the private sector, and the universities seem to be collaborating effectively to support the creation of start-ups, which will hopefully contribute to the greater technological sophistication and diversification of the Chilean economy.

6.9 Green Industrial Policy: The Case of Solar Power in Chile

Designing an effective strategy for development is still a matter for debate. Many mainstream scholars allege that the state should not build capabilities and steer resources to specific sectors because they tend to 'pick losers', thus creating inefficiencies. More heterodox economists, such as Chang (2002), show that developed countries, which had applied highly interventionist policies to promote a leap in their development, are now 'kicking away the ladder' to prevent emerging countries from climbing a few rungs. Some authors may claim that boosting a global green growth strategy to reduce carbon emissions could hamper developing countries' ability to follow the growth path of the global North. However, there is growing consensus that green growth could act as a job-creating, inclusive, developmental strategy, if correctly encouraged.

According to Carlota Perez (in Mazzucato and Jacobs 2016), the next techno-economic paradigm could take a green direction, due to the innovative potential of green projects and their ability to transform linked industries and renovate societal consumption habits. Thus, developing countries seeking to take advantage of this new 'window of opportunity' in development should build capabilities around these technologies (Perez 2010). Latin American countries, such as Chile, highly endowed with natural resources, could use them as a platform for development. Renewable energy technologies (RET), such as solar energy, on which we focus, have the potential to catalyse inclusive growth and sustainable development for various reasons.

Firstly, in Chile, diversifying the energy matrix through the incorporation of renewable energy sources (RES) was necessary to gain more self-sufficiency and stability in energy provision. In the 1990s, Chile's energy generation was based on large hydroelectric projects, insufficient when demand increased and droughts turned more frequent. The country imported gas from Argentina and invested in combined-cycle power stations. However, since the mid-2000s,

Argentina stopped providing gas at a convenient price and Chile suffered provision shortages (Nasirov and Silva 2014). In 2008, Chile, seeking to diversify its energy matrix, launched its Non-Conventional Renewable Energy policy (NCRE). The law established a 10 per cent renewable energy target for 2024. However, the NCRE policy proved so successful that, by 2012, Chile had already met a 7 per cent target. In 2013, a new target of 20 per cent was set for 2025. Stabilizing the energy supply by developing RES has had a huge impact on individual and industrial consumers, who can access energy without interruptions and at a lower price. The incorporation of NCREs to Chile's last electricity tender, in 2015, reduced the price by 40 per cent, from USD 47 MWh to USD 29 MWh.

Secondly, a mission-oriented policy to develop the solar power industry (for which Chile has great comparative natural advantages) is helping to catalyse sustainable and inclusive growth. It incentivizes local producers to develop innovative business models that introduce new technologies and use local natural resources. It fosters dynamic comparative advantages that could position Chile as an internationally competitive producer. Besides this potential for exporting renewables to neighbouring countries, there is also the possibility of exporting industrial products produced with renewable energy, which can reach new market niches and secure higher prices.

Currently, only 17 per cent of the solar energy firms are local, but the target for 2050 is to reach 55 per cent of the market (Fundación Chile 2015). In addition to the limitations that local players encounter as they seek to compete with foreign solar power firms, they also find it difficult to take advantage of the upstream and downstream positive externalities that this new industry creates. Foreign firms have high quality standards, which are not always met by local players. In the case of Chile, most solar firms' suppliers are from China and Europe. Thus, the scope to add local value in the solar energy value chain is reduced. Nonetheless, Fundación Chile's report shows that Chilean companies have a potential niche, as providers of solar power plants' related services, such as the provision of software products to measure and control energy supply or engineering services (2015). The study estimates that more than 45,000 new jobs could be created in Chile.

Thirdly, providing solar energy contributes to reducing inequality and social exclusion, by giving access to electricity to off-grid remote rural areas, based on a cost-effective new business model. One essential aspect for this to work is to grant financial facilities to rural households to acquire the panels and pay for the energy. Digital finance solutions, such as Pay-As-You-Go platforms to pay for solar energy consumption, have become increasingly popular in African and Asian countries, but they need to be developed in Latin America. In Chile, more than 3500 rural communities are still excluded from the interconnected power system (Erlick 2015) and could take advantage of Pay-As-You-Go systems. This figures in the 'Energy 2050' policy, which proposes energy access to 100 per cent of Chile's vulnerable households by 2050. Furthermore, the Ministry of Energy encourages the use of solar panels on the rooftops of every household, small and medium businesses, and public buildings. This initiative targets energy self-sufficiency for regulated clients, who can also provide their surplus energy to the grid (Relac 2016b).

The impact of using technology innovations to grant access to decentralized energy solutions is immediate. It bolsters job creation as it enables business to grow by giving them more time to operate and improves education conditions by giving children more time to study. This could bring new opportunities to achieve transformational social change and development outcomes in developing countries. According to Ban Ki-Moon (2011), former Secretary General of the United Nations, USD 48 billion per year need to be invested to reach universal energy access by 2030.

A final reason to deploy a green growth strategy is to enhance environmental impact. In 2015, Chile committed to the Paris Agreement and its global goal of mitigating climate change by reducing fossil fuel energy sources and carbon emissions. According to the Natural Resources Defense Council (NRDC) Issue Brief (2013), targeting the 20 per cent would reduce CO_2 emissions by 83 million tons. In addition, if hydro projects are replaced by NCRE, savings in water consumption will represent 11 per cent, significant when considering Chile's lack of access to water.

Currently, Chile is among the highest energy consumers in Latin America, with 3568 kWh per capita, but it produces less than 35 per cent of what it consumes. Thus, encouraging diversification of energy sources is crucial for a long-term development strategy. The government's decision to set a green policy direction was initially reflected in the National Energy Strategy 2012–30, documented by Chile's Ministry of Energy (Agostini et al. 2015). Later, the current government launched a new energy policy, called 'Energy 2050', which established a 70 per cent threshold of NCRE to be reached by 2050.

Within non-conventional sources, the generation distribution is even between wind, with 28 per cent of the market, small hydro with 23 per cent, bioenergy with 23 per cent, and solar with 21 per cent (Centre for Innovation and Development of Sustainble Energy (CIFES) 2015). Installed capacity for electricity generation based on renewables is also evenly distributed, but varies substantially by region (see Figure 6.2). However, solar power in Chile is regarded as one of the sources with the largest estimated potential. The Atacama Desert, in north Chile, has the world's most powerful solar radiation. The location of these photovoltaic (PV) panels is strategic, because they feed energy into the Northern Interconnected Power System (SING) used by mining companies, which are the largest energy consumers in Chile (Griffith-Jones et al. 2017).

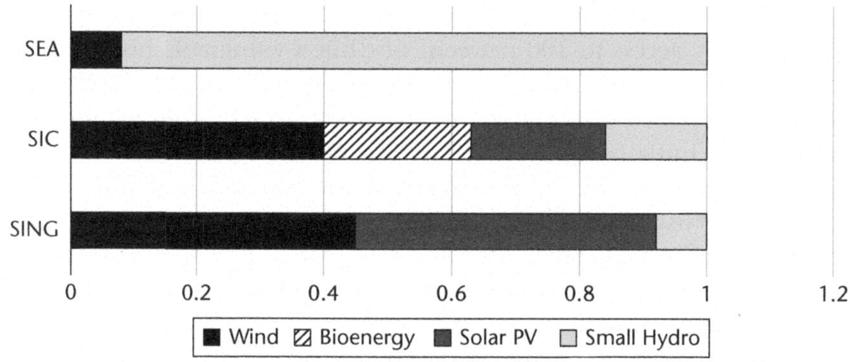

Figure 6.2. Non-conventional renewable energy (NCRE), installed capacity by region
Source: Own elaboration based on CIFES (2015)

However, both financial and non-financial barriers impede the deployment of renewables at full capacity in Chile. As Nasirov et al. (2015) show, many renewable energy projects approved by Chile's Environmental Evaluation Service have not gone to market yet. In 2015, only fifty-two projects with capacity to generate power for 2338 MW were under construction, while approvals reached a power generation capacity of 17,543 MW (CIFES 2015). While this section will mainly focus on the financial constraints, many other limitations may be involved in preventing these projects' deployment.

Among the many non-financial barriers to development are, for instance, price instability, contract negotiations, path dependence, and infrastructure conditions related to the poor grid connection between the SING and the Southern Interconnected Power System (SIC) are also factors. All these issues impose constraints on the supply side. However, policymakers should also focus on the demand side, which may frustrate promising projects from taking place if, for instance, local communities oppose PV solar projects because they occupy vast land portions. This has been raised by 'Energy 2050', which introduced a requirement for community-firm 'associativism' in every green energy project. Greater efforts to involve local representatives are needed to prevent opposition (Moguillansky 2016). In this regard, Germany's 'Energiewende' ('Energy Turnaround') green policy is well known for its capacity to involve the local community in the construction process, providing them with clear information on the benefits of green energy (Zoellner et al. 2008). In fact, many of the actions taken by KfW, Germany's national development bank, went far beyond funding green energy producers; they also targeted consumers by helping to promote the green economy and funding (and even subsidizing) households to increase their energy efficiency. Considering both sides of the green economy when designing and implementing renewable energy policy seems key.

However, one of the main barriers to the deployment of renewable energy projects is financial. Long-term innovative projects have limited access to traditional financial sources due to their particular characteristics. Their future cash flows are uncertain, their projects' payback periods lengthy, and their technical specificities difficult for credit-rating evaluators to assess and monitor. Finally, positive externalities from green growth projects, such as carbon emission reduction or job creation, are not internalized by private investors. States conducting mission-oriented policies that intend to shape the market in a 'green direction' ought to support NRCE projects with long-term, patient, public funding (Culpeper 2012). In particular, Chile's solar projects have a payback period of eight or nine years on average and the private financial sector is not familiar with potential risks (Moguillansky 2016). Moreover, local bankers have limited experience with project finance structures, the mechanism through which these projects are usually funded (Nasirov et al. 2015). Local companies that intend to enter the solar industry often have no track record or real collateral. On the contrary, the players in the electricity market that can use contracts as collateral are the traditional providers, who are frequently reluctant to diversify into green energy.

Traditional electricity generation firms in Chile did not show an interest in the new market, but they are gradually being compelled to diversify their services into new venues such as desalination, due to the sudden increase of players in the electricity market and its plummeting price. However, they are still protected by national regulation, which ensures a 30 per cent technical minimum for traditional companies with large variable costs. This norm, in fact, prevents solar power companies located in the North from injecting electricity into the SING.

As a consequence of this lack of market for renewables, many solar firms located in the Atacama Desert are facing severe restrictions from both local and foreign financial institutions, which have become more risk-averse and increased their requirements for NCRE projects. In this regard, representatives of private banks in Chile have declared their concerns about new actors entering the market without proper expertise, and have made it difficult for them to borrow (Relac 2016a, 2017). This additional restriction poses a serious danger for the achievement of the renewable energy production target, set by Acera. According to Acera, the Chilean Association for Renewable Energy, 2017 could deliver investments for USD 2300, estimated based on 1500 additional MW of installed capacity, at USD 1.5 million per MW. However, it is worth noting that reaching this challenging target, which would reflect a 40 per cent MW rise, would necessarily entail a steep increase in the available public financial mechanisms for the sector.

CORFO designed special financial mechanisms to provide a solution to the aforementioned concerns. As part of the productivity agenda, carried out by the national government and the Ministry of Economy, in 2014, CORFO designed a National Strategic Solar Industry programme, within the Transform initiative. As part of this programme, CORFO designed specific credit lines, whose funds are offered through public tenders.

The main financial support programme that CORFO has launched is a scheme to co-finance up to 70 per cent of solar PV projects, the PV Solar Energy for Desert Weather and High Radiation, to encourage adaptation of the solar energy industry to the local environment. Its main goal is to nudge developers' adaptation to local conditions (for example, very high heat in the sun) and diminish the energy price. Among the requirements, CORFO demands that beneficiaries innovate, associate with technology centres, and strengthen local value-added and exports. Also, public funding will be provided to incentivize self-sufficient solar models, quality certification, and R&D.

Finally, CORFO has designed a credit line to support and help create value for local suppliers to develop prototypes, scale them, and take them to market. Considering the government has detected a niche in service and product provision to the solar industry, this programme could catalyse local sustainable growth throughout the value chain. However, even if many of these programmes are promising, they are relatively underfunded by the Ministry of Economy. As with many other programmes, the target is not always clear and the bureaucratic procedures reportedly deter firms from applying (Moguillansky 2016).

6.10 Conclusions

From 1939, the year it was created, until today, CORFO has played very varied roles, being seen overall by governments of different persuasions as an efficient instrument to serve their development objectives and strategies.

Unlike many developing countries' national development banks, and despite a high level of non-performing loans in the late 1980s, CORFO proved resilient to policy recommendations that advocated for its dismantling, with a highly positive outcome in the Chilean case (Rivas 2012). The prevailing position argued that CORFO was essential to tackle market failures that could hamper SMEs' development potential, as well as to support greater innovation and diversification.

Over the years, CORFO's instruments evolved and it stopped granting direct loans, to continue as a second-tier bank, on-lending through financial intermediaries. Later, it shifted further from granting credit through financial intermediaries to focusing more on guarantees for credit (through financial intermediaries) and on subsidies. Currently, it concentrates mainly on innovation and entrepreneurship, by granting subsidies through public tenders as well as guarantees.

CORFO has emphasized strategic collaboration with the private sector. Furthermore, it has given importance to a careful evaluation of the impact of many of its activities, which is a positive feature.

In recent years, CORFO has been very innovative in several of its instruments. We have discussed in some depth the Start-Up Chile programme, which has received international recognition and been emulated by other Latin American countries; there is, however, room for improvement: for example, by increasing its impact on variables, such as employment and sales, as well as decentralizing its activities more to the provinces. We have also detailed in depth the support that CORFO instruments have granted, in specific sectors, illustrating it with the case of solar energy development, which, combined with a very favourable policy framework, has positively contributed to the highly successful growth of solar energy. It is noteworthy that private financial mechanisms played a significant role in financing solar energy in Chile. However, the Chilean case clearly shows that private funds will discontinue their support towards RES projects as soon as price volatility scenarios or other risks emerge. Private financial institutions are not capable, nor willing, to take the risks that green growth investment demands. Thus, relying only on their funding, without support from public financing, could jeopardize the green economy national strategy. The role of CORFO is essential to provide stable funding to producers capable of adapting to special local conditions and fostering local value added, as CORFO does through its credit line encouraging PV Solar Energy for Desert Weather and High Radiation.

More broadly, with the Transform programme, launched in 2014, the government decided to enhance CORFO's goals by selecting strategic sectors with the potential to create dynamic competitive advantages, foster innovation, support structural transformation, and increase productivity. This seems very valuable, and CORFO has undertaken the task with great enthusiasm; this is especially crucial at a time when the urgency of undertaking structural diversification has increased due to the sharp fall in the price of Chile's main exports, particularly that of copper. Though many valuable steps have already been taken by CORFO, and by the government more broadly, and great efforts are being made to increase coordination with the private sector, it would seem desirable to improve the coordination between government agencies, including CORFO, to better focalize resources and efforts, as well as improve collaboration with the private sector on both sides.

It is noteworthy that an important part of the funding provided is non-reimbursable, instead of loans. Furthermore, as pointed out, guarantees play a large and growing role. Thus, as already discussed, CORFO's main instrument is not its loan granting, but its loan guarantees, which indirectly enabled loans for over USD 2000 million in 2016. There seems to be a strong case for revisiting this approach, as credit instruments may be valuable and necessary for the task of major diversification, as the experience of KfW and renewable energy seems to demonstrate, for example (Griffith-Jones 2016; Moslener et al. in Chapter 3 of this book).

A further, very important issue to consider is whether CORFO's capital and operations are sufficiently large in scale given the magnitude of the existing challenges, even though CORFO has grown in recent years, and overall is a very effective and efficient institution.

CORFO's activity is much smaller than some of the other national development banks, in proportion to the size of the economy and to the total size of credit to the private sector. A larger scale may be needed, particularly given the growing consensus that productive diversification and innovation are necessary for Chile to achieve more dynamic, sustainable, and inclusive growth, as well as higher productivity increases. In this case, mission-oriented finance on a sufficiently large scale may be especially valuable. It would be feasible to increase CORFO's scale with a small contribution from fiscal resources, as CORFO can raise funding at low cost on international capital markets, given Chile's fairly high credit rating, and especially, given the depth of Chilean capital markets, also find funds at fairly low cost and long maturities on domestic capital markets. This would allow greater leverage for fiscal resources.

Furthermore, CORFO, in coordination with other parts of the Chilean government, and in dialogue with the private sector, has already clearly defined important sectors and activities that need support to achieve structural transformation. CORFO is carrying out a number of programmes, many of them innovative, which have a very positive impact on the Chilean economy. Furthermore, CORFO is broadly seen as an efficient institution. It also has good teams, which can help design a more detailed industrial strategy, in close collaboration with the private sector. However, it lacks sufficient scale to deliver significant impact. It is therefore clearly necessary for CORFO to reach an appropriate scale to have a sufficient effect on helping to fund the major structural transformation needed; the proposed mechanism, raising funds in capital markets, seems to offer a tested and effective way of doing so. It could also help deepen and further develop Chilean capital markets, and possibly encourage the use of new financial instruments, with CORFO playing the role of 'market maker'.

Finally, like many national development banks, CORFO has a vast range of programmes. Though most of them seem very effective (which is verified by evaluations regularly carried out), the question can be asked if it may not be more efficient to streamline them somewhat, to allow greater focus. Better information and transparency on application procedures (and CORFO's operations), as well as a simplification of these procedures, also seem important for users. Finally, another question to ask would be whether

CORFO programmes should be made more flexible, to respond even better to companies' needs, that are not already met by the private financial sector.

List of People Interviewed and who Provided Information

Carlos Álvarez
Sergio Bitar
Eduardo Bitran
Claudia Bobadilla
Fernando Carmona
Mario Castillo
Álvaro Diaz
Mauricio Escobar
Patricio Feres
Joao Ferraz
Ricardo Ffrench-Davis
Jorge Katz
Christian Larrain
Claudio Maggi
Oscar Munoz
Edison Marchant
Inti Núñez
Luis Felipe Oliva
Joseph Ramos
Daniel Titelman

References

Agostini, C. A., S. Nasirov, and C. Silva. 2015. 'Solar PV Planning Toward Sustainable Development in Chile: Challenges and Recommendations', *Journal of Environment and Development* 25(1): 25–46.

Alide (Secretary General). 2009. Papel contracíclico de la banca de desarrollo frente a la crisis económica internacional. Estudio Básico para la Asamblea General de ALIDE 39.

Bertay, A. C., A. Demirgüç-Kunt, and H. Huizinga. 2015. 'Bank Ownership and Credit over the Business Cycle: Is Lending by State Banks Less Procyclical?', *Journal of Banking and Finance* 50: 326–39.

Bitran, E. 2016. *Innovation and Productive Transformation: Strategic Selectivity*. Panel 'Innovation Hubs and Regional Advantages: Sharing Experiences and Ideas to Promote Innovation in the Public and Private Sectors in Chile and California', CORFO.

Centre for Innovation and Development of Sustainable Energy (CIFES). 2015. 'Renewable Energy in the Chilean Electricity Market', CIFES Report (September).

Chang, Ha-Joon. 2002. *Kicking Away the Ladder: Development Strategy in Historical Perspective*. London: Anthem Press.

Chile Transforma. 2017. 'Sobre Transforma'. Available at <http://www.chiletransforma.cl/sobre-transforma/>, accessed May 2018.

Culpeper, R. 2012. 'Financial Sector Policy and Development in the Wake of the Global Crisis: The Role of National Development Banks', *Third World Quarterly* 33(3): 383–403. Available at: <doi.org/10.1080/01436597.2012.657470>, accessed 15 December 2016.

Durán, S. and J. Fermandois. 2011. 'La corporación de fomento y reconstrucción en Chile como el espíritu de la economía política de una época, 1939–1970', in M. Rougier (ed.), *La Banca de Desarrollo en América Latina*, 183–226. Fondo de Cultura Económica.

Erlick, J. C. 2015. *ReVista: Harvard Review of Latin America: Energy, Oil, Gas and Beyond*, 15(1). Available at <http://revista.drclas.harvard.edu/files/revista/files/energy_fall_2015.pdf>, accessed 8 December 2016.

Ffrench-Davis, R. 2010. 'Latin America: The Structural Fiscal Balance Policy in Chile: A Move Toward Counter-Cyclical Macroeconomics', *Journal of Globalization and Development* 1(1), doi.org/10.2202/1948-1837.1051.

Fondo de Inversión Estratégica. 2017. 'Memoria 2016–2017'. Available at <http://www.fie.cl/wp-content/uploads/2017/12/FIE-memoria-2016-2017.pdf>, accessed 6 May 2018.

Fundación Chile. 2015. *Programa Estratégico Nacional en Industria Solar (PES)—Informe de Levantamiento de Brechas*.

Griffith-Jones, S. 2016. *National Development Banks and Sustainable Infrastructure: The Case of KfW*. GEGI Working Paper 006. Available at <https://www.bu.edu/pardeeschool/files/2016/07/GriffithJones.Final_.pdf>, accessed 18 April 2018.

Griffith-Jones, S. and G. Cozzi. 2016. 'Investment-Led Growth: A Solution to the European Crisis', in M. Jacobs and M. Mazzucato (eds), *Rethinking Capitalism: Economics and Policy for Sustainable and Inclusive Growth*, 119–33. London: Wiley Blackwell.

Griffith-Jones, S., S. Spratt, R. Andrade, and E. Griffith-Jones. 2017. *Investment in Renewable Energy, Fossil Fuel Prices and Policy Implications for Latin America and the Caribbean*. ECLAC, Financiamiento del Desarrollo.

Hermann, J. 2014. *Estudio sobre programas de crédito con garantía estatal*. CORFO website.

Ki-Moon, Ban. 2011. *Sustainable Energy for All: A Vision Statement*. New York: United Nations.

La Porta, R., F. Lopez-de-Silanes, A. Shleifer, and R. Vishny. 2002. 'Government Ownership of Banks', *Journal of Finance* 57(1): 256–301.

Luna-Martinez, J. de and C. L. Vicente. 2012. *Global Survey of Development Banks*. Policy Research Working Paper No. WPS 5969. Washington, DC: World Bank. Available at <http://documents.worldbank.org/curated/en/313731468154461012/Global-survey-of-development-banks>, accessed 18 April 2018.

Mazzucato, M. and M. Jacobs. 2016. *Rethinking Capitalism: Economic Policy for Sustainable and Equitable Growth*. New York: John Wiley & Sons.

Mazzucato, M. and C. C. R. Penna. 2015. 'The Rise of Mission-Oriented State Investment Banks: The Cases of Germany's KfW and Brazil's BNDES'. ISI Growth Working Paper, October.

Micco, A. and U. Panizza. 2005. 'Public Banks in Latin America'. Background paper prepared for the conference 'Public Banks in Latin America: Myths and Reality'. Washington, DC: Inter-American Development Bank.

Moguillansky, G. 2016. *Informe sobre seguimiento Programa Estratégico Solar*. Mimeo, Santiago de Chile.

Muñoz Gomá, O. (ed.) 2009. *Desarrollo productivo en Chile: La experiencia de CORFRO entre 1990 y 2009*. Santiago, Chile: CORFO.

Nasirov, Shahriyar and Carlos Silva. 2014. 'Diversification of Chilean Energy Matrix: Recent Developments and Challenges'. *International Association for Energy Economics*, IAEE Forum, 27–31.

Nasirov, Shahriyar, Carlos Silva, and Claudio A. Agostini. 2015. 'Investors' Perspectives on Barriers to the Deployment of Renewable Energy Sources in Chile', *Energies* 8(5): 3794–814.

OECD Development Centre. 2016. 'Start-Up Latin America 2016: Building an Innovative Future'. Available at <www.oecd.org/dev/americas/Startups2016-Assessment-and-Recommendations.pdf>, accessed 5 February 2017.

Perez, C. 2010. 'Technological Revolutions and Techno-Economic Paradigms', *Cambridge Journal of Economics* 34(1): 185–202.

Relac, N. 2016a. 'Corfo lanzará en enero de 2016 créditos para nanciar proyectos ERNC', *Electricidad: La revista energética de Chile*, 26 October. Available at <www.revistaei.cl/2015/10/26/corfo-lanzara-en-enero-de-2016-creditos-para-financiar-proyectos-ernc/>, accessed 5 January 2017.

Relac, N. 2016b. 'Generación distribuida: Casi 500 proyectos instalados totalizan 4, 6 MW', *Electricidad: La revista energética de Chile*, 16 December. Available at <www.revistaei.cl/2016/12/16/generacion-distribuida-casi-500-proyectos-instalados-totalizan-46-mw/>, accessed 10 January 2017.

Relac, N. 2017. 'Acceso a financiamiento bancario se ha vuelto complejo para las ERNC', *Electricidad: La revista energética de Chile*, 10 January. Available at <www.revistaei.cl/2017/01/10/acceso-a-financiamiento-bancario-se-ha-vuelto-complejo-para-las-ernc/>, accessed 10 January 2017.

Ribeiro de Mendonça, Ana Rosa, and B. Sibin. 2008. *Public Banks and Recent Anticyclical Policies: A Comparative Study of the Experiences of Brazil and Chile*. Available at <https://www.boeckler.de/pdf/v_2015_10_24_mendonca.pdf>, accessed 10 December 2016.

Rivas, G. 2012. 'La experiencia de CORFO y la transformación productiva de Chile: Evolución, aprendizaje y lecciones de desarrollo'. Serie Políticas Públicas y Transformación Productiva 3. Available at <publicaciones.caf.com/media/17638/caf_libro_corfo_web.pdf>, accessed 15 December 2016.

Sapienza, P. 2004. 'The Effects of Government Ownership on Bank Lending', *Journal of Financial Economics* 72: 357–84.

Verde. 2016. 'Evaluación del Programa Start-Up Chile de CORFO'. Informe Final. Available at <ctie.economia.cl/wp-content/uploads/2017/07/Evaluación-Start-Up-Chile-2016.pdf>, accessed 8 January 2016.

Zoellner, J., P. Schweizer-Ries, and C. Wemheuer. 2008. 'Public Acceptance of Renewable Energies: Results from Case Studies in Germany', *Energy Policy* 36(11): 4136–41.

7

Colombia's System of National Development Banks

José Antonio Ocampo and Paola Arias

The major feature of Colombia's national development banks is that they constitute a system of multiple, specialized institutions. They were created at different times to promote sectors that were considered strategic for the country's development: agriculture, manufacturing, non-traditional exports, regional and local infrastructure,[1] energy, and, more recently, public–private infrastructure partnerships. In economic terminology, it can be said that they were meant to counteract market failures, including, in particular, helping to overcome the risks inherent in the development of new firms, the inadequate supply of long-term credit in a financial system with a strong short-term bias of financial assets, and limited financial inclusion. The system survived the domestic financial liberalization that took place around 1990, when it was restructured as the system of specialized institutions in place now. Some of these banks have been subject more recently to significant and still ongoing restructurings.

This chapter analyses the characteristics of the system of national development banks in Colombia, with a focus on specific market failures. It is divided into five sections. The first looks at the history and current structure of the system. The next three examine how the system is managing three major market failures: infrastructure financing (the major case of market failure in long-term financing), financial inclusion, and the promotion of entrepreneurial growth. The last presents some conclusions. Since the system has not addressed

[1] By regional and local infrastructure, we refer here to investments made by different departments (the major regional political divisions that are equivalent to provinces or states in other countries). However, in the rest of this chapter, we will use the term 'local' to refer to investments both by departments and municipalities.

in particular the issues associated with environmental sustainability, we leave this topic out of the analysis.

7.1 The History and Structure of the System

Colombia has a long history of public sector banks, going back to the Banco Nacional in the late nineteenth century (a quasi-central bank) and Banco Central in the early twentieth century (despite its name, a commercial bank), but particularly to the 1920s and 1930s, which saw the creation of several institutions to serve the rural sector (Banco Agricola Hipotecario in the 1920s and Caja Agraria in the early 1930s, to be joined in the 1950s by Banco Cafetero and Banco Ganadero), housing (Banco Central Hipotecario in the early 1930s, which also absorbed the assets of mortgage banks, public and private, that had been created in the 1920s and went bankrupt during the Great Depression), and access to finance (Banco Popular in the 1950s, as well as Caja Agraria).[2] This was part of a larger set of interventions in the financial sector, which also included several norms forcing financial institutions to allocate credit to particular sectors ('directed credit'), strong regulation of interest rates, and strict specialization of financial intermediaries (commercial banks and a series of non-banking institutions)[3] based on the principles introduced by the 1923 Kemmerer reforms, which also created a modern central bank (Banco de la República).

The first development bank[4] was Instituto de Fomento Industrial (IFI), created in 1940 as part of a Latin American wave with the major objective of promoting manufacturing development through equity investments (in partnership with private investors) and long-term lending. A second push came with the banking reforms of 1951, which gave development functions to the central bank that were reflected in particular in the establishment, in the 1950s and 1960s, of several 'Development Funds', which created rediscount facilities directed to sectors that were prioritized in the policy agenda (agriculture, small and medium-sized manufacturing, non-traditional exports, local

[2] The Corporación Colombiana de Crédito was also created in the early 1930s, but basically to absorb the bad loans from private institutions. A few banks would be nationalized in the 1980s to manage a domestic financial crisis, but were later reprivatized.

[3] They initially included commercial and mortgage banks, to which Corporaciones Financieras (private investment banks) were added in the 1960s, Corporaciones de Ahorro y Vivienda (for housing finance, which operated with inflation-indexed deposits and loans) in the early 1970s, and Compañías de Financiamiento Comercial in the mid-1970s. To this we can add credit unions (the largest being supervised by the Superintendencia Financiera since the mid-1990s) and, more recently, microfinance institutions.

[4] For the history of the development banks and funds through the 1980s, see Gómez (1990) and Ocampo (2015: chs 1 and 2).

infrastructure, and electricity).[5] The Funds were financed from reserve requirements, directed credit obligations, bonds issued by Banco de la República in the domestic market, and credit lines from multilateral development banks (MDBs). They provided credit under preferential interest rates and maturities. Interest rate subsidies were reduced and in some cases eliminated by the first (moderate) domestic financial liberalizations of the mid- and late 1970s. A different type of fund was launched in the early 1970s to guarantee the liquidity of a new financial intermediary created at the time for housing construction financing (Corporaciones de Ahorro y Vivienda), with the central bank basically facilitating the transformation of the short-term liabilities of these intermediaries into long-term inflation-indexed financing for the housing sector. In turn, the urban development fund was transferred to Banco Central Hipotecario in 1975. IFI equity investments were sharply reduced from the mid-1970s. A new development bank, Financiera Eléctrica Nacional (FEN), was created in 1982 to finance the electricity sector, which at the time was essentially state-owned; the central bank's electricity development fund for the sector was transferred to the new institution.

The main reforms of the system were introduced from 1989 to 1991, and were part of a major domestic financial liberalization. The liberalization included the privatization of most first-tier public sector banks (the only exception being Caja Agraria, which was restructured and transformed into Banco Agrario) and the development of universal banks—thus eliminating the historical specialization of domestic financial institutions. It also encompassed sharp reductions of reserve requirements, the full liberalization of interest rates, and free access by financial institutions to external capital markets (subject, during some periods, to reserve requirements on capital inflows) (Ocampo 2015). More importantly from the point of view of this chapter, the central bank's development functions were eliminated, as part of a broader reform of Banco de la República, which became an autonomous institution in charge of monetary and foreign exchange policies with the 1991 Constitution.

In the transition from the old to the new policy regime, three development banks were established to manage the old development funds: (i) Financiera de Desarrollo Territorial (FINDETER), created by Law 57 in 1989 to finance local development infrastructure;[6] (ii) Fondo para el Financiamiento del Sector Agropecuario (FINAGRO), launched by Law 16 in 1990 to finance the

[5] They included Fondo Financiero Agropecuario, Fondo de Promoción de Exportaciones, Fondo de Desarrollo Industrial, Fondo para Inversiones Privadas, Fondo Forestal, Fondo de Desarrollo Urbano, and Fondo de Desarrollo Eléctrico. The Fondo de Capitalización Empresarial was also created during the domestic financial crisis of the 1980s to support the financial restructuring of non-financial firms facing high levels of indebtedness.

[6] These include a myriad of local infrastructure needs: roads, water and sanitation, social infrastructure (education and health), sports and cultural centres, and housing.

agricultural sector, under the policies set by the Comisión Nacional de Crédito Agropecuario, CNCA (National Commission for Agricultural Credit); and (iii) Banco de Comercio Exterior (BANCOLDEX), which was set up by Law 7 in 1991[7] to finance non-traditional exports and started operating in 1992. These institutions took over most of the development funds managed by the central bank; the remaining funds, those for industrial development, were transferred to IFI in 1994. In turn, FEN was transformed into the Financiera Energética Nacional in 1990, with the objective of financing energy activity. Domestic financial liberalization thus left a network of five development banks: IFI, FINAGRO, BANCOLDEX, FINDETER, and FEN. The system was mostly designed as a system of second-tier banks, though with some first-tier functions in the case of IFI and FEN. Directed credit was essentially dismantled with one major exception:[8] the agricultural sector, for which there is still the commitment to allocate 15 per cent of all commercial bank credits. If banks fail to do so, they have to buy bonds issued by FINAGRO (Títulos de Desarrollo Agropecuario—Agricultural Development Bonds—or TDA),[9] which provide the funds that are then used to rediscount loans from other institutions—notably from Banco Agrario. Other development banks must get their resources from the domestic or external markets, or from government equity contributions or securities (see Figure 7.1).

Later reforms included broadening the responsibilities of these institutions, with greater attention to financial inclusion. They also included two major transformations. The first was the absorption of IFI by BANCOLDEX in 2002, essentially to manage the financial strains faced by the former, but mixing two entirely different business models. In turn, growing access by private commercial banks to external financing has reduced the demand for rediscount facilities for exporters, the major historical role played by BANCOLDEX. This fact, together with the old functions of IFI that it had absorbed, led to a redefinition, in 2015, of the role of BANCOLDEX as a bank for entrepreneurial growth—supporting rapidly growing firms, including Colombian firms investing abroad. In turn, due to the restructuring of the energy sector in the 1990s, which included a large-scale privatization of state-owned enterprises in this sector, there was a decision to reduce FEN's capital. The major reform in this case was, however, its transformation into the Financiera de Desarrollo Nacional (FDN) in 2011, with the broader objective of financing infrastructure in partnership with the private sector. Interestingly, a large part of the capital

[7] This law also created an export promotion agency, PROEXPORT, managed by Banco de la República, together with the rediscount facilities of the development fund for non-traditional exports. This institution has more recently been renamed PROCOLOMBIA and given the additional responsibility of promoting foreign direct investment in Colombia.

[8] Special commitments to allocate credit for the housing of low-income households were also preserved for some time, but were eventually discontinued.

[9] There are two types of bonds, one carrying a lower interest rate, which is used to finance lending to small agricultural producers.

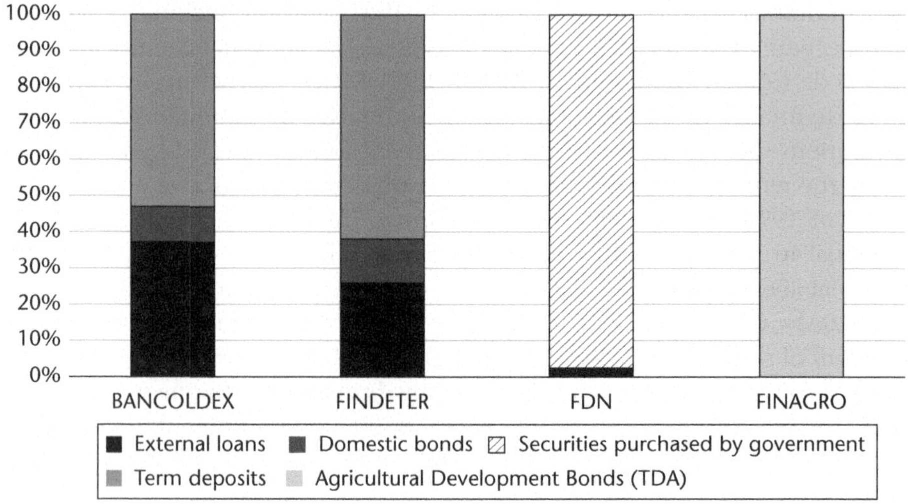

Figure 7.1. Source of funding, percentages (December 2016)
Source: Superintendencia Financiera de Colombia

Table 7.1. Colombia's system of development banks

Entity	Predecessor funds (managed by Banrep)	Sector	Date of creation
Instituto de Fomento Industrial IFI		Industrial development	1940–2002
Financiera Energética Nacional/ Financiera de Desarrollo Nacional FDN	Electric Development Fund	Infrastructure	1982, 2011
Financiera de Desarrollo Territorial FINDETER	Urban Development Fund	Urban and regional infrastructure	1989
Fondo para el Financiamiento del Sector Agropecuario FINAGRO	Agricultural Development Fund	Agriculture	1990
Banco de Comercio Exterior BANCOLDEX	Export Promotion Fund	Non-traditional exports/ business development	1991

of the new institution has come from the privatization of the major remaining electricity generator in which the central government had partial ownership, ISAGEN.

Table 7.1 briefly summarizes the history of the five, now four national development banks. Three of these institutions essentially operate as second-tier institutions that facilitate the flow of funds to banks through their rediscount facilities. FDN does first-tier lending and BANCOLDEX, as part of its recent transformation process, has started to do so again (using the old IFI faculties) and is planning to continue expanding its first-tier operations to co-finance strategic projects that require larger amounts of long-term financing. All these institutions can also undertake equity investments, but have done so only sparingly. The major exceptions are special investment funds of sectorial interest: BANCOLDEX, FINDETER, and FDN have invested in different funds with their own equity, as partners of other domestic or foreign investors, while FINAGRO administers capital funds with the resources of the national government, but is planning to change its strategy to invest in funds instead (Table 7.2). FDN also offers guarantees and credit enhancement facilities, while FINDETER and BANCOLDEX are planning to do so.

Table 7.2. Investments in private equity and capital funds (December 2016)

BANK	FUND	SECTOR	COMMITMENTS (COL$ million, or US$ million when indicated)
BANCOLDEX	Aureos	Small and medium-sized businesses in Latin America	14,000
	Escala	Companies that have a proven and successful business model	11,000
	Progresa Capital	Colombian firms that have developed innovative products or services	3,723
	Fondo de Infraestructura Colombia Ashmore I- FCP	Infrastructure investments	37,686
	Brilla Colombia	Tourism sector	9,600
	Amerigo Ventures Colombia	Digital economy	2,763
	Velum Early Stage Fund I	Companies with high technological and innovative value associated with information management	7,468
	MGM Sustainable	Energy efficiency and renewable energy sectors in Colombia, Central America, and the Caribbean	12,003
FINDETER	Fondo de Infraestructura Colombia Ashmore I- FCP	Infrastructure investments	40,000
FDN*	FCP 4G Credicorp Capital—SURA AM	4G toll-road projects and unsolicited proposals	50,000
	Fondo de deuda senior para infraestructura en Colombia CAF-Ashmore I	4G toll-road projects and unsolicited proposals	50,000
FINAGRO**	Fondo de Inversión Forestal de Colombia	Forestry projects	US$ 10
	Fondo de Inversiones de Capital de Riesgo	Agriculture and agro-industry	

* Commitments.
** These funds are administered by FINAGRO.
Sources: BANCOLDEX, FINDETER, FDN, and FINAGRO

Except for FINAGRO, which benefits from the only remaining mechanism of directed credit, the others must fund their operations in the domestic or external markets. BANCOLDEX and FINDETER mix domestic term deposits and bond issues with loans from MDBs and international banks. FDN is essentially financed from equity investments from the national government or the government's purchase of securities issued by this institution (Figure 7.1). They also provide other services, including advising, project structuring, technical assistance and training, and portfolio administration. All of them are subject to the oversight of the Financial Superintendence (Superintendencia Financiera de Colombia).

FINDETER and BANCOLDEX are controlled by the national government and state institutions have a large majority ownership (99.7 per cent in both cases). FINAGRO and FDN have a more complex shareholding structure. In the case of FINAGRO, 78 per cent of the capital is owned by the national government and Banco Agrario, and the remainder by two private banks (Davivienda and BBVA, which bought the two public sector agricultural banks that were privatized—Banco Cafetero and Ganadero, respectively). Aside from a large capital contribution from the national government, which controls 67 per cent of FDN's capital, the government has actively sought to attract strategic investors to this bank, which now include the International Financial Corporation (IFC) with a 17 per cent share, and the Development Bank of Latin America (CAF) and Sumitomo Mitsui (SMBC) with 8 per cent each.

All banks are linked to one ministry, their majoritarian shareholder, aligning them with national government policies. BANCOLDEX and FINAGRO are each connected to the ministries in charge of policy design and coordination for their sectors, which are the Ministry of Commerce, Industry, and Tourism, and the Ministry of Agriculture, respectively; while FINDETER and FDN are linked to the Ministry of Finance and Public Credit.

Despite this common feature, the shareholding structure has obvious implications for the governance of the institutions: whereas the government names the presidents of FINAGRO, BANCOLDEX, and FINDETER, and the relevant Minister heads the boards of these institutions and board members are designated by law or appointment by the President of Colombia, in FDN, the strategic investors chair the board and have veto power over crucial decisions. There is still an ongoing discussion (as of mid-2017) on whether the boards of other development banks should cease to be chaired by Ministers to meet OECD standards. Regardless of the involvement of public capital in their equity, all banks can hire their employees (with minor exceptions) under the private law regime, allowing them to find high-level executives and build a qualified technical team, competitive with the market.

In terms of their weight in the Colombian economy and financial sector, the evolution of the four institutions has been very uneven. FEN was by far

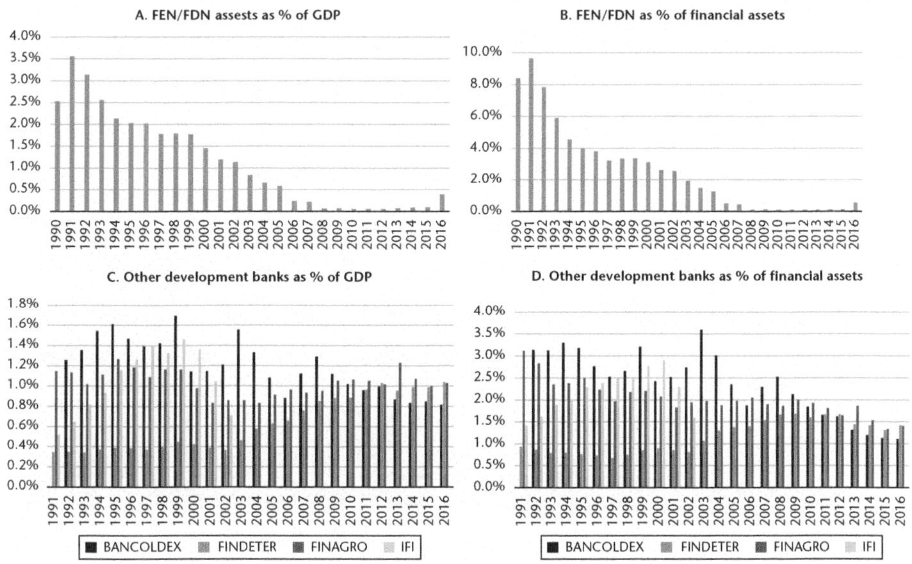

Figure 7.2. Assets of development banks as percentage of GDP and of assets of the domestic financial system

Source: Superintendencia Financiera de Colombia

the largest bank in the early 1990s, at the time of the major financial liberalization, with its assets peaking at 3.5 per cent of GDP and about 10 per cent of financial institutions' assets in 1991(Figures 7.2A and 7.2B).[10] Those shares came down dramatically in the 1990s and 2000s and were very small by the late 2000s. This is also true of FDN today, but it is growing fast and will again be an important institution in the future (see section 7.2). BANCOLDEX (together with IFI until 2002) has also shrunk relative to the economy from close to 3 per cent of GDP in the early 1900s to a third of that level in recent years (Figure 7.2C). In contrast, FINAGRO lending has remained around 1 per cent of GDP and FINDETER has expanded in relative terms since the turn of the century: it now represents about 1 per cent of GDP, about three times its weight in the economy in the early 1990s. As a share of financial institutions' assets, all the banks, with the exception of FINDETER, have shrunk (Figure 7.2D).

The net result is that the share of development banks as a percentage of GDP has declined relative to the economy and, furthermore, they have lagged behind the dynamic growth of the domestic financial sector after

[10] From its creation until 2000, FEN lent around $8.9 billion, funded by domestic and external bond issues and financing from MDBs and international banks. It was the first Colombian institution to get an international credit rating, after the national government.

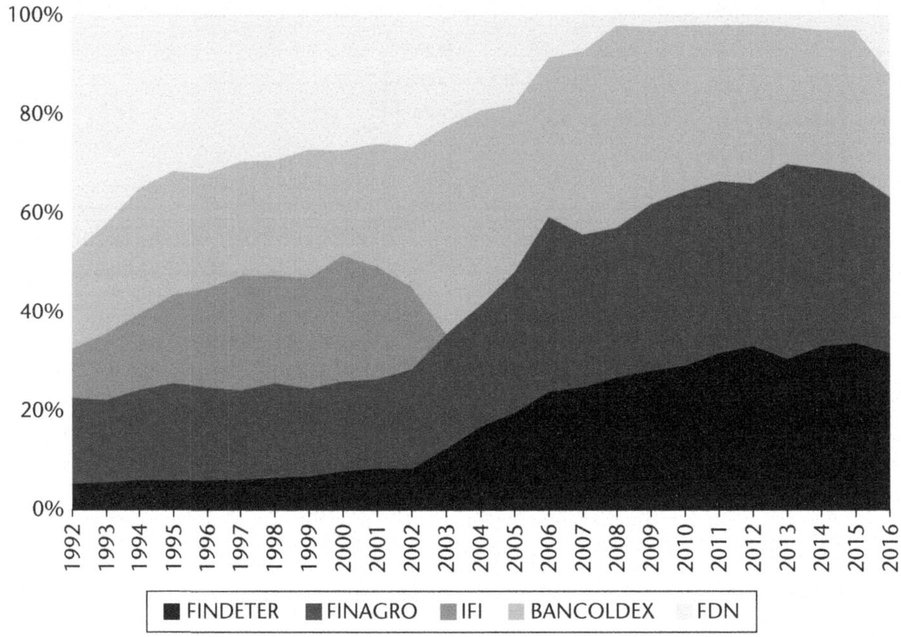

Figure 7.3. Share of development banks in the system
Source: Superintendencia Financiera de Colombia

liberalization. This is true even if we exclude FEN. Overall, the share of development banks, excluding FEN, has been around 3 per cent of GDP in recent years vs a peak of 4.4–4.8 per cent of GDP in the second half of the 1990s. As a proportion of financial institutions' assets, the share of the banks, again excluding FEN, has declined even more: from close to 10 per cent in the early 1990s to less than half that level in recent years. The dynamic restructuring of several development banks in Colombia reflected the recent recognition of the central role played by these institutions in public policy, and their declining share in the economy represents, therefore, a suboptimal performance.

Over this period, development banks have assumed a moderate countercyclical role by slightly scaling up their lending activities during times of crisis, when private banks were finding it hard to expand their loan portfolio. Indeed, all five banks (including IFI at the time) moderately increased their share of financial institutions' assets in the aftermath of the 1998 Colombian financial crisis, while all, except for BANCOLDEX, did the same after the 2008 North Atlantic financial crisis.

The structure of the system has also changed dramatically. FDN is the smallest institution today, whereas FEN was by far the largest in the early

1990s. Jointly, BANCOLDEX-IFI became the largest institution by the mid-1990s, peaking at close to half of all development bank assets around the turn of the century, but then it too fell in relative terms, while FINAGRO and, particularly, FINDETER expanded their shares in the system (Figure 7.3).

7.2 Infrastructure Financing

7.2.1 *The National Infrastructure Programme*

The infrastructure lag of Colombia is unquestionable. According to the World Economic Forum's global competitiveness indicator, Colombia ranked 113th among 138 countries in 2016, based on the quality of its overall infrastructure, and 120th in terms of the quality of its roads. Furthermore, according to government data, the quality of infrastructure has deteriorated during the first decade of the current century. The proportion of paved national road infrastructure in good condition managed by Instituto Nacional de Vías fell from 71 per cent in 2003 to 48 per cent in 2010 (Yepes et al. 2013). This raises the transportation and logistics costs for all activities, affecting both domestic market integration and exports—a substantial problem given the rugged geography of Colombia.[11]

As a result, the government has placed this issue at the centre of its policy agenda since 2010 (DNP 2010). One of its major components is the attraction of private investment into infrastructure, notably roads, through public–private partnerships (PPP), to leverage the resources and administrative capacity of the private sector. This is also necessary to overcome fiscal constraints, which have become more severe with the fall of oil prices in recent years.

For the fourth generation of highway PPPs (4G) now in place, the government redesigned the legal and institutional framework and strengthened the public institutions in charge, in order to overcome the problems experienced during the previous three generations of that programme. These included construction delays relative to schedules and multiple demands that led to several disputes being brought to arbitrage tribunals. According to an OECD study, which compares the renegotiation of concession contracts of Colombia with those of Chile and Peru (Bitran et al. 2013), the twenty-five Colombian contracts done under the first three generations of PPPs were renegotiated approximately seventeen times per contract. The

[11] According to World Bank estimates for 2016, Colombia had a Logistics Performance Index of 2.66 (out of five maximum), and it scored 2.43 for infrastructure (World Bank 2017). Internal transportation costs for a container travelling from the main city to the main port are US$1,535 (2014 prices) vs $280 for Peru, $450 for Chile, and $900 for Mexico. Given geographical conditions, this last comparison is probably the most relevant.

study concluded that the major problems were bids without adequate studies and designs, deficient contractual processes, and opportunistic behaviour on the part of the private contractors, such as submitting artificially low bids in the expectation that contracts would be renegotiated. The fiscal costs of renegotiations were outrageous: an average 280 per cent increase in contract costs versus around 15 per cent in Chile and Peru. A third of the additional costs were due to the inclusion of new stretches of road in the renegotiated contracts (about 50 kilometres on average). There is no doubt that, despite close cooperation with World Bank experts, the guarantees granted in the contracts were excessive.

Institutional restructuring is an essential element of the new strategy. It has included: (i) the creation in 2011 of a Vice-Ministry of Infrastructure in the Ministry of Transportation, in charge of the sectorial coordination for planning, policy formulation, strategies, and studies related to multimodal infrastructure; (ii) the transformation of the Instituto Nacional de Concesiones into the Agencia Nacional de Infrastructura (ANI), an agency with great autonomy and technical resources to structure and administer the concessions; (iii) the already-mentioned transformation of FEN into FDN in 2011; (iv) the development of a new legal framework, through Law 1508 of 2012, which designed a new institutional framework for PPPs, which redistributed the risks between the private sector and the government in these partnerships. The new framework prohibits advanced public sector payments, imposes limitations on additions to the contracts and their extension, and ties government payments to the level of service already achieved.[12]

The 4G programme includes thirty-three PPP projects to build approximately 5600 kilometres of highway for a total cost of COL$55 trillion (about US$19 billion at 2017 exchange rates). There could also be additional projects, as the programme allows for unsolicited proposals by private parties. ANI had awarded thirty-one projects at the end of 2016, but financial closure had been achieved for only eight of them, costing a total of COL$12.6 trillion. As we will see, a major challenge is the size of debt requirements for these projects relative to the size of the Colombian financial sector and of individual financial institutions. The mobilization of resources through different modalities of finance—not only *corporate finance*, the basic instrument used during the past three generations of PPPs, but also *project finance*—is therefore one of the major challenges that the programme faces.

[12] An additional legal instrument is Law 1682 of 2013, which among other things speeds up the purchase of land required by infrastructure projects, which caused major delays in the past.

7.2.2 *Market Failures*

Major market failures in transport infrastructure financing have led to the inadequate supply of long-term lending with adequate risk profiles. In the case of domestic commercial banks, the problems are both the size of the sector and the lack of experience in project financing. The twenty-four projects of the first three generations of PPPs (1993–2013) were largely financed by public sector advances based on the progress of the investments, with no attention paid to the level of available services. Domestic banks provided corporate financing to the firms in charge of concessions, with 10- to 12-year maturities, which complemented public sector advances. If domestic commercial banks were to finance the whole 4G programme, which demands COL$45 trillion, 22 per cent of their current loan portfolio would be required (see Table 7.3). This would significantly increase the concentration of risks in infrastructure financing, as it would more than triple current lending in this area (which reached COL$14.3 trillion in December 2016). Furthermore, individually, these institutions can only contribute 25 per cent of their net worth to a specific project, according to prudential standards that financial institutions must meet. This implies that only the largest domestic financial institutions can participate by themselves in individual 4G projects; indeed, given their net worth, smaller institutions not detailed in the table could finance at most COL$100 billion per initiative, which represents between 5 and 20 per cent of the needs of individual projects. Since banks have to add up all lending to specific borrowers to estimate the 25 per cent of their net worth, even the largest banks have limited capacity if they primarily use corporate finance and the same firms

Table 7.3. Banks' assets and loan portfolios (December 2016, COL$ million)

BANKS	ASSETS	LOANS	COMMERCIAL LOANS	EQUITY	25% of NET WORTH
BANCOLOMBIA	137,880,703	99,591,827	73,121,746	18,433,048	4,608,262
BANCO DE BOGOTA	80,149,713	51,487,757	38,957,651	14,982,759	3,745,690
DAVIVIENDA	72,706,965	56,650,646	28,718,565	9,076,663	2,269,166
BBVA	51,660,690	39,618,528	16,021,097	5,394,457	1,348,614
OCCIDENTE	32,837,103	26,280,751	18,551,253	3,783,943	945,986
BANCO CORPBANCA	30,784,905	21,428,365	14,113,132	3,297,553	824,388
BANAGRARIO	23,860,857	13,146,873	6,868,836	1,752,027	438,007
RED MULTIBANCA COLPATRIA	23,694,300	19,872,450	8,922,021	2,474,174	618,544
BANCO POPULAR	20,595,634	16,351,840	6,984,543	2,053,373	513,343
GNB SUDAMERIS	19,866,911	7,519,989	4,178,340	1,833,276	458,319
OTHER BANKS	54,156,790	42,475,222	11,104,484	7,197,705	1,799,426
TOTAL	**548,194,571**	**394,424,247**	**227,541,668**	**70,278,976**	

Source: Superintendencia Financiera de Colombia

are involved in several PPPs. Therefore, only the largest domestic financial institutions can participate in the 4G programme.

For their part, major domestic institutional investors and pension funds have concentrated their portfolio in low-risk instruments with fixed yields, high levels of liquidity, and high ratings. Therefore, they have very limited appetite for infrastructure bonds, even highly rated ones. Most of these institutions also lack the risk assessment capacity to invest in these instruments. In the case of pension funds, the Financial Superintendency establishes minimum yield requirements, which are largely based on the effective yields of the portfolios of different funds. There is, therefore, no incentive to buy infrastructure bonds if other pension funds do not invest in these instruments. Furthermore, the concentration of the pension fund industry is extremely high, with the two largest holding 80 per cent of the funds in 2016. Furthermore, the owners of the largest funds are also proprietors of major financial institutions, and in some cases investors in the firms undertaking the PPPs, a fact that generates additional risks and potential conflicts of interest.

International banks and institutional investors also face important problems. Due to international prudential standards (Basel II and III), there is a clear disincentive for banks to lend with the 18–20-year maturities that these projects require. Given this constraint, a clear framework must be put in place to refinance the loans with the 7–10-year maturities that they normally offer, to eliminate the maturity mismatch between the project requirements and the loans. International financing is also limited by currency mismatches associated with the fact that the revenues from these projects are mainly in local currency. In this case, the problem is the short maturities of the available hedging instruments, as well as the fact that only a portion of future fiscal commitments (*vigencias futuras*) is denominated in dollars.

7.2.3 *The Role of FDN*

These constraints set the stage for the actions of the new development bank that are given the responsibility of supporting infrastructure financing. FDN has been involved in a rapid and very interesting process of defining its business model to play a key role in helping to overcome market failures. It has defined its mandate around three clear areas for action: (i) directly providing part of the financing required by PPP infrastructure projects; (ii) creating incentives for other market agents to participate in the financing of these projects by mitigating some of the market failures that limit the availability of long-term financing with adequate risk profiles; and (iii) supporting the creation of an infrastructure 'project bank' for all types of initiatives (including local projects and social infrastructure), in collaboration with ANI, FINDETER, and FONADE (Fondo Financiero de Proyectos de Desarrollo).[13] The major objective is to guarantee that projects are well structured to have access to market financing. As indicated, the major constraints are the limited size and concentration of the domestic financial sector and the limited development of the domestic capital market, as well as the high and sometimes insufficiently known risks that these projects face and the limited capacity and experience in this type of financing of all domestic, and even international, agents involved.

FDN has been developing an innovative set of financial instruments, which include the following:

- Direct long-term financing facilities: as a development bank that can undertake first-tier operations, FDN has offered senior and subordinated loans with longer maturities than those provided by other domestic institutions, but otherwise under market conditions. In practice, other financial institutions then match FDN's terms. FDN has also been offering guarantees to firms in charge of the concessions, as well as credit enhancement facilities to guarantee sponsors' equity contributions and to improve the financial structure of different projects, such as covering some risks and stabilizing cash flows through the development of the projects, to allow them to access international financing. By December 2016, FDN had participated in five of the eight projects that had already achieved financial closure with commitments and disbursements totalling about COL$780 billion in liquidity lines, COL$300 billion in senior debt, and COL$37 billion in guarantees of sponsors' equity contributions.
- Support for the creation of debt funds for infrastructure financing, with FDN's participation providing a strong incentive for the involvement of other institutional investors. The board has approved contributions for up to COL$200 billion, of which half has already been made effective. These investments are meant to generate confidence in these new instruments, and are complemented with active advice to support the creation of new funds. Two funds have already been created with FDN contributions,[14] which have provided partial financing for three projects, and two additional funds are on the way.
- Product standardization to facilitate access to the capital market: FDN has also worked on the design, standardization, and promotion of financial

[13] FONADE is an institution that supports pre-investment financing. It is part of the national planning institutions.

[14] They are Fondo 4G Credicorp Capital/Sura Asset Mangement and CAF/Ashmore Group (the first are domestic investors, the second external ones, including a MDB). See Table 7.2.

instruments that facilitate the participation of institutional investors in infrastructure financing. The instruments are designed for two specific moments in the project history: in the initial stages, participating in long-term financing of the project, and during the operation of the project facilitating the refinancing and improvement of credit conditions. Notably, two of the first 4G projects successfully issued project bonds with support from FDN, and the bank designed a 'prototype' instrument for the second phase of the project, which offers partial liquidity guarantees. The project bonds got a BBB– international and a AA+ rating from Fitch, and the prototype instrument a AA+ rating. Additionally, FDN has bought 4G project bonds in the primary market for COL$18 billion.

Aside from the design of new financial instruments, FDN has also promoted regulatory changes that facilitate the participation of institutional investors in debt and equity funds for infrastructure investment and enable lending by commercial banks and FDN by increasing the individual loan limits to 25 and 40 per cent of net worth, respectively. It has also contributed to increase the technical capacity and standards of private and public institutions involved through different training courses, jointly undertaken with universities and industrial associations, the dissemination of guides on good international practices on project finance, and broad-based socialization of the 4G programme.

In addition, FDN has played an important advisory role, providing technical assistance, structuring projects, and conducting research on good management practices in infrastructure to support other institutions in the public sector, and also to provide infrastructure bank projects with adequate pre-investment standards, thus helping increase the availability of bankable projects. Together with IFC, it created in 2013 a pre-investment fund to help design projects in sectors where the private sector has been traditionally absent. It has also participated in a myriad of plan and project designs such as the 2015–35 Master Plan for Multimodal Transportation, the financial structuring for the first metro line for Bogotá and the light metro line in the 80th street in Medellin, the deepening and expansion of the access channel to Cartagena Bay, and the structuring of pilot projects for educational infrastructure.

FDN had assets of COL$725 billion in December 2015, made up essentially of liquid investments and a few remaining energy loans from its predecessor institution, FEN. Growth was very fast in 2016, with assets increasing to COL $3.3 trillion by December, thanks to the transfer of the funds obtained by the government in the privatization of ISAGEN. Liabilities also increased rapidly, from COL$21 billion to COL$2.6 trillion, during the same period. A basic reason for this is that the funds from this privatization were transferred in the form of a purchase of FDN subordinated bonds by the national government. The net worth of the institution has thus remained relatively constant at just over COL$700 billion.

7.2.4 *Local Infrastructure and the Role of FINDETER*

As indicated in the first section of this chapter, FINDETER was created in 1989 to support local infrastructure investments, and has been the fastest growing development bank in Colombia. Its assets in December 2016 were COL$8.9 trillion, equivalent to about 1 per cent of gross domestic product (GDP), and its net worth was close to COL$1trillion. Its major assets are rediscount lending, which represented about 87 per cent of the total. The maturity of 90 per cent of these credits is over five years and for 45 per cent of them, it is over eight years. As for its major liabilities, they were term deposits, borrowing from domestic and international banks, including MDBs, and some bonds in circulation. A bond issuance was carried out during 2015 in the international market for an amount equivalent to US$500 million. The 10-year note was rated BBB by Fitch Ratings and Standard and Poor's.

FINDETER's main responsibility is to correct the market failures that lead to very limited availability of long-term financing for local infrastructure, but also to help strengthen the technical capacity of departments and municipalities to design infrastructure plans and bankable projects. It operates essentially as a second-tier bank that rediscounts lending by financial institutions, mainly commercial banks. Its facilities finance new investments but also working capital and debt restructuring for local infrastructure projects under favourable maturity, grace period, and interest rates. In contrast to FDN's financial innovations, FINDETER's rediscount facilities follow a very traditional model and, in some cases, include subsidies.

The sectors that benefitted the most from its facilities in 2016 were health (40 per cent), energy development (22 per cent), transportation (20 per cent), urban development and housing (8 per cent), and education (6 per cent). Lending comes in three modalities: ordinary rediscounts, those with subsidized interest rates, and special credit lines. The first are rediscounts at market conditions. The second are provided at subsidized interest rates and longer maturities, with funds provided by the Ministry of Finance or another national or local public sector institution to cover the differences in interest rates. Today, they benefit specific sectors: water and sanitation, health infrastructure, and environmental projects. The special credit lines also benefit specific sectors: renewable energy, sustainable cities, water and sanitation, and education.

FINDETER lending is complemented by its supply of non-financial services, as it supports the regional and local governments through the whole infrastructure project cycle. This includes, in particular, the development of three programmes—'Sustainable and Competitive Cities', 'Emblematic Cities', and 'Diamante Caribe and Santanderes'[15]—to help cities in the planning, identification, and prioritization of strategic projects, with the support of other organizations and, in particular, of the Inter-American Development Bank. Additionally, FINDETER supports local governments in the structuring of projects, to guarantee that they are viable from a technical, legal, and financial point of view. For this purpose, it is supported by a pre-investment fund created in 2012, which provides both non-refundable financing and support, subject to a payment by the local institution undertaking the project. In terms of technical assistance, it provides a diverse array of services: financial advisory to public and private sector entities, training on fiscal issues to mayors and governors, revision of local PPP projects, and formulation and revision of projects that local governments finance with their share of the oil royalty payments.[16] It also supports the national government in its strategic projects for the regions, including the formulation, implementation, supervision, and evaluation of strategic projects such as the '100,000 Free Houses' and 'Water for Prosperity'—the major national programmes for social housing and water and sanitation, respectively.

7.3 The Role of Development Banks in Financial Inclusion

7.3.1 *The Level of Financial Inclusion (and Exclusion) in Colombia*

According to the report on financial inclusion, now regularly prepared in Colombia by the Financial Superintendency and Banca de las Oportunidades—the major institution in charge of promoting financial inclusion—74.3 per cent of the adult population (24.9 million persons) had access to at least one financial product in 2015, a proportion that has systematically increased over the past five years (by about ten percentage points). In terms of active banking products, the proportion was 64.5 per cent (21.1 million adults)

[15] 'Sustainable and Competitive Cities' is a platform led by the IADB and FINDETER to promote strategic projects, focused on the transformation of middle-sized cities through orderly planning. Seventeen cities have joined this programme and COL$4.1trillion in loans have been mobilized for the development of these territories. 'Emblematic cities' is a programme designed to close inequality gaps and support the planning and development processes of cities that are strategically important for the country, located in areas of vulnerability. Thirty-one municipalities are part of this programme, which has already disbursed COL$750 billion. 'Diamante Caribe and Santanderes' is a programme implemented by FINDETER in partnership with Microsoft, Fundación Metrópoli, and Colciencias to identify and manage physical or digital projects to consolidate a sustainable mega-region (the Colombian Caribbean and the Departments of Santander and Norte de Santander). This programme has already identified sixty-five key projects for this region.

[16] According to legal provisions, oil royalties in Colombia are distributed between the national government and the departments.

(Superintendencia Financiera and Banca de las Oportunidades 2015a). Despite the fact that these levels of access are high relative to other Latin American countries, the actual meaning of this high level of financial inclusion is questionable, particularly in terms of effective use of banking products.

In particular, although Colombia surpasses the standards set by the international Alliance for Financial Inclusion of 250 access points per 100,000 adults, it is below the standards in relation to savings accounts and access to loans (Superintendencia Financiera and Banca de las Oportunidades 2015b). The share of people with access to savings accounts in 2015 was 50 per cent, with large disparities between major cities (65 per cent) and low-density rural areas (9 per cent). In terms of lending facilities, access to credit cards stood at 25 per cent, but it was very low for microcredits and housing loans—9 per cent and 2 per cent, respectively—again with large urban–rural disparities. In fact, the financial system is mainly used as a system for payments (transactions), rather than for savings or borrowing; this is in part due to the fact that government subsidies (conditional cash transfers, in particular) are paid through the financial system, by depositing them in the savings accounts of the beneficiaries (see in this regard Ocampo 2015: 181–3).

In terms of access of firms to banking products, there has also been a rapid growth over the past five years—10 per cent a year, according to the 2015 report on financial inclusion. However, there are large differences according to firm size. According to the World Bank's Enterprise Survey, access to bank accounts for firms is high in Colombia, but whereas 92 per cent of large firms had access to bank loans in 2010, only 64 per cent of medium-sized and 50 per cent of small firms did (World Bank and IFC 2010). According to a recent study, the major determinants of access to credit for the latter two groups are the size and the technological capacity of the firms (Botello 2015).

In 2006, the government launched a major programme of financial inclusion, Banca de las Oportunidades, to coordinate the actions of the public and private sectors to enhance access to finance. This initiative included the formulation of new regulatory norms to facilitate and generate incentives for the development of special products to serve the needs of low-income households and small firms, including special channels and institutions to provide them (Comisión Intersectorial de Inclusión Financiera 2016). This includes special mechanisms to support the geographical spread of the financial sector, particularly the broader use of 'bank correspondents' in rural areas and poor neighbourhoods in urban areas.

In 2015, the government reformulated its strategy of financial inclusion, with four specific areas of action: (i) promotion of the effective use of financial services; (ii) incentives to increase access and use of financial services in rural areas; (iii) new frameworks to finance small and medium-sized enterprises; and (iv) increased financial education/literacy. Financial inclusion is seen as a major instrument of poverty reduction, increased standards of living, and formalization. It is consistent with research that shows that Colombian firms that have access to lending tend to grow and invest more (Zuleta 2016).

7.3.2 *The Role of BANCOLDEX*

BANCOLDEX inherited from IFI the responsibility to facilitate access to credit for small and medium-sized firms (PYMES, according to the Spanish acronym), to which a special focus on microenterprises has been added in recent years.[17] This includes administering Banca de las Oportunidades as well as a series of special credit facilities: microcredits, micro-insurance facilities, and credits for entrepreneurial formalization. As indicated earlier, BANCOLDEX has recently redefined its role as a bank for entrepreneurial growth. So, aside from the special credit lines mentioned, young and dynamic small and medium-sized firms can access the special credit lines and guarantees to promote rapid growth, which encourages innovation, redefinition of markets for the expansion of the firms, and production sector development.

In 2016 BANCOLDEX disbursed almost COL$2 trillion for small and medium-sized enterprises through financial institutions, non-governmental organizations (NGOs), and credit unions, which represented 51.4 per cent of its overall lending. However, the share of microenterprises and PYMES in the total lending portfolio of BANCOLDEX has been falling in recent years (Zuleta 2016). Access to the rediscount facilities is complemented by the guarantees provided by the Fondo Nacional de Garantías of the Ministry of Trade, Industry, and Tourism, or by the regional guarantee funds it supports (nine currently), which provide this service for both working capital and longer-term investment loans, with a smaller ceiling in the first case.

BANCOLDEX is also in the process of designing a new unit of financial inclusion specialized in microfinance, which will provide special credit facilities for institutions that have no access to existing rediscount facilities, as they are not supervised by the Financial Superintendency. This includes not only non-banking institutions specialized in microcredit but also NGOs and smaller credit unions (the largest of them are subject to traditional prudential supervision). Credit facilities will be complemented with technical assistance to these institutions.

Banca de las Oportunidades was created in 2006 to promote access to credit and other financial services for small firms and poor households. It was also

[17] Microenterprises are defined as firms with less than ten workers and assets of less than 500 minimum wages (equivalent today to COL$369 million or somewhat above US$120,000 dollars at current exchange rates). In turn, PYMES are defined as those with assets in the range of 500 to 30,000 minimum wages, i.e. currently up to around US$7.5 million.

in charge of guaranteeing the spread of financial services to all municipalities. It does not directly provide financial services but it channels subsidies and other services to promote financial inclusion. They include: (i) subsidies to strategic activities or products that can enhance financial inclusion and can be standardized for broad market use, but that are not profitable in the short term; (ii) co-financing of strategic pilot projects that cannot be standardized, as they have to be custom-designed for each institution; and (iii) technical support to microfinance institutions, credit unions, and NGOs, as well as the promotion of research that can increase knowledge about the country's financial inclusion needs.

Among the achievements of Banca de las Oportunidades, we must underscore the design and promotion of the programme of bank correspondents in municipalities or poor urban neighbourhoods where financial institutions are absent. In 2016, there were 94,260 correspondents in stores, drugstores, post offices, telecommunication centres, and credit unions that provided financial services from one or more banks, thus guaranteeing access to those services in all Colombian municipalities. Since the launch of this programme in June 2007 to the end of 2016, there were 702 million transactions carried out through these correspondents totalling COL$178 trillion. This programme also includes subsidies to promote the opening of new offices in targeted localities.

Another major achievement of Banca de las Oportunidades is the programme of financial education provided physically, virtually, and through mass communication media. This programme also serves to overcome the tendency of small firms to claim that they do not need credit, which may be associated with the lack of financial education. The broader provision of financial services and associated education is also essential to break informal channels of credit and the associated usury.

7.3.3 *Promoting Financial Inclusion in Rural Areas*

Financial exclusion is more severe in rural areas (Superintendencia Financiera and Banca de las Oportunidades 2015b). This problem is enhanced by Colombia's rough geography, as well as the large areas characterized by low population density, notably in the Pacific coast, and the Orinoco and Amazon basins. A historical reason for the creation of Caja Agraria but also Banco Cafetero, as well as the decision to keep Banco Agrario as the only state commercial bank, was precisely to provide financial services in rural municipalities. The development of the new model of bank correspondents has lessened the need for such an institution, but the largest network of rural offices of any bank remains that of Banco Agrario.

The provision of financial services in rural areas is indeed quite limited. According to the 2014 agricultural census, only 27 per cent of producers have access to credit (Comisión Intersectorial de Inclusión Financiera 2016). The problem is particularly severe for smallholders. The 2011 household survey on living conditions indicates that the major reason for the limited access to credit is the lack of guarantees. This is associated, in turn, with the high level of informality of land property. To this we should add limited knowledge and the high transaction costs of formal credit. This leads to the use of costly informal credit channels. Limited financial inclusion has been a constraint for the sector's competitiveness and for the supply of foodstuffs, which, in Colombia, depends largely on smallholders (Misión para la Transformación del Campo 2016: vol. 3, ch. 18; Moreno et al. 2011). It has not only affected the standards of living of the rural poor, but also their capacity to mitigate adverse shocks, which also cause a deterioration of their living standards (Marulanda et al. 2010).

The 1990 reform of the agricultural credit system included the creation of FINAGRO and the agricultural credit commission (CNCA), for which FINAGRO serves as the technical secretariat. As indicated in the first section, this is the only case in which directed credit was maintained after the domestic financial liberalization that took place at the time. The credit system includes three basic resources for the agricultural sector:[18] (i) the rediscount facilities that FINAGRO provides, financed by the TDA that banks must buy when they fail to reach the 15 per cent of credit allocated to the sector; (ii) the substitution portfolio (*cartera sustitutiva*) that is made up of the credits directly allocated to the sector, and therefore reduces the amount of TDAs that banks must purchase; CNCA regulations have generated an incentive to provide credits to small producers through this channel;[19] and (iii) other credits extended by commercial banks that do not meet the requirements of agricultural credits according to CNCA. Credits to small producers through the first two channels also benefit from access to a special guarantee fund, Fondo Agropecuario de Garantias (FAG) that FINAGRO administers.

In 2016, the total agricultural credit portfolio amounted to COL$16.9 trillion, of which 44 per cent was financed by the rediscount lines, 52 per cent was made up of the substitution portfolio, and 4 per cent came from other bank loans. Credits to small producers represent 91 per cent of the number of credits but absorb only 27 per cent of their value versus 25 per cent and

[18] For a detailed analysis of the system, see Misión para la Transformación del Campo (2016: vol. 3, ch. 18).

[19] The portfolio that is used to estimate the reduction in the obligation to buy TDAs is a weighted one, with weights of 25 per cent for large, 50 per cent for medium-sized, and 150 per cent for small producers.

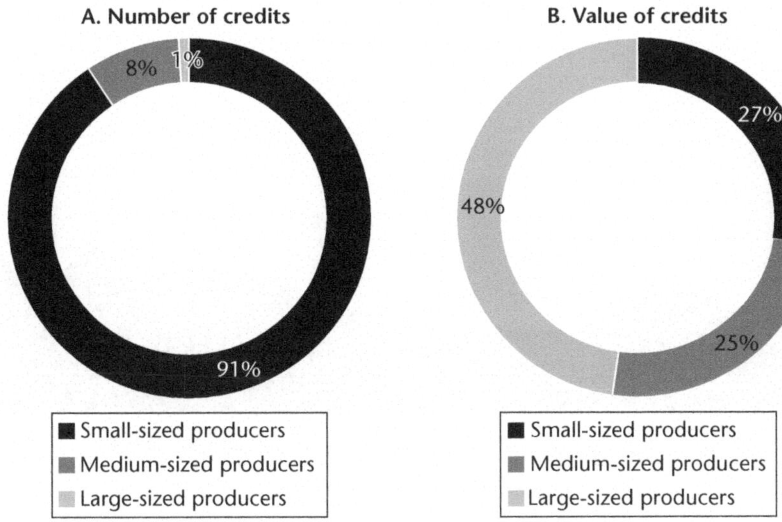

Figure 7.4. Agricultural credit according to size of producers
Source: FINAGRO

48 per cent for medium-sized and large-scale producers, respectively (Figure 7.4). An overwhelming majority of smallholder loans and associated discounts and guarantees have been provided by Banco Agrario. However, these credits do not generally reach the poorest producers.

As indicated, FINAGRO is financed by the subscription of TDAs by institutions that do not meet the 15 per cent directed credit threshold. There are two types of TDAs. TDA-A have a yield equivalent to the market interest rate for term deposits (DTF according to the acronym used in Colombia) minus four percentage points (DTF-4), and are used to rediscount lending to smallholders at subsidized interest rates. They now represent 50 per cent of the TDAs, this proportion having been raised in December 2015 from 37 per cent previously. TDA-B can be used for any rediscount, and have a yield of DTF-2. As Figure 7.5 indicates, total TDAs have fluctuated between 0.7 and 1.1 per cent of GDP. This has largely determined the total size of the rediscount facilities. Though FINAGRO can access other facilities, they would have a higher cost than the TDAs—which, as shown, pay interest rates under the domestic market rates.

Since existing smallholder credit lines do not really reach the poorest producers, there has been an attempt in recent years to develop new financial solutions for the bottom of the pyramid in the rural sector. This includes three facilities: (i) a new microcredit line; (ii) a special programme for rural microenterprises, Programa de Apoyo al Desarrollo de la Microempresa Rural

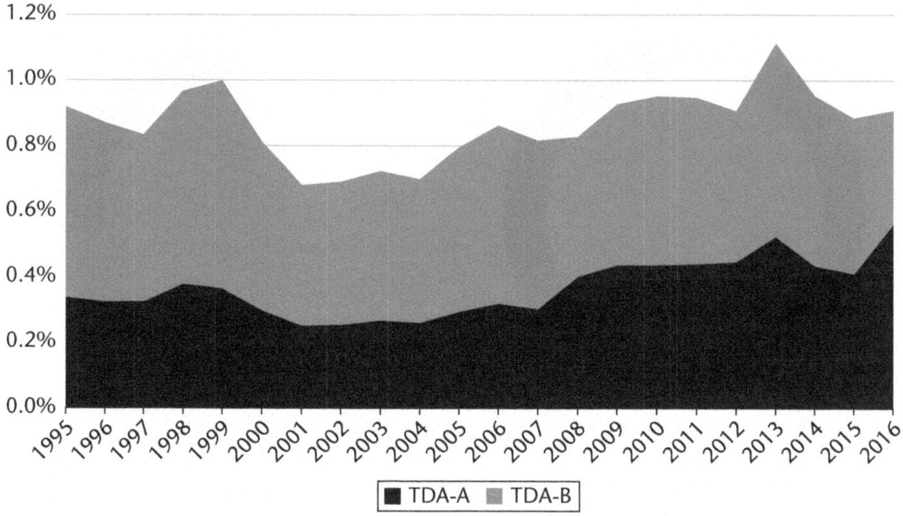

Figure 7.5. Agricultural Development Bonds (Títulos de Desarrollo Agropecuario, TDA) as percentage of GDP
Source: FINAGRO

(PADEMER); and (iii) a special fund for microfinances, Fondo para las Microfinanzas Rurales (FMR).

The first of these facilities is aimed at formal financial intermediaries that have access to FINAGRO's rediscount facilities, but in this case for lending to microenterprises that have no access to formal credit, and in smaller amounts than the traditional loans for smallholders. The average loan has been COL $1.8 million, much below the traditional loans for small producers (COL$8.6 million on average). However, this facility has been used on a very limited scale, reflecting the fact that traditional banking institutions are not the major providers of microcredit. There is, however, a subset of financial institutions specialized in microcredit, some of which have become banks and are now under the supervision of the Financial Superintendency: Bancamia, Mundo Mujer, and Women's World Bank (WWB) Colombia. These three institutions only represent 0.8 per cent of the assets of the banking sector but hold 28 per cent of microcredits.

There is also a larger set of non-banking institutions active in the provision of microcredit, including small credit unions, NGOs, and producer associations. This led to the creation of the second mechanism in 2005, PADEMER, a programme from the Ministry of Agriculture. This instrument operates through direct loans from special facilities administered by FINAGRO that create rotating funds managed by the non-banking institutions, which then lend to the relevant microenterprises. Until 2016, PADEMER had provided 70,585 microcredits for COL$131 million, mostly for working capital (84 per cent) and benefitting women to a large extent (62 per cent) (FINAGRO 2016). This programme has therefore familiarized FINAGRO with these non-banking institutions—also a way forward for similar BANCOLDEX facilities. Interestingly, the default rates for these loans have been significantly lower than for bank loans.

The third mechanism, FMR, is a joint initiative of FINAGRO and the Inter-American Development Bank, with technical assistance from Banca de las Oportunidades. The new FMR, which started operating in 2016, based on the experience of PADEMER, wants to offer a more integral solution for rural inclusion that, in addition to credits aimed at non-banking institutions, also includes technical assistance for these institutions as a key pillar. FINAGRO is expected to capitalize the FMR with resources from PADEMER and has already provided COL$6500 million for credits to 2600 producers by 2016. Currently, FINAGRO is developing FMR's strategy to get new resources and operationalize its funding procedures.

Furthermore, FINAGRO changed the requirements for the associative loans in 2016 to promote more financial inclusion. To have access to these credit lines, associations are now required to have at least 50 per cent of small producers. Finally, as indicated, FINAGRO also administers the guarantee fund (FAG), which supports lending to smallholders, including micro-entrepreneurs. This is a similar mechanism to the Fondo Nacional de Garantías but exclusively for small agricultural producers. It has been critical to expand access to credit: in 2015, 89 per cent of producers who had access to credit for the first time benefitted from FAG guarantees (FINAGRO 2016).

7.4 Business and Entrepreneural Growth

Structural transformation has always been at the centre of the development funds and banks' priorities in Colombia. In the 1940s and 1950s, equity investments and lending by IFI were crucial to create firms to produce steel, cement, and tyres, among others, and in the 1960s and 1970s to support the development of the petrochemical, metal mechanic, and automobile assembly sectors. This role has been reduced significantly since the first (moderate) financial reform of the second half of the 1970s. During the 1980s, equity investments by this institution focused on the support to firms and sectors that faced difficulties as a result of the domestic financial crisis the country faced at the time. For its part, the Export Promotion Fund (Fondo de Promoción de Exportaciones), the predecessor of BANCOLDEX, was created in 1967 to promote export diversification—a task that was fulfilled in a relatively successful way, like that of IFI promoting industrial diversification.

With the market reforms of the early 1990s, the focus of structural change policies shifted to enhancing competitiveness, through several committees and actions that were much less effective than past policies in terms of the structural diversification of the economy. The export promotion activities continued to be exercised by BANCOLDEX, using its rediscount facilities, and by an export promotion agency, PROEXPORT, which inherited the activities that in that regard had also been a responsibility of the central bank's Export Promotion Fund; it was transformed into PROCOLOMBIA in 2014, with the tasks of also promoting tourism and foreign direct investment. A special subsidy for agricultural investment, the Incentivo a la Capitalización Rural (ICR), was created in 1993. It is managed by FINAGRO and operates as a reduction in the principal of investment loans that the institution rediscounts (up to 40 per cent for small producers, and up to 20 per cent for medium-sized and large producers). The most recent mechanisms, on which we will focus in this section, are the redefinition of BANCOLDEX as a bank for entrepreneurial growth and the specific innovation programme it manages, which was created in 2012, iNNpulsa Colombia.

The redefinition of BANCOLDEX's role is a response not only to reduced demand for its export rediscounting facilities but also to the identification of the strong links between innovation and the growth of firms. According to the institution's analysis, the average growth of firms' revenues in Colombia is only 2 per cent in real terms (according to tax records), a reflection of the fact that 78 per cent of them have one-digit or negative growth. In contrast, firms that grow at two-digit rates, which represent 22 per cent of all firms, generate more employment, more social inclusion, and pay 63 per cent of corporate taxes. A major feature of these firms is that they innovate in their respective regions and sectors.

BANCOLDEX thus defined as one of its major tasks supporting the entrepreneurial modernization of firms of all sizes and in all regions—including the expansion abroad of firms that see such strategy as part of their business growth. Its major instrument is medium- and long-term rediscount facilities that help them in their growth strategy. Out of its lending portfolio of COL $3.89 trillion at the end of 2016, COL$1.56 trillion focused on its programme of entrepreneurial modernization (BANCOLDEX 2017). This is complemented by its platform of 'dynamic ecosystems' that supports organizations that promote competitiveness and business growth in different regions through three tools: (i) structuring of projects in science, technology, and innovation relevant for business growth; (ii) training to build up entrepreneurial capacities, such as the programme 3E for entrepreneurs active in export activities; and (iii) information to the regions on how to improve the entrepreneurial 'ecosystem'.

The institution has also been very active in promoting private equity venture funds to support business growth. It has supported them with its own equity investments as well as the promotion of good practices. As of 2016, it has leveraged around COL$1.5 trillion in different funds active in the sectors of infrastructure, agro-industry, information technologies, reforestation, and energy (BANCOLDEX 2017). As part of this activity, it signed an agreement with the Inter-American Development Bank to develop a catalogue of private investment funds in Colombia, which includes information on investment policies and relevant contacts. It also promotes forums and other events to increase connectivity among firms and investors. It is in the process of designing a 'fund of funds' to enhance its activities in this field.

The iNNpulsa programme supports innovation for business growth for firms of all sizes and ages, and in all sectors and regions of Colombia. It starts from the identification of a strong correlation between business growth and innovation (iNNpulsa 2015). It has defined three strategic areas of action: (i) interventions to generate a culture favourable for business growth based on innovation; (ii) correction of market failures, in particular by connecting actors active in the supply and demand for innovation; and (iii) strengthening regional agents promoting innovation and entrepreneurial development.

During its four years of existence, it has supported entrepreneurial communities of interest through promotional tours, fairs/festivals, the 'week of entrepreneurship', and the news agency iNNPulsa (in alliance with the Spanish agency EFE). In terms of market failures, its activities have focused on three areas: financing of firms in their early stages of development; promoting knowledge relevant for entrepreneurial growth; and access to information and business connections. Among its specific instruments, we should underscore the national network of 'angel investors' (Red Nacional de Ángeles Inversionistas), which it co-finances, and different regional initiatives to promote the incubation and growth of firms, encourage training in technology transfer and commercialization, and support strategies to promote rapid business growth.

According to a study by Estupiñán et al. (2015), the fact that iNNpulsa is housed in BANCOLDEX has been critical to give it flexibility in the execution of its programme and enable it to make adjustments according to emerging demands. In 2016, INNpulsa mobilized COL$85 billion through its co-financing instruments (BANCOLDEX 2017). It is expected that this programme will be transferred to Fiduciaria BANCOLDEX, a fiduciary trust owned by the bank, which is a specialized vehicle to administer programmes of this kind.

7.5 Conclusions

Development banks are organized in Colombia as a system of four (initially five) specialized institutions, with sectorial priorities. This system was adopted during the major reforms that took place around 1990, which eliminated the development functions of the central bank and liberalized the domestic financial sector but, interestingly, kept a strong development banking system. Two of these institutions, FINDETER and FINAGRO have increased or kept their share in the economy, while the other two, BANCOLDEX and FDN (previously FEN) have shrunk, but are now also in a process of restructuring and growth, notably in the case of FDN. Except for the agricultural sector, which kept instruments of directed credit, the other institutions must fund themselves in the local or international markets, or count on government resources for specific programmes (very large now in the case of FDN).

We have explored three areas of market failure in which these banks are very active and in most cases have significantly redefined their instruments in recent years: infrastructure development (and associated long-term lending), financial inclusion, and entrepreneurial growth. They operate mainly through rediscount facilities—except FDN, which is a first-tier institution, and BANCOLDEX, which is starting again to use first-tier facilities—but are also very active in the promotion of debt and equity funds in their areas of activities, manage investment incentives and innovation funds, administer or link with guarantee funds that support financial inclusion, and do a myriad of technical assistance activities, many of which support regional processes in their areas of interest.

FDN was recently restructured to support investment in infrastructure, particularly the fourth generation of highway PPPs (4G), in association with the private sector. It has developed numerous instruments to overcome the market failures that limit long-term infrastructure financing from both local and foreign investors. It was conceived as a catalyser of lending and investment in different infrastructure programmes. It faces major challenges, particularly guaranteeing the development of a dynamic local capital market and market instruments to cover the long-term currency risks that foreign investors face.

FINDETER, the bank specialized in local infrastructure, has been the most dynamic institution in the development banking system, particularly since the turn of the century. It has been very instrumental in the implementation of a series of programmes with a strong regional content in the areas of local and urban infrastructure for social services, transportation, housing, and water and sanitation.

Two institutions are active in financial inclusion. Almost half of BANCOLDEX's rediscounts are destined to micro, small, and medium-sized enterprises, and this institution manages the major programme to coordinate financial inclusion, Banca de las Oportunidades. A large proportion of FINAGRO rediscounts go to medium-sized and large agricultural producers, but lending to smallholders is largely done by the only remaining first-tier state commercial bank in the country, Banco Agrario, and financed by rediscounts from FINAGRO. FINAGRO has also been developing new instruments to promote microcredit through non-banking institutions, and BANCOLDEX is in the process of doing so. Financial inclusion is also supported by two guarantee funds, with FINAGRO managing the fund for agriculture.

The traditional activities of BANCOLDEX (and IFI, which it absorbed in 2002) in terms of structural change were redefined in recent years with a focus on the business growth of firms of all sizes and ages, and in all sectors and regions. It operates for this purpose through rediscount facilities, but is in the process of rethinking its role as a first-tier institution (an activity which IFI had in the past). Although BANCOLDEX does not have specific innovation policies, it manages one of the major policy instruments in this area, the programme iNNpulsa.

The redefinition of the functions of these institutions looks promising, and today, there is probably the strongest support for the role of development banks since the market reforms of the early 1990s. This system of specialized banks has worked well so far as it has allowed cooperation between the relevant ministries—sectorial ministries, the Ministry of Finance, and, in some cases, the National Planning Department. Therefore, the national government should keep it as it is, setting aside any idea of merging these entities into a big national development bank, based, for example, on the experience of BNDES in Brazil or KfW in Germany. Notwithstanding, it is important that they continue operating as a system, with clear policies from the relevant ministries to guide them in the priority-setting and coordination processes. It is also crucial that the banks interact, especially in areas where the mandates of two or more of them intersect: infrastructure development, financial inclusion, and the promotion of debt and equity funds, in particular. Additionally, it is also important to keep technical staff independent, reducing the possibility of political capture, a problem that can become a major source of inefficiency in the lending activities of the banks.

Funding strategies could also be an area of mutual interaction and learning, particularly to guarantee that their lending programmes are consistent with the more competitive financial sector that characterizes Colombia today; indeed, limited competitiveness has caused BANCOLDEX to shrink. There is, however, no institutional mechanism in place that guarantees coordination among development banks.

Except for FDN, which has minority strategic partners who chair the board and have control over critical decisions, the other institutions are controlled by the national government (though with minority private ownership in the case of FINAGRO). There is an ongoing discussion on whether the respective ministers should stop chairing the boards of the other banks to meet OECD standards, and BANCOLDEX is thinking of adopting a governance structure similar to that of FDN. This should not be seen as a crucial reform, and it would weaken an essential characteristic of Colombia's public sector administration and, in particular, undermine the alignment of the priorities of the banks with the plans and strategies of the national government. Also, there are no specific prudential regulations for these institutions. This is also a feature of world financial regulations, and should be corrected, as these institutions face risks that are very different to those of commercial banks.

References

BANCOLDEX. 2017. *BANCOLDEX: Informe Anual 2016*. Available at <www.bancoldex.com/documentos/9691_Bancoldex_Reporte_Anual_2016.pdf>, accessed 30 April 2017.

Bitran, E., S. Nieto-Parra, and J. Robledo. 2013. *Opening the Black Box of Contract Renegotiations: An Analysis of Road Concessions in Chile, Colombia and Peru*. OECD Development Centre, Working Paper No. 317. Available at <www.oecd.org/officialdocuments/publicdisplaydocumentpdf/?cote=DEV/DOC(2013)2&docLanguage=En>, accessed 30 April 2017.

Botello, H. 2015. *Determinantes del acceso al crédito de PYMES en Colombia*. Ensayos de Economía No. 46, January–June, 135–55. Bogotá: Universidad Nacional de Colombia.

Comisión Intersectorial de Inclusión Financiera. 2016. *Estrategia Nacional de Inclusión Financiera*. Available at <http://www.minhacienda.gov.co/HomeMinhacienda/ShowProperty?nodeId=%2FOCS%2FP_MHCP_WCC-041673%2F%2FidcPrimaryFile&revision=latestreleased>, accessed 20 April 2018.

DNP (Departamento Nacional de Planeación). 2010. *Bases del Plan Nacional de Desarrollo 2010–2014: Prosperidad para todos*. Available at <https://colaboracion.dnp.gov.co/CDT/PND/Bases%20PND%202010-2014%20Versi%C3%B3n%205%2014-04-2011%20completo.pdf>, accessed 20 April 2018.

Estupiñán, F., F. Castro, H. Garcia, M. Reina, and N. Rincón. 2015. *Análisis y documentación de los resultados de diez instrumentos de iNNpulsa*. Bogotá: FEDESARROLLO.

FINAGRO. 2016. *Informe de Gestión Sostenible 2015*. Available at <https://www.finagro.com.co/sites/default/files/informe_de_gestion_2015_web2.pdf>, accessed 20 April 2018.

Gómez, H. J. 1990. 'Antecedentes y evolución del crédito de fomento y su relación con el banco central', in *El Banco de la República: Antecedentes, evolución y estructura*. Bogotá: Editorial del Banco de la República, ch. XVIII.

INNpulsa. 2015. *Informe de gestión de INNpulsa Colombia: Tres años impulsando el crecimiento empresarial extraordinario: Febrero 2012 a diciembre 2014*. Available at <www.innpulsacolombia.com/sites/all/themes/sitetheme/assets/Informe-de-gestion-iNNpulsa-Colombia-2012-2014.pdf>, accessed 30 April 2017.

Marulanda, B., M. Paredes, and L. Fajury. 2010. *Acceso a servicios financieros en Colombia: Retos para el siguiente cuatrenio*. Bogotá: CAF and FEDESARROLLO. Available at <https://www.caf.com/media/3786/Bancarización.pdf>, accessed 30 April 2017.

Misión para la Transformación del Campo. 2016. *El campo colombiano: Un camino hacia el bienestar y la paz*. Informe detallado, Departamento Nacional de Planeación.

Available at <www.dnp.gov.co/programas/agricultura/Paginas/Informes-misión.aspx>, accessed 30 April 2017.

Moreno, D. F., J. P. Gordo, and D. Estrada. 2011. *Report de Estabilidad Financiera. Financiamiento del sector agropecuario: Situación y perspectivas.* Temas de Estabilidad Financiera No. 59. Bogotá: Banco de la República.

Ocampo, J. A. 2015. *Una historia del sistema financiero colombiano.* Bogotá: Portafolio and Asociación Bancaria de Colombia.

Superintendencia Financiera de Colombia y Banca de las Oportunidades. 2015a. *Estudio de demanda para analizar la inclusión financiera en Colombia.* Available at <http://bancadelasoportunidades.gov.co/es/publicaciones/encuestas-de-demanda>, accessed 30 April 2017.

Superintendencia Financiera de Colombia y Banca de las Oportunidades. 2015b. *Reporte de Inclusión Financiera 2015.* Available at <http://www.bancadelasoportunidades.gov.co/documentos/RIF-2015.pdf>, accessed 30 April 2017.

World Bank. 2017. *International LPI Global Ranking.* Available at <http://lpi.worldbank.org/international/global/2016>, accessed 30 April 2017.

World Bank and IFC. 2010. *Enterprise Survey: Colombia Country Profile.* Available at <http://www.enterprisesurveys.org/~/media/GIAWB/EnterpriseSurveys/Documents/Profiles/English/colombia-2010.pdf>, accessed 30 April 2017.

Yepes, T., J. Ramirez, L. Villar, and J. Aguilar. 2013. *Infraestructura de transporte en Colombia.* Cuaderno de Fedesarrollo No. 46. Bogotá: FEDESARROLLO.

Zuleta, L. 2016. *Inclusión financiera de la pequeña y mediana empresa en Colombia.* Serie Financiamiento para el Desarrollo No. 262. Santiago: ECLAC.

Additional Reading

Schwab, K. and X. Sala-i-Martín. 2016. *The Global Competitiveness Report 2016–2017.* Geneva: World Economic Forum (WEF).

Vesga, R. 2015. *El caso de INNpulsa Colombia: La evolución de una política pública para el crecimiento empresarial extraordinario.* Serie Políticas Públicas y Transformación Productiva No. 19. Bogotá: Banco de Desarrollo de América Latina CAF.

8

The Experience of Development Banking in Peru

1990–2015

Óscar Dancourt and Renzo Jiménez Sotelo

8.1 Introduction

At the start of the 1980s, the overall lending of the state financial entities, which exercised the functions of a development bank,[1] amounted to 15 per cent of gross domestic product (GDP). By 1993, following Alberto Fujimori's neoliberal reforms, which entailed the liquidation and privatization of almost all of Peru's state-owned enterprises, whether productive or financial, the overall lending of the state-owned financial institutions had fallen drastically to 3 per cent of GDP.

However, the Peruvian economy grew at an average annual rate (GDP) of 5.7 per cent, with very low inflation (consumer price index (CPI)) of 2.8 per cent per year, during the period 2002–15. The country's notable performance over this fourteen-year period, which was based on the commodities super-cycle; minimal state intervention in the economy besides effective monetary and fiscal policies, except for 2014–16; negligible productive diversification; and maximum commercial and financial openness to globalization, seems to have had no connection whatsoever with the role of these state-owned financial institutions. Peru's commodities export economy did not require a state development bank.

[1] According to Ferraz, Além, and Madeira, development banks are 'a non-monetary financial intermediary providing long-term loans, which often are government-controlled institutions and operate in segmented markets aiming at promoting the capital development of the economy' (2013).

In 2014–15, the external context deteriorated markedly. In tandem with the slump in international metal prices, GDP growth slowed significantly to an annual average of 2.8 per cent. The question is whether the Peruvian economy will survive the acid test of all commodity-exporting economies: extending growth beyond a long cycle of favourable prices for its export products. Is it, then, time to rethink the role that development banking could play in diversifying the Peruvian economy's production and in closing the infrastructure gap?

Diversification of the Peruvian economy's production structure remains incipient (see, for example, Hausmann and Klinger 2008). The administration of Pedro Pablo Kuczynski inherited in 2016 a less than promising mining-exporting economy, integrated into an urbanized society.[2] The external forces—high commodity prices and capital inflows—that drove economic growth over the past fifteen years will lie dormant for the foreseeable future (see IMF World Economic Outlook 2015 and 2016). Sooner or later, the new administration will be compelled to try to diversify the Peruvian economy in some shape or form. Without the expansion of industries besides mining or the components of aggregate demand other than investment in the extractive sectors, there will be no economic growth in the cities as well as insufficient urban job creation. This process of diversifying the productive apparatus requires a master plan underpinned by public investment, a higher exchange rate, and a genuine state development bank.

This international context has revived interest in the relevance of credit for economic development as highlighted by Schumpeter (1967 [1934]), and on the conditioning effect of the financial system in the short term as signalled by Keynes (2003 [1943]). From there comes the importance of the development banking activities of state financial institutions as a policy instrument to help mitigate those market failures that could hinder a sufficient and adequate credit supply, especially in countries such as Peru where the stock markets are underdeveloped.[3] While several state-owned financial entities exist, to date the Peruvian government does not have an effective development bank as a long-term public policy instrument.

In Peru, the preponderant view of the state's role in the economy is marked by the radical experience of privatization of state-owned companies and financial deregulation accomplished during the dictatorial regime of Fujimori (1990–2000). The 1993 Constitution established that the state can subsidiarily undertake business activities only where expressly authorized by law. This peculiar political-legal context accounts for the performance of development banking in Peru since the 1990s. It is often said that state-owned enterprises can only engage in that which is expressly and specifically provided for by law,

[2] Direct employment in the mining industry does not even account for 1 per cent of the workforce.

[3] For an analysis of financial restrictions on economic development, see Hermann (2014).

unlike private enterprises, which can engage in whatever the law does not expressly prohibit.

On the basis of this controversial 'subsidiary role of the state', state-owned companies are not allowed to compete with private firms on an equal footing, unlike in the Organization for Economic Cooperation and Development (OECD) countries (for example, see OECD 2011 or 2016). In the case of financial companies, this means that their sources of funding in local currency are not competitive and, on the contrary, have often ended up adding to the external debt while contributing to the extensive dollarization of the financial system and the underdevelopment of the securities market (Jiménez Sotelo 2009 and 2010b).

This chapter is organized in ten sections. The second and third sections provide a brief overview of the privatization and dollarization of the financial system, as well as the circumstances regarding the three main market failures in the Peruvian financial system. The fourth reviews the political and legal framework in which state-run financial enterprises have operated since the 1990s. The fifth, sixth, seventh, and eighth sections describe, in broad terms, the legal framework and the economic situation of the four state-owned financial entities currently in existence in Peru. The ninth section outlines the possible strategy and vision of the future to build a true development bank in Peru. The final section contains the conclusions.

8.2 Privatization and Dollarization of the Financial System

At the start of the 1970s, the ECLAC-inspired structural reforms implemented by the military regime of Velasco (1968–75) created a strong sector of public enterprises, productive and financial, which came to control more than 30 per cent of GDP and endured without major changes until the 1990s. This process entailed the nationalization of a considerable proportion of foreign investment and much of the real assets owned by the oligarchy of the day.[4]

The neoliberal structural reforms applied by Fujimori's authoritarian regime in the 1990s can be understood (see Dancourt 1999) as a near-perfect antithesis to Velasco's reforms. An essential component of these reforms was the privatization of the strong public enterprise sector (see Ruiz Caro 2002), as well as the liquidation of almost all state development banking, which accounted for a sizable share of the loans and deposits market.[5] Foreign

[4] According to Fitzgerald, 'the state assumed responsibility for three-quarters of the exports, half of the imports, over half of the fixed investment, two-thirds of the bank credit, and a third of all employment in the corporate sector' (1983). Translation by authors.

[5] In 1992 the five state development banks created prior to the Velasco administration were liquidated; see Castillo Torres (2005).

capital, oriented towards the extractive export sector and public services, recovered its standout role in the economy upon acquiring much of the privatized state companies.

The relative size of the state-owned financial entities varied substantially with these radical yet diametrically opposed changes to the state's intervention in the economy, as shown in Figure 8.1. By the start of the 1980s, the credit channelled to the economy (public and private sectors) by state-owned financial companies accounted for, on average, 15 per cent of annual GDP, while the credit granted by commercial banks amounted to only 7 per cent of annual GDP. From the 1990s, lending by state-owned financial entities plunged to less than 3 per cent of annual GDP and remained at that level for the next two decades.

Lending by state-owned financial entities was subject to only a temporary increase during the banking crisis of 1998–9, which ushered in a steep decline in the loans granted by commercial banks that continued until 2004, as well as a series of bankruptcies and bailouts that included the second- and fifth-largest banks in terms of deposits, according to Rojas and Costa (2002) and Jiménez Sotelo (2010b). In the end, of the twenty-five existing commercial banks, twelve underwent interventions, were absorbed, or were merged. From 2005–6, as can be seen in Figure 8.1, commercial banking grew continuously to the point where the loans granted by the sector exceeded 35 per cent of GDP in 2015.

Figure 8.2 shows the trajectory of the credit-to-GDP ratio for the different state-owned financial entities over the period 1980–2015. The five state-owned development banks (the so-called *bancos de fomento*) liquidated during

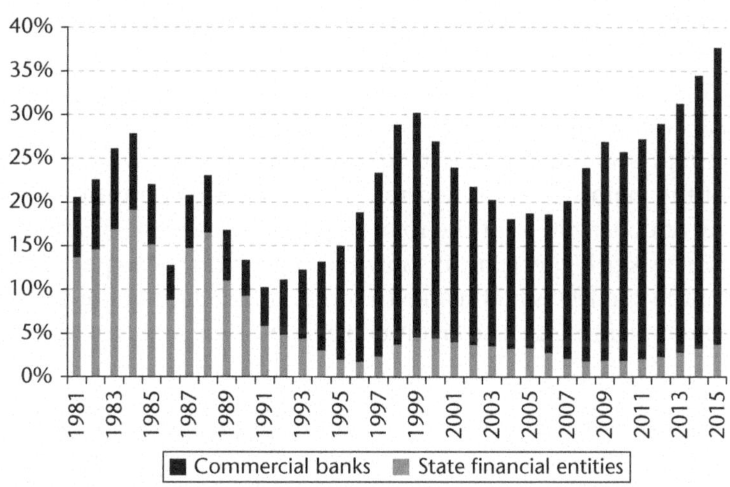

Figure 8.1. Peru: Overall average lending by financial entities, out of GDP
Sources: SBS, INEI, and BCRP. Compiled by authors

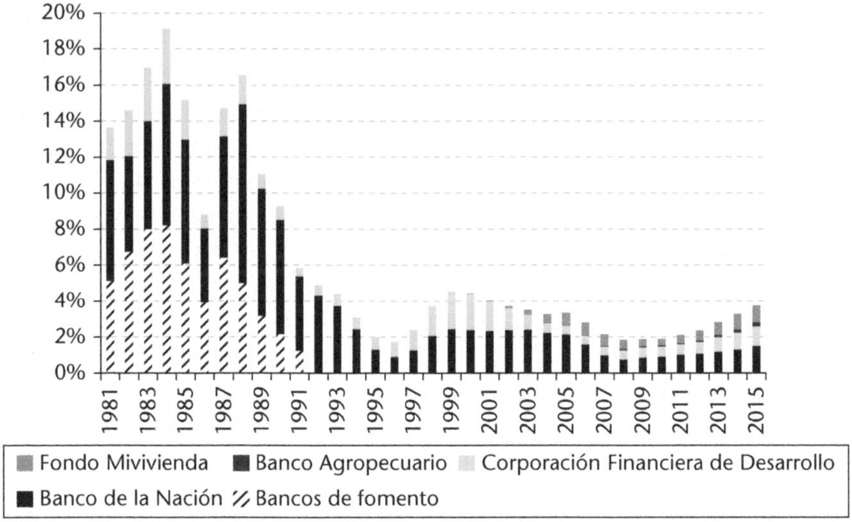

Figure 8.2. Peru: Overall average lending by state-owned financial entities, out of GDP
Sources: INEI and SBS. Compiled by authors

the banking crisis in 1991–2[6] granted loans worth the equivalent of 6–8 per cent of GDP at the start of the 1980s. Corporación Financiera de Desarrollo and the Banco de la Nación, which account for the lion's share, went from lending 10 per cent of GDP at the start of the 1980s to just 2–4 per cent of GDP from the 1990s; during the banking crisis of 1998–9, they temporarily increased their joint lending when they participated in the state bailout of private commercial banking.[7] The other two state-owned financial companies, Banco Agropecuario and especially the Fondo MiVivienda, took on a degree of importance starting from 2004–5.

The basic processes that transformed the Peruvian financial system in the 1990s were twofold: first, the privatization process that has been succinctly described; and second, the credit dollarization process, which qualifies as another of the main structural reforms of the Fujimori administration.

The level of dollarization of the total credit granted by the financial entities climbed to a peak of 80 per cent, as shown in Figure 8.3. The hyperinflation that emerged in the late 1980s had sparked a brutal contraction in the credit system and its rapid dollarization. The credit expansion of the 1990s, which occurred

[6] The agricultural, industrial, mining, and housing development banks were wound up by Decree Law No. 25478, leaving the Superintendence of Banking and Insurance (SBS), whose function was to control, oversee, or liquidate both private or state-owned banks. The mortgage bank, for its part, was declared a private legal entity under Decree Law No. 25479 and wound up three months later under Resolution No. 766-92-SBS.

[7] According to Castillo, COFIDE 'had to include commercial loans of [the] liquidated [private financial] intermediaries in its assets' (2005). Translation by authors.

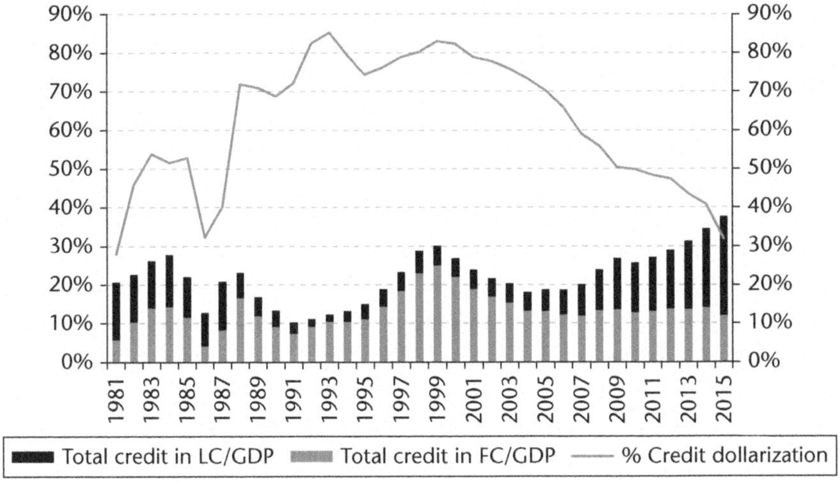

Figure 8.3. Peru: Dollarization of credit from financial entities
Source: SBS. Compiled by authors

in a context of macroeconomic stabilization in which economic activity recovered and inflation dropped to below 10 per cent per year, was basically an expansion of credit in foreign currency, which reached a pinnacle of somewhere above 20 per cent of GDP right before the banking crisis of 1998–9.

This dollarization of credit[8] during the 1990s is explained by the characteristics of a monetary regime based on control of the quantity of money, which impeded an expansion of credit in local currency on the initiative of commercial banking; by the authorization given to commercial banks to extend credit and receive deposits in foreign currency without any limits whatsoever; and by a regulatory system that did not impose reserve requirements on the foreign funding of banks via external debts, according to Jiménez Sotelo (2010b) and Dancourt (2014).

Following the banking crisis of 1998–9, the level of credit dollarization dwindled slowly from 78 per cent in 2002 to 32 per cent in 2015, thus returning to the levels seen at the start of the 1980s. It is also clear, as shown in Figure 8.3, that this gradual de-dollarization of credit reflects an expansion of credit in local currency, which rose from 3 per cent of GDP in 2002 to 25 per cent of GDP in 2015, rather than a contraction of credit in foreign currency, which fluctuated around 12 per cent of GDP over the last decade.

This gradual de-dollarization of credit is associated, first, with the implementation in 2002 of an inflation-targeting monetary regime, whereby a

[8] García-Escribano shows that the level of credit dollarization is greater for loans with longer maturities and for loans to large companies, in comparison with those for small companies or for individuals (2010).

short-term interest rate became the main monetary-policy instrument, replacing the control of various monetary aggregates that had prevailed during the 1990s and enabling the expansion of bank credit in local currency at the initiative of commercial banking; second, with the banking crisis of 1998–9, which temporarily reduced local banks' funding capacity via external debt; third, with the development of a domestic public debt market in local currency from the 2000s, with bonds of increasingly long maturities; and fourth, with an active de-dollarization policy on the part of the central bank, which operated, primarily, by imposing reserve requirements on the foreign funding of commercial banks, to a greater or lesser degree depending upon the specific period (Armas and Grippa 2005, Jiménez Sotelo 2010b, García-Escribano 2010, and Dancourt 2014).

The dollarization of credit not only severely curtails the power of monetary policy, but also increases both the economy's external vulnerability and the likelihood of banking crises. A rise in the real exchange rate prompted by an adverse external shock (a fall in the prices of export commodities or a rise in the international interest rate) increases the debt burden for foreign-currency debtors who receive their income in local currency, which causes a decrease in consumption and investment. This balance sheet effect can impact both the private and public sectors. Typically, delinquency and defaults on foreign-currency loans increase, and runs on local banks by foreign creditors or by depositors may be triggered, as occurred in 1998–9.

8.3 Main Financial Market Failures

Development banking has its origins in the need to mitigate market failures in the financial sector. According to Rezende (2017), 'most development banks were created to promote social and/or economic development'. Of these development banks, 'almost half of them (49 percent) were established during the import-substitution years between 1946 and 1989, nearly two-fifths (39 percent) came into existence during the globalization years between 1990 and 2011. One implication is that irrespective of policy orientation, the failure of private financial markets to deliver adequate long-term finance forces governments to rely on development banking institutions,' according to Chandrasekhar (2016), quoted by Rezende (2017).

In the current Peruvian economy, the main market failures of the financial system are still related to long-term financing, agricultural financing, and the financing of small businesses. Other market failures, such as those related to financing the necessary diversification of production in the Peruvian economy as well as climate change mitigation, are somewhat more convoluted and should be considered in their own right, as the state apparatus does not

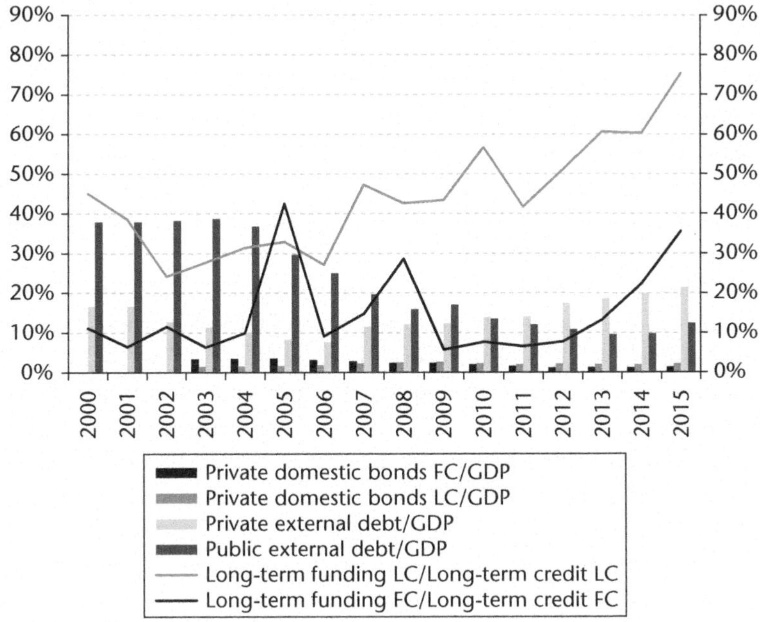

Figure 8.4. Peru: Domestic bonds, foreign debt, and credit funding mismatches
Sources: INEI and SBS. Compiled by authors

today encompass a structured plan[9] concerning these objectives or a national development strategy that differs from the commodities export economy promoted in the 1990s.

The first failure of the financial system in the current Peruvian economy is related to long-term financing. The dollarization of credit and dependence on external debt are primarily a result of insufficient long-term financing in local currency. According to Banco Central de Reserva del Perú (BCRP), the level of dollarization of the extended financing (internal and external debt) of the private sector was 48.6 per cent at the end of 2015. As shown in Figure 8.4, although external public debt fell from more than 30 per cent of GDP at the start of the 2000s to 10 per cent of GDP in 2013–15—a decrease explained in part by the development of a local public bond market denominated in local currency—at the same time, the external debt of the private sector increased over the last decade, exceeding 20 per cent of GDP by 2015. Therefore, overall external debt, both public and private, went up towards the end of this period. In 2014–15 alone, external debt increased from 31.8 per cent to 35.5 per cent of GDP (Moody's 2016). Most of the state-owned financial

[9] For instance, the China Development Bank participates in the nationwide Five-Year Plan, according to Xu (2017).

companies contributed to this result, since their long-term external debt grew by 42.9 per cent in 2015 (MEF 2016a); this is despite one of their general mandates being to develop the domestic securities market.

Figure 8.4 also shows the underdevelopment of the private domestic bonds market in relation to the scale of private external debt. And as the recent experience of the Peruvian public sector proves, further developing this bond market and reducing the dollarization of credit are two sides of the same coin (MEF 2014 and 2015).

However, the problem of long-term financing in local currency for the financial entities themselves is still ongoing. In 2015, as shown in Figure 8.4, almost two-thirds of all long-term credit in local currency (including mortgages, financial leasing, and loans) granted by commercial banks did not have long-term funding in the same currency (including due to banks and other entities and unsubordinated bonds and notes issued), while only a quarter of the credit in foreign currency did not have long-term funding in the same currency. The local-currency mismatch ratio has fallen since 2013, primarily due to the increased supply of longer-term funds granted by the central bank to commercial banking through repurchase agreements guaranteed with deposits in dollars.

A clear area for improvement is associated with the supply of housing loans. State intervention through subsidized withdrawals and guarantees has enabled the expansion of mortgages, albeit in foreign currency through to 2006, as we will see later.

The second failure of the financial system in the current Peruvian economy is related to agricultural financing. According to the SBS, only 4.1 per cent of all business loans granted in 2015 by commercial banks were towards agriculture, livestock, hunting, and forestry, despite the fact that this economic sector employs a quarter of the country's occupied workforce. This failure is exacerbated by the absence of mass agricultural insurance in the country, a key factor that hampers better management of biological and weather risks, which cannot be controlled by either the bank or the farmer (Jiménez Sotelo 2001: 3). Indeed, as 'agricultural activity is exposed to adverse climatic conditions that cause production losses and affect the income of farmers and agro-enterprises [their occurrence ends up impacting] public finances, as it is habitual for governments to contribute financial resources or to waive the [collection] of certain taxes in order to assist the affected population' (Hatch et al. 2012: 4).[10] In 2006, the Countryside and Agricultural Insurance Guarantee Fund (Fondo de Garantía para el Campo y del Seguro Agropecuario, FOGASA), under the auspices of the Ministry of Agriculture and Irrigation (MAR), was created to

[10] Translation by authors.

cover farmers in the poorest and most vulnerable parts of the country; the state participated by co-sponsoring the financing of all premiums alongside two nationwide insurance companies. However, its weak performance was reflected in a volatile claims rate (cost of claims/premium net of general sales tax), which between 2009 and 2015 fluctuated between 28.9 per cent and 71.4 per cent, with an average of 42.7 per cent (Bartra 2015).

To improve this situation, it would be necessary to design agricultural insurance policies suitable for as wide a variety of crops and microclimates as those of Peru, but in the country there are neither the required actuarial studies, nor universities that train professionals versed in actuarial sciences.[11] According to the Peruvian Association of Insurance Companies (Asociación Peruana de Empresas de Seguros, APESEG), there were some ninety professionals engaged in miscellaneous actuarial activities in Peru in 2014, but less than 20 per cent were formally trained in the area, and of this proportion, only 40 per cent were Peruvian, despite the considerable demand for labour (Morris 2014). According to representatives of the International Actuarial Association (IAA), Peru requires 1500 actuaries (Corzo 2015).

Finally, it is worth recalling that much of agricultural financing requires lengthy grace periods, often not only for the principal but for the interest as well, which is not usually true of commercial credit. For example, as they grow and reach their full production stage, the investment process in fruit tree cultivation requires credit with average grace periods of four to seven years (Jiménez Sotelo 2001: 19).

The third failure of the financial system in the current Peruvian economy is related to the financing of small companies. The supply of credit to small and microenterprises[12] is limited; according to the SBS, it accounted for only 7.6 per cent of all direct credit granted by commercial banks in 2015, despite companies with between two and ten employees making up 22.0 per cent of Peru's workforce, according to the Instituto Nacional de Estadística e Informática (INEI).

This credit rationing is reflected in the high interest rates paid by smaller companies. As shown in Figure 8.5, the average interest rate that commercial banks charged small enterprises for loans of less than 360 days fluctuated between 27 per cent and 34 per cent per annum during 2010–16, while the monetary policy interest rate or the borrowing rate paid by banks on deposits of 180 to 360 days did not exceed 6 per cent per annum over the same period. It should be noted that the effective or expected inflation rate likewise did not

[11] An actuary is a 'person versed in mathematical calculation and statistical, juridical, and financial knowledge concerning insurance and the insurance system, who advises insurance companies and acts as an expert in the operations thereof' (RAE 2014). Translation by authors.

[12] The SBS classifies credit to microenterprises as loans of less than PEN 20,000, and credit to small enterprises as loans below PEN 300,000 (1 USD = PEN 3.41).

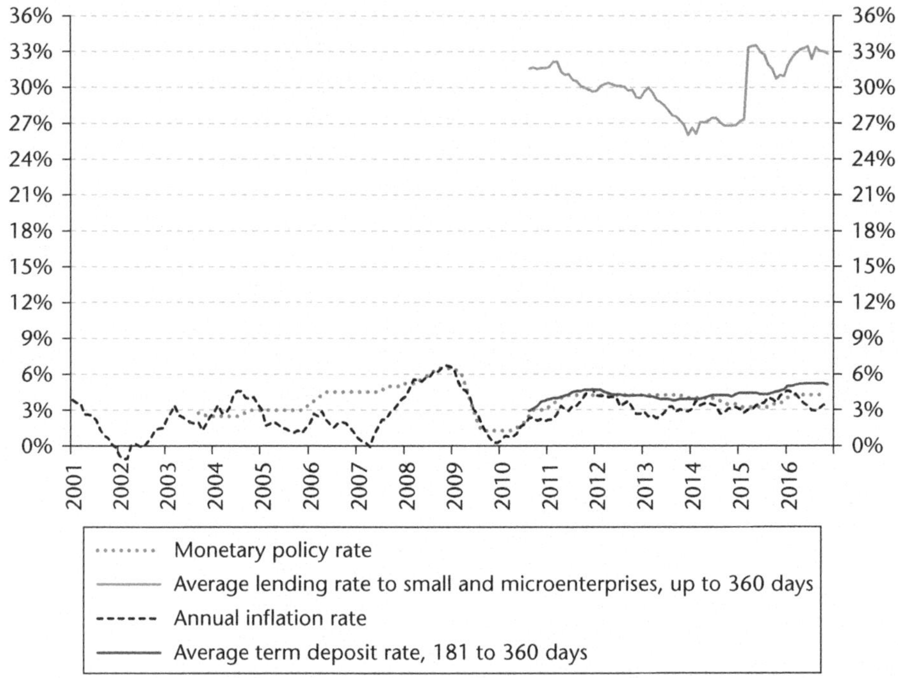

Figure 8.5. Peru: Commercial banks, monetary policy, and inflation rates
Source: BCRP. Compiled by authors

surpass 5 per cent per annum during this period, which implies that the real interest rates paid by small companies are indeed extremely high.

The credit rationing for small and microenterprises has been mitigated by the so-called microfinancing institutions, especially by Municipal Savings and Credit Unions (Cajas Municipales de Ahorro y Crédito) established at the start of the 1980s, whose activities were not affected by the banking crisis of 1998–9. However, the interest rates that these institutions charge small and microenterprises are equal to or greater than the rates set by commercial banks, which have concentrated on the relatively large ones.

According to international experience, 'small companies have greater ease in obtaining financing when: public banks predominate, private banks are domestically owned, smaller and more flexible institutions exist, and there is a national development bank' (Ferraro and Goldstein 2011: 11).[13] As regards the level of concentration of the Peruvian financial system, of sixty-three supervised credit entities, the largest four commercial banks cornered 72.6 per cent of the lending market in 2015.

[13] Translation by authors.

8.4 Political and Legal Framework

Over the last twenty-five years, Peruvian governments have not given state-run financial entities a major role in tackling the market failures in the financial system cited in the previous section, or in participating in strategic tasks such as diversifying the economy's productive apparatus or closing the infrastructure gap. As we have seen, the size of these state-run financial institutions in relation to GDP has been minimal since the 1990s.

As was mentioned in the introduction, the neoliberal view of the state's role in the Peruvian economy is marked by the radical experience of privatization and financial deregulation accomplished during the Fujimori administration.[14] The diminished role of development banking in Peru after the 1990s cannot be explained without referring to this political and legal context or to the controversial subsidiary role of state-owned companies[15] in the 1993 Constitution.

The legal bases of the change of development model were established in 1991, before the change in the Constitution, through four legislative decrees[16] whose objective was to: (i) remove obstacles and restrictions to public investment and create a legally stable regime thereto; (ii) grant private investors the guarantees to acquire shares and assets of state-owned companies; (iii) consolidate the programme of structural reforms by guaranteeing free initiative and private investment; and (iv) recognize the system of concessions for the construction, conservation, and exploitation of public service infrastructure works (MEF 2016b).

In this context, the so-called 'public–private associations' appear as a sequel to the 1990s structural reforms that, including a new legal framework approved in recent years, encompass all those agreements in which the state delegates a series of typically public activities, especially those concerning public investment. In these operations, the state ultimately retains the bulk of the risks by assuming a series of firm and contingent liabilities or commitments that go beyond traditional concessions. In perspective, these risks gradually put pressure on the sovereign risk rating by reducing capacity to pay the public debt (Figure 8.6) in the absence of a state-run development

[14] For example, a textbook recently prepared by MEF states that in 'the decade of the nineties, the Peruvian state undertook a process of promoting private investment, in order to transfer to the private sector the leadership of economic sectors that were in the hands of the state for more than 20 years. This process was carried out within the framework of the policy of economic stability and market liberalization. The central axes of this promotion process were channelled through the privatization of public companies and concessions for the provision of public services, previously delivered by the state' (2016b: 5). Translation by authors.

[15] Article 60 of the 1993 Constitution establishes that only where expressly authorized by law can the state undertake subsidiary business activities, directly or indirectly, for reasons of high public interest or manifest national convenience.

[16] Decretos Legislativos No. 662, No. 674, No. 757, and No. 758.

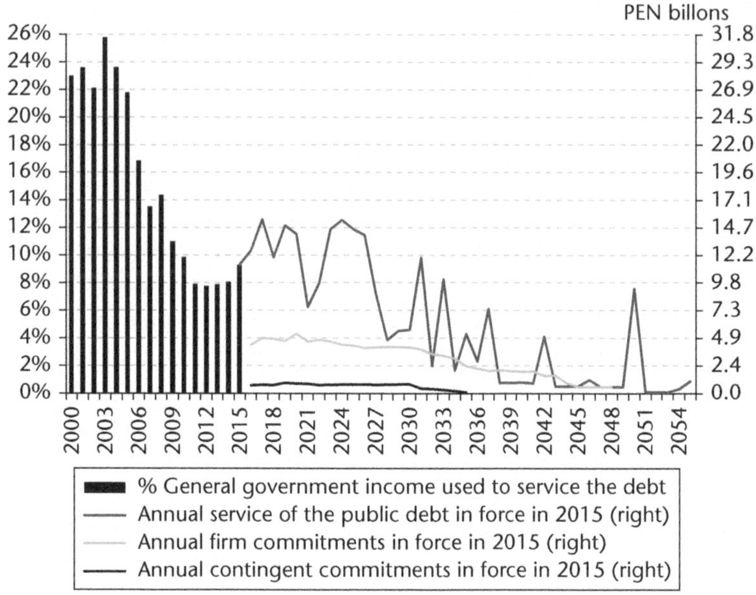

Figure 8.6. Peru: Servicing of the public debt and firm and contingent payment commitments

Sources: MEF and BCRP. Compiled by authors

bank to act as a counterbalance in keeping the private participation incentives aligned—especially as regards the processes of financial structuring and designing bankable feasibility, supervision of economic-financial balance, or advising in the rescue of the concession—as in other countries.

The structural reforms of the 1990s also had dire consequences for the national strategic planning system. A national planning system for economic and social development that had been created in 1962[17] operated during the 1970s and 1980s. The National Institute of Planning (Instituto Nacional de Planificación), which drew on a team of able and experienced technicians, was an important factor in the debate and in the construction of economic policies for the Peruvian state apparatus. However, it was wound up and deactivated in 1992,[18] its staff transferred or made available as surplus to requirements. The Ministry of Economy and Finances (MEF) assumed its functions in theory; but, in practice, no specialized area with responsibility for these matters was created inside it (Jiménez Sotelo 2017: 9–10).

After the fall of the Fujimori dictatorship, the Governance Forum for the National Agreement (Foro de Gobernabilidad del Acuerdo Nacional) revisited the idea of national strategic planning as a state policy agreed between political

[17] Decreto Ley Nº 14220. [18] Decreto Ley Nº 25548.

parties, civil society, religious institutions, and the government, as a basis for democratic transition and consolidation. Although a new national strategic planning system was devised in 2005,[19] it was not implemented and was substituted in 2008[20] by another system, which was given a three-year time frame for the initial implementation of its technical agency, Centro Nacional de Planeamiento Estratégico (CEPLAN), to be attached to the Presidency of the Council of Ministers. It was not until 2014 that CEPLAN approved a directive[21] to commence a real strategic planning process across the public sector.

In consequence, for two decades the Peruvian state acted without planning or calculating the long-term consequences of its actions. This radical neoliberal vision, applied in a specific political and legal context, is a factor that explains both the liquidation in the 1990s of development banks per se (the so-called *bancos de fomento*), and the minimization of development banking activities undertaken by state-owned financial entities that survived or were created subsequently. This vision has not only influenced the financial system but has also had, for example, a negative impact on the development of the country's system of cities, according to the World Bank (2016).[22]

Finally, it is worth noting that in the Peruvian case no special regulations exist for development banks, unlike, for instance, the case of Mexico. As shown in Table 8.1, the four state-owned financial companies engage in development banking activities with different forms of intermediation.

Direct intermediation is carried out through the acquisition and placement of funds or securities involving the general public, and indirect intermediation is triangulated through the acquisition and placement of funds or securities involving other financial entities. In some cases, the indirect intermediation of funds (through deposits and loans) is carried out from the origination through to the maturity of the operation, but in other cases it only applies from their distribution, undertaken by the financial institution that originated it. In some circumstances, indirect intermediation is used due to existing legal restrictions and in others to take advantage of the wide network of agencies of retail financial institutions. Synthetic intermediation is carried out by assuming the risk only, at different levels, through the procurement of bonds, sureties, guarantees, trusts, derivatives, and other contracts with equivalent effects, without the need to place funds or acquire securities. Thus, through

[19] Ley Nº 28522. [20] Decreto Legislativo Nº 1088.

[21] Resolución Nº 026-2014-CEPLAN/PCD.

[22] The World Bank states that 'on a national level, there is a need for an articulated strategy around the development of a system of cities that fosters economic activity' (2016). Translation by authors. In 2015, 31.8 per cent of the Peruvian population lived in the city of Lima, and 81.5 per cent of the credit granted by commercial banks was concentrated there. The near-900,000 inhabitants of the second largest city, Arequipa, amounted to only 9 per cent the population of Lima. On the infrastructure gap, see Perrotti and Sánchez (2011); Bonifaz et al. (2015); World Economic Forum (2015); and Instituto Peruano de Economía (2009).

Table 8.1. Peru: Forms of intermediation of the state-owned financial entities

Principal characteristics by financial entity	Banco de la Nación	Corporación Financiera de Desarrollo	Banco Agropecuario	Fondo MiVivienda
Current target market	Public sector plus exceptions	Public and private sectors[6]	Only agricultural sector	Only real estate sector
Authorization of fund-raising (deposits)	Direct and indirect[1]	Only indirect[7]	Direct[10] and indirect[11]	Only indirect
Authorization of fund placement (credit)	Direct,[2] indirect,[3] and synthetic[4]	Only indirect and synthetic[8]	Direct,[12] indirect, and synthetic	Only indirect and synthetic
Authorization of acquisition of securities (investment)	Direct, indirect, and synthetic	Direct, indirect, and synthetic	Direct[13]	Direct and synthetic[14]
Authorization of placement of securities (issuances)	Direct[5]	Direct[9]	Direct	Direct
Supplementary regulation	General banking	General banking	General banking	Special banking
Current legal regime	Public law	Private law	Private law	Private law
Subsidies from the budget	No	No	Yes	Yes
Trustor and trustee	No	No	No	Yes

Notes:

1 As of 2000, it could accept savings deposits from private sector suppliers, in places where there are no commercial banking branches.

2 As of 1994, it could not grant loans to state-owned enterprises governed by private law, but as of 2001 it could grant credit to private sector employees and pension holders.

3 As of 2006, it could undertake direct placements with small and microenterprises, setting final interest rates.

4 As of 2012, it could carry out synthetic placements for micro- and small enterprises that participate in the financial education programmes promoted by public sector entities.

5 As of 1994, it had required an annual programme to be approved by the MEF.

6 As of 1991, the financing of investment and infrastructure projects, including underdeveloped areas with limited private sector coverage, was added as an objective, and in 1992 the financing of small-business owners and farmers, preferably in deprived areas, was added.

7 As of 1992, it could only raise funds from other intermediaries, and could not receive deposits from the public.

8 Up until 1991 it enjoyed exclusive rights to carry out direct, indirect, and synthetic long-term credit intermediation of state companies, but as of 1992 it could not lend to the public on its own account.

9 Until 1991 the securities it issued were exempt from all taxes for twenty years.

10 Fundraising through deposits subject to SBS authorization, with the favourable opinion of the MEF.

11 Fundraising through credit from other intermediaries and multilateral agencies, subject to agreement with the MEF.

12 Placement of credit with limits per person (maximum of 15 tax units, UIT, in the case of small producers, 300 UIT in the case of medium-sized producers, and in areas of extreme poverty preferential up to two tax units) and per company (3 per cent of the bank's effective equity).

13 Only acquisition of public debt securities, BCRP securities, and securities from shares of agricultural investment funds.

14 As of 2001, and ratified in 2005.

synthetic intermediation it is possible to assume the same or even greater risk than in the case of simple direct intermediation.

8.5 The Case of Banco de la Nación (BN)

BN is the oldest state-owned financial institution currently in existence, having been established in 1966[23] as a public law company to provide the banking services required by the public sector. Despite having been created as a credit entity, in 1972[24] it was granted powers corresponding to an insurance entity to hedge the risks to which individuals, goods, capital, transactions, and operations are exposed and in which the state has a direct or indirect interest. It could, therefore, utilize the operating mechanisms of such entities, directly or through insurance companies. Subsequently, the banking law passed in 1993,[25] later superseded by the current banking law of 1996,[26] established that the activities of the BN would be regulated by its statute, to be enacted by supreme decree approved by the MEF.

Since 2000, the financial operations that can be carried out by BN have been gradually expanded. In 2000,[27] the BN was given authorization to receive demand deposits from individuals and private companies that acted as suppliers to the public sector, and to receive savings deposits from the same entities in places where commercial banks had no branches. In 2001,[28] the bank was authorized to issue money orders and transfers on behalf of individuals and private companies in places where private commercial banks did not have branches, and to grant credit to public sector employees and pension-holders.

In 2006,[29] BN was empowered to execute operations and services with entities that lend to small and microenterprises, and to enter into agreements with these institutions to facilitate access to financial resources; that is, they were authorized to carry out indirect credit intermediation, setting the final interest rate to be charged by each participating credit entity by way of tender. Moreover, in 2012[30] it was authorized to guarantee operations involving credit granted by these institutions to small and microenterprises participating in financial education programmes promoted by public sector entities, which also enabled synthetic intermediation of these credits after their origination.

As to its financial structure, between 2006 and 2015 BN's balance of assets and liabilities grew by an average of 9 per cent per year, as shown in

[23] Ley Nº 16000. [24] Decreto Ley Nº 19569. [25] Decreto Legislativo Nº 770.
[26] Ley Nº 26702. [27] Decreto de Urgencia No. 073-2000.
[28] Decretos de Urgencia No. 045-2001 and No. 120-2001, superseded by Decreto de Urgencia No. 014-2004 and recovered and extended by Decreto Supremo No. 207-2004-EF.
[29] Decreto Supremo No. 134-2006-EF. [30] Decreto Supremo No. 099-2012-EF.

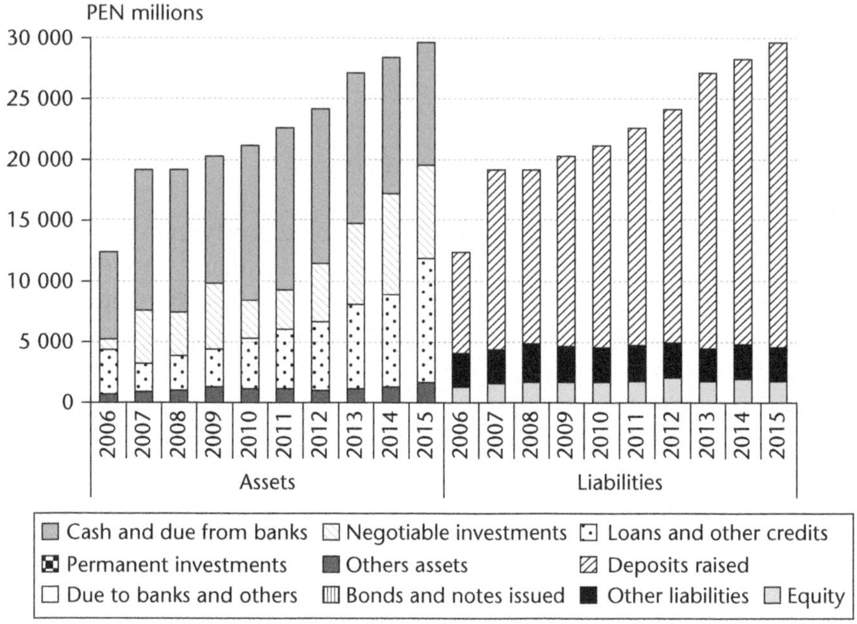

Figure 8.7. Peru: Financial structure of BN, 2006–15
Sources: SBS and audited FSs of BN. Compiled by authors

Figure 8.7—a slower rate than that of the commercial banks, which increased by 16 per cent per year. As regards sources of financing, there has been a sustained increase in the relative share of deposits raised, almost all of them from the public, without resorting to debts due to banks and other entities. In the case of resource usage, it maintains very high liquidity surpluses, both in cash and due from banks and other entities and negotiable investments, despite the slight decline in the relative share since 2013. The bank also held negotiable investments of a value that exceeded its loans and other credits for nine out of ten years, which has diminished the potential aggregate yield on its assets.[31]

Regardless, since 2009, BN has succeeded in maintaining a favourable average differential of +460 basis points between the aggregate return on interest-bearing assets and the aggregate cost of interest-bearing liabilities. The differential from interest and commission alone—not including the effect of exchange rate, market, and derivative risks—was also favourable, at an average of +433 basis points, as shown in Table 8.2.

[31] The commercial banks have historically held available funds totalling less than half of their credit, not to mention the fact that their investments have also been considerably less than those of BN.

Table 8.2. Financial entities: Differentials between returns and costs, 2006–15

Returns and costs by financial entity			2006	2007	2008	2009	2010	2011	2012	2013	2014	2015
Return on interest-bearing assets	All financial revenues	BN	6.50%	6.70%	6.80%	5.50%	4.70%	5.20%	5.20%	5.00%	4.90%	5.20%
		CFD	5.90%	5.70%	5.60%	5.00%	5.00%	5.40%	7.00%	6.30%	5.60%	6.50%
		BA	8.70%	8.00%	9.30%	11.30%	12.70%	15.70%	16.70%	16.80%	14.40%	11.60%
		FMV	3.00%	7.30%	8.30%	7.00%	6.50%	7.50%	6.90%	6.00%	5.40%	8.70%
	Only interest and commissions	BN	6.50%	6.60%	6.60%	4.90%	4.10%	4.70%	4.80%	4.60%	4.60%	4.90%
		CFD	4.90%	4.10%	3.80%	4.10%	4.40%	5.20%	5.40%	5.30%	5.10%	5.00%
		BA	8.70%	8.00%	9.30%	11.20%	12.70%	15.70%	16.70%	16.70%	14.40%	11.60%
		FMV	2.70%	5.90%	6.50%	6.30%	5.80%	6.20%	6.10%	5.70%	5.10%	5.00%
Cost of interest-bearing liabilities	All financial expenses	BN	0.70%	1.10%	1.20%	0.90%	0.60%	0.50%	0.40%	0.40%	0.20%	0.60%
		CFD	6.50%	7.80%	8.60%	5.60%	4.10%	5.00%	7.80%	6.30%	5.50%	6.40%
		BA	18.60%	10.50%	8.40%	10.40%	7.00%	9.90%	8.50%	6.60%	7.60%	5.90%
		FMV	–	–	–	–	–	–	–	13.00%	6.40%	12.10%
	Only interest and commissions	BN	0.50%	0.90%	1.10%	0.80%	0.30%	0.30%	0.30%	0.20%	0.20%	0.20%
		CFD	3.90%	4.50%	3.80%	3.90%	2.60%	3.90%	4.70%	4.00%	4.10%	4.10%
		BA	13.00%	7.50%	8.10%	10.10%	5.60%	8.70%	7.60%	6.60%	7.60%	5.90%
		FMV	–	–	–	–	–	–	–	4.80%	3.50%	3.00%
Differentials between returns and costs (in basis points)	All financial revenues and expense	BN	585	564	559	454	417	479	487	456	469	458
		CFD	−62	−208	−301	−62	91	48	−77	−2	17	11
		BA	−991	−257	86	87	569	587	824	1020	679	571
		FMV	300	728	832	700	651	750	690	−698	−98	−331
	Only interest and commissions	BN	602	562	548	419	383	441	451	437	438	461
		CFD	103	−39	−6	24	177	132	67	136	105	83
		BA	−423	50	115	107	706	700	907	1010	677	572
		FMV	274	590	648	633	579	622	605	87	168	200

Sources: SBS and audited FSs of BN, CFD, BA and FMV. Compiled by authors

In 2015, BN's overall assets equated to 4.8 per cent of GDP, of which 1.8 per cent was comprised of credits; 1.6 per cent of available funds, almost 90 per cent of which was deposited in the central bank with remuneration below the interbank rate; and 1.3 per cent of negotiable investments, more than 80 per cent of them in central bank securities. Its credits were distributed as follows: 54 per cent in the public sector; 8 per cent across other financial entities; and 36 per cent among individuals. Of this total, 33 per cent had maturities of up to one year, 63 per cent from one to five years, and 4 per cent of more than five years.

In 2015, 90 per cent of all its liabilities corresponded to deposits raised, 97 per cent of which were from the public (53 per cent in current accounts and 25 per cent in savings accounts). The bulk of its assets (93 per cent) and of its liabilities (92 per cent) were denominated in local currency, and it has made a greater contribution than any other state-run financial entity to driving the credit de-dollarization process—more than 50 per cent of its loans have been denominated in domestic currency since 2009. Its return on assets ratio was 2.4 per cent, 0.1 times greater than the commercial banks collectively, but the differential between the return on its interest-bearing assets and the cost of its interest-bearing liabilities was +458 basis points, 0.3 times less than that of the commercial banks, or +461 basis points if the effects of exchange rate, market, and derivative risks are not taken into account.

8.6 The Case of Corporación Financiera de Desarrollo (CFD)

CFD was created in 1971[32] during the military regime of Velasco as a public enterprise charged with coordinating the financial and entrepreneurial actions of the state, capturing and channelling savings for priority investments, creating or strengthening companies, and contributing to the expansion of the stock market. That is, it was created primarily as a securities entity to promote business investment. According to Castillo (2005), CFD financed large manufacturing and infrastructure investments in the 1970s.

However, in 1981,[33] during the Belaunde administration, CFD's paid-up capital was reduced and it was ruled that its business promotion and investment activities along with the investments it held until then would be transferred to another public entity, and it would be turned into a state-owned enterprise governed by private law, as a public limited company. Converted into a credit entity, CFD was given the purpose of contributing to Peru's integral development by attracting savings and financial intermediation to

[32] Decreto Ley Nº 18807. [33] Decreto Legislativo Nº 206.

assign it to promoting projects and the financing of new or existing companies, in accordance with governmental plans and policies.

In 1991,[34] during the Fujimori administration, it was ruled that the institution would also assume the role of executing long-term financing operations in infrastructure and investment projects, including in underdeveloped areas where private sector coverage was limited; that foreign funding attracted by CFD and intended for purposes other than financing studies or executing nationwide public infrastructure projects should be channelled preferentially through the national financial system; and that CFD's security issuances would lose the tax exemption to which they were entitled. However, in 1992[35] CFD was prevented from gathering deposits from the public and lending on its own account to individuals or companies that were not classified as financial intermediaries or institutes for the development of rural activities and small-business owners.

As for its financial structure, between 2006 and 2015, CFD's balance of assets and liabilities grew by an average of 14 per cent per year, and at an annual rate that was 20 per cent per year greater than that of commercial banks in 2011–15, as shown in Figure 8.8. As to sources of financing, CFD has

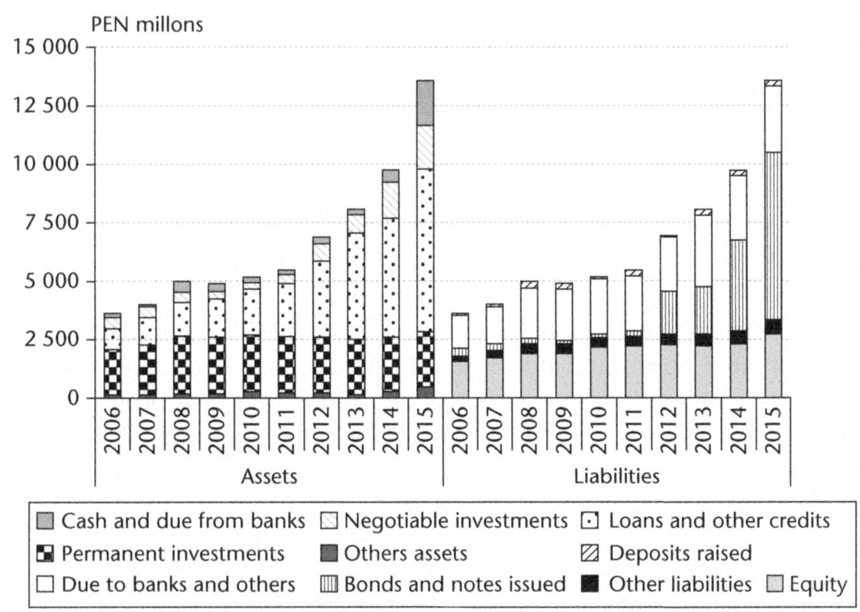

Figure 8.8. Peru: Financial structure of CFD, 2006–15
Sources: SBS and audited FSs of CFD. Compiled by authors

[34] Ley N° 25382. [35] Ley N° 25382 and Decreto Ley N° 25694.

had a volatile funding structure with a high proportion of external debts due to banks and other entities; in the last three years, an explosive growth was recorded in the long-term securities issued abroad. Regarding the use of its resources, CFD has had increasing liquidity surpluses since 2012, both in cash and due from banks and other entities and in negotiable investments. Its credit has also been on the increase, but its returns are very low due to the legal obligation to use another financial entity as intermediary,[36] which leaves it without any bargaining power over the target market or the final financial conditions involved.

Since 2009, CFD has maintained a favourable average differential of just +4 basis points between the aggregate return on interest-bearing assets and the aggregate cost of interest-bearing liabilities. If the effect of foreign exchange differences, variations of market prices, and variations of the derivatives acquired were to be excluded, the differential would be +103 basis points on average, as shown in Table 8.2.

In 2015, its total assets equated to 2.2 per cent of GDP, of which credits accounted for 1.2 per cent, cash and due from banks and other entities for 0.3 per cent, and negotiable investments for 0.3 per cent. Of its credits, 97 per cent are granted to other financial entities (85 per cent to banks, 8 per cent to financiers, and 5 per cent to municipal unions); however, in recent years it has increased its synthetic intermediation, assuming the greatest risk associated with operations and the final debtors involved, rather than only assuming the intermediary risk as in the case of traditional indirect intermediation.

Of the total credits, 40 per cent had maturities of up to one year, 28 per cent from one to five years, and 29 per cent of more than five years. Of all the liabilities, 92 per cent correspond to debts due to banks and other entities and financial obligations (57 per cent to unsubordinated bonds and notes issued, 17 per cent to foreign debts due to banks and other entities, and 10 per cent to subordinated bonds and notes issued), which gives it an uncompetitive funding base. Only 39 per cent of its assets and 23 per cent of its liabilities are denominated in local currency, with CFD's level of credit dollarization having increased to 66 per cent in 2015 from the 30 per cent posted in 2009. In 2015, the return on assets ratio was 0.7 per cent and the differential between the return on its assets and the cost of its liabilities was +11 basis points, +83 if the effects of exchange rate, market, and derivative risks are not taken into account.

[36] It should be noted that most of its assets are committed to the permanent investments it holds in CAF, which neither generate cash dividends nor possess a liquid market.

8.7 The Case of Banco Agropecuario (BA)

BA was created in 2001[37] as a private law company with mixed capital to grant credit to the agricultural sector,[38] directly or through other financial entities, using public and private resources. For the financial and technical support of small-scale agriculture and livestock it draws on the budgetary resources assigned to it by the MEF and the MAR, while it must raise private funds locally and abroad in order to lend to medium-scale agriculture and livestock. In 2006,[39] it was established that the resources assigned to BA by the MEF and the MAR would constitute part of its equity, and that the Guarantee Fund for Small-Scale Agriculture (Fondo de Garantía para la Pequeña Agricultura, FOGAPA) would be transformed into autonomous equity, intended to hedge the risks associated with the credit granted to small-scale producers in the agricultural sector by all financial institutions and transferred in trust for thirty years into the Guarantee Fund for Loans to Small-Scale Industry (Fondo de Garantía para Préstamos a la Pequeña Industria)—a state foundation tasked with strengthening small and microenterprises.

In 2007,[40] the relaunch of BA was approved as the primary state instrument of financial support for the development of the agricultural sector, and its role was defined as undertaking all activities associated with a banking entity. In 2008,[41] following two successive legal amendments—one to reduce the paid-up capital and the other to increase the authorized capital—it was stipulated that the institution should promote private sector participation, both domestic and foreign, without retaining the previous limit of 49 per cent. Moreover, it was established that FOGAPA was an autonomous fund administered by BA, intended to hedge the risks associated with the credit granted by that institution to small-scale agricultural producers.

Between 2006 and 2015, BA's assets and liabilities balance grew by an average of 23 per cent per year, although it remains a very small institution. As to the sources of its resources, starting from 2012, BA embarked upon a drastic change in its funding structure, concentrating both internal and external debts due to banks and other entities but without gathering deposits, whereas in previous years its funding was almost 80 per cent equity-based, as shown in Figure 8.9. With respect to the use of its resources, the increase in the relative share of credits has been sustained since 2012, but still with a very high proportion of new credits. However, since 2009, BA has succeeded in maintaining a favourable average differential of +619 basis points between the

[37] Ley Nº 27603.

[38] This sector includes agriculture, livestock, aquaculture, and the associated transformation and commercialization activities.

[39] Ley Nº 28818. [40] Ley Nº 29064.

[41] Decreto de Urgencia Nº 007-2008, Decreto Legislativo Nº 995, and Decreto Legislativo Nº 1037.

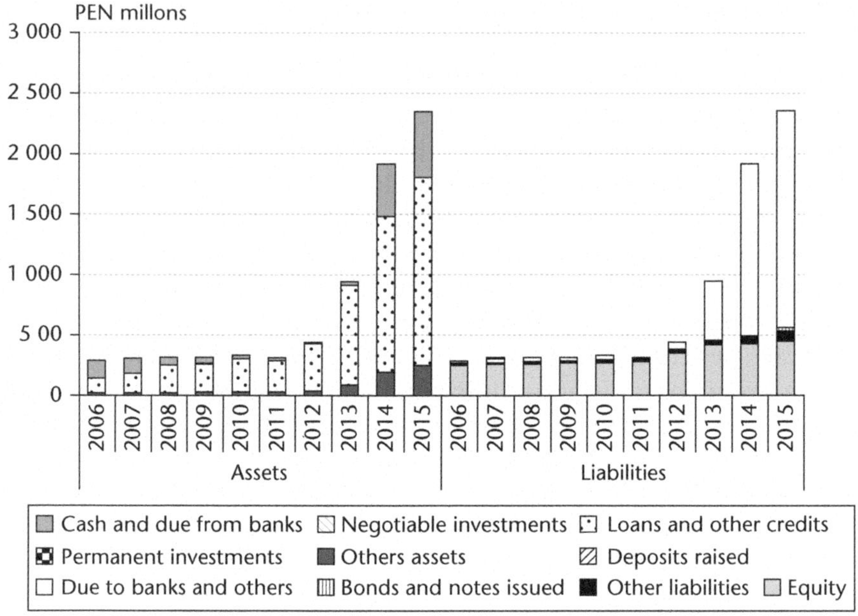

Figure 8.9. Peru: Financial structure of BA, 2006–15
Sources: SBS and audited FSs of BA. Compiled by authors

aggregate return on its interest-bearing assets and the aggregate cost of its interest-bearing liabilities. The differential—not including the effect of exchange rate, market, and derivative risks—was also favourable, at an average of +668 basis points, as shown in Table 8.2.

8.8 The Case of Fondo MiVivienda (FMV)

FMV was created in 1998[42] with the purpose of facilitating the acquisition of housing, especially social housing, and its resources are to be used to complement the financing offered by the private banking system. In 2000,[43] it was authorized to finance housing constructed as a consequence of the partitioning of residential units, subdivision of land, or the completion of urban renewal projects underway. In 2001,[44] it was established that it could guarantee the credit or securities of private financial intermediaries, including securitization firms, associated with housing programmes. In 2002,[45] it was granted the power to administrate and concede the family housing payment (maximum of US$12,000), a subsidy for the

[42] Ley N° 26912. [43] Decreto de Urgencia N° 091-2000. [44] Ley N° 27511.
[45] Ley N° 27829.

acquisition, construction, or improvement of social housing drawn from the budget of the Ministry of Housing, Construction, and Sanitation.

In 2005,[46] the purposes and means of FMV were extended and it was converted into a state-owned enterprise governed by private law. It was able to engage in the promotion and financing of the acquisition, improvement, and construction of housing, especially social housing, activities related to promoting the flow of capital to the housing financing market, participation in the primary and secondary mortgage lending market, and contributing to the development of the capital market. It was authorized to implement products and services to stimulate supply and demand for housing; encourage the timely payment of housing credit; disburse funds to financial entities; promote savings or private sector investment; act simultaneously as trustor and trustee for the financing of housing, as well as improver and beneficiary; issue liabilities and other instruments; participate as structuring agent, underwriter, shareholder, and advisor; and other responsibilities associated with housing financing structures.

As to its financial structure, between 2006 and 2015 FMV's balance of assets and liabilities grew by an average of 12 per cent per year, although from 2011–15 it expanded at a rate in excess of 20 per cent per year. As for the sources of its resources, since 2012 FMV's funding structure has changed drastically, increasing its share of bonds and notes issued, primarily abroad, as shown in Figure 8.10; this is in contrast to what was observed through to 2011, when its funding was largely equity-based. Regarding the uses of its resources, credit picked back up after the decline recorded during the recession of 2008–9; however, during the economic downturn of 2014–15, credit increased more slowly than bonds and notes emissions, generating an increase in liquidity, in cash and due from banks and other entities.

Thus, since 2013, when it started to incur debts due to banks and other entities and issuances of bonds and notes, FMV has faced an unfavourable and volatile differential, greater than −376 basis points, between the aggregate return on its interest-bearing assets and the aggregate cost of its interest-bearing liabilities. If the effect of foreign exchange rate differences and variations in market prices and the derivatives acquired were to be excluded, the differential from interest and commissions alone would be favourable, +152 basis points on average, as shown in Table 8.2.

In 2015, its total assets equated to 1.3 per cent of GDP, of which its credits accounted for 1.0 per cent, 93 per cent of which corresponded to housing credit through a trust with CFD; available funds were 0.2 per cent, and negotiable investments, 0.1 per cent. Of these total credits, 9 per cent had maturities of up to one year, 23 per cent from one to three years, and 69 per cent

[46] Ley Nº 28579.

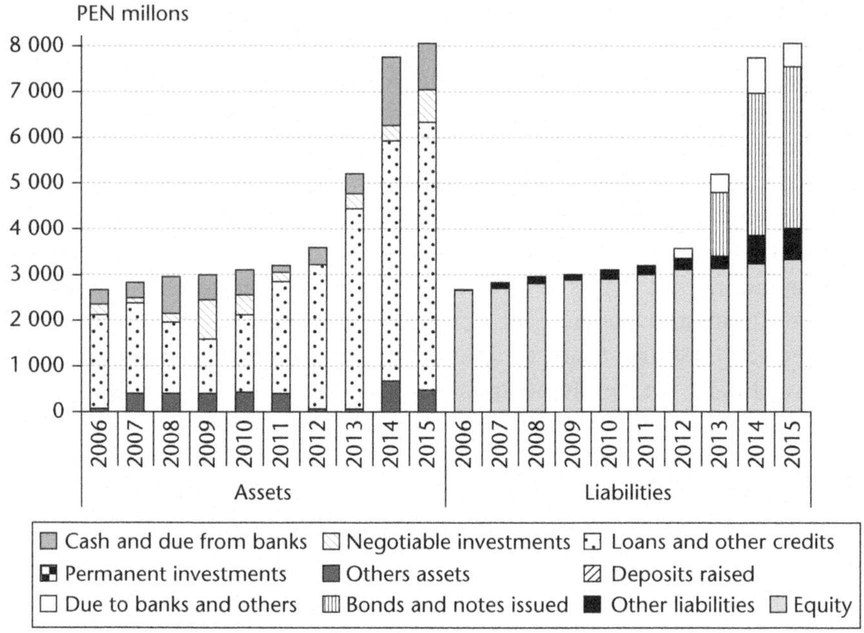

Figure 8.10. Peru: Financial structure of FMV, 2006–15
Sources: SBS and audited FSs of FMV. Compiled by authors

of more than three years. Of all the liabilities, 86 per cent correspond to debts due to banks and other entities and financial obligations (75 per cent to unsubordinated bonds and notes issued, 7 per cent to domestic debt due to banks and other entities, and 3 per cent to foreign debt due to banks and other entities), which gives it an uncompetitive funding base that is further deteriorated by derivative arrangements vis-à-vis the currency mismatch to which it is subject. In 2015, 80 per cent of its assets and 20 per cent of its liabilities were denominated in local currency, although it reached a credit dollarization level of 90 per cent in 2006; thereafter, the dollarization of its loans dropped to 10 per cent in 2013. The return on assets ratio was 1.2 per cent but the differential between the return on its assets and the cost of its liabilities was −331 basis points, but it would have attained +200 basis points without the effect of exchange rate, market, and derivative risks.

8.9 Strategy and Vision of the Future

The economic development of Peru requires a diversified productive structure that reduces dependence on the export of raw materials; but the change will not occur spontaneously. In order to change this, Peru needs to build public institutions that are capable of researching, formulating, and implementing public policies and strategies with a vision of the future. In this sense, the state financial institutions dedicated to development banking remain key players to mitigate market failures. The 'type of finance that innovators receive is not neutral and can affect both the rate and direction of innovation' (Mazzucato and Semieniuk 2017: 25).

However, in the case of the four state financial institutions evaluated here, it is verified that they maintain objectives and goals that are not integrated with each other. On the contrary, in some cases their objectives overlap and their efforts are duplicated, while in other cases they do not take advantage of all possible synergies to obtain economies of scale and economies of scope, not only for administrative efficiency but also for financial economies. For example, BN could help make the concentrated Peruvian banking system more competitive, but it is allowed to operate only in places that are not covered by any commercial bank. By different legal norms, CFD as of 1992 and BN as of 2006 are required to meet the financing needs of small enterprises, but they are not authorized to carry out the direct intermediation of such credit, which means having no bargaining power to alter the prevailing market supply conditions. In fact, the share of microfinance institutions in the balance of credits granted to financial entities by CFD at the close of 2015 was just 5.8 per cent, down on the 6.7 per cent share held by such institutions in overall banking system credit; this is to say nothing of the fact that CFD has assumed synthetically the final credit risk of bigger enterprises in much of the remainder of its loans to other financial entities, without this being explicitly shown in their balance sheets.

As of 1992, CFD must also attend to small-business owners and farmers in depressed regions (where there are no commercial banks and which are only covered by BN, which cannot grant credit to state-owned enterprises governed by private law), but is not authorized to attract deposits from the public or to lend to individuals or companies that are not qualified as intermediaries or financial entities for the development of rural activity or small businesses. Thus, in practice, CFD cannot advance this aim, given the low differential between yields and costs, and it has not opened up so much as a single office of its own in the Peruvian interior. Indeed, the high costs of external liabilities and derivatives incurred from 2010–15 could have been reduced by almost 100 basis points in the case of CFD if it had been funded directly by BN using local currency; at the same time, this would have allowed BN to improve the yield on its assets by utilizing the liquid resources deposited in the central bank.

Given that the rural sector went unattended by CFD and the private insurers, BA was created following prolonged political and electoral negotiations; the institution's funding was primarily equity-based, drawn from the public purse during the first twelve years of its existence. Since 2014, this institution has posted an increase in credit dollarization due to the higher foreign currency debts due to banks and other entities that it has incurred. BA extends credit in foreign currency to medium-sized, small, and microenterprises pertaining to the sector at much lower interest rates (from 360 to 720 basis points) than the local-currency rates, whereby defaults can increase abruptly with a rising exchange rate, according to Jiménez Sotelo (2010a).

Finally, the FMV increased and de-dollarized its credits from 2013–15, but also using funding in foreign currency. In response to this currency mismatch, FMV began to incur a strong negative differential due to exchange rate, market, and derivative risks, which are currently sustainable due to the still-low level of leveraging, albeit without including the part of the final credit risk that was assumed synthetically in its operations with the financial entities.

Therefore, it could be more efficient and effective to bring about a merger between these four state financial entities to accelerate the economic development of the country, and to take advantage of it to match the conditions of public companies with those of private companies (OECD 2011 and 2016). In this way, it would ensure a permanent coordination and integration of its objectives and goals, it could take advantage of the synergies of its operations at national level, and it could constitute a true state development bank. While for the management of loans and investments, practically every entity would become a specialized business unit with differentiated centres of costs and benefits (for example, infrastructure, micro- and small business, real estate, and agricultural sectors), for the management of cash and due from banks, and deposits raised and other liabilities, a single unit of treasury and balance sheet structure would be formed in a manner similar to what would occur with the formation of a single strategic risk management unit, a single unit of trusts, and a single unit of operations. The most viable operational integration would be based on BN, which not only has the largest network of agencies at the national level, but also has a new headquarters of thirty floors, to which the other three state entities could quickly be relocated.

In any case, the mission of this new entity, even if it can retain the trademark of the other three as well, must be firmly linked to its new strategic vision of the future and to the actions necessary to build it.

8.10 Conclusions

The state-owned financial entities in Peru have not been far-removed from the controversial ideological debate on the role the state has played in the economy over the last fifty years. Since the structural reforms of the 1990s, these institutions have not had much significance as instruments of public policy used to mitigate the market failures of the Peruvian financial system (long-term financing and financing for the agricultural and small-business sectors). On the contrary, as with other state-owned companies, they have been subject to discriminatory treatment in comparison with private companies, going against best international practices such as those recommended by the OECD.

Because of the absence of a system of strategic planning in the public sector for more than twenty years, some state-owned financial entities have ended up promoting greater financial dollarization and greater external debt, thereby hampering the development of the domestic securities market despite the lack of investment opportunities for the considerable domestic savings accumulated over the last decade.

Thus, each of the four state-run financial companies analysed has objectives and goals in place that are not aligned with those of the others, but which respond to the regulations that have been implemented over more than fifty years and to the political emergencies that have arisen across the different governments of the day. In some cases, their objectives overlap and their efforts are duplicated, while in others possible synergies borne of administrative efficiencies and economies of scale and scope go unutilized. Therefore, none of these institutions constitutes an effective state development bank such as exists in other countries.

Given this context, the likelihood of the state-owned financial entities displaying pro-cyclical behaviour in the economy is high, since their lack of market bargaining power and of long-term vision often sees them trailing the bigger commercial banks through direct, indirect, or synthetic intermediation of their credits or their preferred or subordinated debt instruments. With the exception of BN, all of the other institutions have ended up as followers of international investment banks through the local intermediation of the greater external debt that these entities offered them and increasing financial dollarization even against the backdrop of efforts by the public treasury to reduce these macroeconomic vulnerabilities. Moreover, their capacity to support countercyclical policy measures is limited, because they are dependent on express approval in the public budget for those funds for specific ends and with a limited life that they manage as trusts, since in the money market too they are usually treated in an unequal and disadvantageous manner in the central bank's operations, in accordance with Jiménez Sotelo (2009).

References

Armas, A. and F. Grippa. 2005. *Targeting Inflation in a Dollarized Economy: The Peruvian Experience*. Working Paper Series, 538. Washington, DC: Inter-American Development Bank. Available at <www.iadb.org/res/publications/pubfiles/pubwp-538.pdf>, accessed 21 April 2018.

Bartra, G. 2015. 'Contexto de los seguros agrícolas en el Perú' ['Context of Agricultural Insurance in Peru']. Paper presented at the exchange and technical training 'La experiencia chilena en la gestión, institucionalidad y procesos operativos de los seguros agrícolas desde el sector público y privado'. Lima: Proyecto Clima, Agro y Transferencia del Riesgo (GIZ/BMUB). Available at <www.agroyriesgo.pe/wp-content/uploads/2015/11/Contexto-de-los-Seguros-Agr%C3%ADcolas-en-el-Per%C3%BA-MINAGRI-DIGNA_GinoBartra.pdf>, accessed 21 April 2018.

Bonifaz, J. L., R. Urrunaga, J. Aguirre, and C. Urquizo. 2015. *Un plan para salir de la pobreza: Plan Nacional de Infraestructura 2016–2025* [*A Plan to Get Out of Poverty: National Infrastructure Plan 2016–2025*]. Lima: Asociación para el Fomento de la Infraestructura Nacional.

Castillo Torres, M. 2005. 'Evolución, perspectivas y diseño de políticas sobre la banca de desarrollo en el Perú' ['Evolution, Perspectives and Policy Design on Development Banking in Peru']. Serie Financiamiento del Desarrollo, 154. Santiago: Inter-American Development Bank & United Nations (ECLAC). Available at <repositorio.cepal.org/handle/11362/5137>, accessed 21 April 2018.

Corzo, S. 2015. 'Actuarios: Una profesión que no se da abasto en el Perú' ['Actuaries: a profession that does not provide enough in Peru']. *Semana Económica*, 15 February. Available at <http://semanaeconomica.com/article/mercados-y-finanzas/banca-y-finanzas/154242-actuarios-una-profesion-que-no-se-da-abasto-en-el-peru/>, accessed 21 April 2018.

Dancourt, Ó. 1999. 'Reforma neoliberal y política macroeconómica en el Perú' ['Neoliberal Reform and Macroeconomic Policy in Peru'], *Revista CEPAL* 67: 49–70. Santiago: Economic Commission for Latin America and the Caribbean. Available at <repositorio.cepal.org/handle/11362/12166>, accessed 21 April 2018.

Dancourt, Ó. 2014. *Inflation Targeting in Peru: The Reasons for the Success*. Working Paper, 386. Lima: Pontificia Universidad Católica del Perú. Available at <http://files.pucp.edu.pe/departamento/economia/DDD386.pdf>, accessed 21 April 2018.

Ferraro, C. A. and E. Goldstein. 2011. 'Políticas de acceso al financiamiento para las pequeñas y medianas empresas en América Latina' ['Policies to Access Financing for Small and Medium-Sized Enterprises in Latin America'], in *Eliminando barreras: El financiamiento a las pymes en América Latina*, 9–60. Santiago: United Nations (ECLAC/AECID). Available at <repositorio.cepal.org/handle/11362/3909>, accessed 21 April 2018.

Ferraz, J. C., A. C. Além, and R. F. Madeira. 2013. 'A contribuição dos bancos de desenvolvimento para o financiamento de longo prazo' ['The Contribution of Development Banks to Long-Term Financing'], *Revista do BNDES* 40: 5–42. Rio de Janeiro: Banco Nacional de Desenvolvimento Econômico e Social. Available at <web.bndes.gov.br/bib/jspui/handle/1408/2284>, accessed 21 April 2018.

Ferraz, J. C., A. C. Além, and R. F. Madeira. 2016. 'Development Banks' Contribution to Long Term Financing'. Produção BNDES. Rio de Janeiro: Banco Nacional de Desenvolvimento Econômico e Social. Available at <web.bndes.gov.br/bib/jspui/handle/1408/7522>, accessed 21 April 2018.

Fitzgerald, E. V. K. 1983. 'Capitalismo de estado en el Perú: Limitaciones de un modelo de desarrollo económico' ['State Capitalism in Peru: Limitations of an Economic

Development Model'], in C. MacClintock and A. Lowenthal (eds), *El gobierno militar: Una experiencia peruana, 1968–1980*, p. 89–117. Lima: Instituto de Estudios Peruanos.

García-Escribano, M. 2010. *Peru: Drivers of De-Dollarization.* IMF Working Paper, WP/10/169. Washington, DC: Western Hemisphere Department, International Monetary Fund. Available at <www.imf.org/external/pubs/ft/wp/2010/wp10169.pdf>, accessed 21 April 2018.

Hatch, D. C., M. Núñez, F. Vila, and K. Stephenson. 2012. *Los seguros agropecuarios en las Américas: Un instrumento para la gestión del riesgo* [*Agricultural Insurance in the Americas: An Instrument for Risk Management*]. San José: Instituto Interamericano de Cooperación para la Agricultura & Asociación Latinoamericana para el Desarrollo del Seguro Agropecuario. Available at <http://repiica.iica.int/docs/B2996e/B2996e.pdf>, accessed 21 April 2018.

Hausmann, R. and B. Klinger. 2008. *Growth Diagnostics in Peru.* Working Paper, 181. Cambridge, MA: Center for International Development at Harvard Kennedy School. Available at <research.hks.harvard.edu/publications/getFile.aspx?Id=435>, accessed 21 April 2018.

Hermann, J. 2014. 'Restricciones financieras del desarrollo económico: Teoría y políticas para los países en desarrollo' ['Financial Constraints of Economic Development: Theory and Policies for Developing Countries'], *Revista CEPAL* 114: 71–87. Santiago: Economic Commission for Latin America and the Caribbean. Available at <repositorio.cepal.org/handle/11362/37437>, accessed 21 April 2018.

Instituto Peruano de Economía. 2009. *El reto de la infraestructura al 2018: La brecha de inversión en infraestructura en el Perú 2008* [*The Challenge of Infrastructure to 2018: The Investment Gap in Infrastructure in Peru 2008*]. Lima: Asociación para el Fomento de la Infraestructura Nacional.

Jiménez Sotelo, R. 2001. *Mejora de prácticas y políticas para créditos agrícolas en el Perú* [*Improvement of Practices and Policies for Agricultural Credits in Peru*]. Lima: Universidad del Pacífico, Facultad de Economía. Available at <mpra.ub.uni-muenchen.de/75307/>, accessed 21 April 2018.

Jiménez Sotelo, R. 2009. 'Acceso de la banca de desarrollo al banco central: El caso de COFIDE y las tasas de interés en el Perú' ['Access of Development Banks to the Central Bank: The Case of COFIDE and Interest Rates in Peru'], *Boletín del CEMLA* 56(3): 119–38. México, DF: Centro de Estudios Monetarios Latinoamericanos. Available at <www.cemla.org/PDF/boletin/PUB_BOL_LV03.pdf>, accessed 21 April 2018.

Jiménez Sotelo, R. 2010a. 'Ciclo crediticio y acelerador cambiario: Evidencia empírica y consecuencias para la regulación prudencial' ['Credit Cycle and Exchange Rate Accelerator: Empirical Evidence and Implications for Prudential Regulation'], *Economía* 33(65): 133–76. Lima: Pontificia Universidad Católica del Perú. Available at <revistas.pucp.edu.pe/index.php/economia/article/view/587>, accessed 21 April 2018.

Jiménez Sotelo, R. 2010b. *Choques externos, regulación y crisis bancarias en el Perú: Una revisión para el periodo 1990–2009* [*External Shocks, Regulation and Banking Crises in Peru: A Review for the Period 1990–2009*]. Lima: Corporación Financiera de Desarrollo. Available at <mpra.ub.uni-muenchen.de/74752/>, accessed 21 April 2018.

Jiménez Sotelo, R. 2017. 'Prospectiva estratégica aplicada a la hacienda pública: Un ejercicio para la gestión de sus activos y pasivos al año 2030' ['Strategic foresight applied to the public treasury: An exercise for the management of its assets and liabilities to year 2030'], *Pensamiento Crítico* 22(2): 7–72. Lima: Universidad Nacional Mayor de San Marcos. Available at <http://revistasinvestigacion.unmsm.edu.pe/index.php/econo/article/view/14018/12398>, accessed 21 April 2018.

Keynes, J. M. 2003[1943]. *Teoría general de la ocupación, el interés y el dinero* [*The General Theory of Employment, Interest and Money*]. México, DF: Fondo de Cultura Económica.

Mazzucato, M. and G. Semieniuk. 2017. 'Public Financing of Innovation: New Questions', *Oxford Review of Economic Policy* 33(1): 24–48.

MEF (Ministry of Economy and Finances). 2014. *Estrategia de Gestión Global de Activos y Pasivos 2014–2017* [*Strategy for Global Asset and Liability Management 2014–2017*]. Lima: MEF. Available at <https://www.mef.gob.pe/contenidos/tesoro_pub/gestion_act_pas/Estrategia_Gestion_Activos_2014_2017.pdf>, accessed 21 April 2018.

MEF. 2015. *Estrategia de Gestión Global de Activos y Pasivos 2015–2018* [*Strategy for Global Asset and Liability Management 2015–2018*]. Lima: MEF. Available at <https://www.mef.gob.pe/contenidos/tesoro_pub/gestion_act_pas/Estrategia_Gestion_Activos_2015_2018.pdf>, accessed 21 April 2018.

MEF. 2016a. *Informe Anual de Deuda Pública 2015* [*Annual Public Debt Report 2015*]. Lima: MEF. Available at <www.mef.gob.pe/tesoro/informe-anual.php>, accessed 21 April 2018.

MEF. 2016b. *Módulo 1: El rol de las asociaciones público privadas en la promoción de la inversión privada en el Perú* [*The Role of Public–Private Associations in Promoting Private Investment in Peru*]. *Asociaciones público privadas en Perú: Análisis del nuevo marco legal.* Lima: Inter-American Development Bank. Available at <www.mef.gob.pe/contenidos/inv_privada/capacitaciones/modulo_1.pdf>, accessed 21 April 2018.

Moody's Investors Service. 2016. *Moody's Statistical Handbook: Country Credit.* New York: Moody's Investors Service.

Morris, F. 2014. 'La situación actuarial en el Perú' ['The Actuarial Situation in Peru']. Paper presented at the 'Primer Coloquio de Actuarios en Perú'. Lima: Universidad ESAN. Available at <www.actuaries.org/FUND/lima/Morris_APESEGL.pdf>, accessed 21 April 2018.

OECD (Organization for Economic Cooperation and Development). 2011. *Directrices de la OCDE sobre el gobierno* corporativo *de las empresas públicas* [*OECD Guidelines on Corporate Governance of Stated-Owned Enterprises*]. Paris: División de Temas Corporativos de la OCDE. Available at <www.oecd.org/daf/ca/corporategovernanceofstate-ownedenterprises/48632643.pdf>, accessed 21 April 2018.

OECD. 2016. *Directrices de la OCDE sobre el gobierno corporativo de las empresas públicas, edición 2015* [*OECD Guidelines on Corporate Governance of Stated-Owned Enterprises, edition 2015*]. Paris: Éditions OCDE. Available at DOI:10.1787/9789264258167-es.

Perrotti, D. and R. Sánchez. 2011. *La brecha de infraestructura en América Latina y el Caribe* [*The Infrastructure Gap in Latin America and the Caribbean*]. Serie Recursos Naturales e Infraestructura, 153. Santiago: United Nations (ECLAC). Available at <repositorio.cepal.org/handle/11362/6357>, accessed 21 April 2018.

RAE (Real Academia Española). 2014. *Diccionario de la lengua española [Dictionary of Spanish Language].* Available at http://www.rae.es/obras-academicas/diccionarios/diccionario-de-la-lengua-espanola>, accessed 21 April 2018.

Rezende, F. 2017. *The Role of Development Banks in the 21st Century*. Manuscript in preparation. Rio, Brazil: Multidisciplinary Institute for Development and Strategies (MINDS) & Hobart and William Smith Colleges.

Rojas, J. and E. Costa. 2002. *Movilidad de capitales y crisis bancaria en el Perú, 1990–2000* [*Capital Mobility and Banking Crisis in Peru, 1990–2000*]. Unpublished manuscript. Lima, Peru: Consorcio de Investigación Económica y Social (CIES).

Ruiz Caro, A. 2002. *El proceso de privatizaciones en el Perú durante el periodo 1991–2001* [*The Privatization Process in Peru during the Period 1991–2001*]. Serie Gestión Pública, 22. Santiago: Instituto Latinoamericano y del Caribe de Planificación Económica y Social (ECLAC). Available at <archivo.cepal.org/pdfs/2002/S027489.pdf>, accessed 21 April 2018.

Schumpeter, J. A. 1967[1934]. *Teoría del desenvolvimiento económico: Una investigación sobre ganancias, capital, crédito, interés y ciclo económico* [*The Theory of Economic Development: An Inquiry into Profits, Capital, Credit, Interest, and the Business Cycle*]. México, DF: Fondo de Cultura Económica.

World Bank. 2016. *Perú—Hacia un sistema integrado de ciudades: Una nueva visión para crecer* [*Peru—Towards a System of Integrated Cities: A New Vision for Growth*]. Lima: World Bank. Available at <http://documents.worldbank.org/curated/en/981211468196152402/Per%C3%BA-Hacia-un-sistema-integrado-de-ciudades-una-nueva-visi%C3%B3n-para-crecer>, accessed 21 April 2018.

World Economic Forum. 2015. *The Global Competitiveness Report 2015–2016*. Available at <reports.weforum.org/global-competitiveness-report-2015-2016/>, accessed 21 April 2018.

Xu, Q. 2017. *CDB: Born Bankrupt, Born Shaper*. Manuscript in preparation. Beijing, China: Institute of World Economics and Politics (IWEP) at Chinese Academy of Social Sciences.

Part II

Thematic Issues

9

Financial Regulation and Risk Management in Development Banks

Lavinia Barros de Castro

This chapter attempts to answer four questions: (1) from a theoretical point of view, should development banks (DBs) be controlled by prudential regulation; (2) is the Basel Accord a suitable framework for DBs; (3) with regard to risk management, do DBs have different characteristics from private banks; and (4) what are the challenges brought by Basel III and 'Basel IV'.

A few habitual answers to those questions include: (1) DBs should not be regulated, because, as they do not receive cash deposits, they do not constitute sources of systemic risk; (2) Basel is an inadequate framework for DB regulation, because its enforcement conflicts with the objectives of funding development; (3) DBs bear greater risks than private institutions, precisely because they operate in areas avoided by the private sector, due to their greater risk and/or longer term; (4) Basel III (or IV) aggravates the situation for DBs due to its tougher requirements. This chapter intends to investigate these responses in greater depth, sometimes questioning, other times qualifying them.

Discussing the regulation of DBs is no simple task, given their institutional diversity. This chapter recognizes that there is no single comprehensive definition that will encompass the multiplicity of existing institutional designs. For this reason, the review is restricted to national public DBs which are non-specialized in specific credit segments, do not accept cash deposits, and are comprehensively defined as 'financial Institutions set up to foster economic development, often taking into account objectives of social development and

The opinions expressed in this chapter do not necessarily represent the views of BNDES. The author thanks Stephany Griffith-Jones, Patricia Barros, Felipe Rezende, Eduardo Ichikava, Leonardo Brazão, Rogerio Studart, Paulo Franco, José Ocampo, Mariana Mazzucato, Juan-Carlos Moreno-Brid, and Shari Spiegel. The responsibility for any errors is solely the author's.

regional integration, mainly by providing long-term financing to, or facilitating the financing of, projects generating positive externalities' (UN-DESA 2005: 10–11). Each section of this chapter discusses one of the above questions.

9.1 Financial Regulation—the Theoretical Justification: Should Development Banks Be Regulated?

There are at least two very distinct groups of arguments in favour of financial regulation: (1) the theoretical framework on *market failures*; and (2) the view that brings together Keynesian, Schumpeterian, and Minskyan contributions. While the former emphasizes the defence of regulations under a microeconomic perspective, the latter does so from a macroeconomic perspective.

Intuitively, the framework on market failures departs from the overall assumption that, under certain conditions, the free market will always arrive at a Pareto-optimal result, where an economic outcome is said to be optimal if it is impossible to make any individual better off without making another worse off (First Welfare Theorem). In that perspective, only in very specific situations will the market 'fail' and government intervention raise economic welfare.[1] These failures occur in situations with the presence of: (i) public goods; (ii) externalities; (iii) asymmetric information; and (iv) market power. The existence of DBs is justified, therefore, to the extent that these institutions are able to reduce such failures and, so, (probably) enhance overall welfare.[2]

Literature on failures agrees, for example, that the government providing financing or producing public goods may bring about improvements in welfare. With regard to externalities, DBs can reduce social and regional disparities, generate positive environmental impact, promote technological spillover, provide signals to the market (e.g. that some companies are eligible for credit support, creating 'crowding-in' effects), provide public information, develop capital markets (helping them to become larger and liquid and so reduce the likelihood of contagion between the credit and stock markets), etc.

Financial regulation, on the other hand, has three purposes: (1) avoid systemic crisis (prudential regulation); (2) increase the allocative efficiency of

[1] Some authors claim that 'government failures' can be higher than market failures and that, theoretically, there is the possibility that a situation is 'Pareto-constrained'. That means, it cannot be improved by any intervention, even if it is not optimal. Stiglitz argues that in financial markets, failure is far more pervasive than 'government failures', making a powerful case for both financial regulation and development banks (1994). I thank Professor Stephany Griffith-Jones for this observation.

[2] In microeconomic theory, the validity of the First Welfare Theorem is conditioned by the existence of: (i) local non-satiation; (ii) complete markets; and (iii) price taker behaviour. Market failures arise, precisely, by a relaxation of the last two hypotheses. See Mas-Colel et al. 1995.

capital, by allowing sectors or regions in surplus to fund those in deficit (allocative regulation); and (3) guarantee consumer and investment protection.

Financing public goods is simply not related to financial regulation. Concerning public goods, someone could argue that DBs should be supervised in order to verify the effectiveness of the credit provided—but not regulated. In the externalities case mentioned above, the situation is the same. Instead of regulation, DBs could be evaluated by cost–benefit analysis (oversight of fiscal costs × the benefits to society).[3] However, the failure literature includes one case that *does* justify financial regulation: banking runs, considered as negative externalities, although it is also remarked that there is always the risk of regulatory action encouraging moral hazard (the 'too big to fail' argument). Traditionally, bank runs are only possible among institutions which accept cash deposits;[4] thus, prudential regulation would only be justified for DBs that took them—but not for the others. Consumer Protection Regulation, also, should apply only to DBs which, once more, serve the public cash depositors directly.[5]

Asymmetric information is precisely the *raison d'être* for the existence of DBs, according to the market failure approach. Here the regulation in focus is allocative (support for small businesses, underdeveloped regions, urban development, etc.). DBs are, in this case, a mechanism against failures, therefore a solution and not a source of failure. They do not require regulation (in the restricted concept of capital requirements, limits on interest rates, and others), but rather, supervision (again) to verify whether they are actually fulfilling their goals.

Finally, the market failures associated with market power (monopolies) must be analysed carefully. For some authors, DBs, upon becoming monopolists in certain credit markets, 'crowd out' private banks. The low interest provided by DBs works as a 'barrier to entry', precluding competition and resulting in smaller amounts supplied in the market—an argument in some sense similar to the old financial repression theory (Gurley and Shaw 1960; McKinnon 1973). Even if so, this case is different from traditional monopolies analysis.

First, the possibility of DBs becoming monopolist in a given credit segment is associated (unlike in the classic case) with the possibility that DBs offer a

[3] It is worth noting that externalities are by definition non-pecuniary (thus hard to measure) and many of the benefits generated by DBs only materialize in the long term. In this analysis, it should be also considered how much would be lost in the absence of the investment promoted.

[4] Someone could argue that an investment bank could have a sort of a banking run (a wave of withdrawals on term deposits). It will face liquidity risk by selling assets with discount. If the investment bank is a big debtor of a commercial bank, its crisis could (at the limit) affect the payment system, but only indirectly. I thank Professor Eduardo Ichikava for that observation.

[5] Luna-Martinez and Vicente note that from a sample of ninety development banks, 41 per cent take deposits from the general public (2012: 10). However, the survey does not make it clear if these are cash or term deposits.

lower interest rate than the market, and not a higher price, as is usually the case in monopoly practices. As such, the theoretical issue of 'dead loss' is not quite clear. Second, assuming that there are niche markets where DBs and private institutions compete, it makes no sense to regulate (through Consumer Protection Regulation, for example) the very party that contributes to the reduction of the average prices.[6] Finally, and more relevant, there are no guarantees whatsoever that a reduction on credit resources by DBs would lead to an increase in supply by the private sector in the same credit segments (long-term projects, small businesses enterprises, innovation, environmental projects, inclusive endeavours, and so forth), precisely because here one faces a situation in which the market fails. In short, the discussion about the monopolistic power of DBs is not the traditional one. It is not a case of avoiding supernormal profits and enlarging supply, by regulation.

In contrast to the previous framework, the Keynesian, Schumpeterian, and Minskyan (KSM) approach emphasizes, as a structural condition, the *inability* of markets to self-regulate.[7] There is some scepticism as to the capability of regulatory activities to completely prevent the outbreak of crises—but it is possible to make them less frequent and mitigate their effects. Unlike the 'failure' approach, public intervention in financial markets is called for, as a rule and not as an exception, in order to: (1) contain systemic risk; (2) act anticyclically, when necessary (through monetary and fiscal policies); (3) foster development.

In the KSM approach, DBs can reduce financial fragility by creating effective demand; offering a stable source of long-term funding in national currency (so reducing exchange and interest rate risks); making investments feasible by reducing uncertainty; and mitigating external vulnerability in primary exporting countries (since they often promote the diversification of production, by funding industrial development), among others (Castro 2009).[8]

The role of DBs in innovation funding is also crucial (Kregel and Burlamaqui 2005)—and this role is seen as one that does much more than 'fixing static market failures' (Mazzucato and Wray 2015). DBs have advantages in

[6] Someone could argue that the marginal cost curve of DBs would be structurally lower, as they access sources not available to others. Potentially, this would open up space for the practice of interest/spreads above their marginal cost—which would also be an exercise of monopoly power. However, considering that spreads are usually quite low in these institutions, the problem is, in our view, immaterial.

[7] The KSM approach is not, in our view, necessarily incompatible with the recognition that 'market failures' might exist. However, it is considered that: (a) the concept of allocative efficiency, adopted in failures, is poorly suited to address the problem of development financing; (b) uncertainty goes far beyond the traditional scope of failures; and (c) funding long-term investments and innovation is crucial for economic growth.

[8] According to Kregel (2014) and Rezende (2015), DBs can, by reducing financial fragility, help solve the 'two masters' dilemma on regulation: assuring a safe and secure payment system versus fostering development (Minsky 1994). I thank Professor Felipe Rezende for that observation.

financing innovation because they can be 'patient and mission-oriented'. Besides, DBs have the technical capacity to analyse innovative projects—since it is a core business. They can provide non-reimbursable funds, in limited amounts, or manage funds (which are not supposed to have returns in the short-term) where the success of one project will make the others financially viable. They can also promote crowding-in on private resources, by joining private equity funds.

In the KSM approach, prudential regulation is made necessary by the recognition of the cyclical nature of capitalism. The phenomenon of 'contagion' is emphasized here, on two levels. First, the very perception of a fragility in a bank can affect others (even if they were *ex ante* healthy). This happens either because of crossed liabilities among banking institutions, or merely due to a 'panic' and 'herd behaviour' in a fractional reserve system. The second level is related to the fact that banks operate the payment system, directly influencing liquidity, which makes the crisis irradiate from the financial sector to the rest of the economy—this is ultimately the reason for regulating the financial system (Carvalho 2009). The payment system being the critical point, financial regulation focuses necessarily on the banks. But as financial markets are interconnected, the need for regulation of other financial institutions is recognized.[9]

Let's apply this discussion to DBs. In the case of DBs that act (exclusively or not) as second-tier banks, fund transfers comprise part of the DBs' assets. Traditionally, the problem of systemic risk occurs, conversely, when a bank is a large debtor (having commercial banks among their liabilities), so that its default spreads to successive breaks. Most likely, only small banks that were fundamentally dependent on the funds transferred by the DB, and had simultaneously assumed short-term liabilities, would not be able to honour their commitments to customers, and thus contaminate the payment system. It is unlikely, however, that the breaking of these small institutions would engender a wave of withdrawals from other banks, thus spawning a systemic crisis.

If a DB only operates through direct operations, its breaking may potentially generate a credit crunch. Companies that receive funds directly from the DB, but also obtain funds from the commercial banking system, could face difficulties in paying back commercial banks, leading to problems for the latter—and in this way a DB break could, indirectly, generate systemic risk. So, the habitual answer to the first question mentioned in the introduction is not precise. However, if it is not impossible for DBs (which do not hold cash

[9] The 1990s–2000s movement to strengthen bank regulation and simultaneously deregulate other financial institutions is seen, in this approach, as a major source of instability. It opens opportunities for regulatory arbitrage, increasing leverage in unregulated areas, which was a key element in the subprime crisis (shadow system).

deposits, but are significant lenders of funds to other banks) to be a source of systemic risk, this could happen only indirectly and that possibility is remote.

Finally, allocative regulation can also be regarded as a KSM concern, but (again) DBs are a solution, and not a source of problems. At most, supervision rather than regulation is applicable. Consumer Protection Regulation is also hardly befitting (as in the case of failures) as this is advocated solely to protect customers from the effects of bank runs, or from selling of products that can lead to individuals' losses.

Realistically one may expect that, if the DB is large, in order to avoid a major credit crunch or economic recession, it will receive additional public funds, so the question becomes fiscal (budgetary space or the ability of the government to raise additional debt in the market, at spreads that are not excessive) or, ultimately, inflationary.[10] In other words, there would be a need for the government to provide additional resources (capital injection or loans—both will enlarge gross public debt) in order to avoid systemic risk. Here another doubt arises: is prudential regulation justified by the fiscal risk? The literature simply does not answer this question.

9.2 The Evolution of Basel Agreements: Is Basel a Suitable Framework for DBs?

The first Basel Accord was established in 1988 and was limited to credit risk, subsequently including market risk, in 1996. The second agreement (Basel II) was launched in 2001 (reviewed in BIS 2004 and 2006), adding operational risk in the minimum required capital.[11] In 2009, BIS, the Bank for International Settlements, launched an amendment focused on trade portfolio improvements (trading book) and the treatment of market risk—which became known as 'Basel 2.5'. Finally, Basel III was released in December 2010 (reviewed in June 2011). Complementarily, in January 2013, BIS announced the rules for dealing with short-term liquidity risk (one month), and in 2014 long-term liquidity requirements (one year), aside from requirements for the exposure of banks to central counterparties.

Quite synthetically, the concepts underlying Basel II involved three pillars: (i) minimum capital requirements; (ii) supervision; and (iii) transparency—and those remain in Basel III. The minimum requirements comprehend: credit, market, and operational risk (defined as the risk of losses resulting

[10] In the KSM approach, it is argued that countries with sovereign currencies have no default risk. In fact, ultimately, the risk is inflationary.

[11] It lies beyond the scope of this work to discuss Basel I and II. For this, see Carvalho (2005); Griffith-Jones, Spratt, and Segoviano (2002).

from failures in processes; people; and systems, including legal risk). Different approaches to deal with each risk were allowed—from standard methods to advanced models. Supervision (Pillar II) oversaw other risks: interest rate risk in the banking book, concentration (BIS 1991), liquidity, reputational, etc. that did not require a priori regulatory capital. Strictly speaking, supervision could require additional capital (the first Pillar is about minimum requirements), changes in the ways of controlling risks, internal limits, provisions and reserves, improvements in internal controls, and other measures. Complementarily, the third pillar was intended to encourage market discipline by developing a set of disclosure requirements in order to provide public information about risk management and capital adequacy.

When Basel II was launched, critics mentioned: (a) its procyclicality; (b) the fact that the agreement hampered access to credit for companies with low ratings, including small businesses; (c) its bias against long-term credit; (d) its bias against smaller banks, since they are probably less able to develop internal models that could (potentially) save capital; (e) the difficulties in measuring operational risk; (f) its indiscriminate use of Value at Risk (VaR);[12] (g) the absence of liquidity risk[13] management enforcement, among others. In particular, Basel II was accused of leaving aside a macroprudential view, focusing exclusively on microprudential issues. Besides, the Basel Accords were applied only to banks, thus creating opportunities for regulatory arbitrage.

The changes made in 2004, still under the scope of Basel II, sought to respond to several of these faults. For example, adjustments were made in credit risk models (to ease the problems of cyclicality and short-term bias) in VaR models, and also some calibration by firm size in the case of internal rating models (credit risk) was added, along with other minor adjustments (see Castro 2007). The more structural criticism regarding the fact that Basel II does not address macroprudential issues and the inadequacy of operational risk models, however, was not dealt with.[14]

What is being called attention to is, in the first place, that several of the criticisms made regarding Basel II were not ignored (even before the subprime crisis), but acknowledged and, to a point, addressed. This, however, was not able to prevent one of the biggest financial crises experienced in the recent

[12] VaR calculates the maximum expected loss in equity due to changes in risk factors, considering volatilities, correlations, and sensitivity measures. For a critique of the use of VaR, see Dowd (2006).

[13] Liquidity risk is a consequential risk (derived from credit, market, and operational risk). It varies according to the severity and duration of events, has no single indicator, capital cannot be used for counterbalances, it is difficult to hedge against, requires contingency plans, and is highly correlated with systemic risk and the other aforementioned risks.

[14] The review of 2006 added new capital requirements for counterparty risk for some portfolio positions (trading activities) and the treatment of double default for credit risk (risk of both the borrower and the guarantor entering into default).

history of capitalism. Secondly, even though the ultimate goal of the framework continued to be avoiding systemic risk, Basel II evolved into a set of risk management usual practices. Thirdly, we can remark that, in Basel II and in spite of the changes made, the focus continued to be on microprudential regulation. The assumption remained that, by good (preventive) risk management practices (market, operational, credit, etc.), the probability of a systemic crisis could be reduced—the argument of levelling the playing field (equal conditions among countries) also remained.

However, from 2008, in face of the severity of the international financial crisis, BIS started to release many documents. Initially, the changes seemed (again) to follow the same strategy as Basel II: to include more and more requirements, and adjust models, without any major conceptual change (BIS 2008). The attentive reader, however, would start to notice a few novelties. The new framework (Basel 2.5), for example, sought to address activities performed by banks such as J.P. Morgan, Citibank Morgan Stanley, and Goldman Sachs, which had investment banking branches, and it was suggested that the framework could be extended to pure investment banks. It was recognized, albeit not explicitly, that regulatory arbitration and the need for more comprehensive regulation might be a possibility. Basel III went much further: not only were a large number of measures introduced, as usual (see Box 9.1), but a new framework was laid down. Also, BIS introduced the 'Supplemental Pillar 2 Guidance' and 'Revisions to Pillar III (Market Discipline)' (2009).

As explained by William Coen, Secretary General of the Basel Committee:

> The global financial crisis highlighted a number of weaknesses in the financial system and the global regulatory framework, including: . . . a high degree of systemic risk; interconnectedness among financial Institutions and common exposures to similar shocks; inadequate capital buffers for banks to mitigate the inherent procyclicality of financial markets and to maintain lending to the real economy in times of stress; and insufficient liquidity buffers and excessive exposure to liquidity risk, both direct and indirect (e.g. through the shadow banking system) . . . The weaknesses in the banking sector were transmitted to the rest of the financial system and the real economy, resulting in substantial costs. (BIS 2016b)[15]

Coen also announced that the current Basel agenda sought a better balance between 'risk sensitivity, simplicity and comparability'. It was admitted that

[15] In 2009, it was already recognized that (a) the boundary between trading book and banking book was susceptible to regulatory arbitrage; (b) the models do not consider extreme events (tail risk—so an additional requirement for losses in extreme situations, Stressed Value At Risk (SVAR), was added), among others. An additional amount of capital was also added, the Incremental Risk Charge (IRC), to estimate default and credit migration risk and another one to better treat correlations (comprehensive risk measure). The treatment of securitization and resecuritization was enlarged and reinforced. It was proposed (albeit vaguely) that calculation be improved for (1) the concentration risk; (2) off-balance-sheet exposures; and (3) reputation risk (thus far, outside the scope of Basel II).

'the regulatory framework became too complex', rendering not only supervision but also the very perception of risk by senior management (board) even more difficult. In addition, the Committee recognized that there were great discrepancies between asset valuations and risk calculations by different banks, which reduced comparability (and possibly revealed low accuracy) among metrics. In this regard, the Committee intends to increase the sensitivity and robustness of the simplest approaches, standardizing them. In particular, changes are underway regarding models of operational risk and interest rate risks in the banking book, and in 'the design and calibration of the leverage ratio and the potential capital floor based on standardized approaches'. In all of these revisions, the sought path seems to be the same: reducing the flexibility of using in-house models—which seems to bear consequences for the DBs, as will be discussed in section 9.4.

Since there are already so many changes in perspective, the bank industry has started talking about a 'Basel IV' approach, instead of mentioning all the new papers. Basel IV is not yet an official name. However, generally speaking, Basel III focuses on higher and more qualified capital requirements (although there are some other changes concerning, for example, liquidity risk). 'Basel IV' is about revisions on the risk assets measures. In other words, Basel III is about the 'numerator' of the Basel index (capital requirements), and Basel IV focuses on the 'denominator' (requirements on the modelling of risks)—both result, in general, in more need for capital. The discussion under 'Basel IV' is at different degrees of maturation. Some of the revisions proposed, like the revision on trading book, are almost finished, while others are still in the form of consultative papers, and we can expect many future changes. The impact of Basel IV on the banking industry is also very diverse, depending on the different banks. Some of the banks can even profit from small reductions on capital requirements, for example, on credit risk, estimated at about 10 per cent by PricewaterhouseCoopers (PWC). Others can have costs highly increased (PWC mentions that they performed tests on different clients and some of them would face a 190 per cent increase in their capital costs for credit risk). On average (an average that does not say much), specialists are considering an increase of total cost of 25 to 30 per cent (PWC 2017). Before dealing with Basel III and Basel IV (section 9.4), a glance may be cast upon the matter of Basel's applicability to DBs.

National public DBs are subject, in general, to specific national rules, and may or may not operate under the aegis of a central bank. Thus, during Basel I, several DBs were not covered by the international framework; to name a few: KfW (the German DB), JBIC (the Japanese DB), and Korea-Exim. BNDES (the Brazilian DB), on the other hand, was under Basel regulations as soon as the rules were laid down in the country, in 1994. The adhesion of DBs to Basel II, however, was much higher, whether imposed or voluntary. The China

Development Bank, the KfW, and the Korean Development Bank, for example, voluntarily joined the framework,[16] as did Latin American institutions (Zendron and Sobreira 2007). Why did this happen?

First, because prudential regulation in Basel stopped addressing only the problem of systemic risk (here understood in the classical sense of bank runs), and focused more directly on the individual risks of financial institutions. This design, as has been seen, is derived from the argument (which would later be belied by the subprime financial crisis) that avoiding individual risks regularly would eliminate the roots of systemic risk. By presenting the rules as a set of risk management best practices (although they always faced some criticism), these became potentially applicable to any organization, including DBs. When imposed, as in the Brazilian case, the justification was the banks' size and the relevance of DBs in the economy (in the broadest sense of the concept of systemic risk: capable of affecting the gross domestic product (GDP) due to their size).

The second reason for adherence to Basel II was, in fact, an increase in the risks undertaken by the DBs, which needed to be managed to ensure financial sustainability. In a context of reduced public resources available for promoting development, it had become necessary (for some DBs) to supplement public resources, abundant until then, and capture market funds (although some DBs, like KfW, already had that practice before). This, however, resulted in structural changes in liability conditions, introducing risks that did not exist before, but now needed to be properly managed. At the same time, the payback terms of DB loans also widened (changes in the terms of assets), since the market, in some countries, assumed funding medium-term projects (five to six years or even longer, in some developed countries), for example.

As a result of this double process (changes in asset and liability conditions), the potential risks to DBs increased, as regards credit, market, and even operational risks associated with assessment of long-term projects. Finally, the assumption of shorter-term liabilities, in order to complement the funding structure (hitherto non-existent or irrelevant), increased the DBs' cash flow risks. Also, the loans for large projects sometimes entailed grace periods that could comprise 'valleys' of cash flows, which also needed to be managed.

Moreover, the financial deregulation process, which gained momentum in the 1990s, inserted an element of competition (national and international). On the one hand, this increased opportunities for raising funds abroad, but on the other, it boosted the risk of mismatches on currencies and terms, and on interest rates, among these institutions, and decreased financial returns. In addition, support for share subscriptions increased the risk of

[16] Since 2016, bank supervisory laws and regulations are oficially applied to KfW—and the Bank has shown concerns about the new requirements proposed by Basel III and IV (KfW 2016).

price fluctuations in DBs' balances. Strictly speaking, when a DB (in order to develop the capital market) supports a firm that has already been awarded loans, through an acquisition of shareholding participation, the institution assumes double exposure on behalf of this company. Furthermore, unlike in the case of loans, there are no longer guarantees to protect it, at least in part, from losses in case of default.[17]

To the extent that DBs' priorities came to emphasize areas such as: (1) innovation funding; (2) micro- and small businesses; (3) large-scale projects in new industries, the challenges have widened once more for managing credit risk (innovation and small businesses) and legal risk (regulatory frameworks for large-scale projects). The greater funding requirements to meet the demand for investment, in turn, required, in some cases, that some DBs create financial products such as a supply of securitized papers or convertible debentures (see BDC 2009). Again, this introduced potential additional market risks for institutions that, historically, did not exist.

The third argument in favour of adhesion of DBs to Basel is that in this same context of financial globalization, not only is better risk management necessary, but also the importance of certifying this management has increased. In many ways (third argument), Basel II became a 'quality seal', used even to attract market resources. This seems to be the reason why some DBs have chosen to adhere to Basel II, even in countries where the rules are not mandatory for them.

According to (informal) reports by risk managers in DBs, adherence to the Basel II framework led, per se, to some improvements in risk management (see Castro 2014). The most relevant gain was the creation of integrated risk management systems, which enabled improvements in management and, above all, improvements in the quality of databases. Other gains included improvements in the corporate governance of risk management, given the imposition of formulating risk management policies, setting limits, segregating functions, greater accountability, etc.

Finally, as Basel II was a relatively flexible framework, allowing internal models, it became difficult to justify to the market why a DB should not join the framework. The DBs saw potential opportunities in saving regulatory capital through the development of internal models, particularly credit risk models, given the low historical default rates and the high recovery rates

[17] From the risk management point of view (exclusively), support through fixed income only, characteristic of the historical role of DBs, was therefore preferable. On the other hand, there are benefits to society in the development of the capital market. It is interesting to note that in Brazil, Law 11.101 states that, independently of the size of debt, if the creditor gives loans and has stocks from the same enterprise above 10 per cent of the share capital, the creditor loses the right to vote. I thank Professor Patricia Barros for that observation.

(low Loss Given Default (LGD)) due to the existence of good-quality guarantees, frequently sovereign or banking.

The voluntary acceptance of Basel II reveals something more important: the Basel requirements were not perceived by these DBs as a hindrance for the exercise of their mission. Why was that? In part, because several of their measures were simply good practices, bringing some important advances. Also, contrary to what is generally thought, in spite of acting in higher-risk credit segments, DBs also rely on risk management instruments that the market does not have access to. If, on the one hand, there are more risks, there are also tools to manage them. Managing risk is not avoiding risk.[18]

9.3 Do DBs Benefit from Distinctive Risk Management Features?

While generalizations concerning DBs are very difficult, it could be argued that DBs do enjoy a few advantages regarding risk management capability:

1. Lower liquidity risks, as a consequence of their own funding structure;
2. The longer terms of DB loans are not imperatively related to higher credit risks for DBs, as will be argued;
3. There are advantages in supporting exports to high-risk countries, because sovereign payments are more easily enforceable among governments and they benefit from specific support mechanisms such as public funds and guarantees;
4. In principle, there is a smaller exposure to market risk in the trading portfolio, vis-à-vis the private sector, since it is not their core business. Also, DBs have, in general, less complex instruments, such as derivatives. The same cannot be said, however, regarding mismatches on indices (different inflation indices on assets and liabilities, different interest rates or currencies), which remain a major source of potential market risk;
5. DBs can renegotiate terms of debt more easily. The existence of crossed assets and liabilities between the Treasury and DBs allows a range of tools for risk management, not available to private institutions;
6. The fact that they interact with higher-risk sectors (small to medium enterprises (SMEs), innovations etc.), once more, does not necessarily

[18] From a Minskyan point of view, but also from other perspectives (see Corden 1990), it would be more important to focus on mechanisms that could guarantee the asset quality and the potential of the investments supported to generate growth, rather than fixing very rigid rules for risk management. Some of the assets must carry risk (especially to DBs). A 100 per cent safe bank would be one that has 100 per cent of capital—it would not foster development. I thank Professor Felipe Rezende for that observation.

imply greater losses. If SME operations are performed as second-tier operations, the risk is assumed by the financial agent. If it is first tier, large portfolios tend to offset losses. As for funding innovation, if done with non-reimbursable funds, risk does not even enter the equation. If done through a fund, capital requirements will look at the sustainability of the fund—not of each individual operation—thus enabling the activity.

It should be added here that the vast majority of Basel requirements for market risks are in the trading portfolio, using VaR or maturity ladder methods.[19] The most significant market risks tend to be: currency risk (in case they support exports or fundraising in the international market); interest rate risk on the banking book; and, if the DB acts to foster capital markets, risk on dividend flow fluctuations in the banking book. However, the latter does not require capital buffers. In relation to mismatched terms on balance sheets, also, DBs are likely to have risk management advantages since the duration of the liability (in spite of the broader loan terms) is greater than that of the asset.

Do all these arguments mean that there are no problems in directly applying Basel rules to DBs? No, it does not. In our opinion, Basel II contained three points of great concern for developmental objectives: (a) maturity adjustment in credit risk models; (b) the treatment of concentration risk; (c) the treatment of operational risk. These points remained, or were even worse, in Basel III—as will be discussed.

As usually occurs in financing, Basel credit risk models consider that the longer the term, the greater the risk.[20] The required capital is calculated (either in standard or in internal models), exclusively appraising the asset's analysis. However, the greater lending periods do not imperatively bring higher risks for DBs in the same proportion as they do to private banks, because their funding is also held in longer term. Upon raising longer-term funding, DBs are capable of renegotiating credit on better terms, reducing default losses without hurting the financial health of the institution. In other words, portfolio management (asset liability management) is more flexible, contributing to financing productive investment, and so reducing the vulnerability of the financial system.[21]

[19] Maturity ladder may no longer be accepted in the near future.

[20] The maturity adjustment is to anticipate possible downgrades and/or changes in mark to market values. It is considered that the chances of downgrading and loss of market value are greater when the probability of initial default is lower. Therefore, when repayment terms are extended, the capital requirement increases—albeit less than proportionally for higher-risk companies (because it is assumed that their quality will improve over time), compared to those with better credit rating (since the latter are more likely to worsen rather than improve in rating over the years by Basel models). See BIS (2005).

[21] On the other hand, non-performing loans can stay for a longer time in a public bank balance sheet (or DB) than they would in a private bank.

Additionally, it can be argued that the existence of long credit relations between banks and clients, as is common in DBs, ultimately reduces default and delinquency, as ties of interdependence grow and flows of information between borrowers and lenders are improved. In addition, as the long-term credit is vital for some sectors, companies often prioritize payments to these institutions. This probably stems from the behaviour of companies in that they prefer (obviously assuming the crisis is not long-lasting) to honour their debt commitments to partners critical to their long-term strategy (even though renegotiation capacity is possibly the most important factor).

Even if we admit that the longer terms somehow involve higher risks, will the risks grow for DBs in the same way as they do for private institutions (exponentially, for example, as several managerial models assume, or linearly as in the Basel format, adjusted to a concave shape by the Probability of Default (PD))? The reality is that the parameter calibration in Basel agreements is based on the experiences of a number of commercial or universal banks located in developed countries, whose characteristics are very different from those dealt with by DBs. The term defined as 'standard' is only 2.5 years, so any longer time-frames are penalized with higher capital charges in Internal Rating Models (IRB) with a cap of five years (higher maturity will be charged as if it was five years anyway) (Barros 2016). It is exceedingly likely that this calibration is inadequate for DBs. In addition, there is the problem of adapting the 'M' (maturity adjustment for capital requirement) to the characteristics of different countries. The reduced average period of credit operations is a feature common to many developing countries, where DBs are the main—or only—alternative for long-term fundraising.

Given that DBs are very different institutions among each other, it is important that the framework be flexible in relation to maturity adjustment, so that it does indeed reflect potential higher risk, but nevertheless without creating a bias against long-term operations, which are essential for economic development and intrinsic to the DBs' mission. It seems to us that the only way to solve this dilemma is to establish a dialogue with the regulator in order to render some points more flexible. The rules should be consistent with the risk profile (which in the case of DBs involves particular characteristics) and also consider the benefits to economic development.

Regarding concentration risk, Basel credit risk models are based on KMV Portfolio Manager type models, where it is assumed that the only significant risk factor is systemic risk, since individual risks are cancelled out due to the law of large numbers (BIS 2005). The Basel models assume, therefore, a granular portfolio. If there is concentration (by borrower, guarantor, industry, or regional/geographic), an adjustment must be made to Pillar II supervision.

The problem is that portfolio concentration in groups, sectors, regionally, or by lender is something almost inherent to DBs. Due to their natural form of action, it is common that their portfolios are concentrated, in certain periods, on industry sectors or regions, following government policies and guidelines. There are funding 'seasons' focusing on certain industries or sectors in large 'National Economic Development Plans'. There is, therefore, a dilemma between the risks of holding a concentrated portfolio and the social damage that the absence of these investments—which need to be large (and often very concentrated, at certain times)—could represent in terms of economic and social development.

In particular, when the infrastructure sector is addressed, the problem is not restricted to industry concentration and the longer terms in the DBs' portfolios. Major infrastructure projects are provided typically by oligopolistic industries: for example, the construction sector. In other words, aside from concentration in an economic sector and region, it will often also involve concentration on a few clients or an economic group or guarantors. The problem is that managing risk concentration (particularly with large exposure) is not a simple matter. Developing forms of mitigation and management of these risks is a clear and present challenge—but *not* treating it in a flexible manner could work against development.

Finally, regarding operational risk, in Basel II three methodologies were established: (1) Basic Indicator Approach; (2) Alternative Standardized Approach (ASA); and (3) Advanced Measurement Approach (AMA), which provided some modelling flexibility. Much criticism targeted the difficulties in estimating this risk, particularly in relation to databases and statistical processing.[22]

With regard to the operational risk for DBs, there is no clarity as to its magnitude. Wyman states that for DB managers, risk management continues to focus on credit and market risks (2016). Several banks identified reputational risk (a demand strengthened in Basel III) as critical, yet few institutions actually manage it.[23] Operational risk, though admittedly relevant, is considered less important in magnitude, and furthermore difficult to measure and treat.

[22] Operational risk data is, in general, of low frequency, and has very different magnitudes between each loss event, making it difficult to use approximations to standard distributions. Besides, some controls are managerial and the items defined by the Committee are not always relevant to the Bank. There are also problems of double counting (operational and credit or market risk); some expenses are estimated from provisions, not always materialized in payments; some events (e.g. labour claims) take much more time to solve than Basel data series allows (the observation period is only five years); other events (e.g. mergers and acquisitions) are unique, etc. It is possible to supplement the analysis with external data, but a careful evaluation of whether the data is suitable for use and applicable to the institution concerned is necessary.

[23] Reputational risk is defined as the risk arising from negative perception on the part of customers, counterparties, shareholders, and other stakeholders, which can adversely affect a bank's ability to maintain normal business practice.

Although from an empirical point of view, there is no clarity regarding operational risk magnitude, one could assume that having a smaller number of operations and not being subject (at least with the same intensity) to typical operational risk events such as, for example, card frauds, DBs would (potentially) face lower operational risk. However, DBs (always remembering that, for the purposes of this chapter, institutions specializing exclusively in small businesses are excluded) tend to have large exposures in less homogeneous, more complex, and longer-termed products. Thus, their operational risk events, even though less likely (lower in frequency), tend to be more severe. Moreover, DBs, given their public nature, may have more difficulties in renewing their IT park (because of the public bidding process requirements), thus raising the risk of system failures and computer system crashes. In short, operational risk management in DBs is particularly challenging, and the proposed models do not seem adequate.

9.4 Basel III: What Are the New Challenges for DBs?

Box 9.1 summarizes the key measures and metrics introduced by Basel III—highlighting in boldface those that appear to be, in our point of view, the most relevant for DBs.

Let us start with the reasons why we maintain that (generally speaking) some of the new requirements in Basel III *are not (or are less)* relevant to DBs than for other banks. First, the short-term liquidity risk indicator (LCR) seeks to assess whether banks maintain an adequate level of liquid assets in a scenario of severe stress. This indicator tends to be irrelevant to DBs, as it is determined with a one-month horizon, for institutions that have few short-term liabilities. The long-term indicator (NSFR) aims to ensure that banks avoid severe term mismatches under normal conditions considering the one-year horizon. The core business in DB risk management is, precisely, managing the mismatch between assets and liabilities. It is expected, therefore, that DBs would have no difficulty in meeting these new requirements. However, the NSFR may increase the short-term bias of the market. Thus, potentially, the need for medium/long-term assets from DBs may increase due to the reduction of their supply on the market—which is why the item is in boldface in Box 9.1 (Barros 2016).

The leverage ratio does not seem to be equally problematic for many DBs, although some institutions could have problems.[24] Regarding the use of

[24] KfW, for example, registered that: 'By nature, a state-owned development bank is bearing a lot of low-default sovereign exposure . . . The question is whether it is expected from development banks to practice a search-for-yield. If so, it is contradictory to the long-term business model of a

Box 9.1 BASEL III

1. Short-Term Liquidity Risk—Liquidity Coverage Ratio (LCR).
2. **Treatment of Long-Term Liquidity Risk—Net Stable Funding Ratio (NSFR).**
3. Leverage Ratio (not risk-weighted).
4. Incremental Charge Risk (ICR)—captures default and migration risk for unsecured credit products held in the Trading Book.
5. Comprehensive Risk Measure—captures price risks as well as incremental default and migration risks in a single measure for correlation of trading portfolio.
6. Higher requirements for Resecuritization.
7. Credit Valuation Adjustment (CVA)—adjusts to take into account the possibility of a counterparty's default.
8. Greater control of credit derivatives—ABS, CDO, and off-balance-sheet vehicles.
9. Disincentive to OTC derivatives.
10. Search for greater integration between market risk and credit risk (Wrong-Way Risk).
11. Back-testing of internal models.
12. Greater robustness in stress tests.
13. Changes in executive compensation rules.
14. Addition of reputation risk control.
15. Pillar II: new requirements to ensure strict guidance and monitoring of banks.
16. Pillar III: Larger set of information requirements.
17. Higher capital requirements for internationally active banks.
18. **Higher capital requirements for nationally active banks.**
19. **Increased requirements of core capital and Tier 1.**
20. **Two additional capital cushions—Absorption and Countercyclical.**
21. **Greater control over concentration risk.**
22. **Disincentive to the use of monoline insurers.**

derivatives (items 4 to 10), they tend to have smaller consequences, relatively, for DBs, due to their lower use. This impression is reinforced by recent research, which showed that several DBs do indeed use derivatives but, as expected, these are often used for hedging purposes (which is not punished with higher capital requirements, but instead encouraged) (Wyman 2016). The most common products used in DBs are interest rates, credit derivatives, and foreign currencies. Of course, for DBs that deal with securitization, an increase in capital may be more significant. Moreover, the disincentive for the use of OTC derivatives may also have some effect. This is because DBs have incentives to create optionalities and OTC derivatives, since tailor-made operations tend to be more common for institutions that deal with projects with non-standard features.

The use of back-testing and more robust stress testing (items 11 and 12), as well as further integration of market and credit risk correlations, are, in

development bank. If not, it limits business volume and thereby the development bank's ability to perform its major task' (KfW 2016: 7).

principle, salutary for risk management, thus are not, a priori, problematic. The addition of Stress-VaR requirements raises capital requirements for all institutions, including DBs. The *Incentives Agenda* in Basel III also does not seem to be of great impact, once these institutions no longer have the objective of profit maximization. As for reputational risk, it is still unclear how its treatment will proceed.

As regards the new capital requirements in Basel III, particularly of Core Capital, this may indeed be a source of concern. Some DBs may face difficulties, depending on each individual case. Compliance with new requirements will depend on the existence of prior capital clearances and fiscal constraints specific to each country. The addition of countercyclical cushions, in contrast, should in our view be assessed carefully for their relevance to DBs. If it is accepted that DBs act anticyclically, does it make sense to apply the cushions to these institutions? (See Chapters 1 and 11 in this book; Luna-Martinez and Vicente 2012.) It may simply be dysfunctional for the economy as a whole, and work against macroprudential regulation goals. DBs should have enough capacity to act fast and decisively in crisis times. In that sense, countercyclical buffers could become part of an agenda applying some rules of Basel III in a more flexible manner for DBs.[25]

Finally, the major requirements for systemically important global banks focus more on banks that operate as commercial banks, because of their global systemic implications. This does not mean that DBs intending to carry out international operations will not be included in the framework in the future. The new rules seem to be, however, more relevant for DBs which are domestically systemic banks (BIS 2012a). To determine whether an institution is domestically systemic, the criteria are size, interconnectedness, the existence of substitutes, and complexity. Thus the concept of being systemic was used in its broadest sense, considering their size relative to the GDP. So, larger DBs may carry additional requirements under Basel III, depending on the judgement of the national monetary authority—which may prove to be problematic in the future.

An important point is that Basel IV diminishes the incentives for the development of internal models (and is moving towards the defence of adjusted standard models), which reduces the flexibility of the framework. In other words, it decreases the possibility that an institution (which has idiosyncratic risk management characteristics, and furthermore, contributes

[25] It should be recognized, however, that DBs may sometimes act procyclically, responding to demands for funding the economy. In fact, when the economy is booming, there is increasing demand for investments, so DBs' disbursements (or other forms of credit support) are higher, whereas the opposite occurs in economic downturns. The DBs' countercyclical behaviour is common, but it is a government or institutional decision.

to development and, it must be emphasized, reduces financial fragility) develop more suitable metrics. It is worth adding that the treatment of the interest rate risk in the banking portfolio (which tends to be relevant for DBs), where the BIS allowed flexibility under Basel II, is also being reformulated into a standard method of treatment, which can be adopted as a requirement by the national regulator or placed as an option (BIS 2016a).

With regard to concentration risk, the problem is far more serious, because its treatment has been systematically revised in the direction of greater severity (BIS 2011, 2012b, 2014). For the purpose of dealing with concentration risk, the use of several metrics (sensitivity analyses, use of scenarios, economic capital models, stress tests) are suggested, setting internal limits and observing the concentrations of counterparties, for both assets and funding sources, currencies, derivatives, etc. (BIS 2014). As of 2019, there will be a default limit for large exposures, of 25 per cent of Tier 1, and, for 'global systemically important banks (G-SIBs)', of 15 per cent of Tier 1 capital.[26]

The issue becomes more serious when one considers that there is a large gap in global infrastructure, with DBs seen as a key instrument to overcome it. This means that Basel III, by demanding higher capital requirements, will be working against the global infrastructure agenda—especially considering greenfield projects, where the risks are higher (and the market does not show appetite without government support). It is worth noting that if project finance structures, on the one hand, allow sharing guarantees and facilitate investment by reducing performance risks, on the other hand, they also introduce new risk management challenges. This is because the guarantee is the project in itself, which is far more difficult to liquidate. In relation to the concentration risk, when a project finance begins its operations, they can be considered as segregated risk—so the 25 per cent limit proposed by Basel III will probably be not binding—but, for the pre-operational phase, it probably will be (Barros 2016). This may be another important point where a dialogue should be maintained with the regulator to enable DBs (and other banks involved in infrastructure financing) some flexibility.

Finally, there are also ongoing changes in the treatment of operational risk (BIS 2011, 2014, 2016b). The Standardized Measurement Approach (SMA) aims to replace the three methods aforementioned. Again, simplicity, comparability, and sensitivity to risk are sought, eliminating the possibility of using internal models. The most relevant issue is that the new DBs' agendas

[26] In Brazil, there was already a similar limit of exposure to a single economic group (financial conglomerate) to 25 per cent of the Regulatory Capital (Tier 1 + Tier 2). BNDES, however, had a (temporary) flexible application of this setting. With the new international rules, the limits are even tighter, because they refer only to Tier 1.

emphasize funding for infrastructure and financing sustainability—segments where the risk of regulatory changes is high.[27] That is, it is possible that in the future, operational risks will grow, once this includes legal risk. In this sense, again, the tendency to use standard metrics could prove inappropriate.

9.5 Conclusions: Answering the Four Questions

Should DBs be regulated? It was seen throughout section 9.1 that, under the aegis of market failures, the rationale for financial regulation was traditionally justified for institutions that collect cash deposits from the public in order to avoid a negative externality. In all other cases, as discussed, DBs pose a solution for such failures and, therefore, do not properly require regulation, but rather, supervision, in the sense used in this chapter. In the KSM approach, financial regulation is justified by systemic risk. Even though there is some theoretical possibility that the illiquidity or, ultimately, the bankruptcy of a DB (that does not collect cash deposits) can indirectly generate systemic risk, this possibility seems remote, from a practical point of view.

However, the negligent or reckless behaviour of a DB (through excessive leverage or poor risk management) could cause potential fiscal damage (ultimately, an inflationary risk), or, more importantly, the risk of a credit crunch. In the latter case, it would cause a loss of investment, probably an increase in unemployment, but the crisis would be concentrated in a few economic sectors. That is, it would not be 'systemic' since the means of payment would not be affected, at least at first. The economic impact that DBs can have is a justification for DBs to be regulated/supervised by the monetary authorities (regardless of the fact that the literature does not consider these issues).

In addition to the macroeconomic costs, it is a fact that DBs that recurrently require additional capital injections due to losses are often questioned by society. DBs are supposed to be self-sustainable. Here lies a political issue that must be considered: any consistently financially unsustainable DBs will hardly have the ability to perpetuate themselves over time, as demonstrated by the 1980s experience, when several DBs became extinct. Moreover, even for DBs that receive fiscal budgetary flows and work with some non-reimbursable projects (besides loans), the return on operations is also an important source of resources. Regulation, however, should not hinder DBs

[27] If these projects involve funds in other currencies (co funding between DBs or DBs and private entities), this will raise market risk (fluctuation of currencies) and add greater risks of interest rate fluctuation in the banking book (associated with longer-term operations and the interest fluctuations in different currencies).

in the fulfilment of their mission. The question, therefore, becomes whether it makes sense to regulate them in the way that prudential regulation is conceived today?

Is Basel regulation a suitable framework for DBs? We sought to clarify and maintain, throughout section 9.2, that Basel II aimed to correct several of the problems raised in Basel I, many of them related to issues with development funding. These adjustments, however, were insufficient—they did not even manage to avoid one of the gravest financial crises in history. However, the fact that many DBs adhered voluntarily to the framework strongly suggests that, contrary to what is generally assumed, Basel II was not seen as incompatible by DBs themselves.

This is so because, first of all, Basel II evolved into a set of good risk management practices, which were therefore also applicable to DBs. Second, because the risks that DBs have to deal with have, in fact, increased over time, more sophisticated management tools were required for the financial sustainability of the institution. Third, many voluntarily adhered to Basel II because it represented a 'quality seal' relevant for banks seeking to raise funds in the market, and it was also considered a relatively flexible framework. Fourth, in spite of working with riskier segments, DBs have different instruments for risk management, which could lead (or so at least it was supposed) to capital savings through the development of internal models. Does this mean that Basel II was an ideal framework for DB management? Far from it! But it also does not seem wholly incompatible with DBs, in the sense of hindering the fulfilment of their mission.

With regard to risk management, do DBs entail different characteristics from private banks? In section 9.3, we sought to demonstrate that if, on the one hand, DBs operate in higher-risk segments, on the other they benefit from instruments to deal with those risks that are not available to the private sector. This enables them to operate in these segments, contributing to funding development, without this threatening their financial health or even jeopardizing their performance. To illustrate the risk management advantages that DBs enjoy, it is worth noting that even in 2009, at the height of the severe subprime crisis, the performance of DBs was not bad—often better than that of the private sector.[28] Evidently, some development projects may have been

[28] Luna-Martinez and Vicente found that in 2009, 14 per cent of the surveyed DBs reported losses. The remaining 86 per cent were profitable or broke even. 'The percentage of DBs reporting losses in 2006, 2007 and 2008 was 15%, 8%, and 9%, respectively... In 2009, 53% of the surveyed DBs had a Return on Assets (ROA) exceeding the average of their banking systems. This was up from 42% in 2006 and 2007, and 46% in 2008. In terms of the Return on Equity (ROE), 19% of DBs exceeded the national average in 2009 (up from 15% in 2006, 13% in 2007, and 18% in 2008)' (2012: 18).

hurt by risk aversion on the part of DBs—which is suggested, incidentally, by the low default rates recorded by many DBs. This aversion to risk, however, would probably also exist without adherence to Basel. It was also pointed out in section 9.4 that, on a few points, Basel regulations need to be more flexible for DBs, in order not to hinder their mission. We discussed three of these points in more detail: maturity adjustment, concentration, and operational risk.

What are the challenges posed by Basel III and IV? In section 9.4, it was argued that some of the new requirements in Basel III do not seem (in principle) problematic for DBs, such as the treatment of liquidity risk and derivatives, amongst others. Some new requirements, however, appear particularly worrisome. This is certainly the case with the new requirements regarding concentration risk, especially in view of the infrastructure agenda that many DBs pursue. The second point is the tendency to abandon internal models and move towards more standardized approaches, which reduces the flexibility in the framework (this is especially relevant in the case of credit risk). With regard to operational risk, in the same vein, the adoption of a single standardized rule may turn out to be quite problematic, especially in the case of legal risk associated with changes in the regulatory structure, which may grow as environmental and infrastructure agendas increase in relevance.

With these analytical considerations, we hope this chapter has contributed to exploring beyond the usual answers given to the four questions above.

References

Barros, P. 2016. Interview conducted on 30 October.

BDC. (Business Development Bank of Canada). 2009. *International Benchmark Study on Development Institutions*.

BIS. (Bank for International Settlements). 1991. 'Measuring and Controlling Large Credit Exposures'.

BIS. 2004. 'International Convergence of Capital Measurement and Capital Standards: A Revised Framework'.

BIS. 2005. 'An Explanatory Note on the Basel II IRB Risk Weight Functions'.

BIS. 2006. 'Basel II: International Convergence of Capital Measurement and Capital Standards: A Revised Framework—Comprehensive Version'.

BIS. 2008. 'Liquidity Risk: Management and Supervisory Challenges'. Press Release.

BIS. 2009. 'Enhancements to the Basel II Framework'.

BIS. 2011. 'Operational Risk: Supervisory Guidelines for the Advanced Measurement Approaches'.

BIS. 2012a. 'A Framework for Dealing with Domestic Systemically Important Banks—Final Document'.

BIS. 2012b. 'Core Principles for Effective Banking Supervision'.

BIS. 2014. 'Supervisory Framework for Measuring and Controlling Large Exposures'.

BIS. 2016a. 'Standards for Interest Rate Risk in the Banking Book Issued by the Basel Committee'.

BIS. 2016b. 'Finalizing Basel III'. Introductory remarks by Willian Coen, Secretary General of the Basel Committee, at the meeting with the European Parliament's Committee on Economic and Monetary Affairs (ECON Committee), Brussels, Wednesday 12 October.

Carvalho, F. C. 2005. 'Basel II: A Critical Assessment'. Rio de Janeiro: UFRJ. Available at <www.ie.ufrj.br/eventos/seminarios/pesquisa/basel_ii_a_critical_assessment.pdf>, accessed 24 April 2018.

Carvalho, F. C. 2009. 'Systemic Crisis, Systemic Risk and Financial Instability Hypothesis', in E. Hein, T. Niechoj, and E. Stockhammer (eds), *Macroeconomic Policies on Sharky Foundation: Whither Mainstream Economics*, vol. 12. Series of the Research Network Macroeconomics and Macroeconomic Policies (FMM). Marburg, Germany: Metropolis-Verlag.

Castro, L. B. 2007. 'Discutindo os Acordos da Basileia', *Revista do BNDES* 14(28): 277–304.

Castro, L. B. 2009. 'Regulação Financeira: Teoria, Acordos da Basileia e a Experiência Recente do BNDES'. PhD thesis. Rio de Janeiro: UFRJ.

Castro, L. B. 2014. 'A experiência da área de gestão de riscos do BNDES', in *Prêmio ABDE: Melhores práticas do Sistema Nacional de Fomento*, 65–95. Rio de Janeiro: ABDE.

Corden, M. 1990. 'Macroeconomic Policy and Growth: Some Lessons on Experience', in S. Fischer, D. de Tray, and S. Shah (eds), *World Bank: Proceedings of the World Bank Annual Conference on Development Economics*, 59–99. Washington, DC: World Bank.

Dowd, K. 2006. *Measuring Market Risk*, 2nd edn. London: John Wiley & Sons.

Griffith-Jones, S., S. Spratt, and M. Segoviano. 2002. 'The Onward March of Basel II: Can the Interest of Developing Countries Be Protected?' Institute of Development Studies, University of Sussex, July.

Gurley, J. G. and E. S. Shaw. 1960. *Money in a Theory of Finance*. Washington, DC: Brookings Institution.

KfW. 2016. 'Regulation of Promotional Banks and Potential Impacts.' KfW Research, November. Available at <www.kfw.de/PDF/Download-Center/Konzernthemen/Research/PDF-Dokumente-Studien-und-Materialien/PDF-Dateien-Paper-and-Proceedings-(EN)/Regulation-of-promotional-banks-November-2016.pdf>, 18 May 2017.

Kregel, J. and L. Burlamaqui. 2005. 'Banking and the Financing of Development: A Schumpeterian and Minskyan Perspective', in S. Paula and G. A. Dymski (eds), *Reimagining Growth: Towards a Renewal of Development Theory*, 141–68. New York: Zed Books.

Kregel, J. 2014. 'Minsky and Dynamic Macroprudential Regulation', *PSL Quarterly Review* 67(269): 217–38.

Luna-Martinez, J. de and C. L. Vicente. 2012. *Global Survey on Development Banks*. World Bank Policy Research Working Paper No. 5969.

Mas-Colel, A., M. Whinston, and J. R. Green. 1995. *Microeoconomic Theory*. New York: Oxford University Press.

Mazzucato, M. and R. Wray. 2015. *Financing the Capital Development of the Economy: A Keynes–Schumpeter–Minsky Synthesis*. Levy Institute of Bard College Working Paper No. 837. New York: Levy Institute.

McKinnon, R. I. 1973. *Money and Capital in Economic Development*. Washington, DC: Brookings Institution.

Minsky, H. P. 1994. 'Financial Instability and the Decline(?) of Banking: Public Policy Implications', in Federal Reserve Bank of Chicago(ed.), *Proceedings of a Conference on Bank Structure and Competition*, 55–64. Chicago: Federal Reserve Bank of Chicago.

PWC. 2017. 'Latest News from Basel IV: Challenges and Implications—28th October 2016'. Available at <www.youtube.com/watch?v=ISs0vIVfAXM>, accessed 18 May.

Rezende, F. 2015. 'Why Does Brazil's Banking Sector Need Public Banks? What Should the BNDES Do?', *Quarterly Review* 68(274): 239–75.

Stiglitz, J. 1994. *Whiter Socialism?* Cambridge, MA: MIT Press.

UN-DESA. (United Nations, Department of Economic and Social Affairs). 2005. 'Rethinking the Role of National Development Banks'. New York: UN-DESA.

Wyman, O. 2016. 'Development Finance Best Practices'. Oliver Wyman Financial Services, January.

Zendron, P. and R. Sobreira. 2007. 'Implications of Basel II for the Development Banks.' In *Quem Controla o Sistema Financeiro?* Rio de Janeiro: Ibase.

10

National Development Banks and Mission-Oriented Finance for Innovation

Mariana Mazzucato and Caetano C. R. Penna

10.1 Introduction

Innovation requires patient long-term finance. Across the world this type of finance has often come from different types of public funds, whether in Research and Development (R&D) agencies (e.g. US Defense Advanced Research Projects Agency (DARPA)), procurement programmes (e.g. Small Business Innovation Research (SBIR) in the USA), public venture capital funds (e.g. Yozma in Israel, Sitra in Finland), or investment funds inside public banks (e.g. EIF inside the EIB) (Mazzucato 2013a; Mazzucato and Semieniuk 2017).

Innovation has not only a rate but also a direction. In the post-war US, the direction of innovation was often spurred by military missions, such as the spillovers that came from the Apollo moonshot programme—many of which ended up in our smart products like the iPhone. The Internet, touchscreen display, GPS were funded by Darpa, the CIA, and the Navy respectively (Mazzucato 2013a). But in more recent decades, US innovation has been also directed by public investments in health- and energy-related missions. Indeed, many of the most revolutionary new drugs have come out of the National Institutes of Health (NIH), which continue to spend over $30 billion a year, and recent advances in fracking, solar, and wind energy have come out of spending in the Department of Energy, including the guaranteed loan that went to the Tesla S car (Angell 2004; Mazzucato 2016).

Mission-oriented policies can be defined as systemic public policies that draw on frontier knowledge to attain specific goals or 'big science deployed to meet big problems' (Ergas 1987: 53). Contemporary missions aim to address broad challenges that require long-term commitment to the development of technological solutions (Foray et al. 2012) and 'a continuing high rate of technical change and a set of institutional changes' (Freeman 1996: 34). The current active role of the public sector in tackling renewable energy investments can be seen as a new mission in relation to the green economy (Mazzucato and Semieniuk 2017). Other new missions include addressing such 'grand societal challenges' as the ageing/demographic crisis, inequality, and youth unemployment (EC 2011). In fact, these challenges—which can be environmental, demographic, economic, or social—have entered innovation policy agendas as key justifications for action, providing strategic direction for funding policies and innovation efforts.

Internationally, there is mounting evidence that patient finance for mission-oriented investments in innovation—in countries like Germany, China, and Brazil, have come from National Development Banks (NDBs) (Schäfer et al. 2004; Fried et al. 2012; Schapiro 2012; Sanderson and Forsythe 2013; Macfarlane and Mazzucato 2018). This is not surprising as there is still too little private finance going into the most capital-intensive and high-risk areas of green technology (solar, wind, biofuels); and such investments have only diminished since the Great Financial Crisis (GFC). Since 2007, it has been 'the development banks [that] have made significant project finance contributions to renewable energy projects across the world' (Fried et al. 2012: 5). Figure 10.1 shows how NDBs have filled the vacuum left behind by private

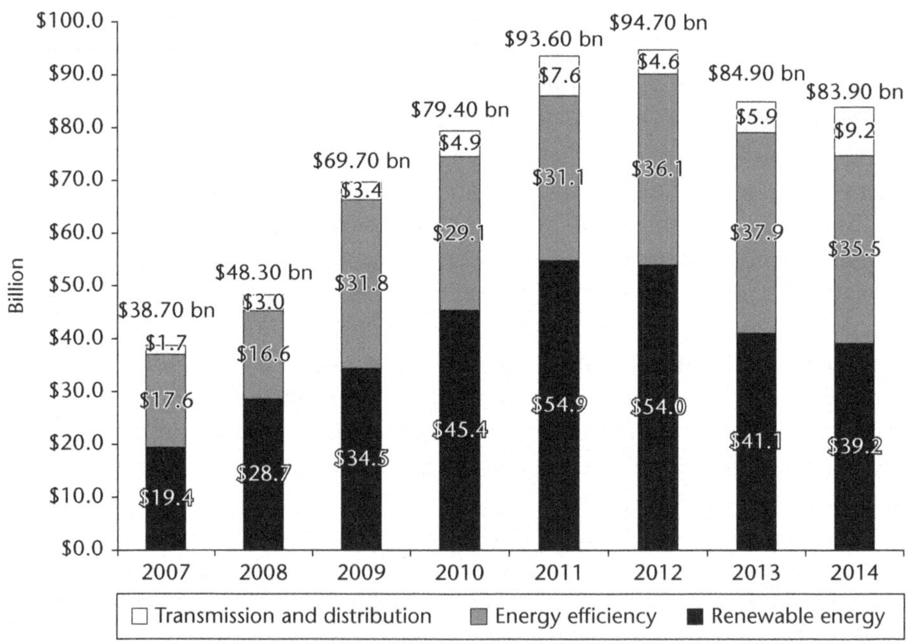

Figure 10.1. National development banks' funds for renewable energy by sector
Source: Based on data from Louw (2014) and FS-UNEP/BNEF (2016)

commercial banks since the outbreak of the crisis, more than trebling their investments in clean energy projects between 2007 and 2012. Indeed, in the context of financialization and pursuit of short-run returns, NDBs are becoming important not only for 'countercyclical' lending or funding catching-up strategies (though both are still crucial), but also for funding the uncertain world of innovation. In this sense, as Sanderson and Forsythe (2013) put it, the China Development Bank (CDB) seems to be 'rewriting the rules of finance', and so are other NDBs such as the Brazilian development bank BNDES and Germany's KfW, to name just a few.

How can one conceptualize this new 'mission-oriented' role assumed by national development banks? The standard perspective on what NDBs do is based on the 'market failure' perspective. Market failures are 'imperfections' in the price system that prevent markets from efficiently allocating resources (Samuelson and Nordhaus 2009 [1948]). Market failures have different types of sources, which can be typified into four broad categories (cf. Ledyard 2008): (1) negative externalities, e.g. air pollution or climate change, for which there is no market; (2) public goods (positive/network externalities), e.g. clean air or knowledge, for which there is no market and/or no equilibrium price (Stiglitz 1989); (3) information asymmetries, e.g. bad vs good borrowers, which result in a non-equilibrium situation (Stiglitz and Weiss 1981); and (4) non-competitive behaviours, e.g. monopolies or monopsonies, where competition is limited. Based on the notion of market failures, NDBs would, for instance, provide finance for investments that internalize the costs associated with 'negative externalities' or that develop 'public goods' to address societal challenges, by subsidizing key infrastructural projects and investing in innovation.

Yet, Market Failure Theory (MFT) provides only a *partial and limited* justification for what NDBs do (particularly in their new 'mission-oriented' role); and it does not explain historical and contemporary developments (Mazzucato 2016). As modern capitalism has become increasingly 'financialized', with a focus on short-run profits rather than long-run development, the financial sector has become more speculative ('short-termist') and disconnected from the real economy (Kay 2012). But companies in the real economy itself have also become financialized (Krippner 2005; Dore 2008). They spend an increased percentage of their net earnings in areas that produce immediate boosts to their share prices—such as share buybacks—at the costs of long-run investments in areas like human capital and R&D (Lazonick 2013). Even venture capitalists—normally thought to be less risk-averse than traditional banks—have sought returns in three to five years, while complex and lengthy innovation cycles require a much longer time horizon (Lazonick and Hopkins 2011; Mirowski 2011). Indeed, sector-based analysis shows that the venture capital funding model is not the appropriate one for innovation in science-based sectors like biotechnology (Pisano 2006). In this sense, lack of finance for capital development and innovation is not a problem of coordination of expectations and risk-taking (as conceptualized by MFT), but is due to a long-term financialization process that has taken place in the capitalist world since the early 1970s—the rise of 'Money Manager Capitalism', as Minsky called it (1996).

MFT also ignores and fails to explain the role that the active hand of the state plays in *shaping and creating markets*—not just 'fixing' their failures (Burlamaqui 2012).[1] Karl Polanyi's historical work showed that '[t]he road to the free market was opened and kept open by an enormous increase in continuous, centrally organized and controlled interventionism' (Polanyi 2001 [1944]: 144). Polanyi described how the state created the conditions for the emergence of a market-based economy, revealing that the 'state vs market' dichotomy is artificial and a myth, because the most capitalist of all markets, i.e. the national market, was 'pushed' into existence through the very actions of the visible hand of the state (Mazzucato 2013a).

Since its origins, the capitalist system—usually portrayed as being 'market'-driven—has been strongly embedded in and shaped by the state (Evans 1995; Reinert 1999). Furthermore, contemporary evidence shows that in the most economically successful and innovative countries, public policies go beyond fixing market failures. In particular, in creating specific technologies and in some cases whole sectors, state investments have not been relegated to only funding 'basic research' (something advocated by market failure theorists); they were the engine behind economic development and industrialization (Wade 1990; Amsden 2001; Chang 2002). The market failure framework does not capture how in countries that have been successful in achieving 'smart' (innovation-led) growth, the *breadth* of such public investments has (always) been driven by broad 'mission-oriented' justifications (Ergas 1987; Mowery 2010; Foray et al. 2012), such as those that drove investments by the National Aeronautics and Space Administration (NASA), DARPA, and the National Institutes of Health, all of which have gone beyond simply funding public goods like research. In fact, mission-oriented policies represent a type of governmental intervention that *shifts* economic priorities and *bias* allocation of resources in the economy towards visionary non-existing areas, creating new technologies, industries, sectors, and, ultimately, new markets.

In this chapter, we combine insights from Keynes, Minsky, Schumpeter, and Polanyi (and works in their tradition) to review the old and new roles of national development banks. We show that the roles of NDBs go beyond the view of the state as 'market fixer'. The chapter is structured as follows: in section 10.2, we identify four roles that NDBs have been playing throughout

[1] Burlamaqui (2012) discusses knowledge governance and describes what he calls the 'market features approach', which would have as a policy counterpart 'market-shaping' policies.

their histories and proceed to discuss the market failure justification behind these roles. Based on concepts and insights from Keynes, Minsky, Schumpeter, and Polanyi, we then show that market failure theory does not account for many aspects of what NDBs have been and are doing. Based on this discussion, section 10.3 examines the four roles of NDBs in light of two important dimensions: (a) the relationship between risks and rewards and (b) the criticisms that NDBs crowd out private investments. Section 10.4 concludes with a brief summary and discussion of the importance of NDBs' mission-oriented finance for the 'great societal challenges' policy agenda (e.g. the EU's Horizon 2020, EC 2011).

10.2 The Roles of National Development Banks in the Economy

10.2.1 *Historical Background on National Development Banks*

National development banks have their historical roots in the monetary agreements of Bretton Woods (1944), which were influenced by Keynes's work, and the reconstruction plans for Europe following World War II (Skidelsky 2011). The idea was to create an institution that promoted financial stability through a permanent flow of finance to fund the reconstruction plan and unleash agricultural production potential, thus preventing deleterious effects that speculative private finance could have on post-WWII economic recovery (World Bank 2013). Following this rationale, the International Bank for Reconstruction and Development (IBRD) was created, providing its first loan to France in 1947 (World Bank 2013). Other NDBs were founded around that time, such as KfW in Germany (1948) (Schröder et al. 2011), with the aim of channelling international (and national) funds to the promotion of long-term growth, infrastructure, and modern industry. While in industrialized countries these institutions focused on niche areas, in Third World countries, NDBs such as the Brazilian BNDES (1953) initially promoted a catching-up agenda (Torres Filho and Costa 2012).

In subsequent decades, NDBs diversified their operations and foci. In the mid-1950s, KfW assumed the responsibility to provide finance for environmental protection and small and medium-sized enterprises (SMEs), roles that were intensified in the 1970s, when it also began to target energy efficiency and innovation development (KfW 2009). Other development banks followed suit: BNDES, for instance, created new credit lines for SMEs in the 1980s, and in the following decade began to experiment with financing programmes targeted at high-tech firms and innovation development (Branco 1994; Sousa 2012). By the 2000s, China Development Bank (CDB) was one of the most active NDBs, investing in regional economic development and industrial catching-up; supporting and nurturing new ventures and innovation development; and, later in the decade, targeting finance to projects aimed at 'green growth' (Sanderson and Forsythe 2013). After the outbreak of the Great Financial Crisis in 2007, NDBs across the world significantly promoted countercyclical credit, increasing their loan portfolio by 36 per cent on average between 2007 and 2009, with some (10 per cent) increasing their loans by more than 100 per cent (Luna-Martinez and Vicente 2012).

This overview highlights four conceptually distinct roles that national development banks have played throughout their histories (Mazzucato and Penna 2016): (1) the countercyclical role; (2) the capital development (or developmental) role; (3) the new venture support (or venture capitalist) role; and (4) the mission-oriented role. The main economic explanation and justification for what NDBs do (or should do) is put forth by market failure theory. From this perspective, all roles performed by NDBs are justified as means to correct a particular failure of the market. But based on insights and concepts from Keynes (and post-Keynesian economics), Minsky (and developmental economics), Schumpeter (and evolutionary economics), and Polanyi (and STI policy research), we point to limitations of the market failure view on NDBs.

10.3 The Four Roles of National Development Banks

10.3.1 *The Countercyclical Role*

Capitalist systems are marked by business cycles (Schumpeter 1939; Freeman and Louçã 2001; Perez 2002), when periods of economic bonanza are followed by periods of recession or crisis. In times of crisis, NDBs play a crucial role, as they supply countercyclical credit that would otherwise be in shortage due to the higher risk aversion of private financial institutions. Public investment thus provides short-term fiscal stimulus for investments that keep the economy running.

Market failure justification. This countercyclical role has usually been justified as a way to address a particular type of 'market failure', namely the 'coordination failure' that arises from private banks' tendency to underreact to countercyclical monetary policy (e.g. lower interest rates), not realizing the fact that by increasing lending they would help the economy out of recession (Levy-Yeyati et al. 2004). The issue is compounded by the fact that private banks' risk aversion is procyclical, whereby lending peaks during the boom and tumbles during the trough. As the state is risk-neutral, the countercyclical role would be further justified by NDBs' ability to absorb risk during an economic crisis and to spread it over time and cross-sectionally (Gutierrez et al. 2011). This market failure view has justified increased state intervention in the economy through national development banks after the outbreak of the 2007 financial crisis, particularly in countries where central banks faced legal and macroeconomic constraints—but not only. Indeed, NDBs played a crucial role in the governmental response to the financial crisis across the world, through a substantive increase in their loan levels to mitigate the impact of the private credit crunch (Luna-Martinez and Vicente 2012).

Limitations. Recent cycles of boom-and-bust have been exacerbated by dysfunctional financial markets that focus on speculative gains even during periods of bust (e.g. betting on further declines in market values by 'selling short'). Thus, the issue is not so much that private agents are risk-averse, but that they became increasingly speculative. As Keynes eloquently put it back in the 1930s:

> Speculators do no harm as bubbles on a steady stream of enterprise. But the position is serious when enterprise becomes the bubble on a whirlpool of speculation. When the capital development of a country becomes the by-product of the activities of a casino, the job is likely to be ill done. The measure of success attained by Wall Street, regarded as an institution of which the proper social purpose is to direct new investment into the most profitable channels in terms of future yield, cannot be claimed as one of the outstanding triumphs of laissez-faire capitalism—which is not surprising, if I am right in thinking that the best brains of Wall Street have been in fact directed towards a different object.
>
> (2006 [1936]: 142–3)

The types of financial structures in an economy (e.g. the quantity and type of banks) are not inconsequential to the workings of the real economy and productive enterprises. Some structures are conducive to what Minsky calls the 'capital development' of the economy, which includes privately owned capital equipment, technologies, skills, and public infrastructure (Minsky 1992). Yet, capital development is hampered when speculative finance targets low-risk, short-term gains through the trade of securities and other investment types that '[amount] to little more than pyramid schemes' (Wray 2012: 310). Minsky called the laissez-faire financial architecture that was established in the 1980s 'Money Manager Capitalism', which he believed was inhibiting the 'capital development of the economy', because it led to speculation, short-termism, volatility, uncertainty, and financial instability (Minsky and Whalen 1996; Papadimitriou and Wray 1998). So, the problem is not so much of risk aversion but of financialization and speculation.

The situation, which repeats itself in capitalist history, does call for public policy intervention, which may take the form of a reform of the financial system and/or of fiscal policies—both of which were indeed policies implemented in the United States through the New Deal, which was influenced by the ideas of Keynes. In the realm of fiscal policy, Keynes called for 'socialization of investments' as 'the only means of securing an approximation to full employment' (Keynes 2006 [1936]: 246). To be sure, Keynes was not so much concerned with underinvestment, as he was with underutilization of productive resources, particularly labour. The goal of his policy proposals was not to increase investments per se, but to decrease unemployment, as explained by Tcherneva: 'Public investment is a direct approach to reducing unemployment. Add to that the secondary employment effects produced by the multiplier effect and we can estimate how much public works spending is needed to close the labor demand gap. Whenever Keynes spoke of how much national income and expenditure are needed to maintain full employment, his "calculations are in terms of equivalent men . . . and women, if they are unemployed . . . " (Keynes 1980, 298)' (Tcherneva 2008: 18).

In summary, while the need for public promotion of countercyclical credit is usually seen as resulting from 'coordination failure', in fact, in this role NDBs do much more than correcting markets. National development banks play an important role in *directing* investment to productive opportunities, laying the groundwork for the capital development of the economy and the full utilization of labour resources.

10.3.2 *The Capital Development (or Developmental) Role*

NDBs also play important roles during periods of economic boom, promoting strategic investments for economic development that lead to a multiplier effect. This was the original role of the IBRD (World Bank) and KfW. Despite Germany being a developed economy, KfW still plays a developmental role to this day, and the original funds from the 'Marshall Plan' are still revolved and invested in promotional areas (KfW 2009).

Market failure justification. Like the countercyclical role, the capital development role of NDBs has been justified by market failure theory (see Levy-Yeyati et al. 2004; Gutierrez et al. 2011): wherever private lenders have limited incentives to finance projects with public goods characteristics (non-excludable, non-rival) or that cause positive/network externalities, the market is not an efficient allocator of resources, and therefore state intervention would be justified. One example is private markets underfunding socially desirable projects (i.e. public goods), which happens in the presence of positive externalities (e.g. infrastructure projects whose value cannot be internalized by private agents). In order to correct for this market failure, NDBs should invest in infrastructure and other public works. Market failures associated with industry structures are another rationale for the developmental role, according to the mainstream view. NDBs provide finance in situations of monopoly and monopsony, in order to promote entry of new agents, increase the pool of producers and consumers, respectively, and foster competition.

Limitations. In Schumpeter (1934 [1912]), economic development is a discontinuous *endogenous* process and result from investments in 'new combinations': new methods of production, new products, opening of new markets, new sources of supply, and new forms of organization. According to Schumpeter, these new combinations disturb the prevailing economic equilibrium. Furthermore, from the entrepreneur or the corporation point of view, the objective of introducing new combinations is the creation of 'monopoly rents'—or 'Schumpeterian rents' (Reinert 2007). Interventions and investments that seek to address a market failure aim at bringing the economy back to the equilibrium of perfect competition, 'killing' Schumpeterian rents. This is at odds with Schumpeter's view of economic development. In fact, in the 'lost' seventh chapter of *Theory of Economic Development*, Schumpeter points to the limitation of the static perspective of mainstream economics that sees development as an exogenous process:

> Our most important result is that such economic development really exists. [...] This conception is the contrary of an alternative explanation which can be expressed as follows: an economic equilibrium, once attained, will be maintained, as long as there is no disturbance coming from the outside. [...] In other words, there is no true economic development, no development emanating from the economy itself, but only development that conforms to one pattern of imagination or does not conform to it. [...] According to this conception the purely economic plays only a passive role in development. Pure economic laws describe a particular behavior of economic agents, whose goal is to reach a static equilibrium and to re-establish such a state after each disturbance. [...] It is true that this way of thinking corresponds to the fundamental principles of static economics. It allows for the precise formulation of static laws... Yet we maintain that the conception described is not sufficient to explain the real development of the economy. (1934 [1912]: 96–7)

The market failure limitation becomes more apparent when we look at the works of developmental economists studying catching-up and industrialization processes (e.g. Prebisch 1950; Singer 1950; Hirschman 1958; Gerschenkron 1962; Nurkse 1966). Abramovitz thus puts forth the 'catch-up hypothesis': 'Countries that are technologically backward have the potential for generating growth more rapidly than that of more advanced countries, provided their *social capabilities* are sufficiently developed to permit successful exploitation of technologies already employed by the technological leaders' [*our emphasis*] (1986: 390). Key in this definition is the 'social capabilities' qualification, a variable that is difficult to measure, but which includes technical competence and political, commercial, industrial, and financial institutions (Abramovitz 1986). In fact, Prebisch (1950), Singer (1950), and Nurkse (1966), among others, had theorized about problems of industrialization, terms of trade imbalances, and insufficient availability of capital in underdeveloped countries, providing the foundation of active development strategies guided by governmental investments and policies.

In this alternative view, NDBs play a central role in developing social capabilities and fostering the catch-up process, and in many instances represent a 'Lead Agency' in latecomer countries' development efforts (Figure 10.2) (Mathews 2006). To do so, an NDB may work as an agency to nurture nascent or knowledge-intensive firms ('infant-industry promotion'); promote strategic trade (e.g. import substitution) and financial leverage; prioritize investments in existing strategic sectors (reinforcing comparative advantages); create 'national champions'; and give coherence to economic policies (Reinert 1999; Mathews 2006; Etzkowitz and Ranga 2009). While the need for some

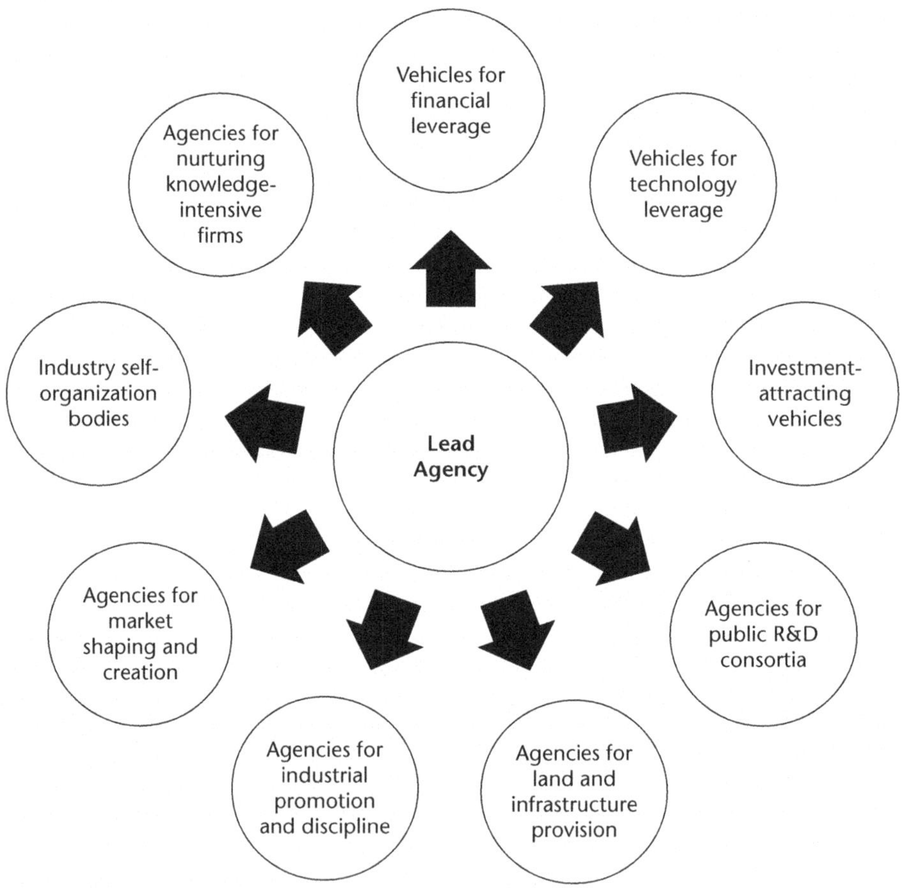

Figure 10.2. Roles, instruments, and functions of a national system of economic learning
Source: Mathews (2006)

of these activities may be explained by market failure theory (e.g. infant-industry promotion as a result of adverse selection by private investors), the fact is that in fulfilling this developmental role, NDBs do much more than provide financial capital to fix failures. Because economic development is an endogenous process, they provide social capital, coordinate initiatives and public–private partnerships, foster synergies, and promote the introduction of 'new combinations' that create Schumpeterian rents.

10.3.3 *The New Venture Support Role*

Investment in new ventures, such as SMEs and innovation development, has been the focus of NDBs since the late 1950s, an activity that was intensified in more recent decades (KfW 2009; Griffith-Jones and Tyson 2012; BNDES 2012). Underlying the initiative is the fact that SMEs—especially those that are developing high-tech innovations—face difficulties in securing external finance due to lack of guarantees and collaterals or of a track record of profitable investments (Tchouvakhina 2013). Indeed, innovation development also presents problems in securing external finance, due to economic and technical risks and uncertainties that underlie the innovation process.

Market failure justification. Market failure theory explains the issue of lack of finance for SMEs as resulting from information asymmetries that lead to adverse selection of potentially good borrowers (Stiglitz and Weiss 1981; Levy-Yeyati et al. 2004; Gutierrez et al. 2011). A similar case happens with R&D and innovation projects, which are risky and uncertain, so that private finance shies away from supporting them. R&D/innovation investments also present 'public good' characteristics (non-rival, non-excludable), and often result in positive externalities. These investments generate new knowledge, which cannot be fully appropriated by the original investor, who cannot 'exclude' other agents from using the knowledge to their own benefit. Private agents tend to underinvest in R&D and innovation not only because they cannot fully capture their benefits, which would compensate for the development costs and make the investments worthwhile, but also because they lack information and technical knowledge about the R&D/innovation project. In these situations, public investments in SMEs and innovation, through loans, equity, or grants, would be justified.

Limitations. The focus on *smallness* is misguided, and we draw on Minsky to show the first limitation of these market failure justifications. Minsky suggested that one form that the Keynesian socialization of investments should take, is that of 'Community Development Banks' (CDBs), which were to fill the gap in banking and financial services for small firms and individuals in certain local communities (Minsky 1993; Minsky et al. 1993). The ethos of CDBs was to promote the financial inclusion of certain strata of the society and certain regions, but this is not an end in itself, as would appear from a market failure perspective: Minsky was concerned with the 'capital development' of the economy, which he conceived as the development of human capital and social capital.

Second, it is not the case that all SMEs face a problem of capital supply due to adverse selection and moral hazard concerns. This idea implies that all SMEs are equal in terms of their propensity to innovate and grow, which is a myth (Mazzucato 2013a). Evidence shows that there is no systematic evidence that a relationship exists between firm size and growth (Haltiwanger et al. 2013). Furthermore, small firms appear to be less productive than larger ones, due to management issues (Bloom and Van Reenen 2007). The challenge for NDBs is not so much the provision of abundant finance for all SMEs, but to find and nurture the so-called 'gazelles' (Birch and Medoff 1994; Nightingale and Coad 2014): young high-tech firms. Nurturing this group requires as much financial capital (in the form of VC) as social capital (sometimes networking and co-management).

Moreover, economists working in the Schumpeterian tradition (evolutionary economists) theorized about technology development and innovation ('new combinations') as an endogenous process to economic growth and development. They showed that the issue is not one of 'information asymmetries', which assumes that some parts know the chances of an innovation project to succeed or fail. Because innovation is a venture that is not only risky, but also fundamentally uncertain, nobody knows the 'odds' of success. Innovation requires finance, but the type of finance received affects the types of investments made (O'Sullivan 2004; Mazzucato 2013b): in fact, innovation requires *patient, long-term, committed finance.* This mutual causation is a key reason why NDBs are increasingly providing long-term committed venture capital for start-ups developing radical innovation projects. But from a market failure perspective, any kind of finance and even tax breaks would do the job in supporting high-tech SMEs and innovation development.

10.3.4 *The Mission-Oriented Role*

The mission-oriented role of NDBs is informed by missions predefined in bold public policy plans, such as Germany's 'energy turnaround' (*Energiewende*), which seeks to phase out nuclear energy and fossil fuel and substitute them with renewable energy sources, in order to tackle climate change, protect the environment (save resources), and promote energy security. Other missions that NDBs are fulfilling around the world are the inclusion of populations to health systems (such as in Brazil) or the transition to a green economy (such as in China and Korea). To name a few examples of mission-oriented investments by NDBs (Mazzucato and Macfarlane 2017, 2018):

- EIB's €14.7 billion commitment (in 2010) to sustainable cities projects (Griffith-Jones and Tyson 2012), such as transport and urban renewals, through which advanced infrastructures substitute for carbon-dependent ones.
- In Germany, KfW invests in the modernization of industries, urban infrastructure, and housing to promote the reduction of CO_2 emissions through the use of new technologies applied to old sectoral systems of innovation (Duve 2007; Schröder et al. 2011).
- China Development Bank's investments in renewable energy projects. CDB has a track record of funding alternative energy firms to develop their technologies, such as the solar company Yingli Green Energy, which received *c.*US$1.7 billion from 2008 through 2012 and has a US$5.3 billion line of credit opened for it at CDB (Sanderson and Forsythe 2013).
- BNDES's technology fund FUNTEC, which targeted resources to very specific technologies (BNDES 2012): (1) alternative energy, specifically bioenergy (such as new-generation biofuels), solar energy, and thermal energy; (2) nanotech and biotech solutions to address issues of waste disposal, land and water pollution; (3) bio-electronics, specifically *organic* electronics and other innovative integrated circuits; (4) new materials; (5) biochemistry; and (6) electric-drive vehicles, particularly technologies for the production, charging, and storage of electricity in automotive vehicles.
- BNDES's programme Profarma, which is the funding leg of the mission of promoting universal access to health products and services for the Brazilian population (Palmeira Filho et al. 2012). To help fulfil this mission, BNDES works in partnership with a network of public and private actors: Brazilian companies and public labs, responsible for the R&D and innovation activities; the Ministry of Health (the lead agency) and the Brazilian National Health System (SUS), which is the main buyer for pharmaceutical products in the country; the regulatory agency, Agência Nacional de Vigilância Sanitária (ANVISA) (equivalent to the US FDA), which established a special biotech pathway to speed up approval of new molecular entities; and the Brazilian Intellectual Property Rights (IPR) office, which also established a fast track for biotech products (Ramundo 2013).

Market failure justification. Societal challenges are often portrayed as resulting from market failures: they are consequences of the production, use, or disposal of certain products (negative externalities). At the system level, these market failures amount to 'system failures'. For instance, climate change is a negative externality from carbon-intensive production methods or the burning of fossil fuels. Negative externalities are not reflected in the price system. There is no 'equilibrium' price, for there is no market for negative externalities. Economists often call for market-based mechanisms (e.g. creation of artificial markets for carbon, carbon tax) or neutral technology policies (e.g. tax breaks) in order to correct market failure. In other words, in the mainstream view, addressing societal challenges is not one of the roles of national development banks and their direct investments—but of markets.

Limitations. Are NDBs just correcting market failures or doing something else here? In our view, NDBs are fulfilling a 'mission-oriented role' (Ergas 1987; Mowery 2010; Foray et al. 2012) that is way beyond addressing a market failure in order to internalize external costs to society. They are making things happen that otherwise would not, as Keynes called for the state to do (Keynes 1926). But more importantly, they are paving the way for a 'Great Transformation', as described by Polanyi (2001 [1944]). In an often-quoted passage from his *magnum opus*, Polanyi explains why market-based mechanisms cannot be expected to provide the solution for societal and environmental challenges:

> To allow the market mechanism to be sole director of the fate of human beings and their natural environment, indeed, even of the amount and use of purchasing power, would result in the demolition of society. For the alleged commodity 'labor power' cannot be shoved about, used indiscriminately, or even left unused, without affecting also the human individual who happens to be the bearer of this peculiar commodity. In disposing of a man's labor power the system would, incidentally, dispose of the physical, psychological, and moral entity 'man' attached to that tag. Robbed of the protective covering of cultural institutions, human beings would perish from the effects of social exposure; they would die as the victims of acute social dislocation through vice, perversion, crime, and starvation. Nature would be reduced to its elements, neighborhoods and landscapes defiled, rivers polluted, military safety jeopardized, the power to produce food and raw materials destroyed. Finally, the market administration of purchasing power would periodically liquidate business enterprise, for shortages and surfeits of money would prove as disastrous to business as floods and droughts in primitive society. Undoubtedly, labor, land, and money markets are essential to a market economy. But no society could stand the effects of such a system of crude fictions even for the shortest stretch of time unless its human and natural substance as well as its business organization was protected against the ravages of this satanic mill. (2001 [1944]: 73)

It is the state that provided and provides this welfare protection and promotes the solution to societal challenges and malaises. While the 'welfare state' has been thoroughly analysed and theorized (Castles and Leibfried 2010), an economic theory of the 'entrepreneurial state' (Mazzucato 2013a) is a job in the making. In particular, the analysis of how NDBs fulfil their entrepreneurial mission-oriented role should be the subject of an important research agenda (see concluding section 10.5), given the pressing need to carry out investments that promote smart, inclusive, and sustainable growth and tackle societal challenges. Such economic theorization must draw in neighbouring disciplines, like economic sociology and public administration, which provide important concepts such as the 'embeddedness' of markets in society (Granovetter 1985; Evans 1995) or 'state and policy capacity' (Skocpol and Finegold 1982; Parsons 2004; Drechsler 2009).

10.4 Discussion: Implications of the Multiple Roles of NDBs

In this section, we discuss two important aspects that make the roles of NDBs differ from one another: (1) their *potential for generating windfall gains*; and (2) whether *the crowding-out hypothesis* applies or not.

10.4.1 *The Risk–Reward Nexus and the Potential for Generating Windfall Gains on Investments*

The risk–reward relationship in economics predicts that the higher the risks, the higher the potential rewards. This is why we propose that the potential for NDBs getting a reward on their investments (windfall gains) increases with the risks and uncertainty involved in the four roles. Yet, rewarding the state for its investments and for its risk-taking is often assumed to happen indirectly via taxation (or the multiplier effect), but this in reality does not always happen (consider, for instance, tax evasion and outsourcing of production to foreign countries). Given the important role that public agencies have played in funding the highest-risk investments (high capital intensity and high technological and market risks) through mission-oriented investments, Mazzucato (2013a) questions why it is that they have not shared in the rewards. The fact that companies like Apple have benefitted greatly from state investments (with all technologies behind the iPhone having been state-funded), and yet they produce mostly abroad and pay very little back to the public purse in taxes to refund such investments, makes the innovation machine less sustainable over time.

This is especially a problem given how uncertain investing in innovation is, with most attempts failing. A return is thus necessary to fund both the inevitable losses and the next round of innovations. Lazonick and Mazzucato (2013) provide a framework through which to consider the risk–reward nexus in innovation, and claim that the need to reap a return is even more important given the highly cumulative nature of innovation. This characteristic means that some actors can enter late, and capture the entire integral under the cumulative distribution curve of returns. In this respect, the ability of NDBs to retain equity in their investments becomes a possible tool to reap a return,[2] rendering the innovation-financing model more stable. The results from BNDES's venture capital fund CRIATEC are striking: in its first four years, the value of the CRIATEC portfolio grew at a rate 50 per cent per annum,[3] with a compound annual growth rate (CARG) per vintage of investments varying between 45 per cent and 160 per cent (Ramundo 2013).

And this is where the framework for understanding the role of NDBs particularly matters. Those who see the role of national development banks as simply fixing market failures often argue that when the 'job' (funding) is done, they (NDBs) should 'get out' and leave the rest (including the rewards) to the markets. However, if instead the job involves much more than fixing market failures, and is actually about actively creating and shaping markets, then the analysis of how deep the investments should be made, in both their risk and return, is different. Indeed, Precisely because innovation often results in failures, it is crucial to make sure that successful investments grant a return that is high enough to both cover (part of) the losses of the failures, as well as achieve a level of return that can help fund the next round of innovation investments.

Indeed, one could make the argument that when funding mission-oriented R&D and innovation, the state *should* reap a share of the profits that are generated so that the funding agencies that are responsible for such investments are 'sustainable' in the future.[4] In this sense, a key issue for mission-oriented innovation policies is how state investments, of any sort, should retain some equity so that returns come back to the state through a more direct mechanism than taxes—precisely because the jobs generated from such investments (hence tax receipts) are often global in nature, and taxes of corporations are often avoided (through loopholes), and are in any case so low that even when paid would not be enough to fund the high costs of (uncertain) innovation. In this respect, some NDBs already employ equity- or income-contingent loans to fund the riskiest and most uncertain components of their innovation portfolio. They therefore represent an interesting alternative to reform the 'dysfunctional' financial system from within.

[2] Other tools include income-contingent loans, equity, and a golden share of the IPR.

[3] See <http://www.fundocriatec.com.br/capital.php?escolha=54>, accessed on 12 June 2013.

[4] It is in this sense that Mazzucato (2013a) asked: had the state reaped back even just 1 per cent of the profits from the investments it made in information technology, how many more billions of dollars would there be today to spend on the next 'big thing': green technology? Instead, we have the dysfunctional situation where in the US, the National Science Foundation (NSF) that funded Google's algorithm is today underfinanced, as is the Small Business Investment Company (SBIC) programme that gave Apple US$500,000 in early-stage funding.

10.4.2 *The Crowding-Out Hypothesis*

Despite theoretical arguments and empirical evidence showing the importance of NDB investments, critics of state intervention in the economy argue that in a free-market economy, the market mechanism is the best allocator of scarce resources, and thus there is no need for any kind of central planning (Friedman 1962). A more developed argument against these institutions takes the form of the 'Financial Repression Hypothesis', according to which the use (by development banks or other central planning institutions) of low or negative (in real terms) long-term interest rates is the cause and not the consequence of the inexistence of a long-term credit market (McKinnon 1973). This is the 'crowding-out hypothesis', derived from mainstream economics (Neo-Keynesian and New Classical) growth models (Hicks 1937; Lucas 1988). Managed long-term interest rates would 'crowd out' credit that otherwise would be supplied by private agents in a free market—inhibiting both the activity of commercial banks and the creation of a capital market (Hemming et al. 2002).

Critics argue that development banks crowd out private investments through a direct and/or indirect route: the former happens when public investments substitute for private investments, the latter when public investments induce changes in interest rates and exchange rates, which in turn lead to lower private investments. In any case, this view sees NDBs as a barrier to the flourishing of private capital markets, i.e. they are the *cause* of (and not the solution to) market failures. Many studies that have attempted to test the crowding-out hypothesis reached contradictory results (for reviews, see Hemming et al. 2002; Hur et al. 2010). And because this hypothesis is derived from specific economic models, its validity remains controversial (Tassey 2013). Thus, demonstrating the direction of causality between state investments and inexistence of a long-term capital market has proved elusive, and to date there is no definitive proof about what is causing what (Hemming et al. 2002; Hur et al. 2010).

In our conceptual framework, the crowding-out hypothesis would be associated only with the countercyclical role (via the indirect route), because in all other cases NDBs are doing precisely what the private sector is not. And yet, the crowding-out hypothesis cannot apply to economies that are not close to full employment of resources or that have not seized all available productive opportunities. In the developmental role, NDBs *crowd in* investments by playing a lead role in the economic development or industrialization strategy in order to create network synergies. In the new venture support role, NDBs *dynamize* the economy, by identifying and supporting young, high-tech firms. And in the mission-oriented role, NDBs help *envision* the future.

10.5 A New Research Agenda

Addressing 'Great Societal Challenges' forms the new agenda of economic growth and development plans (see the EC 2020 Strategy, the OECD Innovation Strategy, or the UK BIS Growth Strategy). These challenges include global, regional, and national problems such as climate change, resource depletion and degradation, water and food supply, energy efficiency and security, obesity, diseases, demographic change, ageing, and well-being, etc. Such challenges are of a different nature than the classic 'mission-oriented' R&D programmes, which had a narrow technological goal. As pointed out by Foray et al. (2012: 1698), in historical mission-oriented R&D projects, such as the Manhattan and Apollo programmes, all funding was provided by public US federal agencies, '[b]ut for current societal challenges, publicly funded R&D, although vital, will be only one of a number of sources of R&D investment'. Indeed, most studies in that special issue organized by Foray and colleagues[5] looked at quite particular types of public funding: non-reimbursable public finance for basic research, such as grants, subsidies (including tax credits), and innovation prizes. New challenges have societal goals aimed at great systemic transitions, which require coordination between public and private actors, and investments in a whole range of sectors.

A different source of public finance for new mission-oriented projects has therefore emerged in recent decades: *national development banks*. In this chapter, we sought to understand this new mission-oriented role of NDBs. To do so, we built our argument by looking at standard market failure justifications for the role of NDBs in the economy. We showed the limitations of the market failure perspective based on insights from Keynes, Schumpeter, Minsky, and Polanyi (and other literatures). Finally, we discussed two important dimensions of what NDBs do: the risk–reward nexus and generation of returns to its investments; and the crowding-out hypothesis—and criticisms often aimed at NDBs—vis-à-vis the four roles.

The new mission-oriented role for NDBs is already a reality, and represents an important alternative to 'old' mission-oriented funding mechanisms. At a time when many countries are trying not only to promote growth but also to address key societal challenges, NDBs seem well positioned to effectively promote the much-needed capital development of the economy in a smart, inclusive, and sustainable direction. Analysing, theorizing, and constructively criticizing what is being done is a new agenda for innovation economists, and

[5] One exception is Edquist and Zabala-Iturriagagoitia (2012), who looked at Public Procurement for Innovation (PPI) as a means to address societal problems. However, as the authors argue, this is not a funding instrument: PPI is a demand-side policy that indirectly supports developmental costs by guaranteeing the acquisition (procurement) of the final product.

we believe our conceptual review represents a first step in this direction. This agenda would improve our understanding of the degree to which the activities of a state investment bank could open up new technological landscapes and economic opportunities—making new 'Great Transformations' happen.

References

Abramovitz, M. 1986. 'Catching Up, Forging Ahead, and Falling Behind', *Journal of Economic History* 46: 385–406.

Amsden, A. H. 2001. *The Rise of 'the Rest': Challenges to the West from Late-Industrializing Economies*. New York: Oxford University Press.

Angell, M. 2004. *The Truth Behind the Drug Companies*. New York: Random House.

Birch, D. L. and J. Medoff. 1994. 'Gazelles', In L. C. Solmon and A. R. Levenson (eds), *Labor Markets, Employment Policy and Job Creation*, 159–67. Boulder, CO: Westview Press.

Bloom, N. and J. Van Reenen. 2007. 'Measuring and Explaining Management Practices across Firms and Countries', *The Quarterly Journal of Economics* 122: 1351–408.

BNDES. 2012. *Apoio à inovação*. Rio de Janeiro: BNDES.

Branco, C. E. C. 1994. 'Apoio às pequenas e médias empresas de base tecnológica: A experiência do contec', *Revista do BNDES* 1: 129–42.

Burlamaqui, L. 2012. 'Knowledge Governance: An Analytical Approach and its Policy Implications', in L. Burlamaqui, A. C. Castro, and R. Kattel (eds), *Knowledge Governance: Reasserting the Public Interest*, 3–26. London: Anthem Press.

Castles, F. G. and S. Leibfried. 2010. *The Oxford Handbook of the Welfare State*. Oxford: Oxford University Press.

Chang, H. J. 2002. *Kicking Away the Ladder: Development Strategy in Historical Perspective*. London: Anthem Press.

Dore, R. 2008. 'Financialization of the Global Economy', *Industrial and Corporate Change* 17: 1097–112.

Drechsler, W. 2009. 'Towards a Neo-Weberian European Union? Lisbon Agenda and Public Administration', *Administrative Culture* 10: 6–21.

Duve, T. 2007. *Financing Environmental Protection and Energy Efficiency*. KfW Institutional Presentation.

EC (European Commission). 2011. *Horizon 2020: The Framework Programme for Research and Innovation (2014–2020)*. Brussels: European Commission.

Edquist, C. and J. M. Zabala-Iturriagagoitia. 2012. 'Public Procurement for Innovation as Mission-Oriented Innovation Policy', *Research Policy* 41: 1757–69.

Ergas, H. 1987. 'Does Technology Policy Matter?', in B. R. Guile and H. Brooks (eds), *Technology and Global Industry: Companies and Nations in the World Economy*, 191–245. Washington, DC: National Academies Press.

Etzkowitz, H. and M. Ranga. 2009. 'A Trans-Keynesian Vision of Innovation for the Contemporary Economic Crisis: "Picking Winners" Revisited', *Science and Public Policy* 36: 799–808.

Evans, P. B. 1995. *Embedded Autonomy: States and Industrial Transformation*. Princeton, NJ: Princeton University Press.

Foray, D., D. Mowery, and R. R. Nelson. 2012. 'Public R&D and Social Challenges: What Lessons from Mission R&D Programs?', *Research Policy* 41: 1697–902.

Freeman, C. 1996. 'The Greening of Technology and Models of Innovation', *Technological Forecasting & Social Change* 53: 27–39.

Freeman, C. and F. Louçã. 2001. *As Time Goes By: From the Industrial Revolutions to the Information Revolution*. New York: Oxford University Press.

Fried, L., S. Shukla,and S. Sawyer (eds). 2012. *Global Wind Report: Annual Market Update 2011*. Global Wind Energy Council.

Friedman, M. 1962. *Capitalism and Freedom*. Chicago: University of Chicago Press.

FS-UNEP/BNEF. 2016. *Global Trends in Renewable Energy Investment 2016*. Frankfurt: FS-UNEP/BNEF.

Gerschenkron, A. 1962. *Economic Backwardness in Historical Perspective: A Book of Essays*. Cambridge, MA: Belknap Press of Harvard University Press.

Granovetter, M. 1985. 'Economic Action and Social Structure: The Problem of Embeddedness', *Readings in Economic Sociology* 91(3): 481–510.

Griffith-Jones, S. and J. Tyson. 2012. 'The European Investment Bank and its Role in Regional Development and Integration', in Marcos Antonio Macedo Cintra and Keiti da Rocha Gomes (eds), *The Transformations of the International Financial System*, 411–40. Brasília: IPEA.

Gutierrez, E., H. P. Rudolph, T. Homa, and E. Blanco Beneit. 2011. *Development Banks: Role and Mechanisms to Increase their Efficiency*. Policy Research Working Paper No. WPS 5729. Washington, DC: World Bank.

Haltiwanger, J., R. S. Jarmin, and J. Miranda. 2013. 'Who Creates Jobs? Small Versus Large Versus Young', *Review of Economics and Statistics* 95: 347–61.

Hemming, R., M. Kell, and S. Mahfouz. 2002. 'The Effectiveness of Fiscal Policy in Stimulating Economic Activity: A Review of the Literature'. *IMF Working Paper Series* WP/02/208. Washington, DC: IMF.

Hicks, J. R. 1937. 'Mr. Keynes and the "Classics": A Suggested Interpretation', *Econometrica: Journal of the Econometric Society* 5(2): 147–59.

Hirschman, A. O. 1958. *The Strategy of Economic Development*. New Haven: Yale University Press.

Hur, S.-K., S. Mallick, and D. Park. 2010. 'Fiscal Policy and Crowding Out in Developing Asia'. ADB Economics Working Paper Series, No. 222.

Kay, J. 2012. 'The Kay Review of UK Equity Markets and Long-Term Decision Making'. *Final Report (July)*. Available at <http://www.ecgi.org/conferences/eu_actionplan2013/documents/kay_review_final_report.pdf>, accessed 22 April 2018.

Keynes, J. M. 1926. *The End of Laissez-Faire*. London: Prometheus Books.

Keynes, J. M. 1980. 'Activities 1940–46. Shaping the Post-War World: Employment and Commodities', in D. Moggridge (ed.), *Collected Works*, vol. 27. London: Macmillan.

Keynes, J. M. 2006 [1936]. *General Theory of Employment, Interest and Money*. New Delhi: Atlantic Publishers.

KfW. 2009. *KfW Annual Report 2008*. Frankfurt am Main: KfW Group.

KfW. 2013. *KfW Annual Report 2012*. Frankfurt am Main: KfW Group.

Krippner, G. R. 2005. 'The Financialization of the American Economy', *Socio-Economic Review* 3: 173–208.

Lazonick, W. 2013. 'The Financialization of the U.S. Corporation: What Has Been Lost, and How It Can Be Regained', *Seattle University Law Review* 36: 857–909.

Lazonick, W. and M. Hopkins. 2011. 'There Went the Sun: Renewable Energy Needs Patient Capital'. *Huffington Post*, 23 November. Available at <www.huffingtonpost.com/william-lazonick/there-went-the-sun-renewa_b_978572.html>, accessed 1 October 2013.

Lazonick, W. and M. Mazzucato. 2013. 'Risks and Rewards in the Innovation-Inequality Relationship', *Industrial and Corporate Change* 22: 1093–128.

Ledyard, J. O. 2008. 'Market Failure', in S. N. Durlauf and L. E. Blume (eds), *The New Palgrave Dictionary of Economics*, 300–3. Basingstoke: Palgrave Macmillan.

Levy-Yeyati, E., A. Micco, and U. Panizza. 2004. *Should the Government Be in the Banking Business? The Role of State-Owned and Development Banks*. IDB Working Paper No. 428.

Louw, A. 2014. 'Development Banks: Less for Green in 2013?'. *BNEF Renewables—Research Note*.

Lucas Jr, R. E. 1988. 'On the Mechanics of Economic Development', *Journal of Monetary Economics* 22: 3–42.

Luna-Martinez, J. de and C. L. Vicente. 2012. *Global Survey of Development Banks*. World Bank Policy Research Working Paper No. WPS 5969. Washington, DC: World Bank.

Macfarlane, L. and Mazzucato, M. 2018. 'State Investment Banks and Patient Finance: An International Comparison'. *IIPP WP 2018-01*. UCL Institute for Innovation and Public Purpose.

Mathews, J. A. 2006. 'Catch-up Strategies and the Latecomer Effect in Industrial Development', *New Political Economy* 11: 313–35.

Mazzucato, M. 2013a. *The Entrepreneurial State: Debunking the Public vs. Private Myth in Risk and Innovation*. London: Anthem Press.

Mazzucato, M. 2013b. 'Financing Innovation: Creative Destruction vs. Destructive Creation', *Industrial and Corporate Change* 22: 851–67.

Mazzucato, M. 2016. 'From Market Fixing to Market-Creating: A New Framework for Innovation Policy', Special Issue of *Industry and Innovation: 'Innovation Policy—Can It Make a Difference?'* 23(2).

Mazzucato, M. and L. Macfarlane. 2017. 'Patient Strategic Finance: Opportunities for State Investment Banks in the UK'. *IIPP WP 2017-05*. UCL Institute for Innovation and Public Purpose.

Mazzucato, M. and C. Penna. 2016. 'Beyond Market Failures: The Market Creating and Shaping Roles of State Investment Banks', *Journal of Economic Policy Reform* 19(4): 305–26.

Mazzucato, M. and G. Semieniuk. 2017. 'Public Financing of Innovation: New Questions', *Oxford Review of Economic Policy* 33(1): 24–48.

McKinnon, R. 1973. *Money and Capital in Economic Development*. Washington, DC: Brookings Institution.

Minsky, H. P. 1992. *The Capital Development of the Economy and the Structure of Financial Institutions*. Levy Institute Working Paper Series, 72.

Minsky, H. P. 1993. *Community Service and Development Banks: A Concept Paper*. Hyman P. Minsky Archive, Paper 279.

Minsky, H. P. 1996. *Uncertainty and the Institutional Structure of Capitalist Economies*. Levy Institute Working Paper Series, 155.

Minsky, H. P., D. B. Papadimitriou, R. J. Phillips, and L. R. Wray. 1993. *Community Development Banking: A Proposal to Establish a Nationwide System of Community Development Banks*. Levy Institute Public Policy Brief, 3/1993.

Minsky, H. P. and C. Whalen. 1996. *Economic Insecurity and the Institutional Prerequisites for Successful Capitalism*. Levy Institute Working Paper Series, 165.

Mirowski, P. 2011. *Science-Mart: Privatizing American Science*. Cambridge, MA: Harvard University Press.

Mowery, D. C. 2010. 'Military R&D and Innovation', *Handbook of the Economics of Innovation* 2: 1219–56.

Nightingale, P. and A. Coad. 2014. 'Muppets and Gazelles: Political and Methodological Biases in Entrepreneurship Research', *Industrial and Corporate Change* 23: 113–43.

Nurkse, R. 1966. *Problems of Capital Formation in Underdeveloped Countries*. New York: Oxford University Press.

O'Sullivan, M. 2004. 'Finance and Innovation', in J. Fagerberg, D. C. Mowery, and R. R. Nelson (eds), *The Oxford Handbook of Innovation*, 240–65. New York: Oxford University Press.

Palmeira Filho, P. L., J. P. Pieroni, A. Antunes, and J. V. Bomtempo. 2012. 'O desafio do financiamento à inovação farmacêutica no Brasil: A experiência do BNDES Profarma', *Revista do BNDES* 37: 67–90.

Papadimitriou, D. B. and L. R. Wray. 1998. 'The Economic Contributions of Hyman Minsky: Varieties of Capitalism and Institutional Reform', *Review of Political Economy* 10: 199–225.

Parsons, W. 2004. 'Not Just Steering but Weaving: Relevant Knowledge and the Craft of Building Policy Capacity and Coherence', *Australian Journal of Public Administration* 63: 43–57.

Perez, C. 2002. *Technological Revolutions and Financial Capital: The Dynamics of Bubbles and Golden Ages*. Cheltenham, UK and Northampton, MA: Edward Elgar Publishing.

Pisano, G. P. 2006. 'Can Science Be a Business? Lessons from Biotech'. *Harvard Business Review*, October: 114–25.

Polanyi, K. 2001 [1944]. *The Great Transformation: The Political and Economic Origins of Our Time*. Boston, MA: Beacon Press.

Prebisch, R. 1950. 'The Economic Development of Latin America and its Principal Problems', *Economic Bulletin for Latin America* 7: 1–12.

Ramundo, J. 2013. *Challenges of Financing Innovation*. Presentation for the Minds' Conference on Financial Institutions for Innovation and Development, 28 June.

Reinert, E. S. 1999. 'The Role of the State in Economic Growth', *Journal of Economic Studies* 26: 268–326.

Reinert, E. S. 2007. *How Rich Countries Got Rich and Why Poor Countries Stay Poor*. London: Constable.

Samuelson, P. A., and W. D. Nordhaus. 2009 [1948]. *Economics*. New York: McGraw-Hill.

Sanderson, H. and M. Forsythe. 2013. *China's Superbank: Debt, Oil and Influence—How China Development Bank Is Rewriting the Rules of Finance*. Singapore: John Wiley & Sons.

Schäfer, D., A. Werwatz, and V. Zimmermann. 2004. 'The Determinants of Debt and (Private) Equity Financing: The Case of Young, Innovative SMEs from Germany', *Industry and Innovation* 11: 225–48.

Schapiro, M. G. 2012. *Rediscovering the Developmental Path? Development Bank, Law, and Innovation Financing in the Brazilian Economy*. SSRN Working Paper.

Schröder, M., P. Ekins, A. Power, M. Zulauf, and R. Lowe. 2011. *The KfW Experience in the Reduction of Energy Use in and CO2 Emissions from Buildings: Operation, Impacts and Lessons for the UK*. London: UCL Energy Institute, University College London and LSE Housing and Communities, London School of Economics.

Schumpeter, J. A. 1934 [1912]. *The Theory of Economic Development: An Inquiry into Profits, Capital, Credit, Interest, and the Business Cycle*. Cambridge, MA: Harvard University Press.

Schumpeter, J. A. 1939. *Business Cycles; a Theoretical, Historical, and Statistical Analysis of the Capitalist Process*. New York and London: McGraw-Hill Book Company.

Skidelsky, R. 2011. 'The Relevance of Keynes', *Cambridge Journal of Economics* 35: 1–13.

Skocpol, T. and K. Finegold. 1982. 'State Capacity and Economic Intervention in the Early New Deal', *Political Science Quarterly* 97(2): 255–78.

Singer, H. W. 1950. 'Comments to the Terms of Trade and Economic Development', *Review of Economics and Statistics* 40: 84–9.

Sousa, F. L. D. (ed.). 2012. *BNDES 60 anos: Perspectivas setoriais*. Rio de Janeiro: BNDES.

Stiglitz, J. E. 1989. 'Markets, Market Failures, and Development', *The American Economic Review* 79: 197–203.

Stiglitz, J. E. and A. Weiss. 1981. 'Credit Rationing in Markets with Imperfect Information', *American Economic Review* 3: 393–410.

Tassey, Gregory. 2013. 'Beyond the Business Cycle: The Need for a Technology-Based Growth Strategy', *Science and Public Policy* 40: 293–315.

Tcherneva, P. R. 2008. *Keynes's Approach to Full Employment: Aggregate or Targeted Demand?* The Levy Economics Institute Working Paper Collection, 542.

Tchouvakhina, M. 2013. *Promotion of Innovations: No Money, No Ideas?* UNECE International Conference 'Entrepreneurship and Innovation', Dubrovnik, Croatia.

Torres Filho, E. T. and F. N. D. Costa. 2012. 'BNDES e o financiamento do desenvolvimento', *Economia e Sociedade* 21: 975–1009.

Wade, R. 1990. *Governing the Market: Economic Theory and the Role of Government in East Asian Industrialization*. Princeton, NJ: Princeton University Press.

World Bank. 2013. *History*. Available at <go.worldbank.org/65Y36GNQB0>, 2 February 2013.

Wray, L. R. 2012. 'The Great Crash of 2007 Viewed through the Perspective of Veblen's Theory of the Business Enterprise, Keynes's Monetary Theory of Production and Minsky's Financial Instability Hypothesis', in E. S. Reinert, and F. L. Viano (eds), *Thorstein Veblen: Economics for an Age of Crises*, 303–16. London: Anthem Press.

11

The Countercyclical Behaviour of National Development Banks in Latin America and the Caribbean

Michael Brei and Alfredo Schclarek

11.1 Introduction

Since the onset of the global financial crisis, the subsequent credit crunch, and the failure to reignite sustained economic growth, the role of national development and public commercial banks has come to the forefront of the policy agenda. Their role in providing credit countercyclically has attracted especial attention given that such lending can mitigate amplifications in business cycles and prevent a crisis from deepening (UN-DESA 2005; Griffith-Jones and Ocampo 2008; Gutierrez et al. 2011; de Olloqui 2013; Rudolph 2010; Griffith-Jones and Gottschalk 2012; World Bank 2012).

On top of this policy focus, there is also a growing body of detailed empirical evidence that state-owned development and retail-oriented banks have played an active role during crisis resolutions in both advanced and emerging market economies (Brei and Schclarek 2013, 2015; Bertay et al. 2015). As will be discussed in this chapter, a number of governments have actively counteracted the crisis-related economic slowdown with increased lending intermediated through national public banks. The government responses have been focused particularly on the provision of working capital for productive purposes and long-term loans for investment in the corporate sector and other key areas such as infrastructure. Privately owned banks, on the other hand, tended to lend procyclically, fuelling booms and exacerbating busts.

Evidently, a certain degree of government involvement in the banking sector appears to be important, particularly in volatile environments where countercyclical policies can help smooth the business cycle. In this context, however, it has to be noted that government interventions in the banking sector are most efficient in countries with sound governance structures and institutional quality (Andrianova et al. 2009; de Olloqui 2013). In countries where institutional quality is low, distortions in governments' allocation of resources are likely to be prevalent, as banks might be used to favour companies with political connections, soften the public sector budget constraint, or to finance electoral campaigns (Krueger 1974; Shleifer and Vishny 1994; Khwaja and Mian 2005; Carvalho 2014). Clearly, in such environments it is unlikely that national development banks would be able to act countercyclically when facing a crisis episode, as they are plagued with non-performing loans due to distorted risk assessments or politically connected lending. Thus, countries have to foster the development of sound institutions that build the ground for well-managed development banks, which can step in and expand lending when the economy is slowing down.

Against this backdrop, the present chapter investigates the lending behaviour of different types of banks, including national development, public, domestic, and foreign banks from thirty-one Latin American and Caribbean countries over the period of 1995–2014.[1] A special focus is hereby set on their lending responses to systemic financial crises. To shed light on this issue, we use the annual financial statements of 336 major banking institutions, of which fourteen are national development banks, thirty-one public banks, and 291 private banks (134 foreign and 157 domestic). Together these banks account for 3.9 trillion USD of assets at end-2014, corresponding to 95 per cent of the assets reported in the Top 200 Latin American Banks Ranking. National development banks accounted for 0.4 trillion USD of assets at end-2014 (or 11 per cent of the sample's assets).

Using dynamic panel regressions that allow for parameter shifts across banks of different ownership during normal times and crises in the bank lending equation, we find robust evidence that national development and public banks have played a countercyclical role in their banking systems. While private banks behaved procyclically, i.e. lending more during booms and less during busts, we observe the opposite for national development and public banks. The different crisis responses are not only statistically but also economically significant. Most responsive to the crises has been the lending activity of national development banks. Their real growth rate of lending increased on average by more than six percentage points relative to normal times, whereas private foreign and domestic banks reduced their lending

[1] In the following, the term 'public banks' refers to commercial, corporate, or savings banks that are owned by a local government; 'domestic (foreign) banks' refers to commercial, corporate, or savings banks that are owned by local (foreign) institutions from the private sector; and 'national development banks' refers to non-deposit-taking development banks that are owned by a local government.

activity by more than three percentage points. Moreover, the econometric evidence suggests that the increase in public bank lending during times of crisis came in the form of commercial and corporate credits. Thus, according to our results, state-owned banks have counteracted the potential adverse economic effects of the slowdown in lending by private banks during crises. To our knowledge, this is the first econometric study that compares the countercyclical behaviour of national development banks and other types of banks during crisis periods.

The remainder of the chapter is organized as follows. A literature overview is presented in section 11.2. In section 11.3, we present the data and descriptive statistics. The econometric methodology is discussed in section 11.4, while the empirical results are discussed in sections 11.5 and 11.6. The final section offers a number of policy conclusions.

11.2 Literature Overview

There is a growing consensus that national development banks should provide countercyclical financing to mitigate amplifications in the business cycle and prevent a crisis from deepening (UN-DESA 2005; Griffith-Jones and Ocampo 2008; Gutierrez et al. 2011; Rudolph 2010; Griffith-Jones and Gottschalk 2012; World Bank 2012; de Olloqui 2013). The empirical evidence based on a number of surveys and case studies seems to be in line with this view. For example, based on a survey of ninety national development banks from sixty-one countries, Luna-Martinez and Vicente (2012) find that their lending volume increased from 1.16 to 1.58 trillion US dollars during 2007–9. This increase of 36 per cent in lending was much higher compared to the 10 per cent increase in private bank credit in these countries. The authors also find that development banks have extended both short- and long-term credits to existing and new customers who were facing difficulties in debt refinancing and in receiving new lines of credit.

An important Latin American national development bank that operated countercyclically in response to the global financial crisis is Banco Nacional do Desenvolvimento Economico e Social (BNDES) from Brazil. For example, BNDES implemented the PSI investment programme (Programa de Sustentação do Investimento) in July 2009 to complement the existing FINAME programme (Financiamento de Máquinas e Equipamentos) for financing the acquisition of machinery and equipment produced in Brazil. The PSI programme involved, on top of a recapitalization of BNDES, a reduction of interest rates charged on these loans, justified by the positive externalities of the programme. Between 2009 and 2010, the disbursements of the FINAME programme increased from 20.7 to 46.8 billion Real, an increase of more than 100 per cent (Machado and Roitman 2015; Ferraz et al. 2012).

Focusing on the European experience, Griffith-Jones et al. (2011) provide evidence that the multilateral European Investment Bank (EIB) increased the signatures for lending to small and medium-sized enterprises (SMEs) by 128 per cent during 2007–9, with a growth in loan disbursements of 57 per cent over the same period. In addition, the number of EU countries with private banks that intermediated EIB lending to SMEs increased from 16 to 24 per cent over the considered period. Such intermediated lending through private banks could avoid the duplication of screening efforts and reduce the costs of acquiring information on individual borrowers (Hainz and Hakenes 2012). As Griffith-Jones et al. (2011) suggest, the increase in lending to SMEs was feasible, because EIB's capitalization had increased significantly in the years prior to the crisis, which implied that the bank had sufficient internal resources and no capital constraints to increase lending once the crisis struck.

In parallel to the recent literature on the lending behaviour of national and multilateral development banks, there exists econometric evidence on the countercyclical behaviour of bank lending when broadening the scope to state-owned commercial and savings banks. The literature finds robust evidence that these banks have played an important countercyclical role in their banking systems, helping economies to recover from the financial turmoil (see, amongst others, Allen et al. 2013; Brei and Schclarek 2013; Cull and Martínez Pería 2013; Bertay et al. 2015; Behr et al. 2017).

The theoretical literature that compares the crisis responses of private and state-owned banks suggests a number of explanations for the distinctive lending behaviour of these two types of banks. As Brei and Schclarek (2015) argue, the objective of state-owned banks is not only to maximize profits given risks, but also to stabilize and promote the recovery of the economy. Thus, given that their objective functions differ, public banks are more willing to take on more risks and expand lending during a crisis period than private banks. A similar argument has been made by Rudolph (2010), who argues that state-owned financial institutions have less volatile risk aversion and therefore provide a more stable source of funding. It is also similar to the argument of Eslava and Freixas (2016), who suggest that a private bank's choice takes into account only the loan repayment, while the other benefits and externalities an investment project may have are not internalized.

Another argument, also put in place by Brei and Schclarek (2015), is that public banks are more likely to be capitalized than their private counterparts during a crisis. Thus, public banks will be in a better position to increase lending during the crisis. The reason for the higher chances of being recapitalized is that the government, which is the owner of the public bank, due to its higher credibility and financial strength during a crisis, is better able to get fresh funds than the private banker. In addition, Brei and Schclarek (2015) also argue that the higher credibility and financial strength of the government, in contrast to that of private bankers, help public banks suffer fewer deposit withdrawals and/or fewer problems in rolling over short-term debt. Having fewer liquidity problems during a crisis allows public banks to lend more than private banks. Note that the increased credibility may be due to an actual recapitalization but could also be due to a credible promise or higher expectation of a future recapitalization.

In line with this literature, Mazzucato and Penna (2016) argue that the procyclical behaviour of private banks is explained by realizing that private banks have become increasingly speculative over the past decades, targeting short-term gains through securities trading and brokerage rather than providing loans to long-term productive and innovative projects. Finally, focusing on public development banks, Eslava and Freixas (2016) study the mechanisms that should be implemented in order to efficiently support the targeted firms. They argue that when national development banks lend indirectly through commercial banks, national development banks should provide funds to commercial banks in the form of lending when commercial banks face a liquidity shortage and in the form of credit guarantees when commercial banks are undercapitalized.

11.3 Data Description

The bank-level data on the annual financial statements are taken from the BankScope database complied by Fitch and Bureau van Dijk. Our data covers banks from thirty-one countries in Latin America and the Caribbean from 1995 to 2014, spanning periods of economic boom and downturns. Where possible, we gather consolidated financial statements of banks, making the assumption that banks manage their entire set of banking activities on a consolidated basis. If no consolidated statement exists, we use the unconsolidated financial statement reported for the bank instead. To avoid double counting, we exclude subsidiaries that have been majority-owned by other banks in our sample.

Our study focuses on the lending activity of national development banks and other deposit-taking institutions. National development banks are hereby identified as development banks that are state-owned, non-deposit-taking, and not foreign- or multilaterally owned. Public, foreign, and domestic banks are deposit-taking banks that are majority-owned by a local government, a foreign, or domestic holding company, respectively. We use BankScope information on the global ultimate owner as the principle source, but we complement the information with Claessens and Van Horen (2015) and publicly available information from the web pages of each of these banks.

Non-bank entities are excluded from the sample.[2] When a bank switched accounting standards, we reconstructed historically the International Financial Reporting Standards (IFRS) statements using the previously reported local Generally Accepted Accounting Principles (GAAP) statements.[3] Finally, whether or not a bank is included in the regressions depends as well on the availability of the information on the control variables (macroeconomic and bank-level information). After applying our filters, our initial sample of 618 financial institutions reduces to our final sample of 336 banks, of which there are fourteen national development banks, thirty-one public banks, and 291 private banks.[4] Out of the 291 private banks, 157 are domestically owned and 134 are subsidiaries of foreign banks. In total, we have 2835 bank-year observations for our regressions.[5]

As can be seen in Table 11.1, the sample of banks is representative of the region, given that the present banks account for 3.9 trillion USD of assets at end-2014, corresponding to 95 per cent of the assets reported in the Top 200 Latin American Banks Ranking of *The Banker* magazine. Most of these assets (83 per cent) are controlled by 172 South American banks that operated in nine countries, followed by ninety-nine banks (with 626 billon USD of assets) from four Central American countries and Mexico, and sixty-six banks from seventeen Caribbean countries with a total of 27 billion USD of assets. In terms of different bank types, national development banks accounted for 0.4 trillion USD of assets at end-2014, corresponding to 11 per cent of the total of the sample's assets, while public banks accounted for 1.0, domestic banks for 1.4, and foreign banks for 1.1 trillion USD of assets; see Table 11.2.

[2] We cross-reference the list of financial institutions obtained from BankScope with the registry of licensed banking entities reported on the websites of the various central banks in the region in order to distinguish deposit-taking entities from other types of financial firms. The manual selection of banks is important as BankScope classifies many non-bank financial entities as commercial banks.

[3] In certain cases, the difference between IFRS and local GAAP can be large, especially for banks with a large trading book. The main reason for this is the different treatment of the derivatives netting on the asset and liability side. However, this mainly affects the value of total assets, whereas loan values (the focus of our study) are much less affected. We have tested whether our results are affected when including an IFRS dummy variable and found that our results are unaffected. Because the IFRS dummy was insignificant, we do not include it in our estimations.

[4] The national development banks included are: Banco Nacional de Fomento de la Vivienda y la Produccion—BNV (Dominican Republic); Banco de Desenvolvimento do Espirito Santo SA—BANDES (Brazil); Financiera de Desarrollo Territorial S.A. Findeter (Colombia); Banco Nacional de Comercio Exterior SNC—BANCOMEXT (Mexico); Nacional Financiera S.N.C. (Mexico); National Export-Import Bank of Jamaica Ltd—EXIM Bank (Jamaica); Banco de Comercio Exterior de Colombia SA—BANCOLDEX (Colombia); Banco Nacional de Desenvolvimento Economico e Social—BNDES (Brazil); Banco de Inversion Y Comercio Exterior SA—BICE (Argentina); Banco Nacional de Obras y Servicios Publicos, SNC—BANOBRAS (Mexico); Corporacion Financiera de Desarrollo S.A.—COFIDE (Peru); Financiera Energetica Nacional (Colombia); Development Finance Limited (Trinidad and Tobago); and Banco de Fomento Agropecuario (El Salvador).

[5] It should be noted that this sample of banks differs from the sample used for the calculation of the summary statistics in the first chapter of this book. The reason for this is that not all banks report the required information on the control variables, which implies that those banks had to be dropped in the regressions.

Table 11.1. Composition and characteristics of the database, by region

Region	No. of banks	No. of dev. banks	No. of foreign banks	No. of public banks	Total assets, 2014 (bn USD)	Growth of lending (%)[1]	Real GDP growth (%)	Real interest rate (%)[2]	CPI inflation (%)	Ex. rate growth, per USD (%)[3]	Return on equity (%)	Capital ratio (%)[4]	NPL ratio (%)[5]	Liquidity ratio (%)[6]
Caribbean	65	4	27	4	26.9	8.0	2.5	3.4	6.0	2.4	13.5	13.4	6.6	19.8
Central America	99	3	51	4	626.5	11.4	4.2	4.7	5.7	1.9	12.2	11.7	3.5	15.7
South America	172	7	56	23	3270.5	12.9	4.3	1.4	9.2	5.3	14.4	11.4	5.8	17.4
Average/sum*	336*	14*	134*	31*	3923.9*	10.8	3.7	3.2	7.0	3.2	13.4	12.1	5.3	17.6

Note: The sample per region is over the period 1995–2014. The Caribbean includes AG, AI, AW, BB, BS, BZ, DO, GD, GY, HT, JM, KN, LC, SR, SV, TT, and VC; South America includes AR, BO, BR, CL, CO, EC, PE, UY, and VE; and Central America is CR, GT, HN, PA, and MX. Average/sum indicates unweighted averages or sums over countries. [1] In national currency and deflated by the consumer price index (CPI). [2] Money market interest rate minus CPI inflation (if not available lending rate minus CPI inflation). [3] National currency per USD. [4] Equity and reserves divided by total assets. [5] NPL ratio denotes non-performing loans divided by total loans. [6] Cash and due from banks plus loans and advances to banks divided by total assets.

Sources: BankScope, IMF-IFS, World Bank WDI, Claessens and Van Horen (2015), authors' calculations

Table 11.2. Bank-specific characteristics across bank types

Bank type	National development banks	Foreign banks	Domestic private banks	Local public banks	All banks
Number of banks	14	134	157	31	336
Total assets (USD bn), 2014	424	994	1448	1058	3924
Interest income on loans/loans	11.34	20.56	15.95	15.41	17.55
Non-interest income/income	13.04	20.31	21.42	29.45	21.60
Return on equity	5.21	12.59	14.28	16.13	13.49
Liquidity ratio	8.17	18.76	16.18	18.02	17.16
Government securities/assets	16.56	12.30	13.47	22.14	14.22
Lending growth, normal times	3.42	11.72	14.42	6.06	11.93
Lending growth, crisis	10.33	9.42	12.31	15.36	11.46
Loans/assets	58.76	55.37	53.85	43.51	53.44
Mortgages/loans	8.58	11.98	14.69	17.10	13.82
Commercial loans/loans	60.49	51.93	53.21	45.64	51.90
Other consumer loans/loans	8.10	25.96	26.57	29.08	25.98
Non-performing loans/loans	3.99	4.56	4.88	8.03	5.08
Deposits/assets	30.03	66.82	62.05	56.45	62.21
Long-term funding/assets	26.78	6.81	7.10	5.48	7.75
Capital ratio	15.28	11.72	11.98	10.22	11.79

Note: In percentages. The sample includes annual data of 336 banks operating in 31 countries from Latin America and the Caribbean over the period 1995–2014. The crisis dummy takes a value of 1 if there was either a banking crisis, currency crisis, or during 2008–12, and zero otherwise. Development banks are state-owned and neither multilaterally owned, nor foreign-owned, nor retail deposit-taking banks. Foreign and public banks are banks that are majority-owned by a foreign holding company or by a local government, respectively.

Sources: BankScope, IMF-IFS, World Bank WDI, Claessens and Van Horen (2015), Laeven and Valencia (2013), authors' calculations

The crisis periods are identified with the banking and currency crisis indicators of Laeven and Valencia (2013).[6] Further, we assigned a crisis period to all countries during the period 2008–12. The reason is that we would like to capture national development banks' lending in response to the recent global financial crisis as well, even though it did not materialize in every country in the form of a financial crisis. In total, our sample covers fourteen banking crises and thirteen currency crises that occurred in the thirty-one countries over the period of 1995–2014.

Our dependent variable, the real growth rate of bank lending, which comprises retail lending (residential mortgages and other consumer loans), corporate loans, and commercial loans, is measured by the BankScope item net loans. To avoid exchange rate valuation effects, we convert loans measured in US dollars into local currency units using the end-of-period exchange rate. Moreover, to avoid inflation effects, we deflate loans in local currency by the consumer price index or the gross domestic product (GDP) deflator, if the former is not available. We exclude observations with extremely low and high growth rates (below the 1st and above the 99th percentile) to avoid the impact of mergers and acquisitions on the growth rate of lending and other noise in the data.

From Table 11.2, which provides summary statistics for our sample of 336 banks across different types, it appears that national development banks recorded on average an annual real growth rate of lending of 3.42 per cent in normal times, while during crisis periods they expanded lending at an average growth rate of 10.33 per cent. The results for public banks indicate a similar countercyclical pattern with a real growth rate of lending of 6.06 per cent in normal times and 15.36 per cent during crises. Domestic and foreign banks, on the other hand, appear to lend procyclically, recording higher growth rates in normal times than in times of crisis. To be more precise, domestic and foreign banks recorded an average annual real growth rate of lending of 14.42 and 11.72 per cent in normal times, whereas during crises they were lending at a growth rate of 12.31 and 9.42 per cent, respectively. Clearly, from these summary statistics, national development banks and public banks showed a countercyclical behaviour, while private banks tended to lend procyclically. While national development banks showed the highest degree of countercyclical behaviour, foreign banks showed the highest degree of procyclical behaviour. These results, however, do not allow

[6] Under their definition, a systemic banking crisis occurs when a country's corporate and financial sectors experience a large number of defaults, and financial institutions and corporations face difficulties in repaying debt on time. The authors combine quantitative data with some subjective assessments by country experts. A currency crisis is defined as an episode during which there was a nominal depreciation of the currency vis-à-vis the US dollar of at least 30 per cent that is also at least ten percentage points higher than the rate of depreciation in the year before.

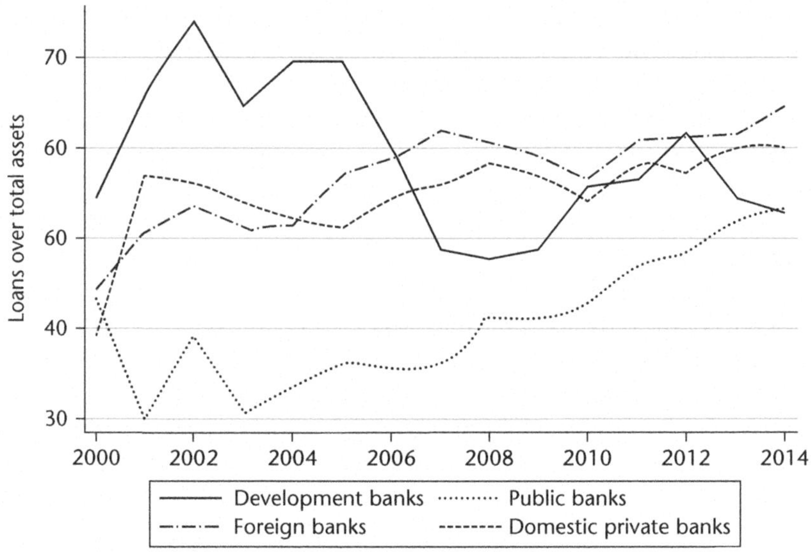

Figure 11.1 Lending activity across bank types

Note: Unweighted averages across banks and years. The sample includes annual data of 336 banks operating in 31 countries from Latin America and the Caribbean over the period 2000–14. There are 157 domestic, 134 foreign, 31 public, and 14 development banks.

us to infer causal relationships and to control for loan demand and other factors. In section 11.4, we will therefore investigate whether these first, tentative results still hold in our regressions on the bank-lending channel.

Table 11.2 also shows that there is some homogeneity in the average loan-to-asset ratio, with national development banks having the highest ratio of 58.76 per cent. Note, however, that public banks are an exception to this homogeneity, having a clearly lower ratio of 43.51 per cent. When considering the evolution of this ratio through time in Figure 11.1, we see more heterogeneity. While private banks were increasing their lending ratio between 2005 and 2007 prior to the financial crisis, national development banks reduced their lending ratio. This is presumably a sign that national development banks were acting countercyclically in the boom period. Then in 2009, national development banks started to increase lending, counteracting the fall in the lending activity of private banks that occurred during 2007–9. Again, this finding suggests that national development banks acted countercyclically in the crisis period.[7]

[7] The use of the loan-to-asset ratio as an indicator of loan availability should be taken with caution. For example, the increase in the ratio for private banks post-2009 may not reflect an increase in lending but a reduction of total assets (the denominator) due to a desire to reduce leverage. Moreover, private banks' lending might have increased because they were intermediating funds from development banks or benefitting from other positive externalities.

Another interesting difference among these types of banks is the heterogeneity in the types of loans they grant. From Table 11.2, it is clear that national development banks have been focused on corporate and commercial lending, with a corporate and commercial loans-to-total-loans ratio of 60.49 per cent, and have concentrated much less on mortgage and consumer loans, with ratios of 8.58 and 8.1 per cent, respectively. The other three types of banks, however, concentrated less on corporate and commercial loans, with ratios of 51.93, 53.21, and 45.64 per cent for foreign, domestic, and public banks, respectively, and much more on consumer loans, with ratios of 25.96, 26.57, and 29.08 per cent, respectively. With respect to mortgages, there is more heterogeneity, with public commercial banks having the highest ratio (17.1 per cent). In addition, we observe that national development banks and public banks have the highest ratios of government securities-to-total assets, ranging between 16.56 per cent and 22.14 per cent, respectively.

In terms of the funding structure, it becomes apparent that national development banks are less dependent on deposits, with a ratio of 30.03 per cent, and more dependent on long-term funding and capital, with ratios of 26.78 and 15.28 per cent, respectively. This more stable long-term funding structure is an important difference with respect to the other types of banks, which makes national development banks less dependent on short-term developments, such as sudden swings in the sentiments of depositors and short-term bond investors. The lower liquidity ratio of national development banks may also be a result of this longer-term funding structure if we consider that they do not need to have as many liquid assets in order to respond to sudden freezes in money markets. Certainly, the more stable long-term funding structure of national development banks has positive consequences for their long-term lending possibilities, as well as the countercyclical properties of their lending, as will be discussed further in section 11.5.

Finally, interest earnings are lower for national development banks, with a ratio over total loans of 11.34 per cent. This lower ratio is probably an indication that they charge lower interest on their loans. As mentioned in section 11.2, this is not a surprise given that development banks do not only take into account the loan repayment, but also the potential externalities and socio-economic impact of the projects. Further, their non-interest income is also lower, with a ratio over total income of 13.04 per cent, which might be an indication that they charge lower service fees, being more dependent on their interest income activities. These lower interest and non-interest incomes show up in their lower return on equity ratio, which is equal to 5.21 per cent. Partly, this lower return on equity can be attributed to their higher capital ratio. Interestingly, the lower return on equity ratio does not appear to be an indication of higher losses on bad loans, given that their non-performing loan ratio (3.99 per cent) is the lowest among the different types of banks.

11.4 Econometric Methodology

To take into account other bank-specific characteristics that determine individual bank lending and macroeconomic factors that affect loan demand, we utilize a specification that has been used before in the bank-lending channel literature (Ehrmann et al. 2003). Given that we are interested in the lending behaviour of the different types of banks during normal and crisis periods, we interact a crisis dummy with the bank-specific indicators on bank type. This allows us to account for potential parameter shifts in the estimated relation between lending and bank type, when the state of the economy moves from normal times to a crisis period. National development, public, foreign, and domestic banks are distinguished by three dummy variables, DB_{ijt}, PB_{ijt}, and FB_{ijt}, which are equal to one when bank *j* operating in country *i* in year *t* is a national development, public, or foreign bank, respectively, and zero otherwise. The dummy for domestic banks is not included due to collinearity, which means that the coefficients associated with the other bank types are interpreted in terms relative to domestic banks.

The approach can be summarized using the following regression model:

$$\Delta L_{ijt} = \alpha_1 \Delta L_{ijt-1} + \alpha + \alpha^* C_{jt} + (\alpha_{DB} + \alpha^*_{DB} C_{jt}) DB_{ijt} + (\alpha_{PB} + \alpha^*_{PB} C_{jt}) PB_{ijt}$$
$$+ (\alpha_{FB} + \alpha^*_{FB} C_{jt}) FB_{ijt} + \beta X_{ijt} + \gamma M_{jt} + u_i + \epsilon_{ijt}$$

where ΔL_{ijt} denotes bank *i*'s annual real growth rate of lending that operates in country *j* in year *t*. C_{jt} is the crisis dummy, X_{ijt} the vector of bank-specific characteristics, and M_{jt} is the vector of macroeconomic control variables specific to each country. One lag of the dependent variable is introduced to limit the omitted variable bias and to allow for persistence in bank lending. The error term includes bank-level fixed effects to control for unobserved time-invariant differences across banks and countries. Note that we estimate the model in growth rates, because lending in levels is non-stationary, as confirmed by the Im-Pesaran-Shin test.[8] The model is estimated using the system GMM estimator introduced by Arellano and Bond (1991), ensuring efficiency and consistency under the assumption that the residuals are not subject to serial correlation of order two and that the instruments used are valid (tested using the Hansen test). The system version of the estimator is employed, because it tends to outperform the difference GMM estimator by the use of both the difference and levels equation (Blundell and Bond 1998).

[8] In principle one could also work with the loan-to-asset ratio as a dependent variable. We prefer, however, working with the growth rate of lending and thus follow the literature on the bank-lending channel (Kashyap and Stein 1995; Kishan and Opiela 2000; Gambacorta and Marques-Ibanez 2011; Brei et al. 2013; Brei and Schclarek 2013).

The vector X_{ijt} includes a parsimonious set of bank-specific variables that have been highlighted in the empirical literature as important determinants of loan supply, notably *bank size, return on equity (ROE), capitalization, non-performing loans*, and *liquid assets*. We lag bank-specific characteristics by one year ($t-1$) in order to mitigate possible endogeneity problems among the bank-specific variables. Finally, we demean the bank-specific regressors for estimation purposes, which implies that the results can be interpreted in terms of the average bank (for which the bank-specific characteristics are equal to zero).

Bank size is measured by the logarithm of total assets, ROE by net income divided by total equity, capitalization by the total equity-to-asset ratio, non-performing loans by the ratio of non-performing loans over total loans, and liquid assets are measured by the share of liquid assets (cash and due from banks, available-for-sale securities, and trading securities) in total assets. The coefficient associated with bank size is ambiguous, given that larger banks might have more resources than smaller banks to expand lending and to absorb country-specific disturbances. It might however also be that smaller banks engage more in relationship lending to faster-growing SMEs (Ehrmann and Worms 2004; Gambacorta 2005; Brei et al. 2013). More profitable banks should be more likely to expand lending if profits are not distributed and retained. The bank-lending literature also tends to find that well-capitalized banks are more likely to expand lending compared to capital-constrained banks, which tend to restore capital ratios by investing in assets with lower risk-weights or by leveraging (Brei and Gambacorta 2016). Banks with a higher non-performing loan ratio are more likely to face asset write-downs and financial difficulties, and as such they are expected to lend at lower growth rates compared to banks with sounder loan books. Finally, the literature tends to find a positive relationship between liquidity holdings and lending, although high liquid asset holdings might also indicate higher involvement in trading and other investment banking activities (Kashyap and Stein 1995; Kishan and Opiela 2000; Brei et al. 2013).

In terms of the macroeconomic variables, we include the annual real GDP growth rate, the real interest rate (measured by the money market rate minus inflation), annual inflation, and the lagged exchange rate depreciation (measured by the annual growth rate of the exchange rate of the local currency vis-à-vis the US dollar). In Table 11.3, we present summary statistics for both the macroeconomic and the bank-specific variables.

Regarding our regression model, the key coefficients are $\alpha, \alpha^*, \alpha_{DB}, \alpha^*_{DB}, \alpha_{FB}, \alpha^*_{FB}, \alpha_{PB}$, and α^*_{PB}. The short-run coefficient α measures the lending growth rate of the average domestic bank in normal times (see Table 11.4). The coefficient α^*, which is associated with the crisis dummy, measures the change in the lending response of the average domestic bank

Table 11.3. Summary statistics of the regression variables

Variable	Description	Obs.	Mean	Std dev.	Min	Max
Lending growth	Annual, domestic currency, deflated	2733	11.7	24.5	−90.7	223.8
Real GDP growth	Annual, real GDP index	2733	4.0	3.3	−18.4	20.3
Interest rate	Annual, real (money market and lending rate minus CPI inflation)	2733	1.8	8.5	−38.9	50.4
Inflation	Annual CPI inflation	2733	7.5	6.7	−2.4	40.6
Depreciation	Annual growth, domestic currency per USD	2733	4.5	23.3	−25.5	232.2
Development banks, α_{DB}	Dummy=1, if development bank	2733	0.0	0.2	0	1
Foreign banks, α_{FB}	Dummy=1, if foreign-owned	2733	0.4	0.5	0	1
Public banks, α_{PB}	Dummy=1, if government-owned	2733	0.1	0.3	0	1
Crisis, α^*	Dummy=1, if banking, currency and financial crisis	2733	0.4	0.5	0	1
Development banks*crisis, α^*_{DB}	Crisis interaction	2733	0.0	0.1	0	1
Foreign banks*crisis, α^*_{FB}	Crisis interaction	2733	0.2	0.4	0	1
Public banks*crisis, α^*_{PB}	Crisis interaction	2733	0.0	0.2	0	1
Bank size (t−1)	Logarithm of total assets	2733	14.1	1.9	9.2	20.1
ROE (t−1)	Return on equity	2733	13.0	12.8	−77.1	50.1
Capital ratio (t−1)	Equity/total assets	2733	11.8	7.3	1.7	98.8
NPL ratio (t−1)	Non-performing loans/loans	2733	5.6	7.3	0.0	75.3
Liquidity ratio (t−1)	Liquid assets/total assets	2733	17.3	11.3	0.0	75.7

Note: In percentages. The sample includes annual data of 336 banks operating in 31 countries from Latin America and the Caribbean over the period 1995–2014 (see Table 11.1 for further information). The crisis dummy takes a value of 1 if there was either a banking crisis, currency crisis, or during 2008–12, and zero otherwise. Development banks are state-owned and neither multilaterally owned, nor foreign-owned, nor retail deposit-taking banks. Foreign and public banks are banks that are majority-owned by a foreign holding company or by a local government, respectively.

Sources: BankScope, IMF-IFS, World Bank WDI, Claessens and Van Horen (2015), Laeven and Valencia (2013), authors' calculations

Table 11.4. Lending responses among different types of banks and states of nature

	Domestic banks, $DB_{ijt} = 0$	*National development banks, $DB_{ijt} = 1$*
No crisis, $C_{jt} = 0$	$\Delta L_{ijt} = \alpha_1 \Delta L_{ijt-1} + \alpha$	$\Delta L_{ijt} = \alpha_1 \Delta L_{ijt-1} + \alpha + \alpha_{DB}$
Crisis, $C_{jt} = 1$	$\Delta L_{ijt} = \alpha_1 \Delta L_{ijt-1} + \alpha + \alpha^*$	$\Delta L_{ijt} = \alpha_1 \Delta L_{ijt-1} + \alpha + \alpha^* + \alpha_{DB} + \alpha^*_{DB}$

Note: For sake of clarity, the table focuses only on the key coefficients associated with domestic and national development banks. Similar relationships apply to differences in lending of domestic banks relative to foreign and public banks.

during a crisis relative to its lending standard in normal times. If it is significantly negative, this means that the average domestic bank's growth rate of lending during a crisis, $\alpha + \alpha^*$, is lower compared to normal times. The coefficient α_{DB} measures the difference in lending across national development and domestic banks in normal times. If this coefficient is significantly negative, it implies that the average development bank's growth rate of lending during normal times, $\alpha + \alpha_{DB}$, is lower than that of the average domestic bank. During crises, the loan growth of the average national development bank is equal to $\alpha + \alpha^* + \alpha_{DB} + \alpha^*_{DB}$. If $\alpha^* + \alpha^*_{DB}$ is significant and positive, this is evidence that the average development bank lends more during a crisis than in normal times. Whether the average development bank lends more during a crisis compared to the average domestic bank is determined by the sum of the coefficients, $\alpha_{DB} + \alpha^*_{DB}$. If this sum is significantly positive, then it follows that the average development bank lends at a higher growth rate compared to the average domestic bank during a crisis. Similar interpretations apply to the coefficients associated with foreign banks and public banks, respectively.

11.5 Econometric Results

The bank-lending equation above is estimated for three specifications: (I) a macro model, which only includes macroeconomic variables; (II) a bank type model that includes macroeconomic variables and the dummy variables distinguishing the different types of banks; and (III) the full bank-specific model, which includes macroeconomic variables, bank-specific variables, and the dummy variables for bank types. The discussion that follows will be focused on the full specification (III), given that any omitted variable bias is minimized. For comparison, we show in addition to the system GMM estimation results, the results obtained by pooled OLS for the full model specification in column (IV).

The estimation results are shown in Table 11.5. Across all specifications and estimators, we find that the real growth rate of lending is significantly and positively autocorrelated confirming our dynamic specification. The estimation results indicate that banks increase lending when economic conditions

Table 11.5. Regression results: Total loans

	Dependent variable: Growth rate of lending							
	Macro model		Bank type model		Bank-specific model		Pooled OLS	
	(I)		(II)		(III)		(IV)	
	Coeff.	Std error	Coeff.	Std error	Coeff.	Std error	Coeff.	Std error
Lending growth (t–1)	0.160***	0.0315	0.158***	0.030	0.142***	0.030	0.148***	0.027
Real GDP growth	1.061***	0.188	1.026***	0.186	1.362***	0.165	1.300***	0.156
Interest rate	−0.325***	0.109	−0.324***	0.109	−0.269**	0.106	−0.196**	0.083
Inflation	0.031	0.111	0.030	0.106	−0.148	0.107	−0.002	0.090
Depreciation (t–1)	−0.317***	0.0422	−0.314***	0.042	−0.240***	0.0374	−0.217***	0.039
α	6.704***	1.330	9.362***	1.634	9.359***	1.561	7.903***	1.432
α_{DB}			−10.31**	4.157	−6.153*	3.586	−7.636**	3.218
α_{FB}			−3.398**	1.406	−2.962**	1.291	−1.920	1.256
α_{PB}			−5.456***	2.033	−3.377*	1.952	−4.513***	1.653
α^*			−3.259**	1.407	−3.190**	1.364	−2.324*	1.398
α^*_{DB}			13.10***	4.215	10.60**	4.212	8.716**	4.127
α^*_{FB}			2.818	2.157	2.090	1.996	−0.005	1.891
α^*_{PB}			10.29***	2.662	6.663***	2.324	6.909***	2.215
Bank size (t–1)					−0.659*	0.347	−0.253	0.264
ROE (t–1)					0.216***	0.055	0.240***	0.046
Capital ratio (t–1)					0.172	0.161	0.023	0.096
NPL ratio (t–1)					−0.060	0.086	−0.068	0.095
Liquidity ratio (t–1)					−0.002	0.065	−0.062	0.044
Observations	2733		2733		2733		2733	
Banks	336		336		336		336	
Hansen	0.155		0.146		0.205		$R^2 = 0.138$	
AR2	0.730		0.701		0.591			

Note: The sample includes annual data of 336 banks operating in 31 countries from Latin America and the Caribbean over the period 1995–2014. There are 157 domestic, 134 foreign, 31 public, and 14 development banks. Robust standard errors are reported. Specifications (I)–(III) are estimated with the System GMM panel methodology, while specification (IV) is estimated with pooled OLS. (***,**,*) denote significance on the 1 per cent and 10 per cent level, respectively.

improve, i.e. when real GDP growth increases. Higher real interest rates and exchange rate depreciation are, on the other hand, associated with significant decreases in bank lending. The only non-significant macroeconomic variable is inflation, indicating that the other macroeconomic indicators capture most of the impact of aggregate economic conditions on individual bank lending.

Regarding the bank-specific control variables, we find that bank size and profitability affect bank lending significantly, while the other variables are not significant. Larger banks tend to have lower growth rates in lending, which is in line with the literature (Gambacorta 2005; Brei et al. 2013). Moreover, as expected, more profitable banks increase their lending activity by more than less profitable banks.

Turning the discussion to our main question of interest, namely, whether the lending behaviour across national development banks and the other types of banks has been different in normal times and crisis periods, we observe significant heterogeneous lending behaviour, particularly during crises. During normal times, development banks expanded their loan portfolio at significantly lower growth rates compared to the other banks. To be more precise, while the average domestic bank expanded lending at growth rates of $\alpha = 9.36$ per cent per year, the real growth rate of lending of the average national development bank was lower and equal to $\alpha + \alpha_{DB} = 9.36 - 6.15 = 3.21$ per cent. Similar results are found for foreign and public banks during normal times, after controlling for macroeconomic conditions and bank-specific determinants of lending. More specifically, foreign banks expanded lending by $\alpha + \alpha_{FB} = 9.36 - 2.96 = 6.40$ per cent and public banks by $\alpha + \alpha_{PB} = 9.36 - 3.38 = 5.98$ per cent.

During crises, however, the lending pattern of banks changes. To be more precise, the average domestic bank reduces lending by $\alpha^* = -3.19$ per cent per year to a level of $\alpha + \alpha^* = 9.36 - 3.19 = 6.17$ per cent. The average national development bank, on the contrary, counteracts the slowdown in the lending activity of domestic banks by expanding lending at a growth rate of $\alpha + \alpha^* + \alpha_{DB} + \alpha^*_{DB} = 9.36 - 3.19 - 6.15 + 10.60 = 10.62$ per cent per year. The lending behaviour of the average foreign bank does not differ significantly from that of domestic banks during crises, and its lending activity decreases significantly to a level of $\alpha + \alpha^* + \alpha_{FB} = 9.36 - 3.19 - 2.96 = 3.21$ per cent, given that α^*_{FB} is not significantly different from zero. In line with the findings of Brei and Schclarek (2013), public banks increase lending relative to domestic private banks. To be more precise, the average public bank increased its lending activity during times of crisis by $\alpha + \alpha^* + \alpha_{PB} + \alpha^*_{PB} = 9.36 - 3.19 - 3.38 + 6.66 = 9.45$ per cent per year. The results are summarized in Table 11.6.

The estimation results corroborate the tentative results of Table 11.2, suggesting that both domestic and foreign private banks have been lending at higher rates in tranquil times, while cutting down on lending in times of crisis.

Table 11.6. Real growth rate of lending across normal and crisis periods

Type of bank	Lending in normal times	Lending during crisis	(ΔCrisis—normal)
Private domestic bank	9.36	6.17	−3.19
National development bank	3.21	10.62	+7.41
Foreign bank	6.40	3.21	−3.19
Public bank	5.98	9.45	+3.47

Note: This table summarizes the regression results of Table 11.5 (column III), focusing on the different lending responses of the different types of banks during normal and crisis periods, after controlling for bank-fixed effects, bank-specific and macroeconomic factors.

National development and public banks, on the other hand, had lower lending growth in normal times, but they expanded credit once a crisis hit their economies. In other words, foreign, and domestic private banks have been lending procyclically, whereas national development and public banks behaved countercyclically.

The differential lending pattern between these types of banks, as discussed in section 11.2, might be explained by a combination of several factors. In the first place, national development banks and public banks have a higher willingness (or risk tolerance) to provide lending in an unstable crisis environment (Brei and Schclarek 2015). Such behaviour may demonstrate that their objective is not only to maximize profits given risks, but also to mitigate the ensuing credit crunch and the negative spillovers to the real sector. Secondly, it might also be that national development and public banks increase their capital by more than private banks during crises, given that they may find it easier to access additional capital during a financial turmoil or the government may issue debt on financial markets at lower costs compared to private bank owners. Thirdly, it might be that national development and public banks suffer fewer liquidity problems in times of crisis because they face fewer deposit withdrawals and/or have fewer problems in rolling over short-term debt. The lower liquidity problems would be explained by the higher credibility these state-owned banks have, given that an actual and/or future recapitalization is more likely due to the higher credibility and financial strength of the government, in comparison to private bankers.

Finally, the distinct funding structure of development banks, which, as can be seen in Table 11.2, is more dependent on long-term financing (long-term bonds and equity), may also explain why they face fewer liquidity problems and can lend more during a crisis than other types of banks. A long-term funding structure presumably implies a more extended and evenly distributed cash outflow structure that is less dependent on short- and medium-term developments. Thus, it implies that they have fewer maturity mismatches between their assets and liabilities, meaning that when payments for issued long-term bonds are due, a similar amount is received by the repayment of extended loans. This means that at any point in time, if a crisis strikes and there is a run on deposits or an unwillingness to refinance expiring bonds, development banks have fewer liquidity problems than other types of banks that rely more on short-term funding. Moreover, the short-term liquidity problems due to a sudden run on banks have medium- and long-term effects on affected banks, not only implying medium- and long-term liquidity problems but also threatening solvency through losses they make when selling liquid assets in the crisis environment. Thus, development banks are not only better able to lend countercyclically during a crisis but also in the aftermath of it, becoming a key player to reignite growth.

11.6 Commercial Lending

In this section, we investigate the cyclical pattern of lending to businesses across bank types. In doing so, we re-estimate our econometric model using the real growth rate of corporate and commercial loans, measured by the corresponding BankScope item. Due to reporting limitations on this variable, our sample is reduced to 132 banks covering eleven countries from Latin America and the Caribbean over the period 2001–14. There are fifty-two domestic private banks, fifty foreign banks, twenty public banks, and ten national development banks. The total number of bank-year observations reduces to 1294.

The estimation results are shown in Table 11.7. Focusing on the full specification (III), we observe significant heterogeneity in the provision of corporate loans across banks. The average domestic bank was lending at a real growth rate of $\alpha = 12.91$ per cent per year, both in normal times and crisis periods (given that α^* is not significant). Similar results are reached for the average foreign bank in the region (α_{FB} and α^*_{FB} are not statistically different from zero). National development banks, on the other hand, increased corporate lending once the state of the economy moved to a crisis period. More precisely, during normal times the average development bank expanded business lending at $\alpha = 12.91$ per cent (α_{DB} is not significant). However, once a crisis struck, they expanded lending to the real sector at a rate of $\alpha + \alpha^*_{DB} = 12.91 + 21.05 = 33.96$ per cent per year. Finally, the average public bank's lending to the real sector has been shrinking during normal times at a growth rate of $\alpha + \alpha_{PB} = 12.91 - 13.88 = -0.97$ per cent. During crises, on the other hand, public banks expanded lending to the real sector at a rate of $\alpha + \alpha_{PB} + \alpha^*_{PB} = 12.91 - 13.88 + 24.43 = 23.46$ per cent.

Our estimation results thus suggest that both domestic and foreign bank lending to the corporate and commercial sector was acyclical, whereas national development and public banks reacted countercyclically. The countercyclical

Table 11.7. Regression results: Corporate and commercial loans

	Dependent variable: Growth rate of commercial lending							
	Macro model		Bank type model		Bank-specific model		Pooled OLS	
	(I)		(II)		(III)		(IV)	
	Coeff.	Std error	Coeff.	Std error	Coeff.	Std error	Coeff.	Std error
Com. loan growth (*t*−1)	−0.048	0.049	−0.053	0.050	−0.049	0.048	0.024	0.041
Real GDP growth	0.715*	0.366	0.854**	0.394	0.808**	0.383	0.737*	0.408
Interest rate	0.425	0.401	0.432	0.382	0.167	0.422	−0.230	0.284
Inflation	0.381	0.360	0.336	0.357	0.211	0.355	0.023	0.247
Depreciation (*t*−1)	−0.235***	0.0599	−0.228***	0.0582	−0.236***	0.0559	−0.257***	0.057
α	10.07***	3.111	11.79***	4.135	12.91***	3.984	17.02***	4.172
α_{DB}			−11.08	7.240	−10.04	8.051	−12.47**	5.623
α_{FB}			−2.056	4.019	−1.574	3.546	−2.787	3.645
α_{PB}			−13.33**	5.433	−13.88***	5.179	−12.97**	5.251
α^*			−1.415	3.230	−1.607	3.230	−3.923	3.343
α^*_{DB}			23.80**	11.15	21.05*	12.33	24.93**	12.04
α^*_{FB}			0.328	3.887	−0.606	3.925	1.474	4.647
α^*_{PB}			23.13**	9.264	24.43**	9.547	19.09***	6.620
Bank size (*t*−1)					0.177	0.891	0.148	0.654
ROE (*t*−1)					0.232**	0.117	0.198*	0.116
Capital ratio (*t*−1)					0.290	0.301	0.337	0.353
NPL ratio (*t*−1)					0.119	0.285	0.346	0.316
Liquidity ratio (*t*−1)					−0.180	0.197	−0.208	0.192
Observations	1294		1294		1294		1294	
Banks	132		132		132		132	
Hansen	0.334		0.173		0.164		$R^2 = 0.057$	
AR2	0.354		0.395		0.210			

Note: The sample includes annual data of 132 banks operating in 11 countries from Latin America and the Caribbean over the period 2001–14. There are 52 domestic, 50 foreign, 20 public, and 10 development banks. Robust standard errors are reported. Specifications (I)–(III) are estimated with the System GMM panel methodology, while specification (IV) is estimated with pooled OLS. (***,**,*) denote significance on the 1 per cent and 10 per cent level, respectively.

response of national development and public banks has been more pronounced than when considering total lending, which includes residential mortgages loans and other consumer loans, suggesting that development and public banks have been especially active in the corporate and commercial lending segments during times of crisis.

11.7 Conclusion

This chapter investigated empirically the lending responses during normal times and crisis periods across national development, public commercial, domestic private, and foreign private banks. To this purpose, we employed dynamic panel regressions that allow controlling for loan demand and other factors using an extensive dataset on the financial statements of 336 banks from thirty-one Latin American and Caribbean countries over the period of 1995–2014.

Our main findings are the following. We find robust evidence that national development and public banks increased total lending in response to crisis periods relative to normal times, while domestic and foreign banks decreased their lending relative to their normal lending pattern. It is interesting to observe that the average national development bank lends at a lower lending growth rate than the average domestic bank in normal times (3.21 per cent per annum compared to 9.36 per cent). However, once a crisis strikes, national development banks expanded lending at a higher rate (10.62 per cent per annum compared to 6.17 per cent for private banks). This countercyclical behaviour of national development banks is even stronger when considering corporate and commercial lending rather than total lending. While foreign bank lending did not differ much from domestic bank lending, we observe that public banks have played a similar countercyclical role during times of crisis, as did national development banks.

The differential lending pattern is to a certain extent related to the different objectives banks have and the fact that national development and public banks presumably have a higher willingness (or risk tolerance) to provide lending in an unstable crisis environment. The higher risk tolerance of state-owned banks may reflect their objective which is not only to maximize profits given risks, but also to mitigate a private bank credit crunch and the negative spillovers to the real sector. It might also be that national development and public banks have been able to increase their capital base by more than private banks during crises, given that they may find it easier to access new capital during a period of financial turmoil or that governments issue debt on financial markets at a lower cost than private bank owners. Further, it might be that national development and public banks have suffered fewer liquidity problems in times of crisis because they are less likely to be subject to deposit withdrawals and/or problems in rolling over debt. The higher trust in state-owned banks and their stronger credibility derive, in turn, from a more likely current and/or future recapitalization due to the higher financial strength of the government, in comparison to private bankers. Finally, development banks may also have faced fewer liquidity problems owing to their particular funding structure, which is more dependent on long-term financing (long-term bonds and equity). A more extended and evenly distributed cash outflow structure implies a better maturity match with extended loans. Thus, development banks are better at coping with the liquidity problems that arise when there is a sudden bank run on deposits and/or difficulties in rolling over debt due to a crisis. As these liquidity problems not only have short-term consequences but also medium- and long-term consequences, development banks are not only better suited for carrying out countercyclical lending during a crisis but are also particularly suited to reignite growth after a crisis. Most likely, the observed difference in the lending responses between the different bank types is explained by a combination of all these four factors.

From a policy perspective, our results suggest that governments can play an active countercyclical role in their banking systems directly through national development and public banks. However, the relative size of these banks with respect to the rest of the financial system is an important determinant of the success of this countercyclical policy. Clearly, a sufficiently large state-owned banking sector will have higher chances of contributing to the stability of the economy. Moreover, as many national development banks lend to companies indirectly through private commercial banks, they may also help private banks to act more countercyclically. Another important determinant of the success of the countercyclical policy is the governance structure and institutional quality of these banks. Clearly, well-managed national development banks that keep out narrow private and political vested interests are more likely to be in a better financial shape in times of crisis, which would allow them to react strongly when needed. Further, it is important that national development banks design specific credit lines that take into account the special needs that companies face when a crisis strikes. For example, it is unlikely that companies demand long-term loans for capital investments at times when production capacity is not fully utilized due to lower demand. Instead, it seems more important for companies to access credit lines for working capital or new innovative credit lines that reflect the special needs of companies during recessions. In addition, the countercyclical lending could be concentrated on public infrastructure projects that foster production and export capabilities.

References

Allen, F., K. Jackowicz, and O. Kowalewski. 2013. *The Effects of Foreign and Government Ownership on Bank Lending Behavior During a Crisis in Central and Eastern Europe.* Wharton Financial Institutions Center Working Paper No. 13–25.

Andrianova, S., P. Demetriades, and A. Shortland. 2009. *Is Government Ownership of Banks Really Harmful to Growth?* Discussion Papers in Economics No. 09/11, University of Leicester.

Arellano, M. and S. Bond. 1991. 'Some Tests of Specification for Panel Data: Monte Carlo Evidence and an Application to Employment Equations', *Review of Economic Studies* 58: 277–97.

Behr, P., D. Foos, and L. Norden. 2017. 'Cyclicality of SME Lending and Government Involvement in Banks', *Journal of Banking & Finance* 77(C): 64–77.

Bertay, A., A. Demirguc-Kunt, and H. Huizinga. 2015. 'Bank Ownership and Credit over the Business Cycle: Is Lending by State Banks Less Procyclical?', *Journal of Banking & Finance* 50: 326–39.

Blundell, R. W. and S. R. Bond. 1998. 'Initial Conditions and Moment Restrictions in Dynamic Panel Data Models', *Journal of Econometrics* 87: 115–43.

Brei, M. and L. Gambacorta. 2016. 'Are Bank Capital Ratios Pro-Cyclical? New Evidence and Perspectives', *Economic Policy* 31(86): 357–403.

Brei, M., L. Gambacorta, and G. von Peter. 2013. 'Bank Rescue Packages and Bank Lending', *Journal of Banking and Finance* 37: 490–505.

Brei, M. and A. Schclarek. 2013. 'Public Bank Lending during the Financial Crisis', *Journal of Financial Stability* 9(4): 820–30.

Brei, M. and A. Schclarek. 2015. 'A Theoretical Model of Bank Lending: Does Ownership Matter in Times of Crises?', *Journal of Banking and Finance* 50 (January): 298–307.

Carvalho, D. 2014. 'The Real Effects of Government-Owned Banks: Evidence from an Emerging Market', *Journal of Finance* 69(2): 577–609.

Claessens, S. and N. Van Horen. 2015. 'The Impact of the Global Financial Crisis on Banking Globalization', *IMF Economic Review* 63(4): 868–918.

Cull, R. and M. S. Martinez-Pería. 2013. 'Bank Ownership and Lending Patterns during the 2008–2009 Financial Crisis: Evidence from Latin America and Eastern Europe', *Journal of Banking & Finance* 37(12): 4861–78.

Ehrmann, M., L. Gambacorta, J. Martinez Pagés, P. Sevestre, and A. Worms. 2003. 'Financial Systems and the Role of Banks in Monetary Policy', in I. Angeloni, A. Kashyap, and B. Mojon (eds), *Monetary Policy Transmission in the Euro Area*, 235–69. Cambridge: Cambridge University Press.

Ehrmann, M. and A. Worms. 2004. 'Bank Networks and Monetary Policy Transmission', *Journal of the European Economic Association* 2: 1148–71.

Eslava, M. and J. Freixas. 2016. *Public Development Banks and Credit Market Imperfections.* Documentos CEDE 014234, Universidad de Los Andes-CEDE.

Ferraz, J. C., C. Figueiredo Coelho Leal, F. Silveira Marques, and M. Trindade Miterhof. 2012. 'O BNDES e o financiamento do desenvolvimento', *REVISTA USP*, Universidade de São Paulo, No. 83 (March–May): 69–80.

Gambacorta, L. 2005. 'Inside the Bank Lending Channel', *European Economic Review* 49: 1737–59.

Gambacorta, L. and D. Marques-Ibanez. 2011. 'Bank Lending Channel: Lessons from the Crisis', *Economic Policy* 20 (April): 135–82.

Griffith-Jones, S. and R. Gottschalk. 2012. 'Exogenous Shocks: Dealing with the Only Certainty: Uncertainty'. Paper prepared for the Commonwealth Secretariat, September 2012, for the Commonwealth Finance Ministers' Meeting, Tokyo, 10 October.

Griffith-Jones, S. and J. A. Ocampo. 2008. 'A Counter-Cyclical Framework for a Development-Friendly IFA', in José Maria Fanelli (ed.), *Macroeconomic Volatility, Institutions and Financial Architectures: The Developing World Experience*, 25–44. New York: Palgrave Macmillan.

Griffith-Jones, S., J. Tyson, and P. Calice. 2011. 'The European Investment Bank and SMEs: Key Lessons for Latin America and the Caribbean'. *CEPAL—Serie financiamiento del desarrollo*, No. 236.

Gutierrez, E., H. P. Rudolph, T. Homa, and E. Blanco Beneit. 2011. *Development Banks: Role and Mechanisms to Increase their Efficiency*. World Bank Policy Research Working Paper No. WPS 5729. Washington, DC: World Bank.

Hainz, C. and H. Hakenes. 2012. 'The Politician and his Banker: How to Efficiently Grant State Aid', *Journal of Public Economics* 96(1–2): 218–25.

Kashyap, A. and J. Stein. 1995. 'The Impact of Monetary Policy on Bank Balance Sheets'. *Carnegie Rochester Conference Series on Public Policy* 42: 151–95.

Khwaja, A. I. and A. Mian. 2005. 'Do Lenders Favor Politically Connected Firms? Rent Provision in an Emerging Financial Market', *Quarterly Journal of Economics* 120(4): 1371–411.

Kishan, R. and T. Opiela. 2000. 'Bank Size, Bank Capital, and the Bank Lending Channel', *Journal of Money, Credit, and Banking* 32(1): 121–41.

Krueger, A. O. 1974. 'The Political Economy of the Rent-Seeking Society', *American Economic Review* 64: 291–303.

Laeven, L. and F. Valencia. 2013. 'Systemic Banking Crisis Database', *IMF Economic Review* 61(2): 225–70.

Luna-Martinez, J. de and C. L. Vicente. 2012. *Global Survey of Development Banks*. World Bank Policy Research Working Paper No. 5969, February. Washington, DC: World Bank.

Machado, L. and F. Brener Roitman. 2015. 'Os efeitos do BNDES PSI sobre o investimento corrente e futuro das firmas industriais', *Revista do BNDES, Rio de Janeiro* 44: 89–122.

Mazzucato, M. and C. Penna 2016. 'Beyond Market Failures: The Market Creating and Shaping Roles of State Investment Banks', *Journal of Economic Policy Reform* 19(4): 305–26.

de Olloqui, F. 2013. 'Public Development Banks: Toward a New Paradigm?'. IDB Publications (Books), Inter-American Development Bank, No. 82671, November.

Rudolph, H. P. 2010. *Can They Be Relied on to Kick-Start Lending?* Crisis Response Note, No. 12. Washington, DC: World Bank.

Shleifer, A. and R. W. Vishny. 1994. 'Politicians and Firms', *The Quarterly Journal of Economics* 109: 995–1025.

UN-DESA. 2005. *Rethinking the Role of National Development Banks*. Background document for the Ad Hoc Expert Group Meeting on 'Rethinking the Role of National Development Banks', New York, 1–2 December.

World Bank. 2012. *Global Financial Development Report 2013: Rethinking the Role of the State in Finance*. World Bank Publications, No. 11848.

12

Financial Sustainability and Infrastructure Finance

The Role of Development Banks

Felipe Carvalho de Rezende

12.1 Introduction

The creation of new sources of financing and funding is at the centre of discussions about promoting real capital development. It has been suggested that access to capital markets and long-term investors is a possible solution to the dilemma faced by countries' increasing financing requirements (such as infrastructure investment and mortgage lending needs) and limited access to long-term funding. This argument is based on the assumption that traditional banks and existing financial structures are unable, due to funding constraints, to meet the growing financing needs of modern economies. In spite of the introduction of several initiatives to mobilize private capital to fund long-term projects and assets, private finance schemes have fallen short of their targets. Notwithstanding the great potential among institutional investors to fund long-term assets such as infrastructure—due to the longer-term nature of their liabilities—and the availability of private financing mechanisms and instruments, their fund allocation has remained below their target allocations to infrastructure (OECD 2015a).

This article on which this chapter is based was prepared for the project 'The Future of National Development Banks', funded by BNDES and CAF, Development Bank of Latin America administered through the Initiative for Policy Dialogue (IPD). The author thanks BNDES, CAF, and IPD for supporting this research. I have benefitted from comments at an IPD/BNDES/CAF seminar in Washington, DC on 20 April 2017.

Though there was a consensus over the past decades in favour of the development of the debt securities and securitization markets to foster local capital markets and long-term funding, since the onset of the 2007–8 global financial crisis, there has been a renewed interest in development banks (DBs). That is, their roles in promoting and financing investment, dampening the effects of financial instability, and creating benchmark assessments on national DBs performance have been investigated (Luna-Martinez and Vicente 2012). There is a growing consensus on the value of DBs and the role they play promoting the capital development of the economy during non-crisis and crisis periods while mitigating the effects of financial fragility, both domestically and internationally. Moreover, development banks have enhanced policymakers' macroeconomic toolkit by acting as countercyclical policy instruments,[1] extending their traditional roles by providing financing aimed at enhancing productivity growth, supporting socioeconomic infrastructure and knowledge-specific activities, and promoting the development of organized liquid capital markets (Rezende 2015).

Even though development banks play an active and strategic role promoting economic development in advanced and developing economies at different stages of their development process (Chandrasekhar 2016), there is little discussion about their macroeconomic role. To be sure, much of the discussion focuses on the role of financial markets in economic growth and development.[2] This is in part a result of the conventional view that, as Robert Lucas put it, finance does not matter much.[3] This approach, in turn, leads to different perspectives on policy for development banks.

Development banks (DBs) are widespread across the world and 'have served as an institutional substitute for crucial "prerequisites" such as prior accumulation of capital or the availability of adequate entrepreneurial skills or technological expertise' (Chandrasekhar 2016: 22). They 'are also involved in early stage decisions such as choice of technology, scale and location, requiring the acquisition of technical, financial and managerial expertise' (23). It is well known that development financial institutions play a strategically role at various stages of economic development. For instance,

[1] A recent IMF study concludes that '[f]irms in sectors that are more financially dependent cut investment more sharply than other firms, particularly early in the crisis. Firms in sectors that are more sensitive to policy uncertainty also reduced investment by more than other firms' (IMF 2015: fig. 4.12). This result reinforces the macroeconomic role played by development banks offsetting swings in lending by private financial institutions, especially during times of stress.

[2] See, for instance, Fischer 2003.

[3] Lucas then said: 'I will ... be abstracting from all monetary matters, treating all exchange as though it involved goods-for-goods. In general, I believe that the importance of financial matters is very badly over-stressed in popular and even much more professional discussion and so am not inclined to be apologetic for going to the other extreme' (Lucas 1988: 6).

> the capitalisation of income earning assets was also the basis for Crédit Mobilier and Société Générale formed in France and Belgium at the middle of the 19th century. These banks served as the pattern for the German Effektenbanken or Kredit banks and the Italian industrial banks. The French proposals in fact went beyond simple industrial financing, and proposed a sort of central bank for Industry which would oversee the industrialisation of the country by arranging associations and mergers, rather than by wasteful competition. (Kregel 1998: 7)

Moreover, 'historically it has been public banks that have led the way in financing the long-term investment necessary for the economic industrialization of developing countries. Second, that financial innovation in the "essential function" of the "creation of money" has had a major impact on the evolution of financial structure and in particular the evolution of the mix of private and public finance for investment and innovation. Third ... the recent dominance of private financial institutions and the presumption of their efficiency advantage have reduced the availability of long-term finance for development' (Kregel 2015: 1).

From this perspective, as Chandrasekhar (2016) put it:

> finding the capital to finance the industrial take-off represents a major challenge ... Gerschenkron believed that they served as institutional substitutes for crucial 'prerequisites' for the industrial take-off, such as the prior accumulation of capital or the availability of adequate entrepreneurial skills and technological expertise.
>
> As Gerschenkron (1962: 13) argued: 'The difference between banks of the crédit mobilier type and commercial banks in the advanced industrial country of the time (England) was absolute. Between the English bank essentially designed to serve as a source of short-term capital and a bank designed to finance the long-run investment needs of the economy there was a complete gulf.'
>
> (Chandrasekhar 2016: 22)

Despite the widespread presence of development banks their evolution has been different, adapting their roles to different stages of economic development. Advanced and developing economies continue to rely on DBs, including Germany's KfW and Japan Finance Corporation (JFC), Development Bank of Japan[4] (DBJ), China Development Bank (CDB), and Brazil's BNDES to name a few (Chandrasekhar 2016; Ferraz et al. 2016). The availability of patient credit allows for industrial take-off, catching-up, and leapfrogging (Burlamaqui and Kattel 2014).[5]

[4] The DBJ still works as a DB, but is being privatized (Ferraz et al. 2016: 17, n. 14).

[5] It is worth noting that 'the Republic of Korea was also a late industrializer in which development finance (supported by the State through the budget and the central bank) played an extremely important role and contributed in no small measure to the success of its late industrialization. However, the DB's role here included support for borrowing from abroad to acquire foreign technology, which was subsequently leveraged to launch a successful export-oriented strategy' (Chandrasekhar 2016: 28).

In spite of the historical importance of development banks promoting capitalist development, they have often received harsh criticism: 'fuelled by the neoliberal economic policies of the Washington Consensus ... a more critical view on DBs emerged in the 1980s and 90s. Particularly national DBs were regarded by many as an instrument of unacceptable state interventionism ... The popularity of DBs gained ground again when the Millennium Development Goals (MDGs) were adopted by the United Nations in 2001' (UN–DESA 2005: 7).

For instance, the chapter 'Mobilizing Domestic Financial Resources for Development' of the Monterrey Consensus noted that '[d]evelopment banks ... can be effective instruments for facilitating access to finance, including equity financing, for such enterprises, as well as an adequate supply of medium- and long-term credit' (United Nations 2003: 7).

However, much of the discussion involving DBs is usually set in different theoretical frameworks. The conventional view about the existence of DBs relies on market failures, in which they play a remedial role (Torres Filho and Zeidan 2016; Wruuck 2015; UN-DESA 2005). This association of DBs with the concept of market failure leads to the view that with the development of financial markets, DBs are no longer needed. For instance, Torres Filho and Zeidan (2016) have suggested that 'as countries develop their financial markets, NDBs should share this role with other local banks and specialize their focus, *eventually disappearing altogether*' (emphasis added).

From this perspective, it is essential that the theoretical discussion about the role of DBs be grounded on a solid framework beyond market failures. Among the lessons that can be drawn from the global financial crisis is that in spite of a rapid increase in financialization, the dominance of private financial institutions failed to promote the capital development of the economy (Levy Institute 2011; Mazzucato and Wray 2015). The global crisis has shown once again that there is no guarantee that developed financial markets promote the capital development of the economy. This has important implications for policymaking, that is, 'during the pre-crisis period, developed countries' regulatory systems had been considered as "best practice" and formed the basis for recommendations to developing countries seeking to liberalize and expand their domestic financial markets' (Rezende 2015: 241). However, since 'the financial structure that emerged in the USA in the past thirty years failed to provide support for the development of the economy and to improve living standards, an alternative design of the financial structure that meets the needs of developing nations needs to be developed' (Rezende 2015: 242).

In what follows (section 12.2), building on the insights of Jan Kregel (2015), I will briefly discuss Hyman Minsky's work on financial regulation and what he labelled as the 'dilemma of financial regulation' as a theoretical framework to analyse the macroeconomic role played by development banks—not only in providing the long-term funding necessary to promote economic development, but also to prevent fragility.

In section 12.3, this broader theoretical framework will provide the basis for the proposition that public financial institutions are needed to provide support for infrastructure and sustainable development projects. I will then discuss in section 12.4 the main challenges faced by the private sector in providing long-term finance in the emerging and developed world to meet some of the infrastructure requirements—and the strategic role national development banks and government policy should play, given the inherent risks of infrastructure projects. Section 12.5 offers lessons for enhancing the role of development banks as catalysts for mitigating risks associated with infrastructure projects, while section 12.6 makes concluding remarks.

12.2 What Is the Appropriate Financial Structure for Emerging Market Economies Promoting Capital Development?

Hyman Minsky wrote extensively about the nature of money and banking. In his model, '[e]veryone can create money; the problem is to get it accepted' (Minsky 1986). As he put it: 'Banking is not money lending; to lend, a money lender must have money. The fundamental banking activity is accepting, that is, guaranteeing that some party is creditworthy' (256). In general, those IOUs are denominated in the state unit of account, but they can also be denominated in foreign currency. That is, banking is liquidity creation. Though traditional banks are liquidity creators—that is, they buy assets through the issuance of liabilities—not all liquidity is created by them.

However, one of the main challenges, in terms of increasing traditional banks' exposure to long-term assets, is related to interest rate and liquidity risks and the returns required to induce investors to be exposed to infrastructure assets. This is because interest risk is significantly increased by the lengthening of the portfolio's duration. The expansion of long-term loans as a share of total assets tends to increase the maturity mismatch between assets and liabilities. A prudent banker might not undertake to increase the risk of maturity mismatches, such as financing long-term assets by issuing long-term liabilities in a volatile interest rate environment. Bankers are unwilling to be exposed to increasing maturity mismatches, particularly when the current macroeconomic policy brings about high interest volatility to fight inflation. That is, bankers are unwilling to increase the duration of assets relative to liabilities and carry this risk on their balance sheets.

Even though maturity matching by bankers is a source of banking stability, it limits financing of investments in long-term capital assets and infrastructure-type products. That is, the financing of these types of investment are limited in a volatile interest rate environment. Though traditional banks are the most important source of long-term financing (see, for instance, Peria and Schmukler 2017), the concentration on shorter maturities in financial instruments is typically the outcome of information asymmetries (Stiglitz and Weiss 1981), coordination problems—which may trigger a dynamic towards short maturities known as the 'maturity rat race' (see, for instance, Brunnermeier and Oehmke 2013)—and incentive problems including short-termism in incentives (Lazonick and O'Sullivan 2000). Macroeconomic risks and lack of an adequate legal framework (such as weak institutions and poor contract enforcement) can also contribute to excessive reliance on short-term financing.

This means that policy should focus on those issues to adjust to the needs of users of long-term finance and their providers. From this perspective, development banks play a strategic role focusing on long-term goals, providing long-term patient finance, and contributing to address the fundamental institutional weaknesses that prevent the mobilization of funding for private investment.

Second, the 'use of long-term finance can be best understood as a risk-sharing problem between providers and users of finance' (World Bank 2015: 24). From this perspective, regulations can be introduced to better manage and transfer risks to parties abler to bear them. The important question is related to the costs of carrying a mismatch between the duration of assets and liabilities on the bank balance sheet, that is, if interest and funding risks are carried on banks' balance sheets. As Kregel (1993) pointed out, different financial structures are created to reduce price risks, such as the risks associated with financing investments in long-term capital assets. German banking regulations imposes matching between assets and liabilities on banks' balance sheets (Kregel 1993). For instance,

> banks issued long-term bonds, which were held within the financial sector, and then slowly started to be held by the public. In this way fixed interest liabilities matched the term lending of the banks to firms and the reliance on bond finance may be seen as a structural result of the way in which price risks are hedged in the German system and as a substitute for the pre-war use of the equity market. The German mixed bank system is thus no less dependent on capital markets to reduce risk than segmented bank systems, both require them to provide a reduction in price risks. (Burlamaqui and Kregel 2005: 45)

So, the question is how to design a financial structure for emerging market economies that promotes capital development and mitigates financial fragility. From this perspective, it has already been suggested that financial regulation should serve two conflicting objectives (Kregel 2015). One master requires leverage and taking risks, since financing capital development and innovation are inherently risky activities—in an environment in which crises are systemic—while the second requires a safe and sound payments system. The question then becomes how to design a financial structure that serves the two contradictory masters within a conceptual framework in which financial crises are systemic.

12.3 Massive Need for Infrastructure in the Emerging and Developed World

Insufficient or inadequate infrastructure in both developing and developed economies has sparked a debate about whether financing is sufficient to sustain infrastructure investment to at least keep pace with projected global GDP growth. The task of keeping the minimum investment required to maintain current levels and fostering incremental spending to close the infrastructure gap has revived the debate over the role played by each actor in closing the gap and how to finance this process (see, for instance, G-20 2013; OECD 2013b; World Bank 2015). One of the major post-crisis challenges is that in spite of an ultra-low interest rate environment or even negative nominal and real rates, investment has been anaemic in developed and developing economies (IMF 2015). This is particular important because since the crisis, investment has collapsed across all sectors (public, business, and household sectors) in Europe (McKinsey 2016: 2). And, in the United States, 'the trajectory of net fixed capital formation, which decreased from 12 percent of GDP in 1950 to 8 percent in 2007, then fell to only 4 percent in 2014. Average depreciation rates accelerated by about 20 percent during the 1980s as companies invested in shorter-lived assets such as ICT equipment but did not compensate in terms of higher gross investment rates. This amplified the decline in net investment' (ibid.). To make matters worse, most governments in developed nations and developing nations (with the exception of a few cases) are cutting back on infrastructure spending due to fiscal consolidation (Figure 12.1), generating a public-funding shortfall in infrastructure investment.

Moreover, insufficient private investment and declining real public investment have contributed to reduce the stock of public capital as a share of output over the past three decades (Figure 12.2).

Furthermore, the economic collapse in the wake of the global financial crisis has contributed to permanent effects on potential output levels across advanced and emerging market economies (IMF 2015; Ollivaud and Turner 2014). Equity requirements and the cost of capital have increased for many infrastructure investments (McKinsey 2013a: 23). This, combined with the decline in public investment as policymakers opted for austerity measures, has contributed to lower potential output (IMF 2014; McKinsey 2016). This decline in government investment has been exacerbated by the short-termism of financial markets and corporations. Additionally, an IMF report pointed out that 'the initial hopes that the privatization wave of the 1980s would fuel a private-sector funded greenfield infrastructure investment boom have fallen well short of expectations' (Samama et al. 2016: 3).

The perverse combination of inadequate direct public investment, increasing cost and availability of long-term financing, and a higher proportion

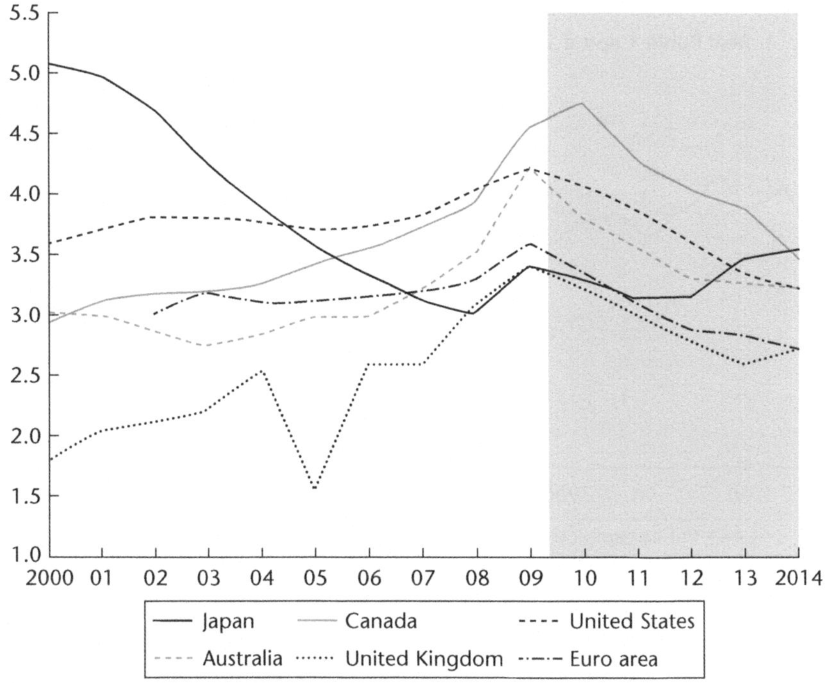

Figure 12.1. General government gross fixed capital formation (percentage of GDP)
Source: McKinsey (2016: 11)

of higher-risk projects (i.e. greenfield projects in developing countries) that are in the investment pipeline has contributed to widen the infrastructure gap (McKinsey 2013a: 19). That is, though 'infrastructure development has been found to have a positive and significant impact on long-run growth and a negative impact on income inequality' (Calderon and Serven 2014), the combination of growing investment needs, low investment, and the imperative to channel investments for sustainable development goals has resulted in massive infrastructure gaps (UNSDSN 2015; UNTT 2013; McKinsey 2016).

Against this background, there are several estimates—using different approaches—that indicate massive global infrastructure needs (Schmidt-Traub 2015). For instance, the McKinsey report estimates that $57 trillion in investments will be required until 2030—which is more than the estimated value of today's infrastructure—to just keep pace with projected global GDP growth (see McKinsey 2016: 1). The McKinsey report suggests that the world will need 'to invest about 3.8 percent of global GDP in infrastructure over the period from 2016 to 2030—or an average of $3.3 trillion a year—just to support expected economic growth. Emerging economies account for some

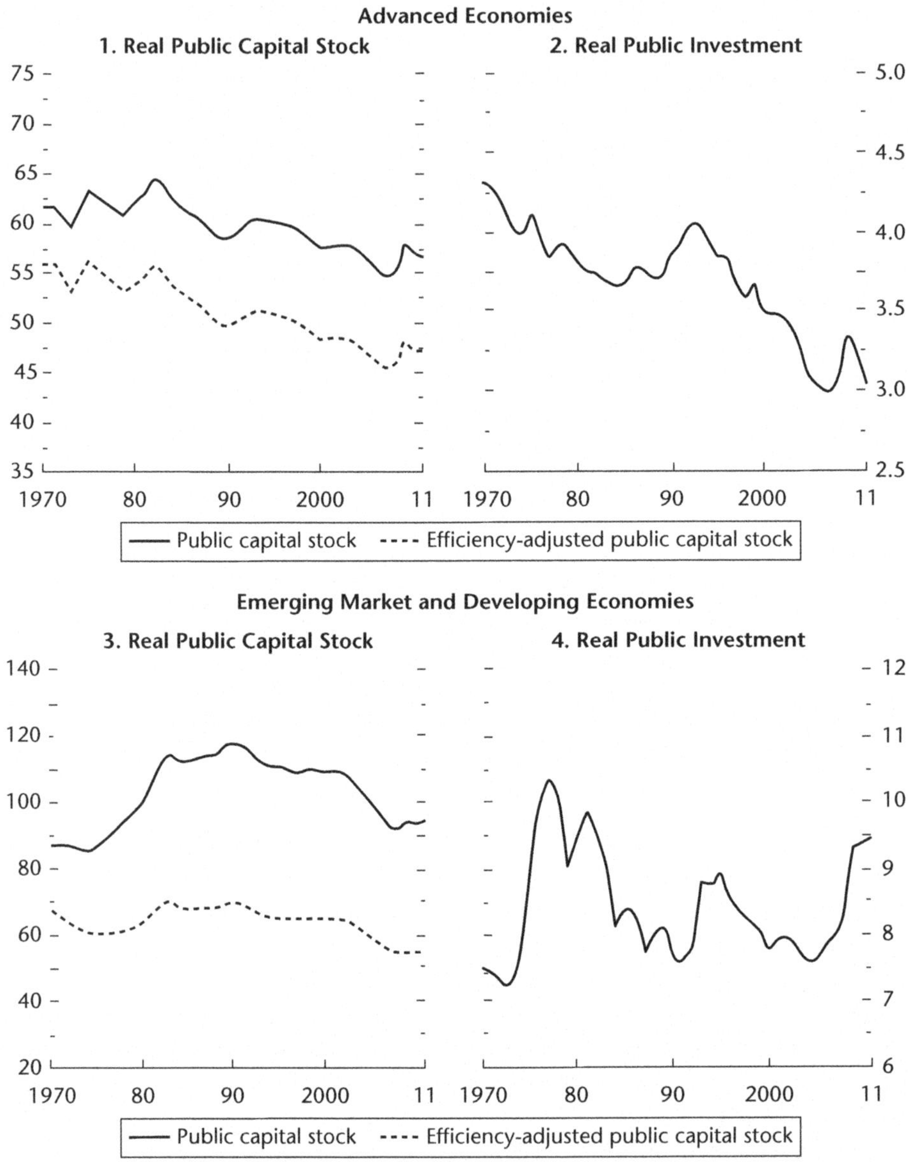

Figure 12.2. Evolution of public capital stock and public investment (percentage of GDP, PPP weighted)
Source: IMF (2014: 80)

60 percent of that need' (McKinsey 2016: 9). The report concludes that '[i]f they maintain their current trajectories, a number of countries will continue to underinvest to such a degree that the world could fall about 11 percent short of the necessary infrastructure investment. The shortfall could amount

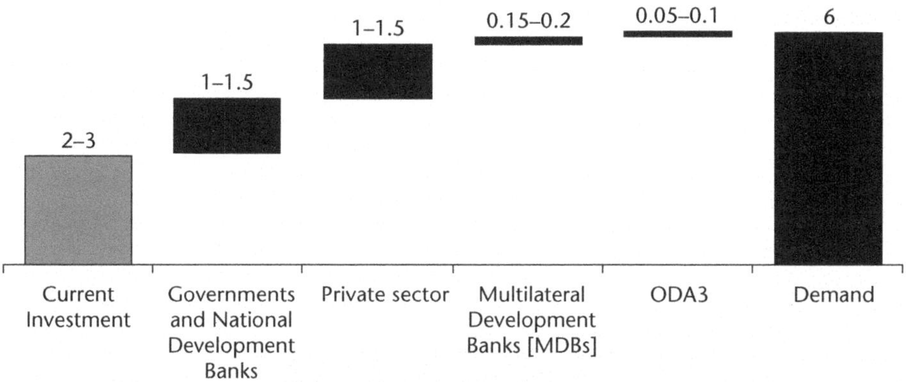

Figure 12.3. Proposed annual incremental spending to close the infrastructure debt (in trillion constant 2010 $)
Source: Bhattacharya et al. (2015: 26)

to some $350 billion a year . . . This size of the gap roughly triples, however, when we take into account the additional investment required to meet the UN's new Sustainable Development Goals' (10).

According to estimates from the Organization for Economic Cooperation and Development (OECD) the investment required is equivalent to US$70 trillion by 2030 (OECD 2015d). The World Bank (2015) estimates that approximately US$1 trillion per year is needed in emerging markets and developing economies (EMDEs), while the G-20 (2013) suggests that developing countries will need to invest an additional $1 trillion a year through 2020.

McKinsey points out that the current annual investment on infrastructure is at US$2 trillion to US$3 trillion and it estimates that required investments could reach the equivalent of US$6 trillion a year, based on demand for about $93 trillion over fifteen years. This means that the government sector, national development banks, and the private sector will have to substantially increase current rates of investment to meet the global demand for infrastructure services. In particular, governments and development banks could be responsible for US$1–1.5 trillion in annual incremental spending while the private sector could contribute with equivalent amounts (Figure 12.3).

12.3.1 *Banks, Capital Markets, and Institutional Investors as Providers of Long-Term Finance*

From 1990 to 2012, the stock of global financial assets increased from $56 trillion to $225 trillion. In 2012, it included a $50 trillion stock market, $47 trillion public debt securities market, $42 trillion in financial institution bonds outstanding,

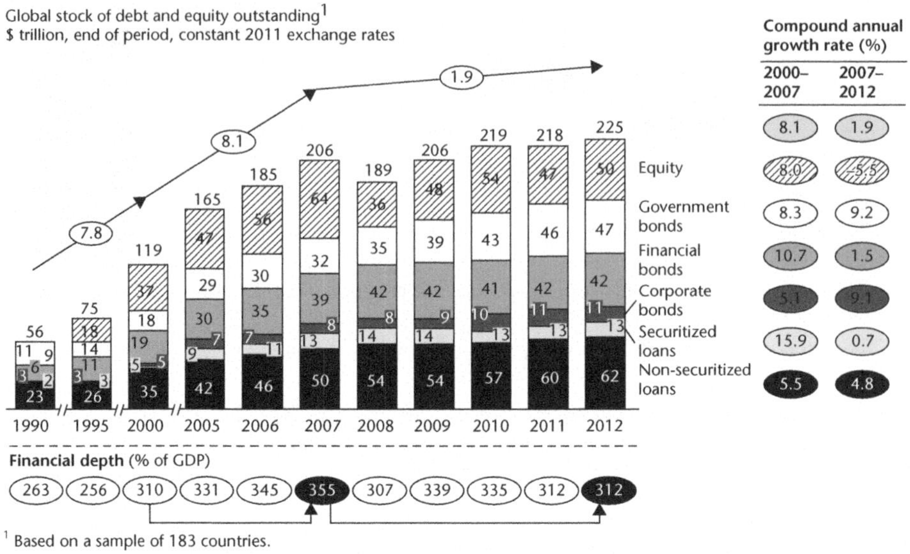

Figure 12.4. Stock of global financial assets (USD trillion)
Source: Lund et al. (2013: 2)

$11 trillion in non-financial corporate bonds, and $62 trillion in non-securitized loans and $13 trillion in securitized loans outstanding (Figure 12.4).

From 2007 to 2012, government debt securities increased by 47 per cent (Figure 12.3) while financial depth rose to 355 per cent of global GDP in 2007 from 120 per cent in 1980 (Lund et al. 2013: 2). In spite of a massive increase in the stock of global financial assets—equivalent to 302 per cent between 1990 and 2012—'[m]ost of the increase in financial depth prior to the crisis was due to financial system leverage and equity valuations' (Lund et al. 2013: 2). Yet the world needs more and better infrastructure, and redirecting finance towards sustainable infrastructure will require a major shift in policy coordination with various stakeholders. For instance, Standard & Poor's estimated that 'institutional investors could provide as much as $200 billion per year—or $3.2 trillion by 2030—for infrastructure financing' (Standard & Poor's 2014: 2). But, 'if the right levers are pulled, there is potential to increase investment from private institutional investors by ~$1.2 trillion per year' (Bielenberg et al. 2016: 28). Thus, the problem is not necessarily one of funding but how to direct the finance created by the financial system towards productivity-enhancing investments.

In this regard, a number of mechanisms are available to finance long-term investments, and yield-seeking potential investors could contribute to close the financing gap (Figure 12.5). The OECD estimated that institutional investors held over US$70 trillion in assets as of December 2011 (Della Croce 2014: 8).

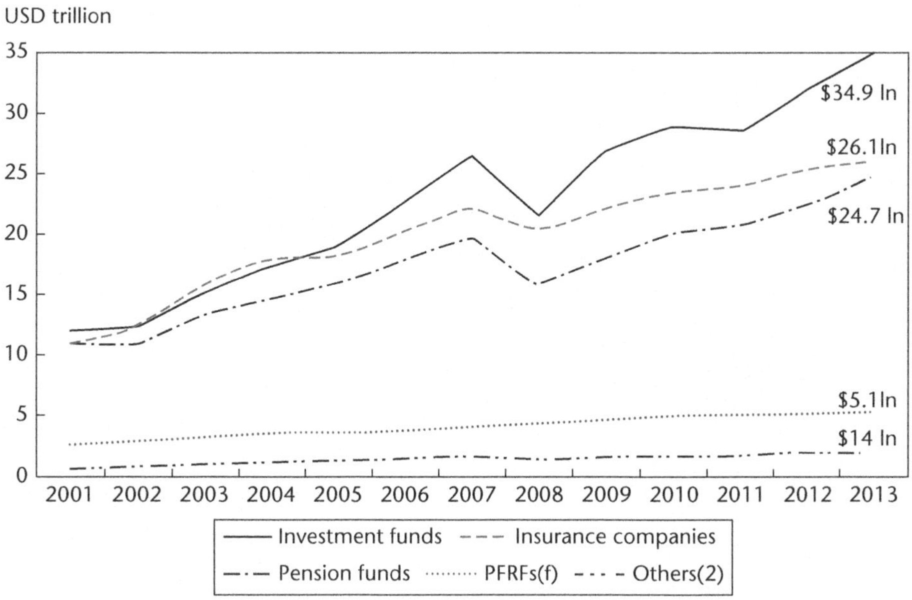

Figure 12.5. Total assets by type of institutional investor in the OECD, 2001–13
Source: OECD (2015b: 10)

Many of these investors are moving towards socially and environmentally responsible investment strategies. Also growing rapidly are Sovereign Wealth Funds (SWFs), with assets under management exceeding US$6 trillion in January 2014 (Della Croce 2014: 9). From this perspective, in the past few years, infrastructure has been more widely accepted as a distinct asset class (BlackRock 2015; Roberts et al. 2015; Russ et al. 2010). Infrastructure investments are diverse as they offer a broad universe of investments ranging from mature assets to opportunistic investment strategies with a variety of risk/return profiles (Figure 12.6).

A study by Russ et al. (2010) concludes that 'the asset class's risk/return characteristics could help pensions mitigate duration risk, due to the long-term nature of many of the sub-asset classes, as well as the return streams associated with certain types of infrastructure. The asset class's potential to mitigate the impact of inflation on portfolios has also been a driver of investor interest' (8).

However, inadequate allocation and assessment of risks of large infrastructure projects are one of the key factors holding back private finance throughout the projects' life cycles. From this perspective, a true understanding of investor's risk appetite and the proper identification of risks and returns over the life cycle of infrastructure assets are essential to design risk mitigation mechanisms and incentives to attract institutional investors. For instance, the

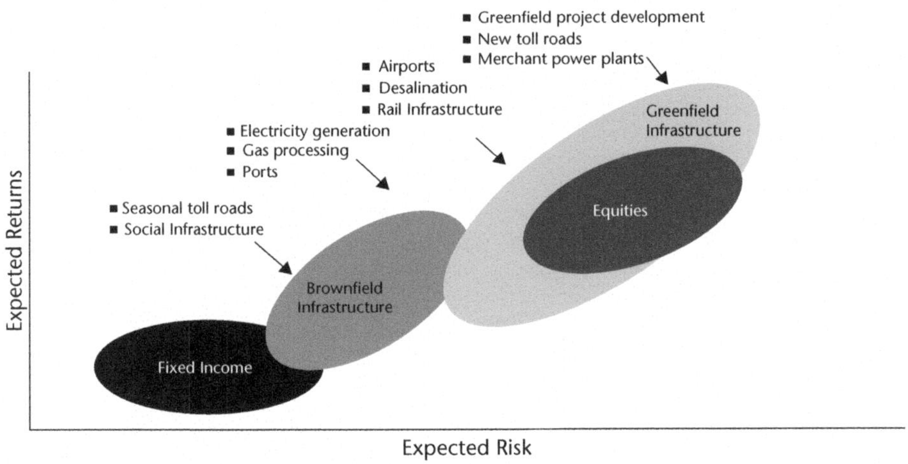

Figure 12.6. Risk/return profiles of infrastructure investments in relation to traditional asset classes
Source: Russ et al. (2010: 3)

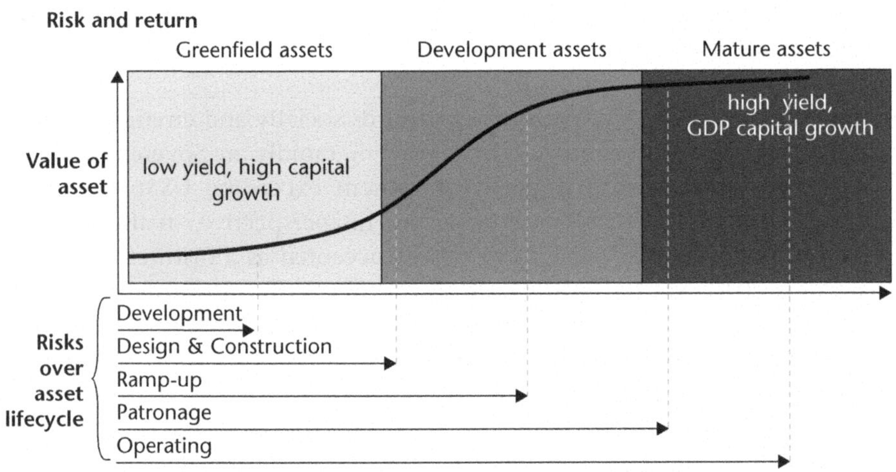

Figure 12.7. Risk return profile of infrastructure assets
Source: AMP Capital (2013: 5)

asset class can be classified by risk buckets, such as core, core plus, value-added, and opportunistic infrastructure (Figure 12.7).

Mature infrastructure (such as large brownfield assets) has core and value-added investment strategies, that is, it typically has income return and capital growth potential. For core assets, most of their returns come from cash yield generating stable cash flow streams. Investors who seek this option look for stable and income-oriented returns with comparatively low risk. Higher-risk

Unlisted infrastructure: comparison with other asset classes		
Asset class	Analogies with unlisted infrastructure	Comparative strengths of unlisted infrastructure
Real estate	Real asset class	Higher barriers to entry
	Cash-flow indexation potential	Exposure to economic cycle more limited
	Cash yield as key return component	–
Fixed income	Long-term cash flow predictability	Asset control
	Inflation hedging potential (e.g. Inflation-linked bonds)	Potential for more limited interest rate risk exposure (depending upon sector and leverage)
	–	–
Private equity	Asset control	Long-term investment horizon
	Scope for management improvements	Higher barriers to entry and exposure to market risk
	–	Potential for ongoing distributions
Listed equities	Asset ownership/control	Long-term cash flow predictability
	Capital appreciation potential	Higher barriers to entry and exposure to market risk
	–	Lower liquidity, but lower volatility potential

Figure 12.8. Unlisted infrastructure: comparison with other asset classes
Source: Roberts et al. (2015: 8)

growth-oriented infrastructure is often associated with value-added investment strategies. This option, however, has substantially more risks relative to low-risk core infrastructure assets and requires expansionary capex to unlock growth potential.

Investors who are looking for potentially higher risk-adjusted returns—or private equity type returns that are more common to greenfield infrastructure assets—tend to invest in opportunistic investment strategies to take advantage of greater total return. However, development infrastructure exposes investors to higher risk–return and capital appreciation potential. This classification is particularly useful to compare infrastructure assets with other asset classes (Figure 12.8) and different possible investment strategies.

Figure 12.8 displays for illustrative purposes the various types of infrastructure investments that usually fall under those risk categories. By identifying these risks, they can be properly managed and allocated between the public and private sectors in a way that unlocks the provision of funding necessary at different phases over the life cycle of the project. This is particularly important because infrastructure investments are capable of providing relatively stable returns, portfolio diversification, and liability management for institutional investors. As investors gain exposure to this asset class, their target returns remain optimistic given its risks. For instance, 'Preqin reports a net IRR target of 15.8 percent on average (12 percent for developed markets and 19.3 percent for emerging markets). Forty-three percent of funds fit into the target IRR band of 10.1–15 percent and 32 percent into the 15.1–20 percent band. Essential to the achievement of such high IRRs are the substantial levels of leverage in underlying infrastructure projects... Nonetheless, target gearing

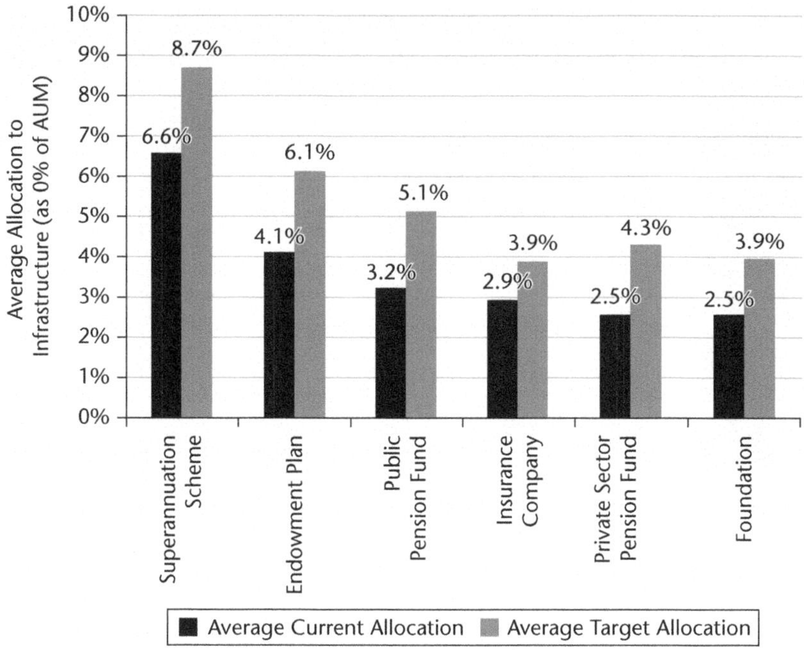

Figure 12.9. Institutional investors, infrastructure asset allocations, and targets as of December 2015

Source: Preqin (2016: 36)

levels are still predominantly in the 60–70 percent and 70–80 percent ranges' (Inderst 2010: 79).

In spite of the huge potential in infrastructure investment—such as portfolio diversification, liability matching, inflation-hedging characteristics, ability to generate consistent long-term cash flows, and potentially high risk-adjusted returns—several factors, which will be discussed later, prevent institutional investors from increasing their exposure to infrastructure assets (Mackenzie 2016). Despite the growing importance of institutional investors, the question is whether there is risk appetite for new infrastructure allocations among them. Even though investors are targeting an allocation of 3 per cent to 9 per cent of their assets under management to infrastructure assets, the Preqin (2016) survey pointed out that institutional investors have current allocations well below their targets for infrastructure projects as the challenges facing the sector have increased, including regulatory, political, and macroeconomic risks. For instance, as of 2015, public pension funds were on average targeting a 5.1 per cent allocation, but had only a 3.2 per cent actual allocation while for insurance companies the allocations were a 3.9 per cent target, but only 2.9 per cent actual. For private pension funds, their target was 4.3 per cent as against 2.5 per cent actual allocation (Figure 12.9).

In spite of the growing interest of pension funds in infrastructure investments as strategic asset allocation, 'all funds that reported a separate target allocation to infrastructure were below targets at the end of 2014' (OECD 2016: 19–20). Notwithstanding several attempts to create all forms of private finance mechanisms, instruments, and incentives to attract private investors, private infrastructure investment has remained low to meet targeted needs—especially during the development stage (Della Croce 2014; OECD 2015a, 2015b). The OECD survey of pension funds shows that they 'prefer the more stable investment profile of operational (brownfield) assets and remain opportunistic in their emerging market interest in infrastructure. Prospective risk and return are perceived as higher in new greenfield assets and may require more due diligence on the part of the investor' (OECD 2015c: 20).

Attracting investors to bridge the financing gap is no panacea. For instance, 'attempts by the UK government to use private funding to pay for infrastructure upgrades . . . show it is easier said than done. Six years after the UK's then chancellor, George Osborne, announced a flagship scheme to persuade pension funds to invest billions of pounds in hundreds of new transport and energy projects, there has been little take-up' (Primmer 2017). In this regard, Mike Weston, chief executive of the Pensions Infrastructure Platform (PIP) in the UK concluded that '[m]ost pension funds believe their obligations are best matched by investing in assets that are already delivering predictable cash flow. This means projects that have an operating track record, or at least predictable payment streams' (Primmer 2017). Moreover, a BlackRock report notes that '[t]he infrastructure story is tantalizing—trillions of dollars needed in infrastructure upgrades and a global wall of money seeking yield. Yet the investable universe is small and funds take a long time to invest. Infrastructure debt is long-duration (up to twenty-five years or more) with limited liquidity. This is fine, as long as you are in for the long haul and get paid for your patience. We typically avoid riskier greenfield projects' (BlackRock 2014: 7).

In a nutshell, even in advanced economies where there exist deep and sophisticated financial markets and regulatory, macroeconomic, and political risks are relatively low compared to other economies, institutional investors shied away from infrastructure development. For instance, 'UK pension funds investing in UK infrastructure projects has been touted by politicians for years as an obvious win–win but actual deals are almost non-existent' (Primmer 2017).

To sum up, despite attempts to develop mechanisms and incentives to attract institutional investors for greenfield projects (see, for instance, World Bank 2015), studies suggest that investors prefer to invest in the lower end of the risk spectrum such as brownfield (or established) projects or in existing infrastructure such as airports and toll roads—to avoid completion and usage risks—and not to invest in the construction phases. Instead, they prefer to invest in built assets, which generate more stable income streams, thus reducing the uncertainty of the cash flows, cost overruns, and delays associated with the early stages of an infrastructure project. This is partially due to its inherent risks and negative cash flows during the construction phase (BlackRock 2015; Bhattacharya et al. 2012: 14; Standard and Poor's 2014). That is, investors focus on investments with attractive risk-adjusted returns such as brownfield projects and already-built and operating assets, which offer predictable revenue streams and lower risks (BlackRock 2016; Bitsch et al. 2010; Primmer 2017). From this perspective, private infrastructure investment is constrained by the inherent risks associated with investing in infrastructure projects (Bitsch et al. 2010).[6]

It is interesting to note that 'around 70 percent of the current pipeline available to equity investors consists of greenfield projects, which they view as much riskier than brownfield projects that have demonstrated returns' (McKinsey 2016: 23). This, in turn, erodes investor interest and prevents the provision of long-term finance by the private sector.

Moreover, '[c]onstrained lending capacity has had a negative impact on infrastructure financing across the board, while wider interest-rate spreads have an adverse effect on the ability to finance greenfield projects' (McKinsey 2016: 21).

This is particularly important for developing economies. The support of private investments for infrastructure in developing countries through the development of local capital markets and efforts to entice private investors are often presented as a solution to the large financing gap for infrastructure (OECD 2013a). To be sure, EMDEs need to address major barriers to infrastructure development such as a weak pipeline of viable projects, high-risk perception, and EMDE infrastructure not being well defined as an asset class (Della Croce and Yermo 2013; Inderst and Stewart 2014). Moreover, public–private partnerships are often discussed 'as the solution for closing infrastructure gaps during periods of tight public funding. However, even in economies that make strong use of them, PPPs typically make up only about 5 to 10 percent of overall investment in economic infrastructure' (McKinsey 2016: 19).

The scarcity of long-term finance in developing economies is well known and well documented. A recent IMF report concluded: 'Although banks are the most important providers of credit, they do not seem to offer long-term financing. Capital markets have grown since the 1990s and can provide

[6] Note that 'Banks, the most important source of long-term financing, lend at significantly shorter maturities in developing economies relative to advanced ones. Moreover, capital markets in developing economies are less developed and are accessible only to a small proportion of total firms. Domestic institutional investors not only have a small participation in developing economies, but also the incentives they face can lead them to invest short-term. However, access to international mutual funds can help developing economies to obtain not only more funds, but also more long-term financing, as these investors hold longer maturities compared to domestic mutual funds' (Peria and Schmukler 2017: 7).

Barrier to Private Investment	Instruments and Initiatives	Rationale
Weak pipeline of viable projects	Upstream Project Preparation Window (operational)	Improve project pipeline by increasing the number of structurally sound and bankable projects
	Project Assessment Tool (proposed)	Improve the quality and completeness of project preparation
Risks are perceived to be high	Downstream Finance Window (proposed)	Mobilize private capital through de-risking critical infrastructure projects
	Asset Recycling Programme (proposed)	Encourage private sector involvement in brownfield projects, when risks are lower
EMDE infrastructure not well defined as an asset class	Emerging Markets Infrastructure Debt Index (proposed)	Position EMDE infrastructure as a recognized asset class

Figure 12.10. Barriers and World Bank Group initiatives to address them
Source: GIF (2016: 5)

financing at fairly long terms. But few firms use these markets. Only some institutional investors provide funding at long-term maturities. Governments might help to expand long-term financing, although with limited policy tools' (Peria and Schmukler 2017: 2).

For EMDEs there are additional challenges to bridge the gap between demand and supply of funds through financial markets. For instance, the Global Infrastructure Facility (2016) identified critical barriers to private investment (illustrated in Figure 12.10), including weak pipeline of viable projects; high risks and high perception of risks; significant regulatory, legal, political, economic, and financial risks; existence of information asymmetries preventing the supply of finance; and infrastructure not well defined as an asset class, which contributes to persistent information asymmetries and prevents the supply of finance (GIF 2016: 15).

The same problems faced by advanced economies are also existent in EMDEs, that is, 'private investors are often unwilling or unable to take project development risk for infrastructure in EMDEs. They are, however, still interested in the returns that the investments can provide once the projects are operational and demand is proven' (GIF 2016: 27). From the investors' standpoint, infrastructure development assets' risk characteristics should be compared to that of private equity. Given the uncertainty and high risks associated with those projects, the economic viability of the project being financed would make the returns needed to attract private investors too high.

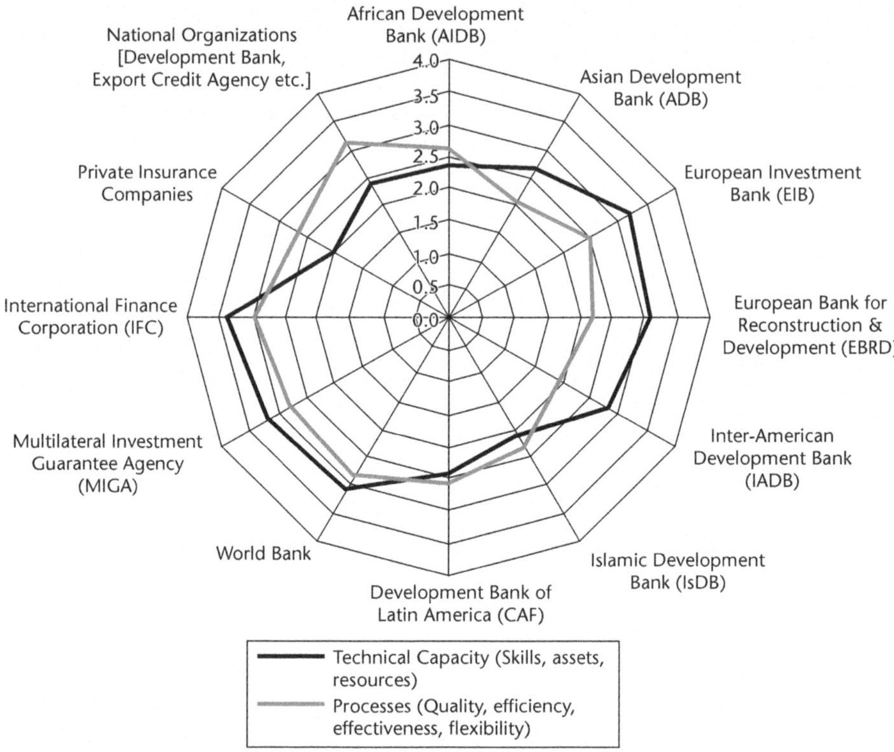

Figure 12.11. Assessment of institutions that provide risk mitigation instruments
Source: World Economic Forum (2016: 34)

In this regard, the combination of 'the regulatory, macroeconomic, and political risks present in many EMDE countries result in a hurdle rate of return that is too high, resulting in limited bankable projects for private investment additionally. Private lenders may be unwilling to lend to projects with high levels of risk unless sufficient credit enhancements or de-risking mechanisms are in place' (GIF 2016: 15), Both national development banks and multilateral organizations are well placed to strategically provide de-risking mechanisms to foster investment by the private sector. However, a recent assessment of institutions that provide risk mitigation instruments show that national development institutions and multilateral organizations can enhance their de-risking instruments (Figure 12.11)—including technical capacity and processes—to better fit investors' needs.

Even though different complementary mechanisms to finance infrastructure deals aim to entice institutional investors to finance infrastructure projects (see, for instance, OECD 2013b; World Bank 2015), Ehlers (2014) notes that 'development banks bring vast expertise and in many cases insurance against political risks to the table and their loan commitments are in some cases a pre-condition for private lenders to make their funding available. In some emerging markets, development banks also serve a key role as the credible auditor of project' (16). In fact, 'Many OECD countries have DFIs to promote the expansion of businesses abroad' (BDC 2009: 62).

It becomes important to 'incentivize institutional investors to work with development banks at earlier stages of the preparation of bankable projects' (Arezki et al. 2016: 33) and 'undertake more comprehensive planning of infrastructure investments and how each individual project may fit into a broader infrastructure network development plan' (Arezki et al. 2016: 36).

12.4 Looking Ahead: Enhancing the Role of Development Banks and Government Support to Foster Investments in Long-Term Assets

Even though much of the conventional discussion about the role of development banks relies on market failures to provide a theoretical basis for their existence, there is little discussion about how development banks operate, their different intervention models, products, and markets targeted, and regulatory issues (Griffith-Jones et al. 2017).

One of the distinguished features of DBs is that their lending products are mainly concentrated in 'long-term loans (90%) followed by working capital loans (85%), whereas syndicated loans [have] consisted of 52% of all DBs, and unsecured loans 25%' (Luna-Martinez and Vicente 2012: 15). Furthermore, and not surprisingly, most loans (84 per cent) offered by DBs have maturity dates greater than five years (Luna-Martinez and Vicente 2012: 16). Comparisons across country groupings show that this is in sharp contrast with the maturity structure of traditional long-term bank loans—that is, over five years' maturity. It averages only 22.5 per cent in upper-middle-income countries and 12 per cent in lower-middle- and low-income countries (Figure 12.12). Though the figures are substantially higher in high-income countries (32.8 per cent of total bank loans) relative to upper-middle-income countries (22.5 per cent), it is still substantially lower than the share of development bank loans (84 per cent) over five years' maturity (Luna-Martinez and Vicente 2012: 16).

It is worth noting that 'DBs are generally mandated to *provide credit at terms that render industrial and infrastructure investment viable*' (Chandrasekhar 2016: 23, emphasis added). Though development banks' operating policies have raised criticisms, the World Bank report notes that 'credit at subsidized interest rates is a practice adopted by 50% of DBs covered in the survey. In this category, 66% of DBs fund these subsidies using transfers from their respective governments' (Luna-Martinez and Vicente 2012: 16). In an environment in which investment returns have declined, credit provisions below market

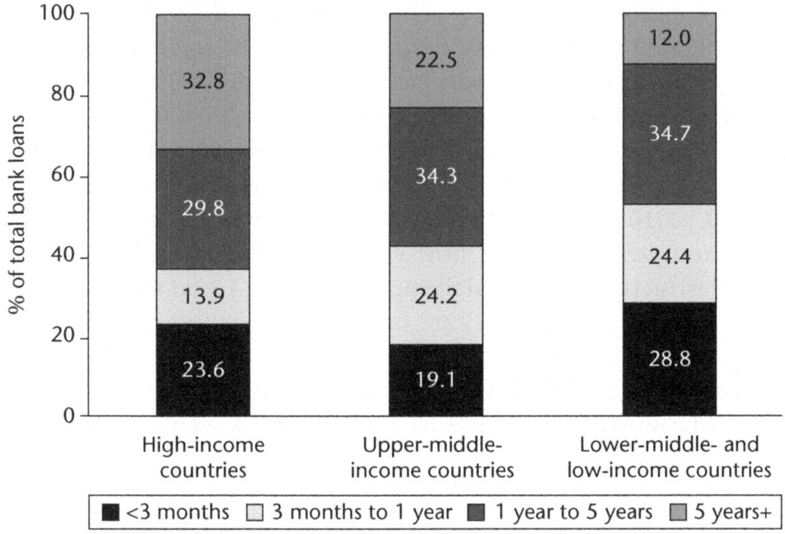

Figure 12.12. Maturity structure of bank loans by country income group, 2000–13
Source: World Bank (2015: 30)

interest rates have an additional impact to stimulate new investments. 'Accordingly, a subsidy or subvention of some kind would be needed to keep interest rates reasonable' (Chandrasekhar 2016: 23). Finally, '73% of all DBs offer loan guarantee products to partially offset the losses faced by a private financial intermediary when a customer defaults' (Luna-Martinez and Vicente 2012: 16).

In addition to long-term loans, developments banks also provide credit for working capital purposes and financing long-term investment, including in the form of equity.[7] Among the best practices used by DBs, Chandrasekhar notes that '[t]o safeguard their investments, they closely monitor the activities of the firms they lend to, often nominating directors on the boards of companies. This allows for corrective action as soon as any deficiencies are detected' (2016: 23).

Among the funding features of DBs, 40 per cent answered that they receive direct budget transfers from the government and 64 per cent reported that the government guarantees their debt; this guarantee is implicitly equivalent to DBs' obligations (guaranteed by the government) having the status of Treasury securities. 'It should be noted that receiving direct transfers from the government does not necessarily mean dependence on government

[7] It has already been suggested that BDs have an additional exposure to companies by investing in equity in firms to which they have extended credit (see, for instance, Castro 2011 for a discussion on risks faced by DBs).

funds. Sometimes, DBs—such as KfW in Germany—receive transfers from the government to fund interest rate subsidies to a particular type of borrower' (Luna-Martinez and Vicente 2012: 10–11). So, not only do DBs offer credit at subsidized—below-market—rates using transfers from their respective governments to make long-term investment viable, but they also rely on direct budget transfers from their governments to expand their balance sheets.

In spite of initiatives to encourage the provision of long-term funds by private finance, development banks continue to play an important role providing long-term funding in traditional sectors and activities in developing and advanced economies. Moreover, precautionary measures imposed on traditional banks such as new capital and liquidity rules under Basel III requirements translate into regulatory and balance sheet constraints, which contribute to reducing the provision of funds by traditional banks (Castro 2017; FSB 2013; Roberts et al. 2015).

The operation of development banks is linked together with uncertainties associated with financing long-lived and expensive capital projects such as infrastructure investments and providing funding for innovative enterprises (Hermann 2010a, 2010b). Risks associated with such initiatives are usually assumed by government policies through development institutions both directly and indirectly (Luna-Martinez and Vicente 2012).

Though there is a growing consensus towards infrastructure investment, in particular by development banks, the focus on infrastructure has a significant impact on the size of the DBs' balance sheet. For instance, 'National development banks in China, Germany, Brazil, India and South Africa all either have strong policies to prioritize infrastructure, significant sustainable infrastructure policies, or both. Significantly, these banks comprise a major portion of the total amount of assets held by NDBs . . . [the top] ten banks have upwards of $2.8 trillion in assets, or roughly three-fifths of all NDB assets in the world economy' (Studart et al. 2016: 22).

Infrastructure projects are complex due to their nature: 'in many economies, but particularly in developing economies, resources to do project planning and elaboration are scarce' (Studart et al. 2016: 25). The literature suggests that successful DBs promoting infrastructure investment are also responsible for taking advantage of their experience in monitoring risks and financing infrastructure projects, which is usually accompanied by high standards when it comes to monitoring environmental risks and classifying their projects according to internationally accepted methodologies (Studart et al. 2016: 25; Ehlers 2014; OECD 2015a).

A study by McKinsey (2013b) suggests that '[p]oorly designed and planned projects lead to significantly higher financing costs and too often even to the inability to mobilize private-sector financing and risk allocation completely. In the absence of private financing and risk sharing, budget-financed public-procurement structures continue to undermanage risk throughout the entire life cycle of the project, leading to even higher rates of project failure and poor results' (McKinsey 2013b: 12). In this regard, a recent initiative—'Sustainable Infrastructure Working Group'—studies the matter and shares best practices (IDFC 2014). 'Not surprisingly, those NDBs who have most success in promoting infrastructure projects seem also to be those that get most involved in identifying and supporting project elaboration. This is the case of the German development bank, KfW, and China Development Bank. In the latter case, the involvement is quite significant, as indicated by Yang (2016: 23)' (Studart et al. 2016: 25). That is, 'There is growing recognition globally that development banks can play an important role in facilitating the preparation and financing of infrastructure projects by private long-term investors' (Arezki et al. 2016: 24). Development banks need to continue to work hand-in-hand with the private sector to contribute with project planning and elaboration and to address poor risk assessment and risk allocation—in particular during the concept and design phase of infrastructure projects.

It is worth highlighting a recent initiative Task Force on Development Banks and Sustainable Development set up 'to examine the extent to which development banks are becoming catalysts for achieving a climate friendly and more socially inclusive world economy' (IDFC 2014). 'Through the IDFC over 100 banks have developed a common criteria for measuring and monitoring green finance, and have made a commitment to provide significant amounts of green finance moving forward' (Studart et al. 2016: 39). In this regard, several BDs are financing 'green' businesses in an attempt to deal with issues related to climate change and energy efficiency (Studart et al. 2016). In the UK, a new 'Green Bank' was established in 2012 to finance environmental projects. However, '[o]n 3 March 2016 the UK Government launched the process to move the Green Investment Bank into the private sector' (Green Investment Bank 2016). They have also fostered investments in activities such as clean energy, biotechnology, and environmental projects. However, one of the challenges DBs have faced throughout their history is the latent pressure to let private financial institutions overtake their role. For instance, 'liberalization led to a decline in development banking and the demise of the major DFIs in India' (Chandrasekhar 2016: 26).

A major enhancement of policy coordination between central banks and development institutions is to encourage monetary authorities to adapt their asset purchase policy to fund development banks. This could be accomplished in the same way that major central banks introduced quantitative easing policies, but instead of targeting sovereign bonds, the monetary authority would buy debt issued by development banks, especially those financing infrastructure and other corporate activities. That is, as I have argued elsewhere (Rezende 2015), the central bank should act as the liquidity provider using the discount window as the main tool to satisfy the liquidity needs of both depository and non-depository institutions, and provide the funding necessary to allow development banks to finance development. This would effectively eliminate funding constraints on the development banks' balance sheet. This proposal has also been embraced by one of the world's most powerful bond managers, which advocated that '[t]he European Central Bank should retool its asset purchase program to fund a wave of new infrastructure spending across the continent' (Foley and Jones 2016). This means 'the central bank has the opportunity to unleash hundreds of billions of dollars in new economic activity by shifting more of its purchases towards bonds issued by the various national and supranational organizations, such as the European Investment Bank, that fund infrastructure and provide trade finance' (Foley and Jones 2016).

This proposal is not new. Hyman Minsky favoured the use of the discount window as a secure source of funds for financial institutions. As he put it, 'Rediscounting was not a lender-of-last-resort activity reserved for a crisis, it was the mechanism by which part of the normal reserve base of banks was brought into being... The use of the discount window as a normal source of financing by member banks legitimated the regulation, supervision, and examination of member banks by the Federal Reserve' (Minsky 1994: 11–12).

To sum up, in spite of deepening capital markets and the greater participation of institutional investors, private investment in infrastructure has not worked in the way it was expected, which has contributed to a growing mismatch between investment expenditures (and available financing) and investment needs. Thus, the question then becomes how to reconcile the growing mismatch between investment expenditures (and available financing) and investment needs.

12.5 Enhancing Government Support to Fund Infrastructure Investments

In EMDEs, public funding of infrastructure accounts for about 70 per cent of total infrastructure expenditure (Inderst 2016: 9). Moreover, 'investor appetite for EMDE infrastructure projects has declined significantly since the 2008 financial crisis. This trend can be attributed, in part, to the tightening of financial regulations. More importantly, the unconducive investment environments in many EMDEs leads investors to associate infrastructure projects in EMDEs with higher credit risk' (GIF 2016: 6). This effect is compounded by the behaviour of private investors, who typically avoid exposure to early stages of infrastructure assets—such as during development and construction phases

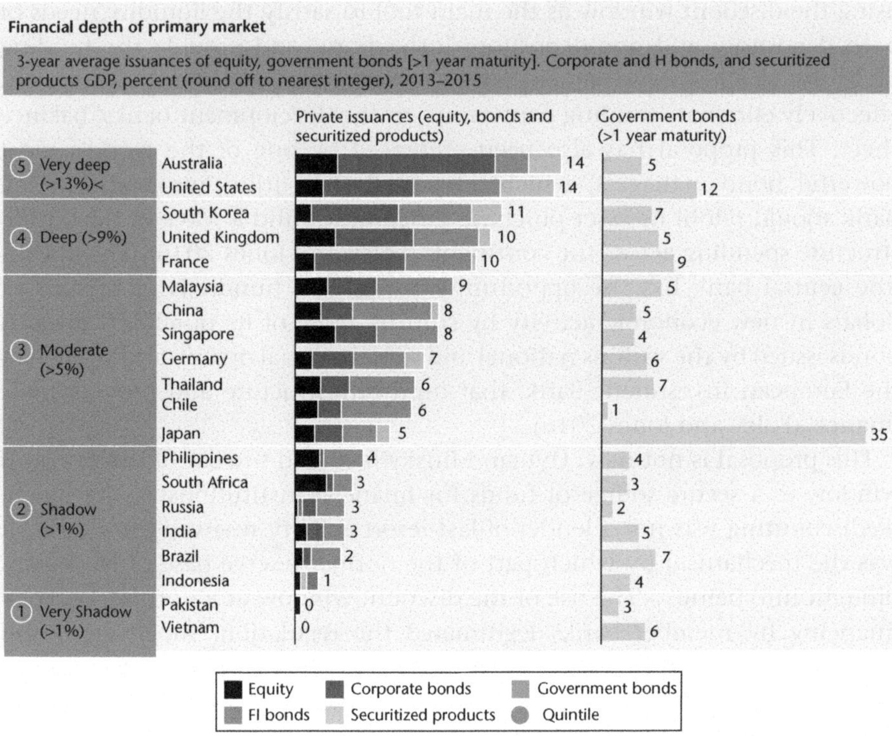

Figure 12.13. Financial depth of primary market
Source: McKinsey (2017: 24)

when the risk exposure is higher (OECD 2015b). As discussed earlier, this is part due to the following factors: high project costs; low-cost recovery; limited public financing; barriers to private investment. As noted earlier, the key factors in the infrastructure financing gap in EMDEs are: projects poorly executed and not well maintained; lack of adequate project planning; weak pipeline of viable projects; high political and economic risks; legal barriers and lack of protection on investments (OECD 2015b: 11–12). For EMDEs, in particular, capital market funding (Figure 12.13) to close the financing gap is limited and issuers either find it difficult or cannot raise affordable capital at scale (World Bank 2004).

The debate over the appropriate level of government spending has sparked considerable controversy—including pressures to promote fiscal consolidation and to reduce public debt—partially due to the conventional narrative about public sector financing capacity. However, there has been a recent shift away from austerity in favour of public investment. For example, a recent IMF report recommends a substantial increase in public infrastructure investment (IMF 2014). As Larry Summers (2014) stated: 'Public infrastructure investments can pay for themselves.' An IMF (2014) study 'finds that increased public infrastructure investment raises output in the short term by boosting demand and in the long term by raising the economy's productive capacity'. It also notes that '[p]ublic capital and infrastructure capital are closely related: a significant component of the public capital stock in most countries consists of infrastructure, and the public sector was and continues to be its main provider' (IMF 2014: 76).

From this perspective, public investment shocks have 'a significant and long-lasting effect on output. They also typically reduce the debt-to-GDP ratio... The level of private investment rises in tandem with GDP' (83). That is, '[t]he effects of public investment on output and debt tend to be stronger when there is economic slack, when public investment efficiency is high, and when public investment is debt financed' (84). It notes that '[p]ublic investment booms in emerging market and developing economies are associated with higher output' (85). Moreover, there is a growing consensus to increase public financing and close the investment gap; this is because 'debt-financed projects could have large output effects without increasing the debt-to-GDP ratio if clearly identified infrastructure needs are met through efficient investment' (75).

Another IMF report concluded that 'increased public investment raises output, both in the short term and in the long term, crowds in private investment, and reduces unemployment. Several factors shape the macroeconomic effects of public investment. When there is economic slack and monetary accommodation, demand effects are stronger, and the public-debt-to-GDP ratio may actually decline. Public investment is also more effective in boosting output in countries with higher public investment efficiency and when it is financed by issuing debt' (Abiad et al. 2015: 2). In a nutshell, public investment is both growth- and productivity-enhancing.

China seems to be following this playbook (Figure 12.14), as it invests more in infrastructure than the other five largest G-20 nations put together (Mohsin 2016). This increase in the share of public investment relative to their economies is particularly important to deal with declining private investment.

In the past, a high share of infrastructure was financed by public budgets. However, the shift towards increasing public investment requires monetary sovereignty. The notion that nations with monetary sovereignty have more fiscal space to promote development—such as increasing public investment—is not new. That is, sovereign countries—those that issue their own currency and adopt flexible exchange rates—have more fiscal space than non-sovereign countries—such as countries that have adopted the euro—to increase public investment. The then Treasury Secretary Jacob J. Lew speaking at the G-20 summit in Hangzhou in 2016 declared that 'the G-20 is no longer debating growth versus austerity, but rather how to best employ fiscal policy to support our economies' (Lew 2016).

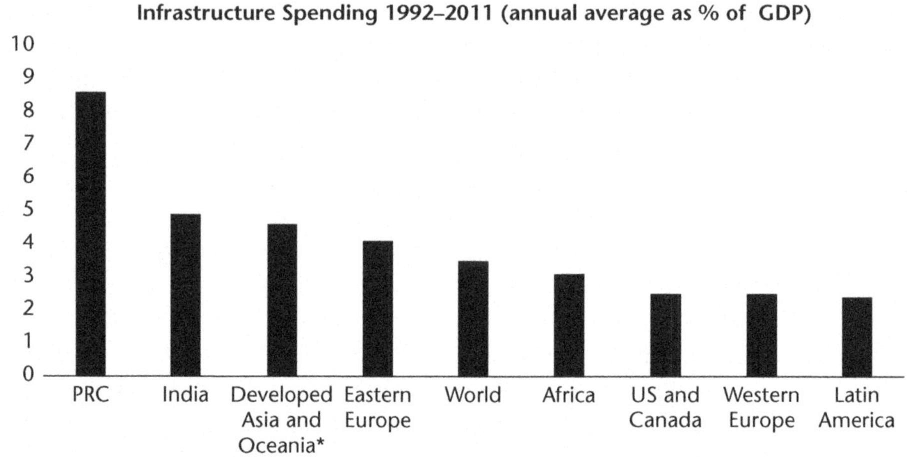

Figure 12.14. Infrastructure spending, percentage of GDP, 1992–2011
Source: Inderst (2016)

12.6 Concluding Remarks

There is a renewed interest in development banks and the growing commitment to use all policy tools to generate sustainable full employment, including coordination between fiscal, monetary, and development policies to promote capital development and stability. Both developed and developing economies need to effectively make the transition to a development strategy based on domestic demand and reduce the dependence policies designed to attract external capital and foreign demand.

In spite of the introduction of mechanisms to attract institutional investors to engage in development finance, results fell short of expectations. Yet, most countries are still struggling to shift their development strategy to foster domestic demand growth. That is, federal public investment is unusually low given countries' infrastructure bottlenecks and investment needs.

The adequate provision of long-term funds will require policy coordination from governments, national, and multilateral development banks, to mobilize private sector banks and institutional investors to unlock their finance potential. In this regard, it is imperative to rethink and reprioritize global and national development agendas in which development banks play a strategic role not only in providing long-term finance but also helping to identify major barriers to investment. DBs can foster capacity-building activities to help deal with barriers to infrastructure development, which contribute to persistent information asymmetries and prevent the supply of finance, particularly in EMDEs.

Meeting the infrastructure challenge goes beyond the lack of funding. The expectation that institutional investors' interest in infrastructure assets would increase has been disappointed by private investors' lack of interest in development infrastructure assets. Bridging the investment gap requires the involvement of DBs and a broad government policy to support economic growth.

In this regard, there is ample policy space to promote private and public infrastructure investment, in which public banks—and in particular national development banks—and private domestic capital markets should play a major and strategic role financing the supply side of this programme. Moreover, macroeconomic support is essential for development banks to be successful. This means that development banks cannot be seen in isolation; instead policy coordination is required so countries can shift their policies to mobilize domestic resources and adopt an investment-oriented growth strategy by increasing government-sponsored infrastructure investment projects. Though the provision of long-term finance for longer-term assets and projects contributes to economic development, financial leverage is a double-edged sword, that is, rising financial leverage and a declining 'cushion' of safety lead to increasing financial fragility. Financial fragility arises as a consequence of the way that corporate funding is structured and financed. In this regard, finance and financial fragility are directly linked. While providing long-term finance, DBs also contribute to mitigating financial fragility by providing funds in the domestic currency and segmenting the financial system, thus serving one of the masters—which requires leverage and taking risks—financing capital development and innovation. This segmentation of the risky activities imparts greater stability to the financial system.

It is noteworthy that despite much controversy, public finance is still the primary source of funding. More broadly, there is a growing consensus towards the use of fiscal policy to support growth and to increase public financing to close the investment gap. In the aftermath of the global financial crisis, unconventional monetary policy—including ZIRP, NIRP, QE—and fiscal austerity failed to support investment growth: that is, even though major central banks moved interest rates into negative territory, this policy failed to reach its goals, such as sparking investment.

Finally, rather than an obsessive concern over budget deficits, the narrative has to centre around the idea of monetary sovereignty. That is, sovereign nations cannot be forced by markets to default on their domestic debt. It should use their fiscal powers of the federal government to increase federal government investment in infrastructure, thus contributing to raising productivity and lowering private sector costs through investment in key areas such as infrastructure, health and education, and research and development.

References

Abiad, A., D. Furceri, and P. Topalova. 2015. 'The Macroeconomic Effects of Public Investment: Evidence from Advanced Economies'. IMF Working Paper WP/15/95, May. Washington, DC: IMF.

AMP Capital. 2013. *Understanding Infrastructure*. Available at <https://bit.ly/2Id5bek>, accessed January 2017.

Arezki, R., P. Bolton, S. Peters, F. Samama, and J. Stiglitz. 2016. 'From Global Savings Glut to Financing Infrastructure: The Advent of Investment Platforms'. IMF Working Paper WP/16/18. Washington, DC: IMF.

BDC. 2009. *International Benchmark Study on Development Institutions*. BDC Strategy & Planning and GY Consulting.

Bhattacharya, A., J. Oppenheim, and N. Stern. 2015. 'Driving Sustainable Development through Better Infrastructure: Key Elements of a Transformation Program'. Brookings Institution Global Working Paper, No. 80, 10 July.

Bhattacharya, A., M. Romani, and N. Stern. 2012. *Infrastructure for Development: Meeting the Challenge*. London: London School of Economics and the G-24.

Bielenberg, A., M. Kerlin, J. Oppenheim, and M. Roberts. 2016. 'Financing Change: How to Mobilize Private Sector Financing for Sustainable Infrastructure'. McKinsey Report.

Bitsch, F., A. Buchner, and C. Kaserer. 2010. *Risk, Return and Cash Flow Characteristics of Infrastructure Fund Investments*. EIB Papers 15: 106–36. Luxembourg: European Investment Bank.

BlackRock. 2014. 'Dealing with Divergence: 2015 Investment Outlook'. Available at <www.blackrock.com/corporate/en-us/literature/whitepaper/bii-2015-investment-outlook-us.pdf>, accessed 27 April 2018.

BlackRock. 2015. 'Infrastructure Rising: An Asset Class Takes Shape'. April. Available at <https://www.laforum.co.uk/download-manager/download-white-paper/220/>, accessed 27 April 2018.

BlackRock. 2016. 'The New Prominence of Private Assets Targeting Outcomes in Today's Markets'. June. Available at <https://www.blackrock.com/co/literature/whitepaper/new-prominence-of-private-assets-en-lai.pdf>, accessed 27 April 2018.

Brunnermeier, M. K. and M. Oehmke. 2013. 'The Maturity Rat Race', *Journal of Finance* 68(2): 483–521.

Burlamaqui, L. and R. Kattel. 2014. 'Development Theory: Convergence, Catch-Up or Leapfrogging? A Schumpeter–Minsky–Kregel Approach', in D. Papadimitriou (ed.), Contributions to Economic Theory, Policy, Development and Finance: Essays in Honor of Jan A. Kregel, 175–95. London: Palgrave Macmillan.

Burlamaqui, Leonardo and J. Kregel. 2005. 'Innovation, Competition and Financial Vulnerability in Economic Development', *Brazilian Journal of Political Economy* 25(2): 5–22.

Calderon, C. and L. Serven. 2014. 'Infrastructure, Growth, and Inequality: An Overview'. Policy Research Working Paper No. 7034. Washington, DC: World Bank Group.

Castro, L. B. 2011. 'Gestão de riscos e regulação em bancos de desenvolvimento', *Revista do BNDES* 36: 89–134.

Castro, L. B. 2017. 'Financial Regulation and Risk Management in Development Banks'. Available at <http://policydialogue.org/files/events/Future_of_National_Development_Banks-_Presentation_-_Financial_Regulation.pdf>, accessed 7 May 2018.

Chandrasekhar, C. P. 2016. 'National Development Banks in a Comparative Perspective', in A. Calcagno, S. Dullien, A. Márquez-Velázquez, N. Maystre, and J. Priewe (eds), *Rethinking Development Strategies after the Financial Crisis, Volume II: Country Studies and International Comparisons*, 21–30. New York and Geneva: United Nations.

Della Croce, R. 2014. *Are Institutional Investors the Answer for Long-Term Development Financing?* Development Cooperation Report 2014, Directorate for Financial and Enterprise Affairs, OECD. See also <www.oecd.org/finance/lti>.

Della Croce, R. and J. Yermo. 2013. 'Institutional Investors and Infrastructure Financing'. OECD Working Papers on Finance, Insurance, and Private Pensions, No. 36. OECD Publishing.

Ehlers, T. 2014. 'Understanding the Challenges for Infrastructure Finance'. BIS Working Papers No. 454, August. Bank for International Settlements.

Ferraz, J. C., A. Além, and R. Madeira. 2016. *Development Banks Contribution to Long Term Financing*. Rio de Janeiro: BNDES.

Fischer, S. 2003. 'The Importance of Financial Markets in Economic Growth'. Lecture presented at International Derivatives and Financial Market Conference of the Brazilian Mercantile and Futures Exchange Conference, Brazil.

Foley, S. and C. Jones. 2016. 'Quantitative Easing Should Fund Infrastructure, Says BlackRock'. *Financial Times*, 7 December.

FSB (Financial Stability Board). 2013. *Financial Regulatory Factors Affecting the Availability of Long-Term Investment Finance*. Report to G-20 Finance Ministers and Central Bank Governors, Basel.

G-20. 2013. 'Long-Term Investment Financing for Growth and Development'. February. Available at <https://bit.ly/2HMJ3DP>, accessed 7 May 2018.

GIF (Global Infrastructure Facility). 2016. *Making Infrastructure Rewarding*. Global Infrastructure Facility Report.

Green Investment Bank. 2016. Available at <http://greeninvestmentgroup.com/about-us/privatisation-process/>, accessed 7 May 2018.

Griffith-Jones, S., J. A. Ocampo, F. Rezende, A. Schclarek, and M. Brei. 2017. *Future of Development Banks*. Framework paper BNDES/CAF/IPD project. Manuscript.

Hermann, J. 2010a. 'Development Banks in the Financial-Liberalization Era: The Case of BNDES in Brazil', *CEPAL Review* 100: 189–203.

Hermann, J. 2010b. 'O papel dos bancos públicos'. Textos para discussão, CEPAL-IPEA 15. Brasília, DF: CEPAL.

IMF (International Monetary Fund). 2014. 'Legacies, Clouds, Uncertainties'. World Economic Outlook (WEO), October. Washington, DC: IMF.

IMF. 2015. 'Uneven Growth: Short- and Long-Term Factors'. World Economic Outlook (WEO), April. Washington, DC: IMF.

Inderst, G. 2010. 'Infrastructure as an Asset Class'. EIB Papers, 15(1). European Investment Bank.

Inderst, G. 2016. *Infrastructure Investment, Private Finance, and Institutional Investors: Asia from a Global Perspective.* ADBI Working Paper No. 555. Tokyo: Asian Development

Bank Institute. Available at <https://www.adb.org/sites/default/files/publication/179166/adbi-wp555.pdf>, accessed 27 April 2018.

Inderst, G. and F. Stewart. 2014. *Institutional Investment in Infrastructure in Developing Countries. Introduction to Potential Models*. Policy Research Working Paper No. 6780. Washington, DC: World Bank.

International Development Finance Club Sustainable Infrastructure (IDFC). 2014. 'Financing Sustainable Infrastructure'. Working Group, October 2014.

Kregel, J. A. 1993. *Financial Fragility and the Structure of Financial Markets*. Working Paper No. 157. Dipartimento Scienze Economiche, University of Bologna.

Kregel, J. A. 1998. *The Past and Future of Banks*. Roma: Ente Einaudi.

Kregel, J. A. 2015. *Minsky's Irreconcilable Masters Governing Financial Regulation and Financial Structure*. The Multidisciplinary Institute for Development and Strategy (MINDS) Discussion Paper No. 4.

Lazonick, W. and M. O'Sullivan. 2000. 'Maximising Shareholder Value: A New Ideology for Corporate Governance', *Economy and Society* 29(1): 13–35.

Levy Institute (Levy Economics Institute of Bard College). 2011. *Minsky on the Reregulation and Restructuring of the Financial System. Will Dodd-Frank Prevent 'It' from Happening Again?* Research Project Report, April. Annandale-on-Hudson, NY: Levy Economics Institute of Bard College.

Lew, J. J. 2016. 'From Pittsburgh to Hangzhou: The Past, Present, and Future of the G-20'. Remarks at the Brookings Institution.

Lucas, R. 1988. 'On the Mechanics of Economic Development', *Journal of Monetary Economics* 22: 3–42.

Luna-Martinez, J. de and C. Vicente. 2012. *Global Survey of Development Banks*. World Bank Policy Research Working Paper No. 5969. Washington, DC: World Bank.

Lund, S., T. Daruvala, R. Dobbs, P. Härle, J. Kwek, and R. Falcón. 2013. *Financial Globalization: Retreat or Reset?* McKinsey Global Institute Report, March.

Mackenzie, H. 2016. 'Myth vs. Reality in the Infrastructure Market'. Deutsche Asset Management, Sponsor Interview, April.

Mazzucato, M. and L. Randall Wray. 2015. *Financing the Capital Development of the Economy: A Keynes-Schumpeter-Minsky Synthesis (May 7, 2015)*. Levy Economics Institute of Bard College Working Paper No. 837.

McKinsey Global Institute. 2013a. 'Infrastructure Productivity. How to Save $1 Trillion a Year'. January.

McKinsey Global Institute. 2013b. *A Risk-Management Approach to a Successful Infrastructure Project. Initiation, Financing, and Execution*. McKinsey Working Papers on Risk, No. 52.

McKinsey Global Institute. 2016. *Bridging Global Infrastructure Gaps*. June. Available at <www.mckinsey.com/industries/capital-projects-and-infrastructure/our-insights/bridging-global-infrastructure-gaps>, accessed October 2016.

McKinsey Global Institute. 2017. *Deepening Capital Markets in Emerging Economies*. Banking & Finance Report.

Minsky, H. P. 1986. *Stabilizing an Unstable Economy*. New Haven: Yale University Press.

Minsky, H. P. 1994. 'Financial Instability and the Decline(?) of Banking: Public Policy Implications,' in Federal Reserve Bank of Chicago (ed.), *Proceedings of a Conference on Bank Structure and Competition*, 55–68. Chicago: Federal Reserve Bank of Chicago.

Mohsin, S. 2016. 'China Growth Playbook on Display to G-20 in City Transformed'. *Bloomberg,* 1 September. Available at <www.bloomberg.com/news/articles/2016-09-01/china-s-growth-playbook-on-display-to-g-20-in-city-transformed?utm_content=buffer690cc&utm_medium=social&utm_source=twitter.com&utm_campaign=buffer>, accessed 27 April 2018.

OECD (Organization for Economic Cooperation and Development). 2013a. *G20-OECD High-Level Principles of Long-Term Investment Financing by Institutional Investors.* Paris: OECD.

OECD. 2013b. *The Role of Banks, Equity Markets and Institutional Investors in Long-Term Financing for Growth and Development.* Report for G-20 Leaders, February. Available at <www.oecd.org/finance/private-pensions/G20reportLTFinancingForGrowthRussianPresidency2013.pdf>, accessed 27 April 2018.

OECD. 2015a. 'Infrastructure Financing Instruments and Incentives'.

OECD. 2015b. 'Risk and Return Characteristics of Infrastructure Investment in Low Income Countries'.

OECD. 2015c. *Annual Survey of Large Pension Funds and Public Pension Reserve Funds.* Report on Pension Funds' Long-Term Investments. Available at <www.oecd.org/daf/fin/private-pensions/2015-Large-Pension-Funds-Survey.pdf>, accessed 27 April 2018.

OECD. 2015d. 'Fostering Investment in Infrastructure: Lessons Learned from OECD Investment Policy Reviews'. OECD, January. Available at <www.oecd.org/daf/inv/investment-policy/Fostering-Investment-in-Infrastructure.pdf>, accessed 27 April 2018.

OECD. 2016. *Annual Survey of Large Pension Funds and Public Pension Reserve Funds: Report on Pension Funds' Long-Term Investments.*

Ollivaud, P. and D. Turner. 2014. *The Effect of the Global Financial Crisis on OECD Potential Output.* OECD Economics Department Working Paper No. 1166. OECD Publishing.

Peria, M. S. M. and S. L. Schmukler. 2017. 'Understanding the Use of Long-Term Finance in Developing Economies'. IMF Working Paper 17/96. International Monetary Fund.

Preqin. 2016. *Preqin Investor Outlook: Alternative Assets, H1 2016.* Available at <www.preqin.com/docs/reports/Preqin-Investor-Outlook-Alternative-Assets-H1-2016.pdf>, accessed 27 April 2018.

Primmer, G. 2017. 'UK Infrastructure Projects Struggle to Attract Pension Funds'. *Financial Times,* April.

Rezende, F. 2015. 'Why Does Brazil's Banking Sector Need Public Banks? What Should BNDES Do?' *PSL Quarterly Review* 68(274): 239–75.

Roberts, M., J. Patel, and G. Minella. 2015. *Why Invest in Infrastructure?* Deutsche Asset & Wealth Management Research Report.

Russ, D., Y. Thambiah, and N. Foscari. 2010. 'Can Infrastructure Investing Enhance Portfolio Efficiency?' White Paper, Credit Suisse Asset Management.

Samama, F., J. Stiglitz, P. Bolton, R. Arezki, and S. Peters. 2016. *From Global Savings Glut to Financing Infrastructure: The Advent of Investment Platforms.* IMF Working Paper No. 16/18. Washington, DC: IMF. Available at <www.imf.org/external/pubs/ft/wp/2016/wp1618.pdf>, accessed 27 April 2018.

Schmidt-Traub, G. 2015. *Investment Needs to Achieve the Sustainable Development Goals: Understanding the Billions and Trillions*. Sustainable Development Solutions Network Working Paper No. 2. Available at <unsdsn.org/wp-content/uploads/2015/09/151112-SDG-Financing-Needs.pdf>, accessed 27 June 2016.

Standard & Poor's. 2014. 'Global Infrastructure: How to Fill A $500 Billion Hole'.

Stiglitz, J. and A. Weiss. 1981. 'Credit Rationing in Markets with Imperfect Information', *The American Economic Review* 71(3): 393–410.

Studart, R., K. P. Gallagher, and A. Bhattacharya. 2016. *Infrastructure for Sustainable Development: The Role of National Development Banks*. Unpublished manuscript.

Summers, L. 2014. 'Why Public Investment Really Is a Free Lunch'. *Financial Times*, October.

Torres Filho, E. and R. Zeidan (2016). 'The Life-Cycle of National Development Banks: The Experience of Brazil's BNDES', *Quarterly Review of Economics and Finance* 62: 97–104.

UNSDSN. 2015. 'Investment Needs to Achieve the Sustainable Development Goals'.

UNTT (UN Inter-Agency Task Force on Financing for Development). 2013. 'Financing for Sustainable Development: Review of Global Investment Requirement Estimates', in *UNTT Working Group on Sustainable Development Financing*, ch. 1.

United Nations. 2003. *The Monterrey Consensus on Financing for Development*. New York: United Nations Department of Economic and Social Affairs.

United Nations–Department of Economic and Social Affairs (UN–DESA). 2005. *Rethinking the Role of National Development Banks*. Revised background document, New York, December.

World Bank. 2004. 'The Challenge of Financing Infrastructure in Developing Countries', in *Global Development Finance 2004: Harnessing Cyclical Gains for Development*. Washington, DC: World Bank.

World Bank. 2015. *Long-Term Finance: Global Financial Development Report 2015–2016*. Washington, DC: World Bank.

World Economic Forum. 2016. 'Risk Mitigation Instruments in Infrastructure Gap Assessment'. July. Available at <www3.weforum.org/docs/WEF_Risk_Mitigation_Instruments_in_Infrastructure.pdf>, accessed 27 April 2018.

Wruuck, P. 2015. 'Promoting Investment and Growth: The Role of Development Banks in Europe'. EU Monitor Global Financial Markets, Deutsche Bank Research Management, December.

13

Conclusions

Stephany Griffith-Jones, José Antonio Ocampo, and Paola Arias

13.1 Introduction

After analysing national development banks (NDBs) in seven countries, we conclude that overall these banks tend to be successful at what they do. They have been broadly efficient development policy instruments in the various countries studied, helping to overcome the major market failures identified in Chapter 1 in this volume, and doing so in a flexible way over time.

NDBs have in several cases been innovative in what they do. They have in the last decade gone into new activities, supporting innovation (China's CDB, Germany's KfW, and Brazil's BNDES) and entrepreneurship (Chile's CORFO, as well as Colombia's BANCOLDEX). They have played an important role supporting key new sectors, like renewable energy and energy efficiency, the latter especially in Germany and China, but also in the other NDBs studied. They have developed new instruments, such as far greater use of guarantees, equity (including venture capital), and debt funds, as well as new instruments for financial inclusion, like correspondent stores. They have also started developing new functions, like funding foreign trade in times of financial crises (e.g. BNDES), encouraging FDI by national companies abroad (e.g. KfW, CDB, and BNDES), and helping to attract foreign investors to the country (e.g. CORFO).

A key question, however, is whether, given major current development challenges, NDBs do enough, especially in several of the Latin American countries analysed in this book, but also more broadly. In particular, is their current scale large enough for the development needs of their countries? Furthermore, do they have the right mix of instruments to perform the existing challenges?

The studies show that there is a great need for a larger scale of NDB activity in Latin America. This is due firstly to the low levels of both private and public investment in the region. In the case of private investment, this is linked in part to limitations of private finance, in particular its capacity to fund long-term investment. Furthermore, Latin American countries have less fiscal space, limiting public sector investment. The leverage of public resources provided by NDBs therefore becomes particularly attractive to boost investment.

At the same time, there is a great need for higher investment in Latin America as the challenges of structural transformation become more urgent, and are linked to the need for a radically different economic model, which is more dynamic, greener (to make growth consistent with the needs of the environment), smarter (with better innovation and its adaptation, to increase productivity more rapidly), and more inclusive (to reduce the large income inequality pervasive in the region).

Furthermore, the new development model may become less reliant on international trade, which since the financial crisis has grown more slowly than in the past, thus turning into a less dynamic engine for growth, and is now also threatened by protectionist tendencies in some major developed economies. Perhaps most importantly, lower commodity prices than in recent decades (linked to the clear end of the super-cycle of commodity prices) mean that investment in new sources of exports and growth is urgently required. As we discussed in Chapter 1, the uncertainty surrounding investments in new sectors and technologies implies that they are unlikely to be funded purely by private financial institutions, which are unwilling to take large risks, especially those associated with long maturities.

Therefore, NDBs' finance, which has the virtue of being long-term (as over 50 per cent of NDB lending is for over ten years' maturity) is needed on a significant scale. This has been understood in the highly successful economies of Germany and China, where the scale of NDB assets, in proportion to the country's GDP, is fairly large (see section 13.2). Within the Latin American region, we see different scales and trends. Brazil's BNDES had continued to be a large and important institution, though recently its scale seems to have been shrinking. On the other hand, countries like Chile, Mexico, and to a certain extent Colombia have seen a reduction in the scale of their NDBs, though in the last case there has been some resurgence in recent years.

As a result, it seems a key conclusion that, in countries like Chile, Mexico, Peru, and Colombia, the scale of operations of NDBs should be quite significantly increased, so they can make a greater impact on increased investment for structural transformation and development. This does not necessarily imply large government resources, as the only public contribution would be an increase in their paid-in capital; then these NDBs could fund their operations on the private domestic market—fairly developed in some of the Latin American countries studied here, notably Chile—as well as international capital markets.

Although this conclusion on the need for larger and more active NDBs focuses on Latin America, where the largest number of banks analysed in this volume are located, it can certainly be extended to other regions of the developing world, notably Africa. It could even be applied to developed countries, where NDBs can play an important role, as the very successful experience of KfW indicates.

A common insight gained from the case studies is also that the broad context in which development banks operate is key to their success. Thus, good macroeconomic policies—in particular, active countercyclical policies, relatively low inflation, fairly low real interest rates, and competitive exchange rates—are essential to the success of NDBs. Thus, for example, BNDES's operations have been constrained in recent years by macroeconomic problems. Furthermore, a well-functioning financial sector is another important precondition for the smooth functioning of an effective NDB. It is, however, interesting to note that NDBs can help develop a deeper and better capital market. Thus CDB, for example, played a key role in the development of the Chinese bond market. More generally, a number of NDBs have helped the introduction of local currency and/or green bonds in their own local capital market.

An NDB can operate far more effectively if the country has a clear development strategy, ideally linked to a modern industrial policy—or, more broadly, to modern production sector strategies, which should focus on promoting innovative sectors and guaranteeing their competitiveness in natural resources, manufacturing, and/or services, depending on the comparative advantages and accumulated capacities of different economies. Development banks like KfW, CORFO, and the CDB operate broadly in the context of a clear strategic direction; in contrast, the Peruvian NDBs seem to operate without such a clear development strategy. Clear policy mandates are particularly valuable if they do not change too much with different governments, allowing continuity and long-term planning for the NDBs and their support for development, as the German example notably indicates.

13.2 General Description and Main Features of NDBs

A set of thirteen national development banks from seven countries of different regions was analysed in the case studies. Five of these countries are from Latin America—Brazil, Chile, Colombia, Mexico, and Peru—and the other two are Germany and China, the most populous and dynamic economies in Europe and Asia, respectively. Moreover, according to the World Bank country classification by income, two of these seven, Chile and Germany, are high-income countries, while the other five are considered upper-middle-income countries.

These thirteen national development banks vary significantly in terms of their scope of operation, history, size, and main features (see Table 13.1). Chile, Brazil, and Germany have universal development banks—CORFO,[1] BNDES, and KfW, respectively—with a broad mandate to support an extensive range of activities and sectors, whereas the other four countries—Colombia, Peru, Mexico, and China—have a system of specialized development banks with a narrow and specific mandate. Colombia and Peru have four specialized development banks, Mexico has seven and China, three. In the case of the former two countries, four development banks were studied in Colombia (FDN, FINDETER, FINAGRO, and BANCOLDEX)[2] and four state-owned financial entities that engage in development banking activities with different forms of intermediation in Peru (Banco de la Nación, CFD, Fondo Mivivienda, and Banco Agropecuario); and in the latter two countries, only one development bank of their system was analysed: NAFINSA in Mexico and CDB in China. These specialized banks explicitly promote key relevant sectors of the economy. For example, CDB, FDN, and FINDETER specialize in infrastructure, NAFINSA in SMEs, an area which is also central to BANCOLDEX, while FINAGRO is specialized in the agricultural sector.

Both models have their own advantages and disadvantages. On the one hand, there is a perception that universal banks, as is the case with CORFO, have too many priority sectors and too many instruments. One observer of CORFO commented: 'for every problem, there is a separate instrument'. The advantage is that they have the benefits of diversification, which may reduce systemic risk in bad times. On the other hand, there is a perception that specialized banks, as in the case of Peru, maintain objectives and goals that are not integrated with each other. In Peru, the four banks analysed are seen to duplicate their efforts and do not take advantage of their possible synergies; therefore, none of these institutions constitutes an effective development bank such as exists in other countries. More broadly, specialized banks do not have the benefits of portfolio sectorial diversification, which may increase systemic risk in times of financial stress.

Although all these banks were established in different periods, the universal banks analysed are older than the specialized ones, except for NAFINSA which was created like CORFO in the 1930s. KfW was founded in 1949 after the end of WWII, and BNDES in 1952. In Peru, Banco de la Nación and CFD were the first two development banks created at the end of the 1960s and beginning of the 1970s, while all the Colombian development banks were created in the

[1] It should be mentioned that in Chile, Banco del Estado, a state-owned bank, does extensive first-tier lending, especially to agriculture. Furthermore, infrastructure is funded via different mechanisms to development banks, both through public and private finance.

[2] It is worth mentioning that Colombia also has Banco Agrario, a commercial state-owned bank to provide financial services in the rural areas.

Table 13.1. Key features of the NDBs studied

No.	Development bank	Year of creation	Country	Region	WB Country classification	Type of DB	Sectors	Second or first tier	Main source of funding
1	CORFO	1939	Chile	Latin America	High income	National Development Bank	Numerous sectors	Second tier	Fiscal resources
2	KfW	1949	Germany	Europe	High income	National Development Bank	Numerous sectors	Second tier	Bond issues
3	BNDES	1952	Brazil	Latin America	Upper middle income	National Development Bank	Numerous sectors	First and second tier	Fiscal resources
4	NAFINSA	1934	Mexico	Latin America	Upper middle income	Sectorial bank—System of DBs	MSMEs	First and second tier	Both internal and external debt
5	FDN	1982	Colombia	Latin America	Upper middle income	Sectorial bank—System of DBs	Infrastructure	First tier	Fiscal resources
6	FINDETER	1989	Colombia	Latin America	Upper middle income	Sectorial bank—System of DBs	Infrastructure	Second tier	Deposits
7	FINAGRO	1990	Colombia	Latin America	Upper middle income	Sectorial bank—System of DBs	Agricultural	Second tier	Mechanism of directed credit
8	BANCOLDEX	1991	Colombia	Latin America	Upper middle income	Sectorial bank—System of DBs	MSMEs	First and second tier	Deposits
9	BANCO DE LA NACION	1966	Peru	Latin America	Upper middle income	Sectorial bank—System of DBs	Public sector	First and second tier	Deposits
10	CFD	1971	Peru	Latin America	Upper middle income	Sectorial bank—System of DBs	MSMEs and infrastructure	First and second tier	External debt
11	BANCO AGROPECUARIO	2001	Peru	Latin America	Upper middle income	Sectorial bank—System of DBs	Agricultural	First and second tier	Both internal and external debt
12	FONDO MIVIVIENDA	1998	Peru	Latin America	Upper middle income	Sectorial bank—System of DBs	Housing	First and second tier	Bond issues
13	CDB	1994	China	Asia	Upper middle income	Sectorial bank—System of DBs	Infrastructure	First tier	Bond issues

1980s and 1990s. The youngest development banks studied are CDB and the two Peruvian banks, Fondo Mivivienda and Banco Agropecuario, created after the mid-1990s.

In the case of Colombia, these dates can be misleading. Thus, it is worth noticing that the first development bank was Instituto de Fomento Industrial (IFI), which was created in 1940, as part of a Latin American wave with the major objective of promoting manufacturing development, and was absorbed by BANCOLDEX in 2002, and the other banks created in the 1980s/1990s were established to administer the old development funds, which were created in the 1950s and were previously managed by the Colombian central bank.

Unsurprisingly, a common feature that the universal development banks share is their large scale. In general, the three universal banks studied are larger than the specialized banks, except for CDB, which is the largest and most influential development bank in China as well as among the set of banks studied in this book. CDB's assets rocketed up from 1.9 per cent of China's GDP in 1994, when it was created, to 18.6 per cent of China's GDP in 2015. Meanwhile, both KfW and BNDES's overall assets represent about 15 per cent of the size of the German and Brazilian economies, respectively. In the case of the system of specialized development banks, the overall share of all four Peruvian state-owned financial entities studied is around 8 per cent of GDP, while the overall share of all four Colombian development banks is about 3 per cent of GDP. One specialized bank, NAFINSA, has been downsized, and its total assets represent at present about 2 per cent of the size of the Mexican economy. CORFO's overall assets, at around only 2.6 per cent of Chile's GDP, are proportionally even smaller, and a much-reduced proportional size of what it was decades ago (Figure 13.1).[3]

As discussed in the introduction to this concluding chapter, in our view the relative size of these development banks in several Latin American countries is insufficient to overcome the challenges faced by their economies and, especially, to make the structural transformation that they require.

These thirteen banks also have different business models to carry out their lending operations. Banks like KfW, CORFO, and the Colombian FINAGRO and FINDETER are exclusively second-tier banks that do not directly lend to businesses or consumers, and instead rely on the network of commercial banks or other financial intermediaries to assess risk, provide the loans and guarantees, and monitor repayment. Meanwhile, FDN and CDB, both oriented towards providing financing to infrastructure projects, are first-tier institutions. There is also a set of banks, such as BNDES and the Peruvian banks, that lend through a combination of first- and second-tier operations.

[3] As pointed out, certain sectors like agriculture and infrastructure are funded through other institutional mechanisms, both public and private, in Chile.

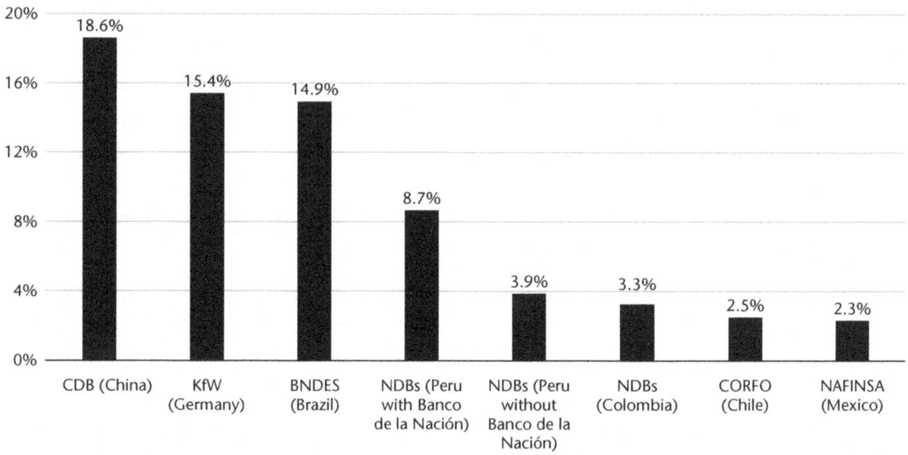

Figure 13.1. Assets of NDBs as a proportion of GDP, 2015
Source: Banscopes and NDBs

NAFINSA and BANCOLDEX also have both operations, but their first-tier credits are very limited.

NDBs offer different financial products, mainly credits, including long-term loans through project finance in the case of the infrastructure projects, subsidized interest rate loans for special projects or sectors, liquidity lines, or credits to help SMEs rediscount their bills. The major exceptions are CORFO and NAFINSA, whose main financial support to the private sector in recent years has been through loan guarantees to financial institutions; NAFINSA has also been innovative in using reverse electronic factoring for supporting SMEs. All banks also provide other non-financial services, including advice, project structuring, technical assistance and training, and portfolio administration.

Regarding their funding strategy, these banks fund their operations in the domestic or external markets with a mix of sources that range from fiscal resources to loans, bond issues, and deposits. BNDES and CORFO are highly dependent on fiscal resources, particularly transfers or loans from the national government. In the case of BNDES, this growth of public transfers revived an old controversy on the validity of its funding strategy, which suffers from a lack of private long-term financing, as capital markets are underdeveloped and real interest rates are high in Brazil. KfW and CDB are essentially financed by the issuance of bonds on the capital markets, with both being the largest bond issuers in their countries. The fact that they receive the same credit rating as the government is an advantage on the bond market as they can borrow more cheaply than commercial banks. CDB has also helped to develop the yield curve of benchmark interest rates as its bonds are now regularly issued and highly liquid. Mexico's NAFINSA and the Peruvian banks (except for Banco de la Nación) are mainly funded by internal and external loans from multilateral development banks and other international banks. This situation has been a problem for the Peruvian banks, as they have ended up increasing financial dollarization, due to their high level of dollar-denominated debt. BANCOLDEX and FINDETER in Colombia mainly rely on domestic-term deposits (about 60 per cent of their liabilities), while FINAGRO has a peculiar funding strategy as it benefits from an old mechanism of directed credit, as discussed in Chapter 7 on Colombian development banks.

Although most national development banks are essentially owned by the national government, as part of its transformation process, Colombia's FDN has a different shareholding structure with participation from multilateral development institutions and one international private bank, that has obvious implications for the governance of the institution: while in the traditional solely public development banks the government names the president and usually a minister heads the board, in the new FDN, the strategic investors chair the board and have veto power over crucial decisions.[4]

13.3 DBs Play Roles and Provide Services that Cannot Be Done by Markets

Development banks have played key roles in the development process, by helping to tackle not just the main market failures in the financial system, but also by contributing funds for structural transformation, via mission-oriented finance (see Chapter 1 in this book and Chapter 10 by Mazzucato and Penna). This is associated with five crucial roles in the development process: counteracting the procyclical behaviour of private financing, promoting innovation and structural transformation, enhancing financial inclusion, supporting the financing of infrastructure investment, and promoting environmental sustainability and green growth. The development banks studied broadly play these roles, and supply the necessary resources for investment, unavailable in the private financing system for those crucial aims.

One possible exception is the Peruvian development banks. Over the last twenty-five years, Peruvian governments did not give the four development banks a sufficiently large role in tackling the main market failures or in participating in strategic tasks such as diversifying the economy's productive

[4] In this regard, FDN follows OECD principles. If boards of development banks cease to be chaired by a minister, this might help avoid possible political capture, an alleged potential source of inefficiency, but it has the disadvantage of potentially undermining the alignment of the banks' priorities with government strategies, so crucial for them to be valuable instruments for national development plans.

apparatus and closing the infrastructure gap. Therefore, the development activities undertaken by these banks were not significant.

A valuable function of development banks is their countercyclical role when private lending falls sharply or collapses, particularly during and in the aftermath of financial crises. Banks such as KfW and CORFO, but also the others studied, have played a relevant countercyclical role. In the case of KfW, once the crisis reached the real economy in the fall of 2008, KfW expanded its on-balance-sheet loans, and its programmes became a major policy tool for the German government when implementing economic stimulus packages, including, for instance, lending programmes and liquidity lines to SMEs. Similarly, during the 1982/3 and the 2008/9 crises, CORFO played a countercyclical role by increasing its credit to enterprises and guarantees for credits to banks. In both cases, the roles played by these banks have been crucial in helping to maintain long-term investment, mitigate the business cycle, and prevent financial crises from deepening.

More broadly, there is also a small but growing body of detailed empirical evidence that national public banks provide countercyclical finance. Brei and Schclarek (Chapter 11) find robust evidence that, during financial crises, national development banks increased total lending in response to crises relative to normal times, while private banks decreased the growth of lending relative to normal patterns. Indeed, once a crisis occurs, national development banks expanded lending at a higher rate: 10.6 per cent per annum compared to 6.2 per cent for private banks. The countercyclical behaviour of national development banks is even stronger when considering corporate and commercial rather than total lending.

Given the procyclical nature of private finance, the countercyclical role of NDBs should be seen as a complement to countercyclical fiscal and monetary policies. Indeed, in the global debate that took place during the North Atlantic financial crises, the countercyclical role that multilateral development banks should play became a widely accepted principle—which of course also applies to NDBs. This means not only expanding NDB financing during crises but also moderating it during booms. And it means, of course, that the additional financing extended during crises should follow sound lending criteria. The overextension of credit should thus be avoided. Some analysts have criticized the countercyclical role of BNDES during the North Atlantic financial crises because of inadequate lending standards and the large-scale use of subsidized credit funded by the national government.

Moreover, development banks have played a key role in fostering innovation and entrepreneurship in national economies. As Mazzucato and Penna argue in Chapter 10, there is mounting evidence that patient, long-term committed finance, for mission-oriented investment in innovation, has been fostered by national development banks. In fact, NDBs are increasingly providing long-term committed venture capital for innovation projects. Because these projects are risky and uncertain, and nobody knows the 'odds' of success, private finance shies away from supporting them, thus making the role of NDBs crucial. If successful, these projects generate positive externalities, inducing further innovations.

KfW, for example, invests in the modernization of industries and has encouraged the development of new sectors, like renewable energy; CDB, as one of the most active NDBs, has supported and nurtured new ventures and innovations since the 2000s; and BNDES began to experiment with financing programmes targeted at high-tech firms and innovation development in the 1990s. BNDES's venture capital fund CRIATEC has shown striking results: in the first four years of its existence, the value of the CRIATEC portfolio grew at a rate of 50 per cent per annum.

CORFO has provided long-term resources to expand the role of risk capital funds, and created initiatives to support the development of non-banking financial intermediaries. Moreover, CORFO created its Start-Up programme, which has received international recognition. This programme has also encouraged the modernization, improvement, and broadening of the policy mix to support these companies in Chile. For example, relevant regulations have been simplified, and financing has also been expanded to support different phases of the projects. Finally, CORFO has helped to design a more detailed industrial strategy. However, it lacks sufficient scale to deliver significant impact.

BANCOLDEX, as a bank for entrepreneurial growth, manages a specific innovation programme, iNNpulsa Colombia. The programme supports innovation for business growth for firms of all sizes and ages, and in all sectors and regions of the country, and has defined three strategic areas of action: interventions to generate a culture favourable for business growth based on innovation, correction of market failures (in particular by connecting actors active in the supply and demand for innovation), and strengthening regional agents that promote innovation and entrepreneurial development. Among its specific instruments are the national network of 'angel investors', which it co-finances, and different regional initiatives to promote the incubation and growth of firms, boost training in technology transfer and commercialization, and support strategies to encourage rapid business growth.

There is also much agreement about the important role that national development banks do and should play in providing access to financing for microenterprises, including family agriculture and SMEs (MSMEs), especially, but not only, long-term credit. A common rationale for development banks to provide financing for MSMEs is that these tend to be too small, implying high transactions costs, and too risky to be of interest to most commercial lenders. Regarding this, development banks like NAFINSA, CORFO, KfW,

BANCOLDEX, and FINAGRO, among others, have provided financing to reach different segments of MSMEs and meet their distinct needs, through a series of instruments, mainly second-tier credits, first-tier lending to associations of producers, and guarantees. These products are channelled essentially through different types of financial intermediaries: commercial banks, specialized financial institutions, and microfinancing institutions.

In the case of NAFINSA, 71 per cent of its second-tier credit has gone to an innovative programme, Productive Chains, which helps potential borrowers rediscount their bill, through an electronic platform. NAFINSA also provides guarantees to improve the conditions under which loans are granted, and to increase the overall supply of credit. These guarantees are *pari passu* and first-loss, and participant firms do not directly apply for the guarantee. In the case of BANCOLDEX, almost half of its rediscounts are destined to MSMEs, and are complemented by guarantees externally provided by national or regional guarantee funds. BANCOLDEX also manages the major government programme to support financial inclusion, Banca de las Oportunidades. Among the achievements of this programme, it is worth mentioning the design and promotion of a programme of bank correspondents in municipalities or poor urban neighborhoods where financial institutions are absent. By 2016, all Colombian municipalities had at least one correspondent. FINAGRO is also active in financial inclusion but exclusively focused on small and medium-sized agricultural producers.

Furthermore, national development banks are especially well-suited for infrastructure financing, as they can provide the long-term financing needed for infrastructure investment to become profitable, given the large scale of the initial investment and the long period of time for amortization. Development banks can finance at relatively low cost, as they often have very high credit ratings and can, therefore, borrow relatively cheaply on capital markets, and pass on that cost advantage to their borrowers. This role is particularly crucial as the deficit in infrastructure investments has created enduring challenges for many countries. Banks like CDB, FDN, FINDETER, and BNDES are very active in long-term infrastructure financing. Additionally, these development banks have been also important players in the financing networks sponsoring sustainable infrastructure projects.

CDB has been a key player in the development of the Chinese financial market and credit system by reshaping the local government credit system, including through a local government financial vehicle (LGFV) model. As local governments had restricted capacity to invest in infrastructure, in 1998, CDB created a model in which the local government creates a company (LGFV), a legal person registered as a local state-owned enterprise. The local government promises to inject its quality assets to the LGFV, and if these assets—e.g. highways—are profitable, the LGFV can take the future profits as collateral and borrow from CDB. Under this model, loans can be bundled and local government revenues—including those associated with profits from managing land owned by local governments—can also be transferred to the LGFV. Despite its benefits, it seems that LGFV model has opened a Pandora's box as regards the explosion of the local government debt burden; this model has also made financial supervision less effective.

BNDES, as part of the government's initiative to build the market of infrastructure bonds, expanded guarantee-sharing clauses in its financing contracts, equalizing the level of seniority of bondholder to loans it co-financed. Through its subsidiary BNDESPAR, it also bought stakes in companies that could prospect for new business in the sector. Thus, BNDES ended up assisting the federal and state governments structure concessions for the private sector and PPP.

In the case of the two Colombian banks, FDN has developed a myriad of products—senior and subordinated credits and credit enhancements—to catalyse the movement of resources into infrastructure projects, mainly highways, using project finance arrangements. In turn, FINDETER has continued to provide rediscount facilities for urban and local projects, and has been very instrumental in the implementation of a series of key programmes of the national government with a strong regional content.

Finally, in terms of green growth, development banks bring the advantages of accumulated expertise, administrative efficiencies, and convening power. They can help mobilize additional funding, design the necessary policy frameworks, and implement effective projects that can showcase the viability of certain green investments, as in renewable energy. Thus, KfW, BNDES, CDB, and CORFO, for instance, have played an important role in supporting the development and use of green technology.

This has been particularly important in the case of KfW. One prominent aspect of this institution's mandate is to support the structural change towards a low-carbon economy. This is particularly evident in two areas: energy-efficient housing for consumers, and energy-saving and renewable energy promotion for businesses. In energy-efficient housing, KfW contributed to the design of the strategy put forward by the Ministry for the Economy, defined the standards for an energy-efficient house, engaged in monitoring and evaluation, and provided loans at slightly below-market rates. In improving energy savings and the use of renewables by businesses, KfW, for example, has engaged in all stages of the policy cycle of a programme targeting SMEs using clean energy.

CORFO helped design a National Strategic Solar Industry programme, and as part of it, designed specific credit lines to provide stable funding to producers capable of adapting to local conditions and fostering local value added. BNDES has a technology fund FUNTEC, which targeted resources to very specific technologies, such as alternative energy, specifically bioenergy, solar energy, and thermal energy; nanotech and biotech solutions to address issues of waste disposal, land and water pollution; bio-electronics, specifically *organic* electronics and other innovative integrated circuits; new materials; biochemistry; and electric-drive vehicles. CDB invests significantly in renewable energy projects as well; this was crucial as Chinese solar panels are playing such a central role in solar energy worldwide. The CDB has a track record of funding alternative energy firms to develop their technologies, such as for example the solar company Yingli Green Energy, which has a US$5.3 billion line of credit opened for it at CDB.

13.4 The Challenges for Development Banks Regarding Financial Regulation

The new financial regulation framework, particularly Basel III, might bring significant challenges for national development banks. According to Barros de Castro in Chapter 9, although some new requirements in Basel III do not seem to be problematic for development banks, such as the treatment of liquidity risk or of derivatives, there are other issues that might be a source of concern, notably the bias that it generates in private finance against long-term lending, the management of concentration risks of NDBs, and the rules regarding countercyclical capital cushions.

Liquidity risks are less relevant to development banks, as they have limited difficulties in managing the maturity mismatch between assets and liabilities. The long-term liquidity risk indicator (NSFR) aims to ensure that banks avoid severe term mismatches under normal conditions, considering the one-year horizon. The core business in DBs' risk management is, precisely, managing the mismatch between assets and liabilities. However, NSFR may increase the short-term bias of the private market, and thus reduce long-term lending. This may increase the demand for medium/long-term lending from DBs, especially for infrastructure.

With regard to concentration risk, the problem is more serious, because its treatment has been systematically revised in the direction of greater severity. This is working against the global infrastructure agenda, for which large project finance leads to high levels of portfolio concentration. DBs are seen as a key instrument to overcome the large gap in infrastructure projects, where the risks are much higher. Revising the associated rules is thus essential if they are going to play a key role in this area.

Furthermore, the addition of countercyclical cushions should be assessed carefully in terms of their relevance to development banks. As Barros de Castro argues, if it is accepted that DBs should act anticyclically, does it make sense to apply the cushions to these institutions? It may simply be dysfunctional for the economy as a whole and work against broader principles of macroprudential regulation.

It is also expected that Basel IV will diminish the incentives for the development of internal models, moving towards the adjusted standard models. This change decreases the possibility that an institution develops more suitable metrics, reflecting their idiosyncratic characteristics and, in the case of NDBs, their development mandate.

Thus, a dialogue should be maintained between national development banks, national financial regulators, and the Basel Committee to enable development banks to have an active role in infrastructure lending and in the provision of countercyclical financing. This includes specific regulation of concentration, which should also apply to other banks involved in infrastructure financing. Maintaining the possibility of internal models relevant to the evaluation of risks may also be a critical issue, given the idiosyncratic features of NDBs.

13.5 The Link of NDBs with National Development Strategies

It is interesting that NDBs do not only operate better with clearer policy mandates, but can also help shape development policies, as has happened especially in Germany and China, and to a certain extent in Brazil, Colombia, and Chile. Thus, KfW helped shape German government policy on energy efficiency, based on its previous experience and technical know-how. More broadly, KfW has impacted how the German government implements domestic economic priorities, and it dynamically engages with the government at all stages of policy design and implementation. It has thus routinely assisted the government in selecting targeted policy areas, designing projects and programmes, implementing and financing them, monitoring the progress, and finally, judging the results and informing the next iteration of the programmes. In this way, KfW can create and expand the policy space in which it operates, achieving policy synergy for maximal benefit.

Indeed, if countries have a fairly clear development strategy, development banks may often be more effective in funding it than government departments, as NDBs may have more technical expertise and accumulated knowledge, and can leverage public resources. Indeed, well-run NDBs seem to be in a privileged position for funding structural transformation, in that they know more about policy than commercial banks and know more about private financing than government departments. In any case, having good governance of NDBs is essential, which means both an important level of autonomy to manage themselves as efficient businesses, but also clear links with both the public and the private sectors. Well-governed NDBs can make a significant difference in terms of strengthening state capacities in areas such as production sector strategies, infrastructure development, financial inclusion, and green growth.

In this regard, it should be emphasized that the nature of financial and other support that NDBs need to give today and in the future is different to that required in the past. In previous decades, NDBs were mainly involved in the developing world in financing 'catch-up growth' based on existing technologies, whereas at present NDBs need to play a role in supporting innovation and its adaptation to new firms and sectors. The new kinds of support needed naturally influence or even determine the appropriate instruments NDBs should deploy.

In this sense, the research in our case studies showed new and interesting trends in the instruments NDBs use. For example, there has been a shift from first-tier to second-tier lending. However, first-tier lending can still be an important instrument, notably in the case of infrastructure. First-tier lending has the virtue of allowing NDBs a more direct impact on implementing development priorities; however, it is far less convenient for loans or other transactions to many especially mid-sized and smaller companies.

In several cases, especially CORFO and NAFINSA, but also more generally, there has been a trend towards far greater use of guarantees, with a relative decline in more traditional lending. Though guarantees are clearly a valuable instrument, especially for providing access to companies without sufficient physical assets to offer as collateral, and can allow for additional leverage of the development banks' capital, they often need to be complemented by other instruments. This is particularly the case for lending to new sectors or activities, where uncertainty and therefore risk are far higher and private commercial banks may be unwilling to take such larger risks, especially in loans of long maturity. In this sense, KfW—with its continued far greater emphasis on lending, in spite of the high level of development of German banking and capital markets—seems to offer valuable lessons for Latin American NDBs.

Direct investment by NDBs in companies used to play an important role in NDBs in Latin America, but has been downsized. There is, however, an interesting surge of indirect investment by NDBs, through equity and debt funds in key sectors, like green energy. There are specific important programmes to support innovative start-ups and lengthy innovation, where private capital is often too oriented towards the short-term, as well as new programmes to support entrepreneurship, like CORFO's Start-Up Chile, emulated in several other Latin American countries.

An important instrument continues to be subsidies or grants to sectors that the state considers important to support, either due to externalities—e.g. environmental benefits linked to lower CO_2 emissions—or for achieving greater financial inclusion—e.g. lower interest rates to smaller producers. It is important that such subsidies are transparent and clearly targeted; it may be desirable that they be temporary, if the effects of an externality tend to decline over time—e.g. a cheaper technology introduced for renewable energy that is gradually adopted by other firms.

More generally, subsidies can be granted through explicit fiscal transfers, for example to fund high-risk R&D, with potentially high social returns, and even commercial impact. They can also be granted to support training and education, so as to increase skills. However, grants can also be given through subsidized interest rates, especially to smaller or poorer producers. Combining loans or guarantees with subsidies is easier for NDBs than commercial banks, as they are closer to policymakers, who can better help design and monitor such schemes.

To conclude, the range of instruments NDBs deploy should be broad. It is clearly valuable to introduce new instruments but also to rely on well-tested effective mechanisms, such as loans.

13.6 Future Research Questions

We hope to have contributed, through our research in this project and book, to an understanding of the positive role national development banks have and can in the future play in the development process, in low-income, emerging, and even developed economies.

There are several outstanding questions for future research. These include:

- A deeper understanding of modalities to best fund NDBs, in countries of different levels of development and depth of capital markets.
- Further research on the most effective instruments for NDBs to channel funds, in the face of old and new development challenges, such as for example innovation in renewable energy. Also, what type of loans and credit lines could be used to make NDB disbursements more countercyclical? How best to capture the upside, in loans that support activities with large potential profits? And, more broadly, what financial mechanisms are best suited to promote innovation and entrepreneurship?
- Are universal national development banks more effective or is it better to have more specialized development banks?
- What are the elements that make an NDB most effective for fulfilling its development mandate? More specifically, how can governance of NDBs best be improved?

- What are the political economy dimensions for generating support for creating NDBs in those countries where they do not exist, and maintaining their scale or even expanding them, where required, to achieve key development objectives? And what is the political economy for ensuring they are well governed and well run?

During the period of strong emphasis on market reforms, NDBs became almost a forbidden topic. The limitations that market reforms have shown in many parts of the developing world, the persistence of strong adverse distributive trends, the major environmental challenges facing the world, and those posed by strong financial crises, some of global impact, have put the issue of the role of NDBs back on the agenda. Contributing to this emerging debate has been the central objective of this volume.

Index

n = footnote; *f* = figure; *t* = table; *b* = boxed section.

The manufacturer's authorised representative in the EU for product safety is Oxford University Press España S.A. of El Parque Empresarial San Fernando de Henares, Avenida de Castilla, 2 - 28830 Madrid (www.oup.es/en or product.safety@oup.com). OUP España S.A. also acts as importer into Spain of products made by the manufacturer.
Printed and bound by CPI Group (UK) Ltd, Croydon, CR0 4YY
14/09/2026
02216305-0013